Timberlake
Los
September

W9-BZH-135

Mechanisms of Syntactic Change

Mechanisms of Syntactic Change

Edited by Charles N. Li

University of Texas Press/Austin and London

*For reasons of economy and speed this volume
has been printed from camera-ready copy
furnished by the editor, who assumes full
responsibility for its contents.*

International Standard Book Number 0-292-75035-8
Library of Congress Catalog Card Number 77-82263
Copyright © 1977 by the University of Texas Press
All rights reserved
Printed in the United States of America

Contents

List of Participants   vii
Acknowledgments   ix
Introduction   xi

I. The Nature of Syntactic Change
1. On the Gradual Nature of Syntactic Change   3
   Sandra Chung
2. Syntactic Reanalysis   57
   Ronald W. Langacker
3. Reanalysis and Actualization in Syntactic Change   141
   Alan Timberlake

II. Word Order Change
4. The Drift from VSO to SVO in Biblical Hebrew: The
   Pragmatics of Tense-Aspect   181
   Talmy Givón
5. Syntactic Change and SOV Structure: The Yuman Case   255
   Margaret Langdon
6. Motivations for Exbraciation in Old English   291
   Robert P. Stockwell

III. Syntactic Change and Ergativity
7. On Mechanisms by Which Languages Become Ergative   317
   Stephen R. Anderson
8. The Syntactic Development of Australian Languages   365
   R. M. W. Dixon

IV. Development of the Copula
9. A Mechanism for the Development of Copula
   Morphemes   419
   Charles N. Li and Sandra A. Thompson
10. From Existential to Copula: The History of Yuman BE   445
    Pamela Munro

V. Clisis and Verb Morphology
11. The Evolution of Third Person Verb Agreement in the
    Iroquoian Languages   493
    Wallace L. Chafe
12. From Auxiliary Verb Phrase to Inflectional Suffix   525
    Mary R. Haas
13. Clisis and Diachrony   539
    Susan Steele

VI. Multiple Analyses
  14. Multiple Analyses   583
      Jorge Hankamer
  Author Index   609
  Language Index   615

List of Participants

Lloyd Anderson
Boulder,
Colorado

Stephen Anderson
Linguistics Department
UCLA

Francesco Antinucci
Consiglio Nazionale
    delle Ricerche
Rome

James Bauman
Linguistics Department
UCSB

Derek Bickerton
Linguistics Department
University of Hawaii

Michael Canale
Linguistics Department
McGill University

Wallace Chafe
Linguistics Department
UC Berkeley

Sandra Chung
Linguistics Department
UCSD

R.M.W. Dixon
Linguistics Department
Australian National University

Talmy Givón
Linguistics Department
UCLA

Georgia Green
Linguistics Department
University of Illinois

Jorge Hankamer
Linguistics Department
Harvard University

Mary Haas
Linguistics Department
UC Berkeley

Hsin-I Hsieh
Asian Languages Depart-
    ment
University of Hawaii

Edward Keenan
Linguistics Department
UCLA

Ronald Langacker
Linguistics Department
UCSD

Margaret Langdon
Linguistics Department
UCSD

Winfred Lehmann
Linguistics Department
University of Texas

Charles N. Li
Linguistics Department
UCSB

David Lightfoot
Linguistics Department
McGill University

Sally McLendon
Linguistics Department
City University of New
    York

(continued on next page)

Pamela Munro
Linguistics Department
UCLA

Michael Noonan
Linguistics Department
San Jose State U.

Carol Justus Raman
Linguistics Program
SUNY Oswego

Gillian Sankoff
Anthropology Department
University of Montreal

Arthur Schwartz
Linguistics Department
UCSB

Dan Slobin
Psychology Department
UC Berkeley

Susan Steele
Linguistics Department
Stanford -- U. of Arizona

Robert Stockwell
Linguistics Department
UCLA

Sandra Thompson
Linguistics Department
UCLA

Alan Timberlake
Slavic Languages Department
UCLA

Acknowledgments

The Symposium on Mechanisms of Syntactic Change where the papers in this volume were presented in their preliminary versions was funded by a grant from the National Science Foundation, Grant No. BNS76-06028. The editor wishes to express his deep appreciation and gratitude to Brenda Bartell and Mora Dewey, Lila Margolis and Naomi Schwartz who helped to make the Symposium a delightful experience to all the participants; to Gay Bradshaw and Mora Dewey for assisting me in preparing the indexes; and especially to Ann Krooth who typed the manuscript of this book.

Introduction

The Symposium on the Mechanisms of Syntactic Change was
held at the University of California, Santa Barbara, May 7-
May 9, 1976. A total of twenty-three papers were prepared
for the Symposium. They were circulated among the participants prior to the Symposium and a discussion session was
held for each of the papers. The outgrowth of the Symposium
is this volume consisting of fourteen articles revised from
their original versions on the basis of the discussions and
input by the participants. The articles are grouped into six
chapters. The first chapter concerns the nature of syntactic
change. Chung provides for this chapter a lucid presentation
of three exciting cases of syntactic change: the passive-to-
ergative reanalysis in Pukapukan, the spread of the ergative
case marking in Samoan, and the extension of the domain of application of certain movement rules in Bahasa Indonesian. The
theoretical implication of her case studies is significant:
syntactic change is gradual and the gradual nature of certain
changes is characterized by a hierarchy of sentence types governing the actualization of change. It is particularly re-
warding that this hierarchy corresponds exactly to our understanding of sentence and rule types in synchronic studies.The
second article in this chapter is a carefully argued and well
documented (based on Uto-Aztecan data) study of reanalysis by
Langacker: the types of reanalysis, its effects, and its
causes. Although this study is by no means exhaustive, it
represents the first theoretical attempt to investigate the
general nature rather than a specific case, of reanalysis. The
third article in Chapter I deals with the two aspects of syn-

tactic change: reanalysis and actualization. Using two case
studies--the loss of subject-to-object raising in the complement of verbs of cognition in Finnish and the replacement of
the genitive by accusative marking for objects in Russian--as
illustration, Timberlake argues convincingly that actualization is a consequence of reanalysis and actualization is gradual, occurring first in "unmarked" contexts before proceeding
to "marked" contexts. Thus, Timberlake's study complements
Chung's. The difference is that in the cases of syntactic
change discussed by Chung, the markedness of the contexts for
gradual actualization is synchronically definable. Timberlake
also implicitly claims that reanalysis typically occurs during
language acquisition by children. This is a point with which
others (including Stockwell in this volume) may disagree.

Chapter II deals with word order change. Word order
change is probably the most drastic and complex category of
syntactic changes. It affects the fundamental syntactic organization of a language. A word order change, for instance
SOV to SVO, usually represents a series of parallel or sequential syntactic changes acting in a coordinated manner to push
the language from one typological category to another. Its ram-
ification, therefore, extends far beyond a mere reorganization
of the order of the basic sentential constituents: subject,
object, verb. Thus, the actualization of word change inevit-
ably spans centuries or even millennia, further complicating
the task of the researcher to recapture the interplay of diachronic processes that initiate and propel the language to
drift from one word order type to another. With the exception of the Chinese case which has developed certain verb-final constructions while the language is still SVO (See Li, C.

N. and S. A. Thompson, 1975, "Historical change of word order:
a case study in Chinese and its implications", in Historical
Linguistics, ed. by J. M. Anderson and C. Jones, Vol. 1, 199-
217.) the only documented types of word order changes that are
not due to language contact are SOV to (VSO) to SVO. Yet we
are far from understanding the precise mechanism and process
of actualization of the change from SOV to VSO. The comment
focusing rule is proposed by Stockwell as a mechanism for developing VSO constructions in SOV languages. It is conceivable that comment focusing might have sparked the change. But
the actualization of the change is completely unknown. In other words, how does a comment focusing construction which must
be highly marked and serving a specific pragmatic function in
a verb-final language, become unmarked and lose its function
as a focusing construction? Could it be a case of reanalysis?
What causes the reanalysis? A series of questions confronts
us squarely. But the answers continue to elude us.

    With regard to the VSO to SVO drift, Givón contributed
a commendable study to this chapter with statistics and documentation painstakingly gathered from Biblical Hebrew text.
The primary driving force of the VS to SV drift, according to
Givón, is the principle of discourse topicality, and he provides us with a number of hierarchies describing the various
contexts through which the drift is gradually actualized. It
is particularly interesting to see that at least in the case
of Hebrew, the change in the tense-aspect system went hand in
hand with the principle of discourse topicality in propelling
the language to drift from VS to SV.

    Langdon's comparative study of constituent ordering in
both the VP and NP of Yuman languages should have a lasting

salutary effect on those who might blindly infer word order
change on the basis of the tentative findings of word order
typologies. The basic word order in Yuman languages is SOV.
But they have certain non-SOV characteristics: adjective follows the head noun; headless relative clauses; an elaborate
prefix system. For each of these characteristics which is
allegedly incongruent with the SOV word order, Langdon convincingly demonstrated with historical and comparative evidence that the characteristic is perfectly natural for Yuman
languages. Thus the non-SOV characteristics are not the relic
of an older variant word order typology, but part and parcel
of a sub-category of the SOV typology. The valuable lesson
to be drawn from Langdon's study is that we must determine
for each specific language family "how much of today's morphology (and constituent ordering of NPs) is still today's syntax and, conversely, how much of yesterday's morphology (and
constituent ordering of NPs) is still yesterday's morphology
(and constituent ordering of NPs)." It has become increasingly clear that the word order typology put forth by Greenberg
over a decade ago, though invaluable as a pioneering source of
stimulation in modern studies of language typologies, does not
constitute an unshakable foundation for diachronic syntax. The
SVO, SOV, VSO typology does not provide a trichotomy of the
vast majority of languages in the world. At best, it represents three points of idealization in the continuum of word
orders and a wide array of ancillary grammatical properties.
The precise nature of this continuum remains somewhat of a
mystery to date.

Chapter III concerns syntactic change involving ergative
languages. Two questions immediately come to mind: (1) how

does an accusative language become ergative? (2) how does an
ergative language become accusative? The primary attested
mechanism by which a language becomes ergative is reanalysis
through passivization, i.e., ergative morphology arises by
generalizing the morphology of a passive construction as the
passive/active distinction is lost. Viewed in terms of rule
change, this mechanism amounts to the replacement of the passive rule by an obligatory ergative case marking rule
applying to active sentences. A consequence of such a
development of ergative morphology in a language is that the
syntactic properties of the language generally remain to be
those of active sentences in an accusative language. Chung's
paper in Chapter I provides a detailed account of the passive-
to-ergative change in a number of Polynesian languages. Anderson, in his article in this chapter, traces the development of the ergative morphology in perfect tense among Indic
and Iranian languages to the same mechanism: passive-to-ergative reanalysis. While the passive-to-ergative reanalysis
appears to be an important mechanism for the development of
ergative languages and thus constitutes an answer to question
(1), we have not yet come to grips with question (2). Anderson reported Braithwaite's account of the origin of the accusative morphology in the present tense series among the Kartvelian (South Caucasian) family, and further provided an alternative suggestion. It is also known that the ergative-to-
accusative change has taken place among a number of Tibeto-
Burman languages (see J. Bauman, Pronouns and Pronominal
Morphology in Tibeto-Burman, Ph.D. dissertation, UC Berkeley,
1975). But we are on less firm ground in those cases than
we are in the cases of change from accusative to ergative.

Among the ergative languages, the Australian languages
are distinct. They are ergative both morphologically and syntactically as Dixon demonstrates in his paper with data from
Dyirbal and Yidin. Dixon postulates an ergative-prone system
in Proto-Australian nominal and pronominal morphology and suggests that both morphology and syntax change in a direction
to avoid disparity between the two. Anderson, however, cit-
ing Hale, disagrees with Dixon's reconstruction for Proto-Australian. It is clear that the nature of the Australian languages, namely syntactic ergativity, bestows on them a special
importance in both the diachronic and synchronic study of ergativity. Further research and studies in the Australian language area will undoubtedly result in significant contributions to our understanding of ergative languages and their
diachronic origins.

Any investigation into the diachronic development of the
copula will reveal that the copula is extremely susceptible
to change. It can be easily lost, borrowed or redeveloped.
This is probably due to the fact that copula is typically unstressed and has little or no semantic content other than serving as a tense bearer. In many languages, the investigators
can easily uncover evidence supporting both the loss and the
emergence of the copula without reaching a great time depth.
However, the diachronic cycle is complex and the processes of
decline and emergence (or borrowing) often overlap, creating
a mesh that is difficult to untangle. Chapter IV presents
two sources and pathways for the development of the copula:
from anaphoric pronoun through reanalysis to copula in Chinese,
Hebrew, Palestinian Arabic and Wappo presented by Li and Thompson; from existential to copula through reanalysis in Yuman

presented by Munro. They represent a small step forward in
the study of the rise and decline of the copula in many languages of the world.

Many scholars of American Indian languages have jokingly
declared on one occasion or another that there is only morphology and semantics but no syntax in American Indian languages.
While it might be wrong to impugn the claim that there is syntax in every language, it is a fact that most American Indian
languages have extremely rich and complex morphological systems that manifest and signal a huge array of semantic and
pragmatic functions, thus eliminating the need of certain syntactic rules (particularly movement rules) for displaying
those functions. It is probably uncontroversial to say that
in most American Indian languages morphology constitutes the
primary surface codification for both meaning and structure.
Thus, in Chapter V, the three articles are concerned with
change involving morphology and all three draw their data
from American Indian languages. Haas' paper traces the development of subject pronominal suffixes on verb systems in Hitchiti and Creek from an old conjugated auxiliary used with intransitive verbs. Steele's paper examines the development of
the second position clitic pronouns and the prefixal subject
pronouns on verbs in Uto-Aztecan languages. Finally, Chafe
presents a significant case of the evolution of verb agreement in the Iroquoian languages. One significant aspect of
this evolution lies in the unusual origin of the third person
verb agreement markers in the Iroquoian languages. They e-
volved from existing verb morphology through reinterpretation
rather than from independent pronouns through cliticization.
Another significant aspect of the evolution lies in the dir-

ection and the nature of the drift. It moved toward greater
complexity through extensions from one semantic category to
another rather than toward greater simplicity through phonological leveling. Thus, the Iroquoian case unfolds a refresh-
ing picture of the diachronic development of verb morphology.

Chapter VI strictly speaking is not a study of mechanisms of syntactic change. As the title, 'Multiple Analysis',
indicates, Hankamer's paper argues for the hypothesis that
given a body of data, it is possible to have two or more conflicting analyses that are simultaneously correct. The hypothesis is highly provocative and has serious theoretical rami-
fications in both synchronic and diachronic studies. Diachronically, multiple analyses may constitute the motivating
force inducing syntactic change. In other words, the existence of multiple analyses for a construction probably immediately precedes the stage of reanalysis of that construction.
Thus, if Hankamer's hypothesis proves correct, the synchronic
description of a language may yield important clues to the
nature and direction of syntactic changes in the language,
opening up new possibilities for the investigation of syntactic changes that are actively at work in present day languages.
One may disagree with the specific analyses proposed by Hankamer for some of the constructions cited in his study. But his
basic thesis that multiple analysis exists is intuitively appealing.

To sum up, this collection of studies covers a wide
range of topics in diachronic syntax, and their conclusions
and hypotheses are documented with a large array of data
drawn from a great variety of language families. There is

no doubt that the field of diachronic syntax is still very
much in its embryonic stage. Yet if the Santa Barbara sympo-
sia can be used as a yardstick, one cannot fail to notice the
significant advances that have been made in the field since
the 1974 symposium on Word Order and Word Order Change. At
this stage, the study of diachronic syntax shows all the prom-
ises of an exciting and bountiful future. It is clear if we
are to reap the harvest, we must be prepared to devote much
more time to empirical investigation. Generative mechanisms
do not explain diachronic processes in syntax. It is only
through the unbiased analysis of data collected from either
historical documents or comparative studies that mechanisms
of syntactic change may be discovered.

                              Charles N. Li
                              Santa Barbara, 1977

I The Nature of Syntactic Change

1 On the Gradual Nature of Syntactic Change

Sandra Chung

It is a widely held assumption in generative historical linguistics that syntactic change is not gradual but discrete. King (1969: 115), for instance, states in a discussion that is basically about phonological change:

> Parenthetically, let it be noted that linguistic change other than phonological is clearly not gradual by any stretch of the imagination. If an adult learns to use whom in place of who in the right places, how could this be anything but sudden and abrupt? When a child says foots instead of feet, what is gradual about it?

King's assumption seems to be that the very nature of nonphonological change (including syntactic change) precludes its occurring in gradual fashion. Since there is no level of syntax corresponding to the phonetic level in phonology, there is no possibility for gradual change in this area of grammar. Although this assumption is not stated as clearly elsewhere, it is implicit in much of the early work on particular problems of syntactic change (Klima 1964; Traugott 1965). These works recognized trends in syntactic change, but assumed that they could be broken down into series of discrete changes, described by the generative mechanisms of rule addition, rule loss, simplification, and reanalysis.

In this paper I present evidence from Pukapukan, a Polynesian language spoken on Danger Island, that argues that

this assumption must be modified in a crucial way. I will
show that one syntactic change in progress in Pukapukan can
be broken down into a series of discrete changes in syntactic
rules. However, this change is actualized gradually, and in
a way that cannot be described by the generative mechanisms
proposed so far. I will further argue that this actualization is governed by the principle in (1):

(1) Syntactic change is actualized for sentences that
undergo superficial rules before it is actualized
for sentences that undergo major cyclic rules.

Since (1) is needed in addition to the devices of rule addition, reanalysis, and so forth, it represents a significant
departure from the standard generative view. As such, it
should be justified by facts from a number of languages. As
a first step towards this, I discuss two other types of
change in Austronesian languages that appear to be governed
by the same principle.

This paper is organized as follows. In Section 1, I
summarize the evidence that a number of Polynesian languages
have reanalyzed an original passive as an ergative construction. In Section 2, I describe the case marking of Pukapukan
and show that this language is in the process of actualizing
the passive-to-ergative reanalysis. Section 3 examines the
interaction of the three types of case marking in Pukapukan
with different syntactic rules. This investigation reveals
that the 'new' ergative case marking is more restricted than
the other, 'older' types, and is restricted in a principled
way. In Section 4, I introduce and argue for the principle
in (1). Finally, Section 5 discusses two unrelated changes
-- one from Samoan and the other from Bahasa Indonesia --

that support and suggest refinements of the principle.

1. The Passive-to-Ergative Reanalysis in Polynesian

The change that I will discuss for Pukapukan can be understood only within the larger context of Polynesian. In this Section, I sketch the synchronic characteristics of the Polynesian languages and argue that some of them have undergone a passive-to-ergative reanalysis.

The Polynesian languages are a group of some thirty languages spoken on islands in the South Pacific. The languages form a closely related subfamily of the East Oceanic branch of the Austronesian language family. Thanks to the transparency of the Polynesian languages and of their genetic relationship to one another, a considerable amount of comparative work has already been done. (2) gives the subgrouping of these languages as established by Pawley (1966, 1967):

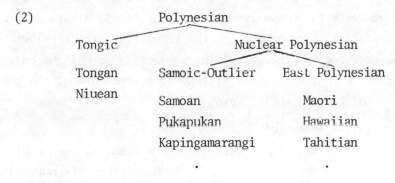

(2)   Polynesian

    Tongic   Nuclear Polynesian

    Tongan   Samoic-Outlier   East Polynesian
    Niuean
                Samoan   Maori
                Pukapukan   Hawaiian
                Kapingamarangi   Tahitian

                    .   .

                    .   .

The languages are alike in having simple phonology and precious little morphology. With the possible exception of some Samoic-Outlier languages, which show a preference for verb-medial word order, all of the languages have the basic word order VSO. Tense and aspect are indicated by a particle

preceding the verb; case marking, specificity, and number are
indicated by particles preceding the noun. Other than this,
nominal and verbal inflection is almost completely absent.

Syntactically, the languages exhibit great diversity in
the area of case marking. There are two principal types of
case marking, _accusative_ and _ergative_, which are distributed
among the different subgroups as follows.

The accusative type of case marking is found principally
in East Polynesian (e.g. Maori, Hawaiian). In this type of
case marking, the subjects of intransitive and transitive
clauses are unmarked; direct objects of transitive clauses
are marked with the particle _i_:[1]

> (3)   Accusative Languages:
>   Tns   Verb   Subj   (intransitive)
>   Tns   Verb   Subj   _i_ DO   (transitive)

Languages with accusative case marking almost always have a
Passive. This rule promotes the transitive direct object to
subject, removes the underlying subject to an oblique case
(marked with the particle _e_), and adds some form of the passive suffix -_Cia_ to the verb:

> (4)   Passive:
>   Tns   Verb-_Cia_   _e_ Agent   Subj
>   (=underlying   (=underlying
>   Subj)   DO)

For our purposes, it is important that the accusative type of
case marking is not limited to East Polynesian, but is found
in a few Samoic-Outlier languages as well. Pukapukan, for
instance, exhibits accusative case marking, as will be shown
below.

The ergative type of case marking is found in Tongic and
in almost all Samoic-Outlier languages. In this type of case
marking, subjects of intransitive clauses are unmarked, as
are direct objects of transitive clauses. Subjects of transitive clauses are marked with the particle e:

(5)   Ergative Languages:

        Tns   Verb   Subj   (intransitive)
        Tns   Verb e Subj   DO   (transitive)

Languages with ergative case marking seem to reserve the
transitive case marking of (5) for clauses whose direct objects are directly affected by the action. Transitive clauses whose direct objects are not directly affected -- such as
clauses involving verbs of emotion or perception -- take a
different type of case marking, which I will refer to as middle. In middle case marking, the subject is unmarked and the
direct object is marked with one of the oblique prepositions
i 'at' or ki 'to':

(6)   Middle:

        Tns   Verb   Subj   i/ki DO

There are two reasons why these two types of case
systems are striking. Synchronically, it is striking that
such closely related languages should choose to organize their
case marking in ways as different as (3) and (5). Diachronically, it is even more remarkable that the two types of case
marking appear to be related systematically. The transitive
case marking of the accusative languages resembles the middle
case marking of the ergative languages:

(7)   Transitive case marking of accusative languages:

Tns   Verb   Subj   i̲ DO

Middle case marking of ergative languages:

Tns   Verb   Subj   i̲/ki̲ DO

Further, the passive case marking of the accusative languages
is essentially the same as the transitive case marking of the
ergative languages:

(8)   Passive case marking of accusative languages:

Tns   Verb-C̲i̲a̲   e̲ Agent   Subj
                     (=underlying   (=underlying
                        Subj)   DO)

Transitive case marking of ergative languages:

Tns   Verb   e̲ Subj   DO

These correspondences hold for case marking throughout
Polynesian, and they suggest that the present syntactic diversity of these languages may have an elegant historical solution. Namely, both accusative and ergative case marking
are descended from a single, original type that has undergone
a number of changes in the daughter languages. Assuming that
the original system resembled one of the attested systems (an
assumption that has been made by all linguists attempting to
deal with this problem), we are left with two possibilities.
Either (A) Proto-Polynesian had an accusative case system,
like (3-4), and the case marking of the ergative Polynesian
languages is a later development; or else (B) Proto-Polynesian had an ergative case system, like (5-6), and the case
marking of the accusative languages is a later development.

The choice of (A) or (B) as the right history for Polynesian is not uncontroversial. Solution (A) has been proposed by Hale (1968, 1970) and Hohepa (1969), while solution (B)
has been proposed by Clark (1973a, 1973b); see Chung (1976b)
for a critique of these proposals. It appears that the
strongest argument for (B) is the appearance of ergative case
marking in two of the three major subgroups of Polynesian
(Tongic and Samoic-Outlier; see (2)). According to proponents
of (B), this distributional fact alone should force us to reconstruct the ergative type of case marking for Proto-Polynesian.[2]

However, while distributional evidence is one criterion
for historical reconstruction, it is not reliable enough to
serve as the only criterion. Comparative linguists since
Schmidt (1872) have recognized that in many instances, the
wide distribution of some feature in a language family is due
to changes that occur after the dissolution of the proto-language. In such instances, distributional evidence would
wrongly predict that the feature was part of the proto-language and not the result of later change. Given this fallibility, it seems to be generally conceded that distributional
evidence can serve only as a secondary criterion for reconstruction. Instead, the kinds of evidence that must be used
ultimately to justify a reconstruction are (i) genuine archaisms in the attested languages, and (ii) sequences of plausible historical changes that relate the reconstructed feature
to its descendants. This is the traditional position of comparative historical linguistics, as set forth by Meillet
(1966).

In my thesis (Chung 1976b), I use these two types of
evidence to argue that Proto-Polynesian had an accusative
case system (proposal (A)). The reader is referred there for
the full account of the evidence. Here I briefly sketch the
arguments that the accusative case marking was original, and
propose an explanation for the rise of ergative case marking
in the Tongic and Samoic-Outlier languages.

There are three sets of archaisms that argue that Proto-
Polynesian had accusative case marking. These are:

(i) In several Tongic and Samoic-Outlier languages, a
suffix -Cia is used in certain nonproductive types of verb
derivation. This suffix, though lexicalized, has exactly the
same semantic properties as a passive suffix. Now given that
lexicalized morphemes are often remnants of older, syntactically productive forms, this suffix can be used to argue that
-Cia was originally a syntactic passive suffix in Proto-Polynesian.

(ii) In one ergative Samoic-Outlier language, Rennell-
Bellona, i is used as a direct object marker for pronouns and
proper names. This i, which can be shown to be distinct from
the oblique preposition i 'at', has several anomalous syntactic properties. These properties can be explained by assuming that they are survivals from an earlier time when i marked direct objects of all types in Proto-Polynesian.

(iii) Finally, all Polynesian languages have a productive mechanism for turning clauses into noun phrases or nominalizations. These nominalizations undergo a rule of Possessive Marking, which places one NP associated with the nominalized verb in the possessive. Possessive Marking can be

reconstructed as affecting subjects and direct objects, but not oblique NPs. Exceptionally, though, the synchronic versions of this rule in the ergative languages do not affect transitive subjects marked with the ergative particle e. It can be shown that it is the specific presence of e that blocks Possessive Marking from applying in these languages -- a fact that is anomalous synchronically. This fact can, however, be accounted for historically by assuming that e was originally the marker of an oblique case. In other words, e must be reconstructed as an oblique preposition, not a subject marker, in Proto-Polynesian.

These archaisms make it clear what the case system of Proto-Polynesian must have looked like. On the one hand, *i can be reconstructed as a direct object marker in Proto-Polynesian. This argues that the accusative-middle case marking of (7), which crucially involves *i, must have been used originally for transitive sentences. On the other hand, *-Cia can be reconstructed as a passive suffix, and *e as an oblique preposition. This argues that the passive-ergative case marking of (8), which crucially involves these morphemes, must have been used originally for passive sentences. Putting these conclusions together, we find that the reconstructed system is point for point identical to the accusative type of case marking in (3-4). Hence Proto-Polynesian had an accusative case system (proposal (A)), and it was organized as follows:[3]

(9)   Proto-Polynesian:

Tns	Verb	Subj		(intransitive)
Tns	Verb	Subj	i DO	(transitive)

Passive converts transitive sentences into:

Tns	Verb-Cia	e Agent	Subj
		(=underlying Subj)	(=underlying DO)

It is important to stress exactly why proposal (A) is superior to the proposal that Proto-Polynesian might have had ergative case marking (proposal (B)). Adopting proposal (A) gives a unified explanation for the archaisms of (i-iii). The comparative method predisposes us to believe that these archaisms should be accounted for historically. On the other hand, adopting proposal (B) would leave these archaisms without any explanation at all.

Archaisms, then, provide one type of evidence for proposal (A). In order for this proposal to be established without doubt, it is also necessary to show that the Proto-Polynesian system can be related to the case systems of the attested languages by means of plausible historical changes. The relationship of (9) to the accusative Polynesian languages is obvious; the systems are almost identical.[4] We can therefore turn our attention to the ergative languages, and the historical relationship of (9) to (5-6).

Note that in Proto-Polynesian, the syntactic functions of the NPs of the passive are in fact ambiguous. The e NP and the unmarked NP are surface agent and subject, respectively; but they are also underlying subject and direct object. This suggests that one possible historical development for the passive would be for its NPs to have their underlying syntactic functions reanalyzed as surface functions. The passive agent would be reanalyzed as a surface subject, and the derived subject, as a surface direct object:

(10)   Passive: Tns Verb-<u>Cia</u>   e Agent   Subj
                                    (underlying   (underlying
                                     Subj)   DO)

                → reanalyzed as →

Transitive: Tns Verb-<u>Cia</u>   e Subj   DO

This reanalysis accounts for the major difference between Proto-Polynesian and the case systems of the ergative
Polynesian languages -- namely, the rise of ergative case
marking itself. The changes required to account for the rest
of the case system of (5-6) are extremely minor (e.g. loss of
the -<u>Cia</u> suffix, and loss of accusative case marking for non-
middle clauses in favor of the newer ergative pattern).

I propose, then, that the case marking of the ergative
Polynesian languages arose through reanalysis of original passive clauses as active transitive clauses. This reanalysis
is a plausible change, since it exploits an ambiguity in the
original surface data (Andersen 1973); the <u>e</u> NP in (10) originally functioned as a surface agent but an underlying subject,
and the unmarked NP originally functioned as a surface derived subject but an underlying direct object. Further, the
reanalysis is motivated in the sense that it decreases opacity (Kiparsky 1971): it realigns the NPs of the passive so
that their underlying grammatical relations are reflected
transparently by their surface relations. Finally, although
it is always risky to speculate on direct causes of change,
it may be that this particular reanalysis was facilitated by
the fact that the passive was more frequent than the active
in Proto-Polynesian. The passive occurs more often than the
active in several attested Polynesian languages; and evidence
from more distantly related Austronesian languages (e.g. Ma-

lagasy, Bahasa Indonesia, Philippines languages) suggests
that this may be characteristic of the Austronesian language
family as a whole. It is conceivable (though by no means certain) that this frequency set up a situation in some Polynesian languages where reanalysis of the passive as transitive
was particularly desirable.

In summary, the evidence indicates that Proto-Polynesian
had an accusative case system, and that case marking in the
ergative Polynesian languages arose through a reanalysis of
passive sentences as transitive. I will assume this in what
follows, and I will refer to the change in (10) as the passive-to-ergative reanalysis.

2. Case Marking in Pukapukan

Having set up the comparative situation, I now turn to
the major focus of this paper: the synchronic status of case
marking in Pukapukan, a Samoic-Outlier language. In this Section I describe the basic facts of case marking in Pukapukan,
and suggest that this language is in the process of actualizing the passive-to-ergative reanalysis.[5]

Pukapukan differs from all other Polynesian languages in
having three types of case marking for (underlying) transitive
clauses. Following the morphology, I refer to these types as
'accusative', 'passive', and 'ergative'. These labels are
somewhat misleading syntactically (see Section 3), but they
have the virtue of corresponding to the names introduced for
different case patterns in Section 1.

The case system can be outlined as follows. Subjects of
(underlying) intransitive clauses are in the nominative, which

is unmarked. This is the normal pattern throughout Polynesian:

(11)   na   we-lele te kau
        past pl-run the people
        'The people ran.'

(Underlying) transitive clauses allow 'accusative',
'passive', or 'ergative' types of case marking. In the 'accusative' type, the subject is nominative and the direct object is marked with the particle i. Clauses that select this
type of case marking tend to be fairly rigidly VSO:[6]

(12)a.   na   patu mātou i   te tamaiti
         past hit we   Acc the child
         'We hit the child.'

    b.   tulituli loa Lua Tulivae ia   i   tana wawine
         chase   Emp L.T.   that Acc his woman
         'Lua Tulivae chased his wife

             ma na   tama
             and the=pl boy
             and the children.' (B1090)

In the 'passive' type, the (underlying) subject is marked with
the particle e and the (underlying) direct object is nominative. In addition, the verb takes some form of the suffix
-Cia, usually -a, -ina, or -ngia. Clauses that select this
type of case marking freely allow VSO or VOS word order:

(13)a.   na   patu-a   te tamaiti e   mātou
         past hit-Pass the child   Agt us
         'The child was hit by us.' 'We hit the child.'

    b.   kai-na   loa na   tamaliki e   te wui aitu
         eat-Pass Emp the=pl children Agt the pl spirit
         'The children were all eaten by the

             pau
             done
             spirits.'   (B1083)

Finally, in the 'ergative' type, the (underlying) subject is marked with e and the (underlying) direct object is nomina- tive. The verb does not take a suffix, but occurs in its stem form. Clauses that select this type of case marking allow VSO or VOS word order, with VSO slightly preferred:

(14)a.   na   patu te tamaiti e   mātou
         past hit the child   Erg we
         'We hit the child.'

     b.   lomilomi ai e   tana wawine ma na   tama
         massage Pro Erg his woman and the=pl boy
         'His two knees were massaged by his wife and

             lua tulivae ia
             two knee   that
             the children.'   (B1089)

Morphologically, the only difference between the 'pas- sive' and 'ergative' types of case marking appears to be the presence of the suffix -Cia. We will see in Section 3, how- ever, that these two types of case marking differ syntacti- cally in several crucial respects. In anticipation of this, I give different glosses (Agt and Erg) to the e's that occur in (13) and (14). These are chosen primarily to relate (13- 14) to the larger comparative situation.

The use of 'accusative', 'passive', and 'ergative' types of case marking deserves a study in itself. There appear to be stylistic differences among the three types: the 'accu- sative' is identified by native speakers as polite/formal/ proper; the 'passive' as neutral; the 'ergative' as casual/ colloquial/slightly improper. This does not, however, pre- vent the three types from being used side by side in elicited sentences, conversation, and narratives. For instance, in (15), taken from a text, the first clause is accusative and the second, ergative:

(15)   patu loa te wenua i   a   Uyo, yangayanga wua
        hit Emp the people Acc pers U.   work   just
        'The people attacked Uyo, they pressed (him) hard,

                e   lātou, kiai loa na   maua ete patu
                Erg they   not Emp past able Comp hit
                but (they) could not kill (him).'

Sentences like these are extremely common; they show that the
three types of case marking occur freely for simple transitive
clauses, regardless of register of speech.

The appearance of the 'ergative' type of case marking
suggests that Pukapukan has undergone the passive-to-ergative
reanalysis of (10); it has reanalyzed former passive clauses
as active transitives and begun to lose the passive suffix
-Cia. In fact, it can be demonstrated that this change has
occurred, and that it operated on an older accusative system.
Evidence that Pukapukan was originally accusative is provided
by the structure of nominalizations; this is discussed in
Chung (1976b). Evidence that passive clauses in this language
have been reanalyzed as active transitives is provided in Section 3.

I consider it established, then, that Pukapukan has undergone the passive-to-ergative reanalysis. This is exactly
what is predicted by the surface morphology of (12-14) plus
our knowledge of the comparative situation. In the following
Section, I turn to the question of how this change is being
actualized, and what the proper mechanisms are to describe it.

3. The Actualization of the Passive-to-Ergative Reanalysis

In a standard generative framework, the passive-to-ergative reanalysis would be realized by two separate and discrete changes. These would be: (i) loss of Passive, and (ii)

addition of a new, Ergative Case Marking rule. Such changes would provide an elegant account of the relationship between the original case system (16) and its reanalyzed counterpart (17):

(16)   Before the Passive-to-Ergative Reanalysis:

        Passive: V NP NP
        (optional)   1   2   3 → 1+$\underline{Cia}$ 3 $\underline{e}$+2

        Accusative Case   V NP NP
        Marking: 1   2   3 → 1   2 $\underline{i}$+3

(17)   After the Passive-to-Ergative Reanalysis:

        Accusative Case   V NP NP
        Marking: 1   2   3 → 1   2 $\underline{i}$+3
        (optional)

        Ergative Case V NP NP
        Marking: 1 2   3 → 1+$\underline{Cia}$ $\underline{e}$+2 3

Later developments in the reanalyzed system would be accounted for in similar fashion. For instance, loss of the -$\underline{Cia}$ suffix could be described as a simplification of Ergative Case Marking, or as the addition of a rule of Suffix Deletion:

(18)   Suffix Deletion: V-$\underline{Cia}$
        (optional)   1   2   → 1 $\emptyset$

Now if this description were correct, the fact that Puka-pukan has undergone the passive-to-ergative reanalysis would lead us to expect that its grammar would look like (17) rather than (16). The 'accusative' clauses of (12) would be derived by Accusative Case Marking; the 'passive' and 'erga-tive' clauses of (13-14) would be derived by Ergative Case Marking followed by optional Suffix Deletion. However, the situation is not so simple. A closer examination of the syntax reveals that the passive-to-ergative reanalysis has been

actualized in Pukapukan only in partial fashion. In this
Section I demonstrate this by considering the interaction of
'passive' and 'ergative' clauses with a number of subject referring rules.

Crucial to the investigation will be which NP of a 'passive'/'ergative' clause acts as a subject for the purposes of
these rules. If the unmarked NP (=underlying direct object)
acts as the subject, we can conclude that the clause must
have been derived by Passive. But if the e NP (=underlying
subject) acts as the subject, we can conclude that the clause
must have been derived by Ergative Case Marking. Given that
the subjecthood of these NPs is open to question, one of the
most difficult aspects of the investigation is finding independent evidence that a rule in Pukapukan is restricted to
subjects. Below I will assume that the interaction of a rule
with the 'accusative' pattern will establish whether it is
subject limited. This assumption seems justified, given that
'accusative' case marking represents the older type and is
not directly involved in the passive-to-ergative reanalysis.
Further, it is supported by the fact that the rules picked
out by this test can be identified as subject limited in other
Polynesian languages.

The way in which these rules apply to 'passive'/'ergative' clauses is subject to a certain amount of variation.
Here some explanation of my use of the term variation is in
order. Studies of variation have traditionally been based on
data from a large sample of the linguistic community. Labov
(1969) has argued that such data reflects the synchronic and
diachronic status of linguistic rules more accurately than
data collected from a small number of speakers. In my field-

work on Pukapukan it was impossible for me to conduct a large
scale study of this type; hence I cannot discuss the passive-
to-ergative reanalysis in terms of variation across speakers.
It is, however, possible to derive some of the same benefits
by examining individual variation in judgements of particular
sentence types. When presented with sentences like those below, native speakers of Pukapukan tended to offer different
grammaticality judgements on different occasions. It seems
reasonable to assume that this variation is principled, and
thus indirectly reflects the larger status of 'passive' and
'ergative' types of case marking. In this sense, individual
variation can be considered analogous to variation across
speakers.

    This assumption about individual variation has the advan-
tage of allowing us to discuss fine differences in grammaticality on the basis of data from only a few native speakers.
It is motivated in the sense that individual speakers are members of the larger speech community, and so can be expected to
reflect some aspects of this community when given a chance
(see Bickerton 1971, 1973; Wolfram 1973). Finally, as far as
the passive-to-ergative reanalysis is concerned, the assumption is supported by evidence from narrative texts. An examination of Beaglehole and Beaglehole's Pukapukan texts (1938)
reveals that the frequency of clause types discussed below
correlates almost exactly with the degree of grammaticality
assigned them by individual native speakers. This suggests
that individual variation can be as reliable an index of usage, in the long run, as variation across a number of speakers.

Let us, then, consider the interaction of 'passive' and 'ergative' case marking with five subject referring rules. These are Equi, Raising, Relativization, Clefting, and Question Movement.[7]

3.1. Equi. Pukapukan has a rule of complement subject deletion that I will refer to as Equi. This rule affects complements of verbs of motion (e.g. yau 'come', wano 'go'), which are normally introduced by the subjunctive tense marker ke:

(19) na wō   te wui tāne ke yī-ika   lātou i
      past go=pl the pl man sbj catch-fish they in
      'The men went so that they could fish in the

      te moana
      the ocean
      ocean.'

If the complement subject is coreferential with the subject of the motion verb, it can optionally be deleted. As a result, the subjunctive tense marker disappears, giving the complement the surface form of a participle:

(20) na wō   te wui tāne yī-ika   i te moana
      past go=pl the pl man catch-fish in the ocean
      'The men went fishing in the ocean.'

Crucially, Equi deletes only NPs of a certain syntactic/semantic type; it is restricted to deleting syntactic subjects that are also semantic agents. Intransitive subjects, for instance, can be deleted by this rule if they are agentive. So can transitive subjects (i.e. the subjects of 'accusative' clauses):

(21)a. ka yau ia Uyo tiaki i te wenua
       aor come pers U. lead Acc the people
       'Uyo will come to lead the people.'

b.   ko   te tangata e   yau yala i   taku
     Pred the man   tense come untie Acc my
     'For the person who comes to untie my wife ...'

     wawine nei
     woman this
     (B1121)

But indirect objects and causes of states cannot be deleted,
although they can be interpreted as agentive, because they
are not the syntactic subjects of their clause. Similarly,
direct objects cannot be deleted because they satisfy neither
the subjecthood nor the agency criterion.

   Consider now the interaction of Equi with 'passive' and
'ergative' clauses. Since the e̲ NPs (=underlying subjects)
of these clause types are agentive, we can expect their interaction with this rule to reveal whether or not they are syntactic subjects. And here the results are rather surprising.
The e̲ NPs of 'passive' clauses can be deleted occasionally by
native speakers; this deletion is attested infrequently in
texts:

(22)a.   ?ka yau koe onoono-wia te tala o te wale
         aor come you look-Pass the side of the house
         'You'll have to come inspect the side of the
              house.'

    b.   ?na   lōmamai lātou patu-a   te toa
         past come=pl they hit-Pass the warrior
         'They came to kill the warrior.'

The e̲ NPs of 'ergative' clauses are rarely, if ever, deleted.
There are no clear examples of this deletion in texts:

(23)a.   ?*ka yau ia   Uyo tiaki te wenua
         aor come pers U. lead the people
         (Uyo will come to lead the people.)

b.   ?*yau koe onoono te tala o toku wale
     come you look   the side of my   house
     (You come inspect the side of my house.)

In both cases, although deletion is possible, it is considerably less acceptable than deletion of transitive subjects in
the 'accusative' pattern (see (21)). (24) shows that this is
a fact about Equi and not about the complement structures
themselves, for when Equi has not applied, both 'passive' and
'ergative' patterns are allowed:

(24)a.   na yau te tāne ke wakayaele-a e-na   te
         past come the man sbj lead-Pass   Agt-him the
         'The man came so that he could lead the

              wenua
              people
              people.'

   b.   lele mai te mango ki te pala ke kakati e-na
         run here the shark to the pala sbj bite   Erg-he
         'The shark rushed for the pala to bite him (lit.
          so that he could bite (him); him deleted by
          zero-pronominalization).' (B1041-42)

   Given that Equi can always delete true transitive subjects, sentences like (22-23) argue that the e NPs of 'passive' and 'ergative' clauses are not fully (or always) the
syntactic subjects of their clause. Hence the actualization
of the passive-to-ergative reanalysis is not yet complete.
Further, the contrast of (22) and (23) reveals that this actualization has proceeded faster for 'passive' clauses than
for 'ergative' clauses, which do not have the -Cia suffix.
These differences are significant, for they are repeated in
roughly the same form for all of the syntactic processes discussed below.

3.2. Raising. More evidence for this gradual actualization

is provided by the Pukapukan rule of Raising. Raising affects sentences formed with <u>kiai</u> 'not', the negative for past
actions and tenseless clauses containing predicate nominals.
This negative is an overt verb (Chung 1970, 1976b) and takes
the entire negated clause as its sentential subject. That is,
a negative sentence like (25):

> (25) kiai na   tū   ake au
>   not past stand up I
>   'I didn't stand up.'

has the structure:

> (26)

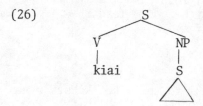

Optionally, an NP from the embedded clause can be
raised to become the subject of <u>kiai</u>. Thus from (25) it is
possible to derive (27), where the raised NP occurs in normal
subject position, immediately after the higher verb:

> (27) kiai au na   tū   ake
>   not I past stand up
>   'I didn't stand up.'

Arguments that (27) involves Raising and not some other rule
are given in Chung (1976b).

What we are interested in is the fact that Raising is
restricted to syntactic subjects. It applies to intransitive
subjects, as in (27), and to transitive subjects (i.e. the
subjects of 'accusative' clauses):

(28)a.   kiai kōlua na   kite i   a   Mili?
          not you=du past see Acc pers M.
          'Didn't you two see Mili?'

    b.   kiai te tamāwine na   patu i   te tāne
          not the girl   past hit Acc the man
          'The girl didn't hit the man.'

But it does not affect direct objects, locatives, causes, or other non-subject NPs. For instance, the accusative direct object nā yakali 'the coconuts' in (29) cannot undergo Raising:

(29)   *kiai nā   yakali na   kai (ai) te kuri
         not the=pl coconut past eat Pro the dog
         (The dog didn't eat the coconuts.)

    Now when Raising is applied to 'passive' and 'ergative' clauses, a close parallel to the Equi pattern emerges. Raising is allowed occasionally for the e NPs (=underlying subjects) of 'passive' clauses:

(30)a.   ?kiai ia   Te Malo na   tiaki-na te wenua
          not pers T.M.   past lead-Pass the people
          'Te Malo didn't lead the people.'

    b.   ?kiai ia-na   na   wakatū-ngia te wale āpī
          not pers-he past build-Pass the house school
          'He didn't build the schoolhouse.'

But it is allowed only rarely (if at all) for the e NPs of 'ergative' clauses:

(31)a.   ?*kiai ia   Te Malo na   pepelu te malo
          not pers T.M.   past don   the loincloth
         (Te Malo didn't don the loincloth.)

    b.   ?*kiai te tamāwine na   patu te tāne
          not the girl   past hit the man
         (The girl didn't hit the man.)

Facts like these argue that the e NPs do not always act as

the syntactic subjects of their clause; further, the e NP
of an 'ergative' clause acts as subject less often than the e
NP of a 'passive' clause.

Raising also reveals a comparable difference between the
unmarked NPs (=underlying direct objects) of these two clause
types. (Recall that these NPs could not be deleted by Equi,
because they failed to satisfy the agency requirement.) Unmarked NPs in the 'passive' pattern can always undergo Raising:

(32)a. kiai ia-na   na   patu-a   e   Yina
        not pers-he past hit-Pass Agt Y.
        'He wasn't hit by Yina.'

   b.   kiai te lā   na   liaki-na   e   te wui tāngata
        not the sail past leave-Pass Agt the pl men
        'The sail wasn't left up by the men.'

In this respect they resemble the unmarked NPs (=syntactic
subjects) of 'accusative' clauses. But unmarked NPs in the
'ergative' pattern are allowed to raise only marginally:

(33)a. ?kiai ia-na   na   patu e   Yina
        not   pers-he past hit Erg Y.
        'He wasn't hit by Yina.'

   b.   ?kiai te lā   na   liaki e   te wui tāngata
        not   the sail past leave Erg the pl men
        'The sail wasn't left up by the men.'

Disregarding for the moment this last difference, which
will be discussed in fn. 11, it is clear that the unmarked
NPs (=underlying direct objects) of 'passive' clauses can always act as syntactic subjects. This means that Passive must
still be productive in Pukapukan. Further, these NPs act as
subjects more often than the e NPs (=underlying subjects) in
(30-31). This suggests that the Ergative Case Marking rule

is only in the process of being introduced. When combined
with the contrast between (30) and (31), these facts reveal
that Pukapukan is very far from the discrete synchronic system of (17-18).

3.3.   Extraction Rules. Roughly the same situation obtains
when we consider the interaction of 'passive' and 'ergative'
case marking with Relativization, Clefting, and Question Movement. These rules are closely related to one another and to
their analogues in other Polynesian languages. For this reason they are treated together here.

     Relativization in Pukapukan deletes or pronominalizes
the relative noun, under conditions to be described below.
This rule produces the relative clauses in:

(34)a.   te wui tāngata na   lōmamai mai o lātou konga
          the pl men   (past come-pl from pl-their place
          'the people who came from their distant places'

          mamao
          far)

    b.   te taime na   maka ai au
          the time (past leave Pro I)
          'the time that I left'

Clefting moves a focused NP to the left and marks it with the
predicate particle <u>ko</u>:

(35)a.   ko   Yinaliulu ya   tu   i te uluulu akau
          Pred Y.   past stand on the   reef
          'Yinaliulu was standing on the outer reef.' (B993)

    b.   ko   te moana na   yi-ika   ai lātou
          Pred the ocean past catch-fish Pro they
          'It's the ocean that they were fishing in.'

Question Movement moves a question word to the left and marks
it with the predicate particle <u>ko</u>, or else (with certain ob-

lique question words) leaves it unmarked:

(36)a.   ko   ai   koa yau nei?
          Pred who? perf come here
          'Who has come here?'

   b.   tiai koe ka ngakaumate ai?
          why? you aor bold   Pro
          'Why are you so bold?' (B1087)

These rules share several syntactic characteristics.
First, each is unbounded. Second, each involves a <u>deletion
strategy</u> (the (a) examples above) and a <u>pronominalization
strategy</u> (the (b) examples above). The <u>deletion</u> strategy simply deletes or chops the focused NP; the pronominalization
strategy copies it with the pronominal <u>ai</u>, which cliticizes
to the verb. Arguments that these strategies are distinct
from the normal processes of pronominalization and zero-pronominalization are given in my thesis (Chung 1976b). Here I
simply assert that (34-36) cannot be produced by ordinary pronominalization, but must involve Relativization, Clefting,
and Question Movement.

As is to be expected by now, the deletion strategies of
these rules are restricted to syntactic subjects. They are
allowed for intransitive subjects, as in the (a) examples
above. They are also allowed for transitive subjects (i.e.
subjects of 'accusative' clauses):

(37)a.   onoono-wia-ake te mea   na wakangayuayua i
          look-Pass-up the thing (past stir   Acc
          'Just look at the thing which stirred the pile

                te   taekele tutae
                the pile   feces)
                of feces.' (B1102; Relativization)

   b.   ko-na   na   tuku i   te kou
         Pred-he past give Acc the gift
         'It was he who gave the present.' (Clefting)

   c.   ko   ai   na   aumai i   te puka?
         Pred who? past bring Acc the book
         'Who brought the book?' (Question Movement)

However, they do not affect direct objects, indirect objects,
causes, or other nonsubject NPs, which must use the pronominalization strategies instead.

     Given their restriction to subjects, the deletion strat-
egies of these three rules can be expected to pick out the
syntactic subjects of 'passive' and 'ergative' clauses. Here
the results are parallel to those for Equi and Raising, though
they are not exactly identical. The deletion strategies are
almost always allowed for the e NPs (=underlying subjects) of
'passive' clauses. Sentences in which this NP has been relativized, and so forth, are not always accepted by native
speakers, but they are attested regularly in texts. I will
indicate this near perfect acceptability with a @:[8]

(38)a.   womamai la   ki te kata   ya   wai-a   tatou
          come=pl that to the shark (past make-Pass us)
          'Come to the shark who injured us.' (B1085; Rela-
             tivization)

    b.   @ko te toa   koa patu-a   te tamaiti
          Pred the warrior perf hit-Pass the child
          'It was the warrior who had hit the child.'
             (Clefting)

    c.   @ko ai   na   kalo-wia   ia   Te Malo?
          Pred who? past look-Pass pers T.M.
          'Who saw Te Malo?' (Question Movement)

But the deletion strategies are allowed only occasionally for
the e NPs of 'ergative' clauses. Consider:

(39)a.   ko   ai   te   kau   e   langa a tatou ui   nei?
         Pred who? the people (unm pull pl-our   taro this)
         'Who is the group who pulls up our talo? (B1128;
         Relativization)

   b.   ?ko   te   toa   na   patu te   tamaiti
        Pred the warrior past hit   the child
        'It was the warrior who hit the child.'
        (Clefting)

   c. ?*ko   ai   na   aumai te   puka?
      Pred who? past bring the book
      (Who brought the book?) (Question Movement)

Further, it seems to be harder to question the e NP
of an 'ergative' clause via the deletion strategy than it is
to relativize or cleft it. This judgement is expressed consistently by native speakers and supported by textual evidence. Thus, relative clauses and cleft sentences like (39a-
b) occur sometimes in texts, though not with the frequency of
their 'passive' counterparts (38a-b). Questions like (39c),
however, do not occur at all. The contrast between (38c) and
(39c) serves to stress two points that are made in 3.1 and
3.2 as well. Namely, the e NPs of 'passive' and 'ergative'
clauses do not always act as syntactic subjects for the purposes of these rules, and the former act as subjects more often than the latter.

The deletion strategies are always allowed for the unmarked NPs (=underlying direct objects) of 'passive' and 'ergative' clauses. I will illustrate this briefly for Relativization. In (40), the unmarked NP of a 'passive' clause has
been relativized:

(40)   ko   ai   te   tāne e   kalo-wia e   māua?
       Pred who? the man (unm   look-Pass Agt us=du)
       'Who's the man who we're going to see?'

In (41), the unmarked NP of an 'ergative' clause has been relativized:

(41)   wakalongo loa te   lulu   i   te   wakapononga
        hear   Emp the village Acc the arrangement
        'The village heard the arrangement told

        na talatala e   te   pule
        (past say   Erg the pule)
        by the pule.' (B1124)

The fact that the deletion strategies can always affect
these unmarked NPs argues that they are true subjects, like
the subjects of 'accusative' clauses. As such, it supports
the Raising evidence discussed above.

    In short, extraction rules give roughly the same pic-
ture of 'passive' and 'ergative' case marking as do Equi and
Raising. This point is of interest because extraction rules
are more superficial syntactically than either of the other
rules. Further, although all rules treat the two types of e
NPs in roughly the same fashion, the frequency with which
these NPs actually behave as subjects is higher for extraction rules. This point will become significant below.

4.   An Explanation

    The results of this investigation can be summarized as
follows. To begin with, it is clear that the unmarked NPs
(=underlying direct objects) of 'passive' and 'ergative'
clauses must be identified as syntactic subjects. These NPs
are always able to undergo the subject referring rules of
Section 3: Equi, Raising, Relativization, Clefting, and
Question Movement. However, the e NPs (=underlying subjects)
of 'passive' and 'ergative' clauses cannot be identified as
subjects in as clear a fashion. The e NPs of 'passive'

clauses are almost always eligible for the deletion strategies
of the extraction rules; but they undergo Equi and Raising only
occasionally. The e NPs of 'ergative' clauses are sometimes
available for Relativization and Clefting; they are rarely
able to undergo Equi, Raising, or Question Movement.

(42)   Availability of Different NPs for Subject Ref-
           ferring Rules:

	Unmarked NP		e NP	
	'passive'	'ergative'	'passive'	'ergative'
Equi			?	?*
Raising	√	?	?	?*
Question	√	√	@	?*
Relativiz.	√	√	@	?
Clefting	√	√	@	?

The arrangement of the chart in (42) suggests that
these facts can be treated synchronically as a squish of subjecthood (Ross 1974). Our historical perspective on Pukapukan makes it more profitable, however, to view them in terms
of a case system in transition. Here several observations
can be made. First, the ability of the unmarked NP in (42)
to undergo almost all of the subject referring rules argues
that Passive is still productive in Pukapukan. Second, the
ability of the e NP to undergo some of the rules, but not
others, argues that Ergative Case Marking has been added to
the grammar in some restricted fashion.

Finally, it appears that Ergative Case Marking interacts differently with Equi and Raising than with the deletion strategies of the extraction rules. This last differ-

ence is important, because it extends beyond the particular
rules discussed in Section 3 to other subject referring rules
in Pukapukan. For instance, besides the Raising of 3.2, Pukapukan allows subjects to raise to the imperative negative
auwae and to certain sentential adverbs (e.g. auwā 'probably',
yaulā 'therefore'). In their interaction with 'passive' and
'ergative' clauses, these processes pattern with Equi and
Raising rather than with the extraction rules. Further, besides the extraction rules discussed in 3.3, Pukapukan has a
rule of Bare Topicalization that simply moves a subject to
the left. In its interaction with 'passive' and 'ergative'
clauses, this rule patterns with the deletion strategies of
the other extraction rules, although it is consistently more
acceptable for e NPs.

The difference between the two types of rules is also
significant because it correlates with their formal properties. Raising and Equi, for instance, are examples of what
can be called major cyclic rules. They are governed, bounded,
cyclic rules that alter the grammatical relations of the
clause. Relativization, Clefting, and Question Movement, in
contrast, are examples of superficial rules. They are ungov-
erned, unbounded, postcyclic rules that usually involve leftward movement, accompanied by some kind of chopping or copying. These formal differences extend to the other subject
referring rules mentioned briefly above. Hence it is possible to say that Ergative Case Marking in Pukapukan interacts differently with major cyclic rules than with superficial rules.

What is interesting about this observation is that it is
relatively hard to capture using the standard generative devices. Since this may not be obvious, I will now consider

two ways of formalizing the Pukapukan facts synchronically
within generative grammar. These involve: (i) transformations and the principle of the cycle, and (ii) variable rules
of the sort described by Labov (1969, 1972).

4.1. Cyclic Solution. Within a discrete theory like transformational grammar, it is difficult to account for the nondiscrete facts of Section 3. Perhaps a first try at an adequate account might look like this. Pukapukan would have a
cyclic Passive rule and a cyclic Accusative Case Marking rule.
The fact that these rules would be cyclic would allow them to
interact freely with other cyclic rules, producing Equi and
Raising sentences like (21), (28), and (32).

In addition, Pukapukan would have a postcyclic rule of
Ergative Case Marking. Being postcyclic, this rule would be
extrinsically ordered after Equi and Raising, which as cyclic
rules would bleed it. However, it would still be able to interact with the extraction rules, which would also be postcyclic. This would account for the relative acceptability of
(38-39).

Such a solution captures the basic difference between
the two types of rules in (42); but it does not account for
much else. In particular, it fails to explain why the e NPs
of 'passive' clauses can sometimes undergo Raising -- a kind
of interaction that should be impossible if Raising is cyclic
but Ergative Case Marking is not. Further, it fails totally
to account for the different syntactic properties of 'passive'
and 'ergative' clauses, which in this solution would differ
only in the presence or absence of Suffix Deletion. It is
hard to see how these differences could be coded into a discrete grammar, since they cannot be described by appealing to

rule ordering.

4.2. Solution Involving Variable Rules. Clearly what is
needed is some version of transformational grammar that is
able to describe a range of variation. One version of transformational grammar that attempts to do this has been developed by Labov (1969, 1972). Labov proposes that transformations
may be accompanied by variables indicating the frequency (in
percentages) with which they will apply under various conditions. Elements whose presence or absence affects this frequency are assumed to be part of the formal statement of the
rule, and they are written into the structural description or
structural change in angled brackets. Such a system is, in
many ways, a notational elaboration of transformational grammar, once the need for accounting for variation in some way
is recognized.

In Labov's framework, a formalization of the Pukapukan
facts might look like this. Passive, Accusative Case Marking,
and Ergative Case Marking would all be cyclic rules, with different variables assigned to them describing their frequency
in simple sentences. In addition, Raising, Equi, and the deletion strategies of the extraction rules would be condition-
od so as to apply less frequently to subjects marked with e
(and still less frequently to these subjects when the verb is
not marked with -Cia). The actual frequencies involved would
be coded into variables attached to each rule. To take a
hypothetical example:

(43)   Raising: Neg Tns V <-Cia> <e> NP X
                  1   2   3   4   5   6   7
                                                  $\longrightarrow$
                  1   6   2   3   4   7

Variables: $(1-k_0)(1-k_1)$ when $\underline{e}$ and $\underline{-Cia}$ are present

$(1-k_0)(1-k_1)(1-k_2)$ when $\underline{e}$, but not $\underline{-Cia}$, is present

$(1-k_0)$ otherwise

Such a system is, in fact, capable of describing the variation in (42). The problem with it is that it provides no explanation whatsoever of why the rules should vary as they do. In particular, it fails totally to capture the unified behavior of the major cyclic rules in their interaction with Ergative Case Marking. This is because this behavior cannot be described in any general fashion, but must be coded separately into the formal statement of each rule. Given this, the variable solution to (42) is not particularly more satisfying than the cyclic solution.

4.3. A Principle Governing Syntactic Change. Other solutions of this sort could be suggested; all would fail, however, to account for the basic generalization embodied in (42). 'Passive' and 'ergative' clauses interact with syntactic rules in a way that is both nondiscrete and systematic. We can conclude from this that the Pukapukan facts cannot be explained by appealing to existing formal devices.[9] Nonetheless, it is clear that the variation in (42) is principled, and that its principled nature is due in part to the different behavior of major cyclic and superficial rules. Here I would like to propose a substantive principle governing this aspect of the variation.

Looking again at (42), we see that the $\underline{e}$ NPs of 'passive' and 'ergative' clauses undergo superficial rules more successfully than they do major cyclic rules. This correlation holds

not only for the rules of Section 3 but also for the others
mentioned briefly above (Raising to sentential adverbs, Bare
Topicalization). Further, it holds despite the differences
between the two types of e NPs ('passive' and 'ergative') in
their interaction with all of these rules. We do not have to
look far to find an explanation for this difference. Generally speaking, major cyclic rules have a more serious effect
on the syntax of the clause than do superficial rules. This
difference is revealed most clearly by grammatical relations;
major cyclic rules alter grammatical relations, but superficial rules do not (Perlmutter and Postal, forthcoming). It
is also revealed by other formal properties.[10] Major cyclic
rules are 'deeper' than superficial rules in the sense that
they apply first (i.e. major cyclic rules precede superficial
rules). Further, in many languages, major cyclic rules have
a more radical effect on the morphology than superficial
rules, since major cyclic rules create infinitives or participles, but extraction rules do not. This difference suggests that the most innocuous way to introduce a change into
the syntax is to let it interact with superficial rules before it interacts with major cyclic rules. Such a suggestion
assumes, of course, that the optimal situation is for syntactic change to be actualized gradually in the grammar.

I propose, then, that the addition of Ergative Case
Marking to the grammar of Pukapukan is governed by the following principle:

(44)   Syntactic change is actualized for sentences that
       undergo superficial rules before it is actualized
       for sentences that undergo major cyclic rules.

This principle insures that Ergative Case Marking will feed

rules like Relativization, Clefting, and Question Movement before it feeds rules like Equi and Raising.[11] Further, I propose that this principle is a realization of the more general requirement that:

(45) Syntactic change must be actualized gradually.

Although (45) allows syntactic changes (such as the passive-to-ergative reanalysis) to be abrupt or discrete, it requires that the effects of all such changes spread through the grammar in gradual fashion. In this sense, it contradicts the standard generative position that syntactic change is entirely discrete.

5. Two Further Examples

The principles that I have just proposed claim that syntactic change is actualized in gradual but systematic fashion. According to (44), the relative chronology with which different syntactic processes interact with a given change will be determined by their formal properties. Processes with more superficial properties will interact with the change first; processes with less superficial properties will interact with it later. In this Section I discuss two further examples of change that support this claim and suggest refinements of (44). These are the extension of ergative case marking to some middle verbs in Samoan, a Polynesian language, and the reanalysis of some subject referring rules in Bahasa Indonesia, a Western Austronesian language, as affecting subjects and direct objects.

5.1. Samoan. Samoan is an ergative Polynesian language, with a case system essentially like (5-6). Transitive verbs whose direct objects are directly affected by the action gov-

ern the ergative case marking of (5). Transitive verbs whose
direct objects are not directly affected, such as perception
verbs and psychological verbs, govern the middle case marking of (6). As in Section 1, I will refer to the latter
type of verbs as middle verbs.

Recently, ergative case marking in Samoan has been extended to a number of middle verbs. Evidence from texts
(Stuebel 1896) indicates that this change had begun by the
end of the nineteenth century; it has certainly gained
ground since then. Today many speakers -- particularly
younger speakers -- allow a wide range of middle verbs to
occur with middle case marking or ergative case marking:

(46)a.   na   tofo 'oia i le kuka
         past taste he   to the cooking
         'He tasted the cooking.'

    b.   na   tofo e   ia le kuka
         past taste Erg he the cooking
         'He tasted the cooking.'

Apparently, the extension of ergative case marking has
progressed to different degrees for different middle verbs.
This can be seen from the semantic/stylistic value associated
with choice of the ergative rather than the middle pattern.
For verbs like va'ai 'see', which almost all speakers allow
to govern ergative case marking, choice of the ergative pattern has almost no semantic/stylistic value. For verbs like
tofo 'taste', which govern ergative case marking less often,
choice of this pattern implies more focus or emphasis on the
subject. Finally, for verbs like fa'alogo 'hear', which few
speakers allow to govern ergative case marking, use of the
ergative pattern is restricted to special semantic or pragmatic circumstances:

(47)a.   'ua 'ou fa'alogo i le agi o le matagi
         perf I   hear   to the blow of the wind
         'I heard the blowing of the wind.'

   b.   sā   fa'alogo a'u e le fōma'i
         past hear   me Erg the doctor
         'The doctor examined me with a stethoscope (lit.
            heard me).'

The extension of ergative case marking can be interpreted in several different ways; as a mere change in lexical
marking of a few middle verbs, or as the beginnings of a
change that will ultimately eliminate middle case marking altogether. Which of these interpretations is correct does not
directly concern us, however. What is important is that
there are middle verbs to which ergative case marking has not
been extended across the board. For instance, the verb tofo
'taste' governs middle or ergative case marking in simple
sentences. But when the subject of this verb has been clefted or cliticized, ergative case marking is not allowed:

   (48)a.   'o ia na   tofo i le kuka
            Pred he past taste to the cooking
            'It was he that tasted the cooking.' (Clefting)

      b.   *'o   ia na   tofo le kuka
            Pred he past taste the cooking
            (It was he that tasted the cooking.)

      c.   sā   'ou tofo i lau kuka
            past I   taste to your cooking
            'I tasted your cooking.' (Clitic Placement)

      d.   *sā   'ou tofo lau kuka
            past I   taste your cooking
            (I tasted your cooking.)

·Compare (49), which shows that the ergative subjects of non-
middle clauses can routinely be clefted or cliticized:

(49)a.   'o a'u sā   togi le tusi i le maile
        Pred I   past throw the book at the dog
        'It was me who threw the book at the dog.'
        (Clefting)

    b.   sā   ia 'aumai se meaalofa o le Easter i-āte a'u
       past he bring a gift   of the E.   to-pro me
       'He brought an Easter present to me.' (Clitic
       Placement)

In short, ergative case marking has been extended to verbs like <u>tofo</u> only in restricted fashion; it is allowed when these verbs occur in simple sentences, but not in sentences whose subjects have been clefted or cliticized. There is a clear sense in which simple sentences are less deformed syntactically than sentences that have undergone any movement or deletion rules. This suggests that the change in (46) is being actualized in gradual fashion, along the lines of (45); it is affecting the most transparent sentence type, the simple sentence, before it affects sentences that have undergone any movement or deletion rules at all.

5.2. Bahasa Indonesia. Bahasa Indonesia belongs to the Western branch of the Austronesian language family, a branch that includes Malagasy, most of the languages of Indonesia and the Malay Peninsula, and the Philippines languages. Although comparative work on the syntax of these languages has not progressed very far, it seems likely that they originally had verb-initial word order (Pawley and Reid 1976). In addition, it seems likely that movement rules in these languages were originally restricted to subjects. These characteristics are attested synchronically in a number of Western Austronesian languages (Keenan 1972).

Along with several other Western Austronesian languages,

Bahasa Indonesia has innovated SVO word order. This change
may (or may not) be connected to the fact that the language
has begun to reanalyze some of its movement rules as affecting direct objects as well as subjects. Since the grammatical tradition of this language is extremely prescriptive, it
is possible to observe two stages of the change by examining
the formal language (as described in Indonesian grammars)
and comparing it with more colloquial versions volunteered
by native speakers. I will do this briefly below.[12]

In formal Indonesian, as mentioned above, the basic word
order is SVO. Transitive clauses have their verbs prefixed
with the transitive prefix meng-, which has a number of phonologically conditioned variants:

(50)   dokter itu me-meriksa   saya
        doctor the Trans-examine me
        'The doctor examined me'

Relativization, Clefting, and Question Movement in the formal
language are restricted to subjects. These rules move the
focused NP to the left and separate it from the rest of the
clause with the complementizer yang:

(51)   dokter itu yang me-meriksa   saya
        doctor the Comp Trans-examine me
        'It was the doctor that examined me.' (Clefting)

Since these rules are restricted to subjects, direct objects
can undergo them only if they have first been turned into derived subjects. There are two mechanisms for accomplishing
this, depending on whether the underlying subject of the
clause is a full noun or a pronoun. If the underlying subject is a full noun, the clause undergoes a Passive rule
whose effect roughly resembles the English passive; we are

not concerned with this rule here. If the underlying subject
is a pronoun, however, the clause undergoes a rule of Object
Preposing (Chung 1976a), which turns the direct object into a
subject and optionally cliticizes the underlying subject to
the verb. Because the resulting clause is superficially intransitive, the transitive prefix does not appear, and no new
morphology is added elsewhere:

> (52)   dokter itu saya periksa
>   doctor the I   examine
>   'I examined the doctor.' 'The doctor was examined
>   by me.'

Once Object Preposing has applied, the underlying direct object (=derived subject) is eligible for Relativization, Clefting, and Question Movement:

> (53)   dokter itu yang saya periksa
>   doctor the Comp I   examine
>   'It was the doctor that I examined.' 'It was the
>   doctor that was examined by me.' (Clefting)

Although colloquial Indonesian differs from formal Indonesian in several respects (Dyen 1964), the crucial difference
for us is that the transitive prefix is optional. Thus, a-
longside (50), we have (54), where the verb appears in its
stem form:

> (54)   dokter itu periksa saya
>   doctor the examine me
>   'The doctor examined me.'

The absence of the prefix in (54) makes it morphologically similar to (52), where Object Preposing has applied --
with the difference, of course, that the underlying direct
object occupies a different position relative to the verb.
This similarity is heightened in relative clause and cleft

constructions like (53), where the direct object has been extracted. And it suggests the following diachronic possibility. Since the clause remnant following yang in (53) looks
like the remnant of an active clause in the colloquial language, it might be possible to reanalyze it as being derived
directly by extraction of the direct object, without the intermediate stage of Object Preposing. As a consequence, leftward movement rules would come to be extended to direct objects as well as subjects.

In fact, reanalyses of this sort seem to have taken
place in the colloquial language. This can be seen from the
fact that constructions like (53), which were formerly restricted to clauses with pronominal underlying subjects, are
now also allowed for clauses with full noun underlying subjects. Such clauses cannot have undergone Object Preposing,
which continues to be limited to pronominal underlying subjects in the colloquial language. Hence their direct objects
must be relativized, clefted, and questioned directly, as syntactic direct objects.[13]

The actualization of these reanalyses, interestingly,
has progressed farther for some leftward movement rules than
for others. For instance, the subject-and-object reanalysis
has been actualized completely for Clefting and Question
Movement. These rules can apply regularly to direct objects
for all native speakers, and they are even attested this way
in some grammars:

(55)a.   hanya nama itu saja yang tukang beca   tahu
         only name the just Comp worker pedicab know
         'It's only this name that the pedicab driver
             knows.' (D19a.4; Clefting)

b.   apa   yang anak itu masak?
     what? Comp child the cook
     'What did the child cook?' (Question Movement)

On the other hand, Relativization seems to lag slightly behind
in the actualization of this change. This rule applies regularly to direct objects for some speakers; for others, it is
allowed to do so only when the underlying subject is a short
common noun or proper name. A few speakers comment that constructions like (56), though common in everyday speech, are
substandard:

(56)a.   kamu me-lihat ikan yang anak itu masak?
         you Trans-see fish Comp child the cook
         'Have you seen the fish that the child cooked?'

     b.   bunga yang ibu   saya beri-kan   sudah mati
          flower Comp mother my   give-Benef Perf die
          'The flowers that my mother gave (to me) already
          died.'

The contrast between Clefting/Question Movement and Relativization may seem surprising at first glance, since all
three rules are usually classified as low level. A closer
look, however, reveals that Clefting and Question Movement
are somewhat more superficial than Relativization. Clefting
and Question Movement are unbounded, for instance, but Relativization must operate in the first clause below the head
noun (i.e. it is downward bounded). Further, Clefting and
Question Movement obey the no-ambiguity condition (Hankamer
1973), but Relativization does not. Finally, Clefting and
Question Movement have productive strategies for prepositional phrases, but Relativization is restricted to subjects and
direct objects. These facts show that Clefting and Question
Movement have more of the properties of superficial rules
than does Relativization. This correlates nicely with the

fact that the reanalysis has progressed farther for the former two rules, again along the lines sketched in (44-45).

Bahasa Indonesia, then, provides a third example of the
gradual actualization of syntactic change. The subject-and-
object reanalysis is actualized faster for Clefting/Question
Movement than for Relativization, whose status as a superficial rule is somewhat ambivalent. It is instructive to compare all three rules with the major cyclic rule of Tough Movement, which in Bahasa Indonesia is limited to underlying objects that have undergone Passive or Object Preposing. Although this rule is subject limited, it applies only to semantic objects; this would seem to make it a particularly good
candidate for a reanalysis of the sort described above. Significantly, though, Tough Movement has not undergone the subject-and-object reanalysis at all. We can connect this to the
fact that Tough Movement has all the formal properties of a
major cyclic rule, and hence can be expected to undergo this
change later than Relativization or Clefting, if it undergoes
it at all.

6. Conclusion

The specific changes discussed in this paper provide
evidence for the following. First, syntactic change interacts with superficial rules before it interacts with major
cyclic rules (Pukapukan). Second, it interacts with simple
sentences before it interacts with any superficial rules at
all (Samoan). Third and finally, it may distinguish between
rules that are more and less superficial, interacting with
the former before it interacts with the latter (Bahasa Indonesia). Putting these conclusions together, we can say that
the actualization of change is governed by a hierarchy like

that in (57):

(57)   Syntactic change implemented first
            Simple sentences
            Sentences that have undergone superficial rules
                Clefting/Question Movement
                Relativization
            Sentences that have undergone major cyclic
                rules
        Syntactic change implemented later

Such a hierarchy is natural in the sense that it corresponds
to what we already know about these types of sentences and
the rules that they involve. Synchronically, that is, it is
possible to classify syntactic rules as more or less superficial, depending on their formal properties; it is also possible to classify sentence types as more or less transparent,
depending on the types of rules that they have undergone.
What is striking is to find these classifications taking part
in the very different area of diachronic syntax. I hope to
have shown that it is plausible and intuitively quite satisfying that they should govern the systematic progress of syntactic change.

*This paper is extracted from Chapter 5 of my thesis
(Chung 1976b). I wish to thank Parepano T. Tukia, Atawua Rō-
bati (Pukapukan); Eteuati Reupena, Ali'itama Sōtoa, Palafu
Tili, 'Ali Pālata (Samoan); Ariet Budiman, Robert Item, Ibra-
him Hasan, Iwan Hirsan, and Johnny Basuki (Bahasa Indonesia)
for providing native speakers judgements on the sentences discussed here. This work was supported in part by Wellesley

College (Alice F. Palmer Travelling Fellowship), Radcliffe
College (Isobel Briggs Travelling Fellowship), the Linguistics
Department of Harvard University (funds from the Packard Foun-
dation), and the Linguistics Department of UCSD.

Examples taken from manuscripts and published sources
are referred to by author (abbreviated) and page number.   B
stands for Beaglehole and Beaglehole (1938); D for Dyen
(1964).

Notes

1. In addition, objects of middle verbs (see below) are marked either with the accusative i or with the oblique preposition ki 'to'.

2. Proponents of (B) have also claimed that the external evidence (i.e. evidence from East Oceanic languages outside the Polynesian family) argues that Proto-Polynesian had ergative case marking. In fact, the external evidence is neutral between the two proposals; see Chung (1976b).

3. In addition, Proto-Polynesian had a special type of case marking for middle clauses, along the lines described in fn. 1.

4. Perhaps the only substantive difference as far as case systems are concerned is that the frequency of the passive has diminished in a number of East Polynesian languages.

5. Following Andersen (1973), I assume that Pukapukan has undergone the passive-to-ergative reanalysis even though this change has only begun to be actualized. Conceivably, one could interpret the Pukapukan facts instead as innovations that will force a reanalysis like (10) at some future date (Klima 1964). Though possible, this approach seems to be less explanatory on a number of counts.

6. It is sometimes suggested that contact with some East Polynesian language might be responsible for the appearance of accusative case marking in Pukapukan, a Samoic-Outlier language. (Recall that the vast majority of the Samoic-Outlier languages are of the ergative type.) But in fact, there is no reason to posit this "extensive influence" other than to

avoid having to deal with the facts at all. See Chung (1976b)
for discussion.

   7. These rules are discussed and justified in greater
detail in Chung (1976b).

   8. Since the e NPs in these examples do not undergo the
deletion strategies perfectly (i.e. they are sometimes rejected by native speakers), the question arises as to whether
they can behave like oblique NPs and use the pronominalization strategies instead. The answer to this is no. It appears that subjects must be relativized by the deletion strategies where possible. If this is not felt to be possible for
the e NPs in (38-39), native speakers will simply use 'accusative' case marking and avoid the whole problem.

   9. For discussion of other types of solutions that
could be suggested for Pukapukan and their inadequacies, see
Chung (1976b).

   10. It might conceivably be claimed that major cyclic
rules have a less serious effect on the syntax of the clause,
because they are structure preserving (in the sense of Emonds
(1970)), and that superficial rules have a more serious effect
because they are nonstructure preserving ('root' transformations). Such a claim, however, is only as good as the theory
on which it is based; and the theory of root and structure
preserving transformations is known to have serious defects.
See Higgins (1971) and Pinkham and Hankamer (1975) for discussion.

   11. As such, it accounts for one major aspect of the
variation in (42). The other major aspect is that 'ergative'
clauses are more inert syntactically than 'passive' clauses

in Pukapukan. Thus, the e NPs of 'ergative' clauses undergo
all rules less successfully than the e NPs of their 'passive'
counterparts; and the unmarked NPs of 'ergative' clauses undergo Raising less successfully than the unmarked NPs of
their 'passive' counterparts. This also can be accounted for
by principles (44-45), if we assume that 'ergative' clauses
are derived from 'passive' clauses by a Suffix Deletion rule,
like (18), which is in the process of being introduced to the
grammar. I discuss this in Chung (1976b), where I also indicate more explicitly what a synchronic grammar of the Pukapukan case system might look like.

12. As is well known, the linguistic and sociolinguistic
situation in Indonesia is extremely complex, due to the fact
that Bahasa Indonesia has been a national language only since
1945 and is still a second language for the majority of speakers. For this reason, I confine my remarks to the speech of
native speakers who I have worked with. All of them are
young, well educated, upper or upper-middle class Indonesians
from Jakarta; all speak Bahasa Indonesia as their first language and do not speak Dutch, Javanese, Chinese, or any of
the other languages of Indonesia. By and large, my description agrees with that of Dyen (1964).

13. Although the conditions on Object Preposing differ
slightly across speakers, for every speaker it is possible to
find direct objects that can undergo Relativization, Clefting,
and Question Movement but cannot undergo Object Preposing. To
my mind, this is particularly strong evidence that the extraction rules must affect direct objects directly.

References

Andersen, H. 1973. Abductive and deductive change. Lg. 49: 765-93.

Beaglehole, E. and P. Beaglehole. 1938. Myths, stories, and chants of Pukapuka. Ms. in Bernice P. Bishop Museum, Honolulu, Hawaii.

Bickerton, D. 1971. Inherent variability and variable rules. FL 7: 457-92.

_____. 1973. Quantitative versus dynamic paradigms: the case of Montreal que, in New ways of analyzing variation in English, ed. by C.-J. N. Bailey and R. Shuy, pp. 23-43. Washington, D.C.: Georgetown University Press.

Chung, S. 1970. Negative verbs in Polynesian. Harvard University senior honors thesis.

_____. 1976a. On the subject of two passives in Indonesian, in Subject and topic, ed. by C. N. Li, pp. 57-98. New York: Academic Press.

_____. 1976b. Case marking and grammatical relations in Polynesian. Ph.D. dissertation, Harvard University.

Clark, D. R. 1973a. Aspects of Proto-Polynesian syntax. Ph.D. dissertation, University of California at San Diego.

_____. 1973b. Transitivity and case in Eastern Oceanic languages. Oceanic Linguistics 12: 559-605.

Dyen, I. 1964. Beginning Indonesian, lessons 1-24, 4 vols. Washington, D.C.: U.S. Department of Health, Education and Welfare, Office of Education (Language Development

Program, NDEA).

Emonds, J. 1970. Root and structure-preserving transforma-
    tions. Ph.D. dissertation, MIT (distributed by Indiana
    University Linguistics Club).

Hale, K. 1968. Review of Hohepa, A profile generative gram-
    mar of Maori. JPS 77: 83-99.

_____. 1970. The passive and ergative in language change:
    the Australian case, in Pacific linguistic studies in
    honour of Arthur Capell, ed. by S. A. Wurm and D. C. Lay-
    cock, pp. 757-81. Pacific Linguistics, Series C, No. 13.

Hankamer, J. 1973. Unacceptable ambiguity. LI 4: 17-68.

Higgins, F. R. 1971. A squib on J. Emonds' analysis of
    Extraposition. Ms.

Hohepa, P. W. 1969. The accusative-to-ergative drift in
    Polynesian languages. JPS 78: 295-329.

Keenan, E. L. 1972. Relative clause formation in Malagasy,
    in The Chicago which hunt, ed. by P. Peranteau, J. Levi,
    and G. Phares, pp. 169-89. Chicago: Chicago Linguistic
    Society.

King, R. D. 1969. Historical linguistics and generative
    grammar. Englewood Cliffs, N.J.: Prentice-Hall.

Kiparsky, P. 1971. Historical linguistics, in A survey of
    linguistic science, ed. by W. O. Dingwall, pp. 576-649.
    College Park, Md.: University of Maryland Linguistics
    Program.

Klima, E. S. 1964. Studies in diachronic transformational
    grammar. Ph.D. dissertation, Harvard University.

Labov, W. 1969. Contraction, deletion, and inherent varia-
    bility of the English copula. Lg. 45: 715-62.

_____. 1972. Sociolinguistic patterns. Conduct and commu-
    nication No. 4. Philadelphia: University of Pennsylvan-
    ia Press.

Meillet, A. 1966. La méthode comparative en linguistique
    historique. Paris: Librairie Honoré Champion.

Pawley, A. 1966. Polynesian languages: a subgrouping based
    on shared innovations in morphology. JPS 75: 39-64.

_____. 1967. The relationships of Polynesian Outlier lan-
    guages. JPS 76: 259-96.

Pawley, A. and L. A. Reid. 1976. The evolution of transi-
    tive constructions in Austronesian. Ms.

Perlmutter, D. M. and P. M. Postal. forthcoming. Relational
    grammar.

Pinkham, J. and J. Hankamer. 1975. Deep and shallow clefts,
    in Papers from the eleventh regional meeting of the Chi-
    cago Linguistic Society, ed. by R. E. Grossman, L. J.
    San, and T. J. Vance, pp. 429-50. Chicago: Chicago
    Linguistic Society.

Ross, J. R. 1974. There, there, (there, (there, (there,..))),
    in Papers from the tenth regional meeting of the Chicago
    Linguistic Society, ed. by M. Lagaly, R. Fox, and A.
    Bruck, pp. 569-87.

Schmidt, J. 1872. Die Verwantschaftverhältnisse der indog-
    ermanischen Sprachen. Weimar: H. Böhlau.

Stuebel, O. 1896. Samoanische Texte. Veröffentlichungen

aus dem Königlichen Museum für Völkerkunde, Band 4, Heft. 2-4. Berlin.

Traugott, E. C. 1965. Diachronic syntax and generative grammar. Lg. 41: 402-15.

Wolfram, W. 1973. On what basis variable rules?, in New ways of analyzing variation in English, ed. by C.-J. N. Bailey and R. Shuy, pp. 1-12. Washington, D.C.: Georgetown University Press.

2 Syntactic Reanalysis

Ronald W. Langacker

Introduction

I will be concerned in this paper with syntactic change. The term "syntactic change" will be construed quite broadly, to include change at the morphological and semantic levels as well as changes in syntax in the narrowest sense. I will discuss and exemplify one broad category of syntactic change, specifically reanalysis, with respect to its types, its causes, and its effects. Not all diachronic developments in the domain of syntax involve reanalysis as I will define the term, but this is clearly a major mechanism of syntactic evolution which we must understand in depth if we wish to understand how and why syntactic change occurs. An overall theory or taxonomy of grammatical change is beyond the scope of this paper, which is however intended as a small contribution in this direction.

My data consists of syntactic changes in the Uto-Aztecan family of American Indian languages.[1] The analysis is in all cases my own. I have restricted my attention to syntactic changes that I have described and documented in publications or at least finished manuscripts,[2] leaving aside many others of a more tentative or less accessible nature. This restricted data base consists of approximately 200 syntactic changes; of these approximately 50 are reanalyses in the sense to be defined below. I cannot claim that this data is fully repre-

sentative of syntactic change in general, but it does cover a
fairly wide array of diachronic phenomena and syntactic constructions from all parts and historical stages of a large
and variegated language family with a time depth approaching
that of Indo-European. It would be presumptuous to claim in-
fallibility for my reconstructions and analyses; however, the
great majority are reasonably well established and straightforward. Moreover, all of my major conclusions are based on
a variety of independent examples and therefore do not hinge
on the full validity of any particular example.

I will define "reanalysis" as change in the structure of
an expression or class of expressions that does not involve
any immediate or intrinsic modification of its surface manifestation. Reanalysis may lead to changes at the surface level, as we will see, but these surface changes can be viewed
as the natural and expected result of functionally prior modifications in rules and underlying representations.

The mechanism of reanalysis is by now quite familiar
from phonology. Here the surface level is the phonetic level,
which derives via phonological rules from abstract, phonological representations. Reanalysis in phonology is thus phonological change that does not involve immediate or intrinsic
phonetic change. In Proto Uto-Aztecan (P-UA), for example,
there was a process of medial consonant lenition, whereby in-
tervocalic consonants lenited or "spirantized". Let us single out for discussion /t/ and take [l] as its lenis allophone.[3] Some morphemes, said to be "geminating" or "unalter-
ing", had the effect of blocking this lenition; we will indicate these by the fortis symbol /'/, which can be regarded as
either a morphological feature or an unmarked or only mini-

mally specified consonant, depending on one's theoretical
predilections. The synchronic situation in P-UA is summarized for /t/ on the left-hand side of (1), where C stands
for a consonant, V for a vowel, and the hyphen for a morpheme boundary.

(1)   /CV'-tV/   /CV-tV/   >   /CV-tV/   /CV-1V/
           ↓   ↓   ↓   ↓
        [CVtV]   [CV1V]   [CVtV]   [CV1V]

Lenition and the resulting alternations are preserved as
active phonological processes in the Numic languages, but outside this subfamily the surface contrast between fortis and
lenis consonants has become phonemic, so that in Luiseno, for
example, /t/ and /1/ are clearly separate phonemes, as shown
on the right-hand side of (1). The change depicted in (1) is
an example of phonological reanalysis. The surface or phonetic representations have not been altered ([CVtV] and [CV1V]
are found at both stages), but the rules and underlying representations responsible for these surface forms have been. We
can speculate about the reasons for this reanalysis -- it reduces the abstractness of underlying representations, and it
relieves the skewed situation in which an abstract property
of one morpheme is responsible for a concrete property of another -- but we can identify this type of change as a reanalysis regardless of whether or not we can identify its causes
with any confidence.

       In discussing syntactic reanalysis, it will be helpful to
adopt certain notational conventions. This notation should
allow us to depict the specifics of individual cases as well
as to show schematically the similarities between superficially different cases. We must also be clear about what consti-

tutes surface and underlying levels of structure in this context. For coherent discussion, moreover, we must distinguish
between types of reanalysis, the causes of reanalysis, and
the effects of reanalysis. Let us go through a typical example for purposes of illustration.

We will consider the origin of the Luiseno absolutive
suffix -ta.[4] The P-UA elements from which this suffix derives
are *-ti, the absolutive suffix, and *-a, the basic accusative suffix. The two occurred in sequence on accusative
nouns, with *-a causing truncation of the preceding vowel
(which we may thus ignore), giving us *-t-a. The accusative
suffix *-a was replaced in the Takic languages by a newer accusative suffix, originally *-yi (used without the absolutive). Expressions with *-t-a were therefore no longer recognizable as accusative in character, but in Luiseno they were
not simply dropped from the language. Instead the sequence
-ta was reanalyzed as a new absolutive suffix, which was retained side-by-side with the original -t absolutive. The
choice between -ta and -t is now morphological rather than
syntactic in character, being determined by the morphological
class of the noun stem. Both occur on nominative forms, showing that they no longer contrast in regard to case. (In fact,
by virtue of a further reanalysis not considered here, accusative forms of nouns ending in -ta came to be marked by the
process of dropping the final vowel, so that too-ta is the
nominative form of 'rock' and too-t the accusative form, despite the fact that a is the reflex of the P-UA accusative
suffix.)

The essence of this change is the reanalysis of a bimorphemic sequence, *-t-a, as a single morpheme, -ta. This

change was caused, or at least facilitated, by the fact that
*-a had no identifiable syntactic or semantic function after
*-yi had replaced it as the basic accusative suffix in Luis-
eno. Once the reanalysis occurred, -ta and -t were both regarded as absolutive suffixes, and their distribution came to
be determined morphologically rather than on the basis of
surface case. We can thus characterize the type of reanalysis
as loss of a morpheme boundary, the change of ta from a bimorphemic to a monomorphemic sequence. The cause of the reanalysis was the occurrence of a surface element, a, with no
apparent meaning or syntactic function. The effect of the reanalysis was a change in the distribution of -t and -ta, from
nominative versus accusative on the same class of nouns to
general absolutive function on different classes of nouns.
While causes and effects for reanalyses may not always be
apparent, it is important for developing a coherent account
of reanalysis that we factor them out whenever we can, so
that we can focus our attention on the central mechanism involved. I will not claim that the division is always sharp
and self-evident, but in most instances it seems reasonably
straightforward.

There are different ways of defining the surface level
for purposes of discussing syntactic reanalysis, and they
naturally define different classes of phenomena as instances
of this category. For our purposes the surface level can be
viewed as the phonemic level of representation, together with
indications of word boundaries, but with no indication of constituent structure or boundaries smaller than word boundaries
(such as morpheme or clitic boundaries). In the example at
hand, then, the surface level can be represented as ta, both

before and after the reanalysis; no changes occur in this representation by virtue of the reanalysis itself. The surface
representation of Bill kicked him might be given as bIl kIkd
hIm, with word boundaries indicated but not morpheme boundaries or any other aspects of syntactic structure. Loss of a
morpheme boundary, as with Luiseno ta, therefore counts as reanalysis by my definition, but loss of word boundary, where
a separate word becomes incorporated as an affix, clitic, or
element of a compound, does not. There is nothing magic a-
bout the definition I have adopted -- others can perfectly
well be considered. It does however isolate a coherent class
of phenomena that lend themselves to reasonable characterization. The definition is also a natural one from the view-
point of the language user. Speakers and listeners are more
aware of an utterance as phonological (or phonetic) sequences
than they are of surface constituent structure. They are also more cognizant of word boundaries than they are of morpheme or clitic boundaries.

The underlying level (or levels) relevant for syntactic
reanalysis may consist of any aspect of morphological, syntactic, or semantic structure, i.e. anything more abstract
than the surface level as defined above. These structural
features include the location of morpheme and clitic boundaries, surface constituent structure, underlying constituent
structure, the semantic value or syntactic function of morphemes, and so on. In discussing reanalysis it is usually
necessary to refer to at least two different underlying levels of representation. One is the surface level together
with information about the placement of morpheme boundaries.
The other is a more abstract level providing information a-

bout the syntactic or semantic role of the morphemes involved, or about their syntactic or semantic configuration. Reanalysis may involve changes at either of these two levels,
or at both. Two levels come into play because morphemes consist in the correlation of form and function or meaning and
because reanalysis typically hinges on the interplay between
the two.

The Luiseno example shows this interplay between two
levels very clearly. The reanalysis is represented in (2),
which illustrates some of the notations to be employed.

(2)(a)   ABS $\emptyset$ ABS   (b)   A $\emptyset$ A
         | | | | | |
         t -   a   ta   X - Y   XY

The top line in (2)(a) is the more abstract level, which consists in this case of the syntactic function of the surface
elements. The vertical bars indicate "realization", the relation between an abstract element and a less abstract manifestation of it, shown in the bottom line. The left-hand
side of (2)(a) thus shows the morpheme sequence t-a and indicates that t had the syntactic function of an absolutive suffix (ABS) and that a had no apparent syntactic or semantic
value ($\emptyset$). The reanalysis consisted in t-a collapsing into
a single morpheme which functions as an absolutive. Note
that the two levels depicted are both more abstract than the
surface level as defined earlier. The surface level is ta
both before and after the reanalysis. The lower level in
(2)(a) is abstract relative to this, since it makes reference
to the morpheme boundary; it is this level which changes,
while the surface level -- the level that is most directly
observable -- is unchanged. The upper level in (2)(a) also

remains constant, but the lack of any element at this level
corresponding to a is what apparently triggered the reanalysis.

The same change is shown schematically in (2)(b). I
will use early capital letters (e.g. A, B, C) for syntactic
or semantic categories and late capital letters (e.g. X, Y,
Z) for sequences of phonological segments. I will use a hyphen (-) for morpheme boundaries, an equal sign (=) for clitic boundaries, and a space for word boundaries. Other notations will be introduced as needed.

I will now proceed to a fairly systematic discussion of
reanalysis, giving a representative sample of the cases that
have come to my attention in Uto-Aztecan. Subsequent sections will focus in turn on types of reanalysis, its effects,
and its causes.

Types of Reanalysis

Two broad types of reanalysis can be discerned, "resegmentation" and "syntactic/semantic reformulation", which I
will abbreviate as "reformulation". These two types are independent, in that a given instance of reanalysis may involve
either one without the other. Frequently both are involved.
Resegmentation pertains to the more superficial side of syntactic structure, namely the occurrence and placement of morpheme boundaries. Reformulation pertains to more abstract
aspects of semantic and syntactic structure.

Three kinds of resegmentation can be expected: "boundary
loss", "boundary creation", and "boundary shift". All three
kinds occur, though with different frequency.* Boundary crea-

tion is probably the least common (though it may be regarded
as one component of the not infrequent process of "selection",
to be discussed below). Boundary loss (in which I include
the downgrading of a boundary from a clitic to a morpheme
boundary) is probably the most frequent. Boundary shift is
apparently intermediate in frequency. These estimates are
naturally very crude, but loss definitely appears to be more
common than creation or shift.

Only one instance of boundary shift happens to occur in
my restricted data base, but it is a fairly common phenomenon familiar to all linguists from English examples involving
nouns and the indefinite article a/an (e.g. apple, apron,
orange, newt, nickname). My Uto-Aztecan example is from
Mono, in which boundary shift is responsible for the innovative accusative suffix -na. The P-UA accusative suffix was
*-a, as we have seen. When this suffix was attached to noun
stems of the type called "nasalizing" (analogous to the "geminating" stems discussed in (1), except that their effect is
to prenasalize a following consonant), the accusative noun
ended in the phonological sequence na. The boundary shift
consisted in the reanalysis of the n, originally contributed
by the stem, as part of the accusative suffix, as shown in
(3)(a); it is shown schematically in (3)(b).

(3)(a)   N   ACC   N   ACC
         | | > | |
         Xn - a   X   - na

   (b)   A   B   A   B
         | | > | |
         XY - Z   X   - YZ

The effect of this change is that -na is now the regular accusative suffix in Mono, not restricted in distribution to

original nasalizing noun stems. Causes or facilitating factors are easy to observe. For one thing, the change brought
morpheme boundaries into line with syllable boundaries, in
accordance with a general tendency in language, one which the
Uto-Aztecan languages seldom violate.[5] A second cause is the
fact that no trace of the final n of nasalizing noun stems
appeared when this would be word-final, and the n or nasalizing feature appeared only as prenasalization with a suffix
beginning in a consonant.[6] This being the case, it would be
natural for speakers to associate the segmental n, which only
occurred as such before a vowel-initial suffix, as being part
of this suffix. This accords with a tendency for morphemes
to have identical realization in all environments.

The question arises of whether we need recognize boundary shift as a distinct type of resegmentation. It is a
trivial matter to reformulate boundary shift as the sum of
two possibly more basic types, boundary loss and boundary
creation. When XY-Z is reanalyzed as X-YZ, we could simply
say that the original morpheme boundary (between Y and Z) is
lost and that a new boundary (between X and Y) is created.
While I wish to leave this question open, I will note that
this alternative formulation of boundary shift becomes far
less trivial if one can demonstrate that in all apparent
cases of boundary shift there are grounds for positing a previous boundary loss or creation which can constitute one half
of the overall process. This is not at all implausible in
the Mono example. Since the final n of nasalizing stems appeared as a discrete segment only before vowel-initial suffixes, the tendency for speakers to generalize one form of a
morpheme to all environments could lead them to dissociate

stem-final n from the noun, leaving it with no apparent function. This would in effect be boundary creation, and a
boundary loss exactly analogous to (2) would then complete
the shift. This two-step version of the reanalysis is given
in (3').

(3')   N   ACC   N   ∅   ACC   N   ACC
        | | > | | | > | |
        Xn –   a   X –   n   –   a   X –   na

Similarly, expressions like an=ewt could be reanalyzed as
a=newt by dissociation of the n from an on the model of a,
followed by loss of the boundary between n and ewt. However,
the occurrence of the opposite development (e.g. a=napple ›
an=apple) casts some doubt on the viability of this interpretation.

Boundary loss is extremely common. It is by far the
most frequent type of reanalysis in my data, and I would be
surprised if this did not prove true of language in general.
For the moment we will restrict our attention mostly to boundary loss that does not also involve syntactic/semantic reformulation; combinations of the two will be considered when we
discuss the latter.

The reanalysis given in (2) is one simple example of
boundary loss. The reanalysis of *-t-a as an absolutive suffix has happened independently at least twice in the history
of Uto-Aztecan, once in Luiseno and once in Proto Aztecan.
Yaqui shows exactly the opposite development; the same -ABS-
ACC sequence was reanalyzed as an accusative suffix due to
(or as part of) the general loss of absolutive inflection in
this language. This boundary loss is given in (4).

(4) (a) $\emptyset$ ACC   ACC   (b) $\emptyset$ A   A
$\quad\quad$ | | | $\quad$ | | |
$\quad\quad$ t $-$ a $>$ ta $\quad$ X $-$ Y $>$ XY

One thing that (2) and (4) (also (3')) have in common is the
elimination of morpheme status for a surface element that
has no syntactic or semantic value; it is evident already
that the pressure to eliminate such elements is a significant cause of language change. There are various ways in
which these elements can arise. Let us consider further examples which illustrate two of these (a third mechanism figures in (14) below).

Since speakers normally do not make up meaningless morphemes (for the purpose of talking about nothing?), their
existence in an expression or class of expressions will usually be due to a prior change of some kind. One type of
change that may be responsible is "loss", the disappearance
from a language of some element or grammatical device. Loss
of the accusative suffix *-a results in the situation leading to the reanalysis in (2), and loss of the absolutive *-t
is the ultimate cause of that in (4). The phenomenon of loss
poses surprisingly deep and difficult questions that I cannot explore here. For present purposes it is sufficient to
note that lost elements do not instantaneously disappear
from a language without a trace. Their disappearance is
gradual, and even after they have been lost as actively employed elements with clear meaning or syntactic value that
speakers are (or can be made) consciously aware of, they may
be retained as relics in fixed expressions or grammatical
patterns. This is the stage at which reanalysis occurs.

A case in point is the reciprocal prefix *na- that is

clearly reconstructable for P-UA. This prefix could be used
with either verbs or postpositions, possibly also with nouns.
In various subfamilies, including Takic, this prefix was lost
in some or all its roles, being superseded by other devices.
One specific sequence that can be reconstructed with some
confidence is *na-w(i), in which -wi is a postposition meaning 'to' or 'with'. This sequence was retained in Proto Cahuilla-Cupeno as the relic form *nəw(i). By that stage the
reciprocal prefix had been lost as a recognizable unit with
separate function, and the sequence was consequently reanalyzed as a single-morpheme postposition (yielding ultimately
-new and -niw in Cahuilla and -nəw in Cupeno).

(5)(a)   ∅   WITH   WITH   (b)   ∅   A   A
         | | > | | | > |
        nə - w   nəw   X - Y   XY

The new postposition resulting from resegmentation was then
attached to nouns or postpositional object pronouns, no longer standing alone as an independent word.

The Tubatulabal reciprocal pronoun ?omohic provides another example. Originally this sequence was bimorphemic,
consisting of ?omohi-, a basic reflexive pronoun, and the
postposition -c, which perhaps meant something like 'between'
or 'across'. I will assume that a reciprocal affix or pronoun consists of two basic components of meaning: the reflexive component (REFL), i.e. the information that the set designated by the subject is the same as (coreferential to) the
set designated by the object; and a component I will call
"skewing" (SKEW) for want of a better term, which implies
that the verbal relation pairs different individuals (in contrast to the non-reciprocal situation where each member of

the set designated by the subject acts only on himself, or
where the whole set acts collectively on itself). It is evident that the reciprocal ?omohic was originally a periphrastic
expression, and while this may be a slight oversimplification,
I will assume that the reflexive pronoun ?omohi- contributed
the REFL component of meaning, and the postposition -c the
SKEW component (in accordance with its probable sense). The
postposition -c was eventually lost as an independent postposition, and there is phonological evidence to suggest that
it is no longer treated as a separate morpheme in the sequence
?omohic. The reanalysis I posit differs a bit in detail from
those previously examined, but the basic mechanism remains
the same. Here the SKEW component is not lost, since ?omohic
remains a reciprocal pronoun, but once -c is lost as an independent element it is no longer identified by speakers as a
separate unit or as that portion of ?omohic which contributes
that particular component of meaning. The reanalysis is
shown in (6); square brackets enclose members of a conjunctive
set.

(6)(a)

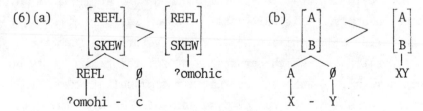

This notation indicates that ?omohi- was still recognizable
as a reflexive pronoun (it still occurs in that role), but -c
had no identifiable function. The whole expression realized
the meaning components REFL and SKEW, enclosed in the square
brackets, but so far as speakers were able to determine this
complex notion was realized through a sequence the first ele-

ment of which had REFL as its value and the second zero. The
boundary loss brings about the more straightforward situation
in which the complex semantic notion is associated with the
sequence as a whole. We will find this notation useful for
other cases.

Loss, then, is one type of development that results in
the occurrence of surface elements with no apparent meaning
or syntactic function. The second type of development having
this effect is semantic extension, where expressions come to
be used in a figurative sense. A nice example is found in
the evolution of the Southern Paiute emphatic reflexive pronoun na'noo. The reciprocal *na- generalized in Proto Numic
to both reflexive and reciprocal value. Proto Southern Numic
*na'noo was originally a postpositional phrase consisting of
*na-, with reflexive value, and the postpositional -noo 'with'
(cognate to Proto Cahuilla-Cupeno *nəw(i) in (5)). The expression thus originally meant 'with oneself' or 'by oneself',
and it still has this locative value in Kawaiisu. As in English, this locative reflexive expression was extended to emphatic reflexive use. When we say He did it by himself in
English, either we may mean that he did it while alone, in
which case by is being used literally in its locative sense,
or we may mean that he himself did it, where by himself is
simply emphatic, with the locative by used only figuratively.
Southern Paiute na'noo is now just an emphatic reflexive; another postposition is incorporated for locative or oblique
uses, so we have good reason to suppose that speakers no longer recognize -noo as a postposition or see na'noo as a postpositional phrase.

It is not obvious to me how to characterize emphatic

reflexives semantically, but since they pertain in some way
to the reference of a nominal, and emphasize the appropriate-
ness of that reference to the exclusion of other possibilities,
I hope I will not distort matters too seriously by positing
the two semantic components REFL and EMPH as a first approximation. The figurative extension of na'noo from locative
reflexive (REFL and WITH) to emphatic reflexive (REFL and
EMPH) thus robs the postposition -noo 'with' of its semantic
content; WITH is present in the literal reading of the expression, but there is no such semantic element in the figurative
sense in which the expression has come to be used. The semantic extension, then, leaves us with the situation shown on
the left-hand side of (7)(a).

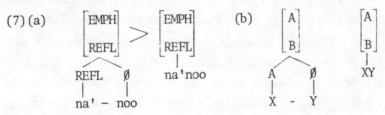

The expression na'noo was emphatic reflexive in sense, but
in form it consisted of two elements, only one of which had
a meaning compatible with this sense. Speakers tend to lose
sight of the figurative character of common expressions, and
to the extent that this happened with na'noo, speakers could
recognize no appropriate semantic value for -noo. Changes
(6) and (7) are of essentially the same type, as shown by the
identity of (6)(b) and (7)(b), but the situation leading to
the two reanalyses was brought about by different processes,
loss in the one case and semantic shift in the other.

Actually, we cannot be sure that loss was not a contributing factor in (7), since the postposition -noo has been

lost as an independent element in Southern Paiute. Let us
therefore consider another example of boundary loss which collapses elements whose value is obscured by the figurative use
of language, this one from Aztec. It involves the emphatic
reflexive pronoun -no?ma, which takes the appropriate possessor prefix to specify the person and number of the nominal
emphasized. The fact that a possessor prefix is required is
good evidence that reanalysis has taken place, since -no?ma
itself contains an element, no, that was originally a possessor prefix. The sequence derives from the periphrastic locution *no-ma-ka, literally 'from my hand', consisting of no-
'my', ma 'hand', and -ka 'from'. To say 'I myself did it',
then, the Aztec speaker would say literally 'I did it by/from
my own hand'. This locution was figurative from its incep-
tion. Since speakers quickly come to ignore the literal
sense of established figurative expressions unless it is somehow called to their attention, the surface units no, ma, and
ka eventually came to be dissociated from their original semantic value in nomaka. No doubt contributing to this dissociation was the reduction of final ka to k, then to ?, which
could hardly still be recognized as the postposition -ka.
This ? was later displaced to medial position.[7] (8) portrays
the situation at the stage where the reanalysis most likely
took place and shows the nature of this reanalysis.

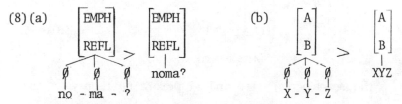

Since speakers did not recognize the identity of the individ-

ual surface elements, or were only dimly aware of their identity, the boundaries between these elements were subject to
loss.

I have included within the category of boundary loss the
downgrading of a boundary from the status of clitic boundary
to that of morpheme boundary.[8] The example we will consider
is an innovation common to Hopi and Proto Takic, in which the
sequence *ʔita=mɨ, consisting of the independent pronoun
*ʔita 'we' and the plural clitic *=mɨ, was reanalyzed as a
single word independent pronoun (reflected in modern Hopi as
ʔitam 'we' and in Proto Takic as *ʔičamɨ 'we' through palatalization of *t to *č after *i). Since mɨ is an obligatory feature of the daughter pronouns (not optional as clitics are),
and since a new plural clitic was added in certain daughters,
it is clear that the reanalysis did in fact take place. As
for the cause of this change, one factor may have been analogical pressure from the other plural independent pronouns,
which ended in the plural suffix -mɨ.

The proper way of representing this reanalysis diagram-
matically is not fully evident. One way is indicated in (9).

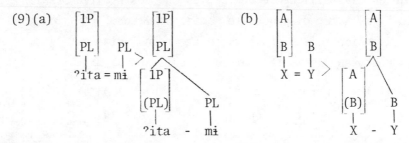

Before the reanalysis, ʔita and mɨ were a unit only at the
level of surface structure, the latter being introduced as a
redundant marker agreeing with the subject but being attached

to the first element of the sentence, which happened to be
the subject pronoun only in certain instances. Once the plural mi is incorporated as an integral part of the pronoun,
though, the two elements ?ita and mi can be viewed as mani-
festing a single unit, shown in the top line of the output
structure; that is, mi came to be introduced morphologically
(as part of the pronoun) rather than syntactically (by agreement and clitic placement). It is likely that the morpheme
boundary before mi is retained, and also that mi is recognized as plural in character, since -mi is retained as a general plural suffix and is found in the other plural pronouns
(with some modification in Hopi). While we may speculate that
the redundancy of marking plurality twice possibly facilitated
the reanalysis to some degree, it would probably be incorrect
to claim that ?ita and mi have been realigned as markers of
first person and plural respectively, thereby eliminating the
redundancy. ?ita has shown no tendency to generalize to first
person singular uses, and it is still distinct in form from
the first person singular pronoun and hence recognizable as
the plural pronoun even without mi.

As I have indicated, boundary creation may be the least
common type of resegmentation. One apparent example involves
innovative third person pronouns in Tarahumara. For P-UA one
can reconstruct two reflexive pronouns: *pɨ-nak^W ayɨ, with
locative and emphatic value (i.e. '(by) oneself'); and the reciprocal *?a-nak^W ayɨ. *pɨ and *?a were originally alternate
third person singular pronouns, but the two reflexive pronouns have undergone extensive modifications and reanalyses in
the daughter languages, and the identity of the first syllable
-- as a pronoun or even as a separate morpheme -- was certain-

ly lost by the time of early Tarahumara. *pɨ-nak^{W}ayɨ evolved
phonologically in Tarahumara to binoy, and semantically it
evolved from locative-emphatic to emphatic, and from emphatic
to being the basic third person singular independent pronoun.
*ʔa-nak^{W}ayɨ remained reciprocal and changed in form to
ʔanagu.

The Tarahumara third person plural independent pronoun
is ʔaboy or ʔaboni, which cannot be traced to any P-UA ancestor. Most likely, then, it was innovated as a plural counterpart to binoy once this became the basic third person independent pronoun, since third person pronouns virtually always
distinguish singular and plural. ʔaboy and ʔaboni both derive
fairly naturally from *ʔa-binoy (through the intermediate
stage *ʔa-bonoy),[9] which would be a natural source if the new
pronoun were innovated specifically as a plural counterpart
to binoy. The only difficulty is that no prefix *ʔa- can be
reconstructed with plural value; *ʔa- has no apparent source
if we compare it to other plural markings in Tarahumara or Uto-
Aztecan generally. I suggest, then, that Tarahumara speakers,
needing a plural counterpart for binoy, turned to the reciprocal pronoun ʔanagu, which had been paired structurally with
binoy since P-UA. Reciprocal pronouns are inherently plural,
and ʔanagu was resegmented as ʔa-nagu, with ʔa- assigned plural value. (10) shows one way of looking at this reanalysis.

I doubt that the situation is as neat as (10) makes it appear
-- that is, I have no reason to believe that -nagu is per-
ceived as a separate unit or that the semantic components are
neatly partitioned as shown -- but it does seem clear that ʔa
was singled out from the rest of the form and contributed
plural sense to *ʔa-binoy. *ʔa-binoy might be regarded as a
blend of binoy and ʔanagu, and boundary creation was one element in the blending process.[10]

Boundary creation may prove considerably more frequent
if we take it as constituting one step in the process I will
call "selection". Selection is the process whereby one portion
of a phonological sequence with a given semantic or syntactic
role is singled out, or "selected", and comes to stand alone
in that role. The evolution of the P-UA passive suffix, which
was originally bisyllabic, shows numerous independent instances of selection, only one of which I will "select" for
presentation here.

The P-UA passive suffix had two or more dialectal variants, one of which was *-liwa. In the evolution of Huichol,
this became *-riwa by regular sound change, and the loss of
medial w from this sequence, though probably not regular, has
parallels in other southern daughters. The resulting sequence
*-ria, more accurately rendered *-riya in phonetic terms, e-
ventually resulted in the passive suffix *-ri(y)e, but we are
concerned here with an alternative course of development leading from *-riya. Specifically, both syllables came to stand
alone as passive suffixes, with the result that both -ri and
-ya occur separately as passive suffixes on different classes
of verbs in modern Huichol. One way of construing the initial
step in this process is given in (11).[11]

(11)(a) PASS   PASS   PASS   (b) A   A   A
           | > | | | > | |
         riya   ri - ya   XY   X - Y

That is, speakers came to consider either syllable of *-riya
as being in itself sufficient to identify a verb as passive,
so that in effect verbs with *-riya were regarded as doubly
marked for the passive. This set the stage for the further
step whereby either new passive suffix could be used alone
without the other. I am fairly sure that selective phonetic
erosion could not account for the origin of both -ri and -ya
and that selection must be recognized as a special kind of
syntactic change. There may however be other ways of construing selection which do not rely so directly on boundary creation.

For a slightly different example of selection, let us
consider the independent pronoun 'we' in Proto Cupan. It will
be recalled from (9) that the Proto Takic form was *ʔitami,
with i palatalizing the t to yield *ʔičami. This is retained
as ʔičam (or ʔačam by vowel harmonization) in Serrano, but in
Proto Cupan the initial syllable is lost; Proto Cupan *čami is
reflected as Cahuilla čemem, Cupeno čəməm, and Luiseno čaam
by further changes. The reduction of *ʔičami to *čami is an
instance of selection that can be diagrammed as in (12). (We
can ignore here the possibility of segmenting *-mi as a plural
morpheme.)

(12)(a) ⎡1P⎤   ⎡1P⎤   (b) ⎡A⎤   ⎡A⎤
         ⎣PL⎦ > ∅   ⎣PL⎦   ⎣B⎦ > ∅   ⎣B⎦
           | | | |
         ʔičami   ʔi - čami   XY   X - Y

*čami was itself sufficient to identify a pronoun as first

person plural, so speakers were free to dissociate the initial
syllable from the semantic content of this pronoun. The initial *?i-, lacking apparent meaning or function, was subsequently dropped.

Having considered the three types of resegmentation, we
turn our attention now to syntactic/semantic reformulation.
Reformulation is reanalysis that involves aspects of structure
more abstract than the occurrence and placement of morpheme
boundaries; these aspects include rules, semantic and syntactic categories, and semantic or syntactic configurations (such
as tree structures). Reformulation often includes resegmentation (both figure in (9), for example), but we will see examples of reformulation in which boundaries are unaltered.
Since its domain is much more complex, reformulation is not
so straightforwardly subcategorized as resegmentation. The
classification below represents only one possible way of or-
ganizing the phenomena for purposes of discussion. It pertains to the nature of the change as it affects semantic representations.

I will assume that semantic representations are related
to surface structures by lexical choice and by a single body
of (syntactic) grammatical rules. In this view syntactic
structures at any level are manifestations or realizations,
derived by grammatical rules, of the underlying semantic structure. Any reformulation that affects semantic representations
also thereby affects syntactic structure, since the semantic
representation of a sentence is the most abstract syntactic
structure underlying it. On the other hand, syntactic reformulation which leaves semantic representations unaffected is
perfectly conceivable when the elements involved are semanti-

cally redundant (e.g. transformationally introduced agreement features) or have purely syntactic function with no inherent semantic value (e.g. absolutive suffixes which occur on uninflected nouns).

One can easily find examples of reformulation that appear to lack semantic consequences (their validity of course depends on precise claims about the nature of semantic representations and the semantic contributions of surface form). One such example involves postpositions in Yaqui. Yaqui has a series of postpositions that can stand as independent words. Most of them begin with the syllable be, which derives historically from the third person singular pronoun *pi- by regular sound change. We may therefore posit a boundary loss whereby the sequence be-X, originally a pronoun-postposition sequence, was reanalyzed as a postposition of the form beX. That such a reanalysis has in fact occurred is demonstrated by the fact that these new postpositions can attach, as a unit, to other pronouns (even non-third person ones).

Although the pronoun is lost by virtue of this reanalysis, and pronouns clearly have semantic value, it can be argued that no semantic change is actually involved, since the reanalysis took place in a construction in which the affected pronoun was grammatically introduced as a semantically redundant element. This construction is a "pronoun copy" construction in which a postposition is attached, not to a noun directly, but rather to a pronoun copy of that noun (marked accusative by the suffix -ta considered in (4)):

(13)(a)
$$N_i \quad ACC \quad PRON_i \quad P \quad N \quad ACC \quad P$$
$$X - ta \quad be - Y \quad > \quad X - ta \quad beY$$

(b) A   B   C   D   A   B   D
     | | | | > | | |
     W - X   Y - Z   W - X   YZ

If the pronoun copy is considered to be transformationally
inserted, with no analog in semantic structure, the reformulation in (13) will leave semantic representations unchanged.
What does change is the syntactic character of the construction -- the copying operation no longer comes into play --
and the phonological shape of the postpositions.

Another development affecting the same construction is
attested in Aztec and resulted in the innovation of a connective -ti- that occurs between nouns and certain postpositions: N-ti-P. The cause of this reformulation was the coalescence of the two-word sequence into a single word, as
shown in the left-hand side of (14)(a).

(14)(a) N_i ABS $PRON_i$ P   N $\emptyset$ P
         | | | | > | | |
         X   -   t   -   i   -   Y   X   -   ti   -   Y

(b) A   B   C   D   A $\emptyset$ D
     | | | | > | | |
     W   -   X   -   Y   -   Z   W   -   XY   -   Z

The suffix *-ta was absolutive in Aztec rather than accusative (cf. (2)), and ti is the expected result of coalescing
ta and i, the third person singular pronoun. Neither the absolutive suffix nor the pronoun copy has independent semantic
content. Moreover, both were syntactically superfluous once
the two words (for whatever reason) combined into one; a pronoun copy is not needed when a postposition attaches to the
noun itself, and an absolutive suffix is not expected on a
noun when a postposition is attached. It is not surprising,
then, that the boundary between the two elements was lost and

that -ti- no longer has any recognizable absolutive or pronominal value. In fact, the term "connective" should not be allowed to obscure the lack of semantic value or specific syntactic import of this sequence, which is simply required by
convention between nouns and certain postpositions.

We turn now to cases of reformulation that clearly do
involve change at the semantic level. At least for purposes
of discussion, it will be helpful to consider separately
changes as they affect individual words and morphemes and
changes as they affect the semantic representations of larger
units such as clauses and entire sentences. Some instances
of semantic reformulation affecting lexical expressions are
essentially localized to these expressions and do not have
any drastic effect on other aspects of the larger constructions in which they occur. In other cases the semantic reformulation of a lexical unit may be viewed as an integral
component of the semantic restructuring of a clause or sentence as a whole. We will begin by examining semantic reformulation that is largely localized to lexical expressions.

As with resegmentation, three kinds of semantic reformulation affecting primarily lexical units might be expected:
the loss of semantic elements, their addition, or shift in
their value. All three kinds do occur. While these quantitative estimates should not be taken too seriously, it appears that semantic shift is the most frequent, and that semantic loss is more common than semantic addition. For the
moment we will limit our attention to a single example of
each.[12]

As I have defined the term, semantic extensions and fig-

urative uses of lexical items are so prevalent and pervasive.
When linguists first started using terms like tree, branch,
and node in their technical sense, they were guilty of this
kind of reanalysis, since these terms did not change in their
surface appearance but did change in their semantic value.
For an example involving grammatical morphemes, consider the
Southern Paiute emphatic reflexive pronoun na'noo, previously
discussed in (7). It will be recalled that this was originally a postpositional phrase, with na- a reflexive prefix
and -noo a postposition meaning 'with'. Originally this expression was a locative reflexive, directly parallel to English by oneself in its literal sense. The extension of this
expression from the literal locative reflexive sense to emphatic reflexive value is shown in (15).

(15)(a)   REFL   WITH   ⎡EMPH⎤   (b)   A   B   ⎡A⎤
            | | > ⎣REFL⎦ | | > ⎣C⎦
           na - noo   X - Y
                           REFL WITH   A   B
                            | | | |
                           na - noo   X - Y

Since -noo 'with' no longer had its literal value in this expression, speakers gradually lost sight of its actual sense,
leading to the situation shown on the left-hand side of (7)(a),
which in turn triggered reanalysis (7). (15), incidentally,
is an example of reformulation that does not involve resegmentation.

We have seen previously several instances of a strong
tendency for surface units with no obvious semantic value or
syntactic function to be eliminated, in particular through
boundary loss. Boundary loss also eliminates as segmentable
units elements with purely syntactic function or with only re-

dundant semantic value, as illustrated in (13) and (14). As
one might expect, boundary loss cannot freely eliminate independently meaningful elements. Semantic loss does occur, but
it tends strongly to affect only minimally meaningful elements, those typically coded by grammatical markers, rather
than lexical units like 'house', 'kangaroo', or 'squalid'.
(One possibly major exception to this statement involves the
figurative use of expressions when this figurative usage becomes standardized or "frozen" and speakers gradually lose a-
wareness of the literal meanings of the individual elements.
In (8), for example, the meaning component 'hand' is lost in
the evolution of the Aztec emphatic reflexive pronoun no?ma.)

As a typical example of semantic loss, consider the Hopi
verb tiivahoma 'wash'. This verb derives from tii-, a prefix
which indicates that the object is unspecified, and the stem
vahoma (cf. naavahoma 'wash (oneself)', incorporating the reflexive and reciprocal prefix naa-). Reanalysis has clearly
occurred, making tii part of the stem, since vahoma cannot
occur alone and since tiivahoma can be used with specified
objects. Thus the highly limited semantic content of tii has
been eliminated, as has the morpheme boundary between it and
the original stem:

(16)(a)   UNSPEC   (b)

$$\begin{array}{ccc} \text{OBJ} & \text{WASH} & \text{WASH} \\ | & | \quad > & | \\ \text{tii - vahoma} & \text{tiivahoma} \end{array} \qquad \begin{array}{ccc} \text{A} & \text{B} & \text{B} \\ | & | \quad > & | \\ \text{X - Y} & \text{XY} \end{array}$$

One might plausibly argue that the value of tii, namely indicating that the direct object is unspecified, is syntactic
rather than semantic, or that if semantic it is redundant giv-
en the absence of a specified object; these are also reason-

able ways of viewing matters, and they are consistent with
the more basic point that loss mainly affects elements devoid
of substantial independent semantic content. Loss of a more
clearly meaningul element, specifically the reciprocal notion
(REFL plus SKEW), will be illustrated when we discuss semantic reformulation affecting entire clauses and sentences.

Like semantic loss, semantic addition tends to be restricted to minimally meaningful elements of the kind typically coded by grammatical markers. Huichol provides a simple example. Huichol has a whole series of innovative plural
suffixes, among them -te, which derives ultimately from the
P-UA absolutive suffix *-ti (the sound change is regular).
Absolutive inflection was lost in Huichol as an active process, leaving nouns with the suffix -te which lacked apparent
meaning or syntactic function. The adoption of this suffix
as a marker of plurality is therefore an example of semantic
creation or addition:

(17)(a) $\emptyset$ PL   (b) $\emptyset$ A
         $|$ > $|$ $|$ > $|$
         te   te   X   X

Note that this change, like (15), exemplifies reformulation
without resegmentation.

Many semantic reformulations are not localized to single
lexical items but involve modifications of the semantic representation of an entire clause or sentence. We may term
this type of reanalysis "constructional reformulation", since
it involves modification of the type of construction the sentence represents.

One such change affected the sequence *pi-ma reconstructable for Pre-P-UA.[13] This sequence consisted of the demon-

strative *pɨ and the pro form *ma 'one', so it meant 'that
one'. It combined with a following noun in what amounted to
an appositive construction; *pɨ-ma N was literally 'that one,
(the) N'. By P-UA times, *pɨ-ma had been reanalyzed as a simple demonstrative. Various daughters preserve a two-syllable
demonstrative deriving from *pɨ-ma, which is also the source
of the ubiquitous demonstrative ma, coming from *pɨma by the
process of selection. The reanalysis of *pɨ-ma as the single-
morpheme demonstrative *pɨma is shown in (18).

(18)(a)　　DEM　　ONE　　　　DEM　　　(b)　A　　B　　　A
　　　　　　｜　　｜　＞　　　｜　　　　　｜　　｜　＞　｜
　　　　　　pɨ　-　ma　　　　pɨma　　　　　X　-　Y　　　XY

This reformulation and boundary loss involves loss of the semantic element ONE, a pro form with very limited semantic content. The change is not restricted to this lexical item, however, since the overall construction also changes from an ap-
positional construction (possibly with a complex-sentence
source) to a simple demonstrative-noun construction. The extent of the constructional reformulation of course depends on
one's conception of the underlying structure of appositive expressions.

Considerably more dramatic instances of constructional
change can be found. Another example that involves semantic
loss is the origin of the Numic postposition *-noo 'with',
from the reflexive and reciprocal prefix *na- and the postposition *-w(i) 'to, with'. (This same sequence was reanalyzed as
the postposition *-nəw 'with' in Proto Cahuilla-Cupeno by the
resegmentation shown in (5); the Proto Numic change was independent of the Proto Cahuilla-Cupeno change, as the two differ in both type and cause.) Once the postpositional phrase

had been reanalyzed as the single-morpheme postposition *-noo
'with', it could be attached to nouns or pronouns like any
other postposition. Proto Numic retained the prefix *na-,
which took postpositions, so *na-noo 'with oneself' was innovated (despite the etymological redundancy) as an emphatic
reflexive pronoun 'with/by oneself', as previously discussed.

While the resegmentation of *nə-w to *nəw in Proto Cahuilla-Cupeno was caused by previous loss of the reciprocal
*na-, the corresponding reanalysis in Proto Numic was caused
by the phonetic merger of *na-w to *noo. As noted, *na- still
existed in Proto Numic (and is retained in the daughters),
but after the phonetic merger it was no longer clearly discernible in the syncretistic *noo. The reanalysis of *noo as a
postposition, with this lexical change viewed in isolation,
is given in (19); we will limit our attention to the reciprocal interpretation.

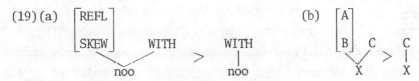

Here the reciprocal notion is lost, eliminating the situation
in which two semantic units were realized by a single phonetic
sequence with no non-arbitrary boundary.

Now we must place this reanalysis in the context of overall sentence structure. Prior to it, *noo was a periphrastic
locution meaning 'with one another' or 'together'. It would
thus occur in sentences having the schematic form $N_1 N_2$ noo V
'N_1 and N_2 V together/with one another' ('and' is often not
lexicalized in Uto-Aztecan). When *noo is reanalyzed as mean-

ing simply 'with' and is attached as a postposition to the preceding nominal, N_2, the result is a sentence structure of the form $\underline{N_1 N_2\text{-with } V}$ 'N_1 V with N_2'. The sentence structure thus undergoes reformulation from one involving a conjoined subject, with the notion 'together' expressed through a postpositional phrase with a reciprocal prefix, to one involving a non-conjoined subject, with the notion 'together' expressed through a comitative postposition on the second nominal. As partial corroboration of this account, observe that -noo does occur in Northern Paiute in sentences such as these, and new expressions (including nanoo) based on the reciprocal na- and meaning 'together' can be added to such sentences to reinforce the notion of reciprocity that was eliminated as an explicit semantic category due to change (19).

Another example of radical constructional change is found in the P-UA locative/emphatic reflexive pronoun *pɨ-nak^{W}ayɨ, already mentioned in the discussion of (10) as the source of the Tarahumara independent pronoun binoy. Originally, at some stage of Pre-P-UA, this expression was an independent clause that occurred with another clause and qualified or elaborated its meaning. The four basic elements of this clause were the third person singular animate pronoun *pɨ-, the reciprocal *na, the postposition *k^{W}a,[14] and the verb yɨ 'be'. The whole clause thus meant approximately 'He is by himself', and appended to another clause (with coreferential subject) it contributed locative reflexive sense, and by extension emphatic reflexive sense. 'The man is working by himself', for example, would be rendered literally as 'The man is working, (and) he is by himself' at the earliest stage.

By the time of P-UA, *pɨ-nak^{W}ayɨ had been reduced from a

clause to a phrase, at least in terms of surface structure.
Some or all of the individual morphemes were still recognized,
in all probability, and it is conceivable that this surface
phrase had a clausal source in underlying structure. Several
daughters of P-UA show reflexes of *$p\dot{i}$-nak^{w}ay$\dot{i}$; in all cases
it is now a phrase or a single word, and in no case is there
any indication that any morpheme boundary is recognized except the one between $p\dot{i}$ and the rest.[15] Our concern is with
the transition between the P-UA stage and the situation in
certain daughters, and in the reduction from an expression
that constitutes a clause (at least in underlying representation) to one that constitutes only a phrase (even in underlying representation, presumably). We will focus our attention on this reduction as it manifests itself in Proto Western
Numic and Proto Central Numic. This same reduction triggers
other reanalyses, similar to varying degrees, in Proto Southern Numic, Proto Takic, Proto Pimic, and probably Proto Taracahitic.

The Western and Central Numic reanalysis is summarized
in (20).

(20)(a)   PRON   REFL   P   BE   REFL   P
          | | | | > | |
          $p\dot{i}$ - na - k^{w}a - y$\dot{i}$ $p\dot{i}$ - nak^{w}ay$\dot{i}$

   (b)   A   B   C   D   B   C
          | | | | > | |
          W - X - Y - Z   W - XYZ

Possibly (20) collapses more than one separate change, but
the overall development seems quite clear. As the expression
loses its clausal character and becomes a postpositional
phrase, the subject pronoun and the (meaningful!) verb BE must
be lost, since these give the expression its clausal status.

The phonological material originally distributed among four semantic elements is redistributed among the two remaining ones, the reflexive and locative postpositional categories. This entails boundary loss within the sequence nak^{W}ayɨ (expected if the separate elements were no longer recognized) and shift of pɨ from simple pronominal to reflexive pronominal. This reformulation is the source of the reflexive use of pɨ in Numic. The reflex of *nak^{W}ayɨ has been lost as a postposition in Numic, but the sequence is retained (in a slightly different role) in Kawaiisu and the reflex of *nak^{W}ayɨ can be seen to be postpositional (after parallel reanalyses) in Takic and Pimic.

Our final example of constructional reformulation pertains to the nominal suffix *-wa in P-UA. This suffix had at least two syntactic roles, each attested in a variety of daughter languages. One of its uses was as a suffix attached to possessed nouns; it co-occurred with a possessor affix and apparently contributed no meaning, having only this (somewhat redundant) grammatical function.[16] This was its original role. Its second role, deriving from the first by reanalysis, was that of a derivational suffix with the meaning 'have'. Attached to nouns, it derived verbs with the meaning 'have N'. It is the innovation of the derivational use of *-wa that interests us.

Many languages, including various Uto-Aztecan languages, use existential locutions such as 'His N is' to express the meaning 'He has a N'. In this existential locution, the noun N would naturally take the possessed suffix *-wa, and the verb might be expected to be zero, which can in fact be reconstructed for 'be' in P-UA and was clearly used in existential

sentences. Another, less common possessive locution found
in various Uto-Aztecan languages in 'He has his N'. I propose that the 'have' sense of *wa came about through a constructional reformulation in which expressions of the type
'His N is' were reanalyzed as representing locutions of the
type 'He has his N' (which later simplified to 'He has N').
This change is shown in (21).

(21) (a) N_i POSSR$_i$ N   POSSD   BE   > N_i POSSR$_i$ N   HAVE
         | | | | | | | | |
         X   Y   -   Z - wa   Ø   X   Y   -   Z - wa

     (b) A   B   C   D   E   >   A   B   C   F
          | | | | | | | | |
          W   X   -   Y - Z   Ø   W   X   -   Y - Z

The pronoun copy construction (in which a nominal possessor stands alone as an independent word and possession is
marked by a possessor prefix coreferential to it) is ubiquitous in Uto-Aztecan and can be presumed without question for
P-UA. (21) is a clear example of substantial reformulation
occurring without resegmentation. The cause of the reanalysis
is easy to perceive -- an overt element, *-wa, occurs with no
meaning and only redundant syntactic function, while a unit of
meaning, BE, remains without overt expression. It was natural,
then, for *-wa to be reanalyzed as the meaningful element in
the post-nominal sequence, and since it was a noun suffix the
meaning HAVE was more likely than BE. This affected more than
just the suffix, however, since the overall locution changed
from the existential 'His N is' to the non-existential 'He has
his N'. The possessor noun, as part of this reformulation,
changed from being part of the nominal functioning as the subject of BE in underlying structure to being the underlying
subject of HAVE. Finally, since the new meaning component

HAVE was introduced as part of this constructional reformulation, it counts as well as an example of semantic addition.

Effects of Reanalysis

Little of a truly systematic character can be said about the effects of reanalysis. The nature of these effects depends on the particulars of each individual case. If there is a generalization to be made, it is the obvious one that the behavior of the elements affected by reanalysis changes in just the manner one would predict given the way in which they have been modified. For example, when the nasalizing feature of noun stems in Mono was reanalyzed as part of the accusative suffix in change (3), the resulting accusative suffix -na was generalized in distribution, so that -na as a unit (rather than just -a) is now the basic accusative ending in the language; in fact, prenasalization has disappeared in Western Numic as an active phonological process (nasalization has merged with gemination), but the n of -na was left unaffected because it had been reanalyzed as the first consonant of the accusative suffix and was no longer a "final feature".

The effects of reanalysis nevertheless merit a certain amount of attention, for several reasons. First, as observed earlier, the effects of reanalyses must be distinguished from these reanalyses per se if we wish to develop a coherent account of the process. Second, it is the ultimate effects of a reanalysis that provide the clearest evidence that the reanalysis has in fact occurred, since by definition this type of change leaves surface representations unchanged. Third, the effects of reanalysis interact in an interesting way with substantive language universals. Finally, they show clearly

the "local" nature of much syntactic change, which is important for understanding why languages change continually rather
than ultimately achieving stability.

Before examining some of these matters, let us briefly
survey various kinds of effects that the reanalyses presented
here have had. One possible effect is that an originally independent element becomes dependent. In both (5) and (19),
the sequence *na-w(i), originally a postpositional phrase
(RCPR-WITH) that stood as an independent word, is reanalyzed
(by different mechanisms) as a single-morpheme postposition.
This postposition can no longer stand alone as a separate
word; rather it is attached to the noun or pronoun that functions as its object.

It is not uncommon for an element that is lost from a
construction to be reintroduced into that same construction.
When the reciprocal prefix *na- was reanalyzed as part of the
postposition *noo in Proto Numic by (19), the whole resulting
sequence *noo was reattached to *na- to yield the locative reflexive *na-noo; since *na-P remained as an active construction and *-noo was a new postposition, nothing prevented its
attachment to the *na- which spawned it. When the plural
clitic *=mi was reanalyzed as part of the pronoun 'we' in Hopi
and Proto Takic by (9), this new pronoun could and did itself
take the clitic *=mi when it happened to be the first element
in a sentence. After the Yaqui reanalysis in (13), yielding
postpositions of the form beX incorporating the pronoun be-
(‹*pi-), these new postpositions could attach as a unit to
other pronouns. The Aztec reflexive pronoun noʔma discussed
in (8) takes an appropriate possessor prefix, including no-
'my', even though the first syllable of noʔma ultimately de-

rives from this prefix. This reintroduction of elements swal-
lowed up by reanalysis is the clearest evidence one could desire that the reanalysis in question has indeed taken place.

Another indication that a reanalysis has taken place, in
particular a resegmentation, is a shift from the optional occurrence of an element to its obligatory occurrence. In (9),
just discussed, the plural *=mɨ occurred optionally with the
pronoun 'we' in Hopi and Proto Takic whenever this pronoun
happened to be initial, but after it was incorporated as part
of the pronoun its occurrence was of course obligatory. Similarly, the Hopi unspecified object prefix tɨɨ became an obligatory component of tɨɨvahoma 'wash' by (16), so that vahoma cannot now stand alone. In both these examples the element in question is now morphologically determined -- it functions as an intrinsic part of a lexical item -- rather than
being syntactically introduced.

Reanalysis may lead to radically new uses of an element.
In (10), the ʔa of the Tarahumara reciprocal pronoun ʔanagu
was reanalyzed as a marker of plurality, and as such it was
added as a plural prefix to the third person independent pronoun binoy. The Numic pronoun pɨ became reflexive in (20); as
a result of this change pɨ was extended to various other reflexive uses, occurring without *-nak^{W}ayɨ, though it has none
of these uses elsewhere in Uto-Aztecan. Even when the uses
of a reanalyzed element do not drastically change, and it occurs in the same position (say as a noun suffix), its distribution may change as a result of its change in value. We saw
in (2) that the absolutive-accusative sequence *-t-a was reanalyzed as a simple absolutive in Luiseno (and Aztec), and
as such its distribution came to be determined by the morpho-

logical class of the noun rather than by syntactic case. The
same sequence became an accusative in Yaqui by (4), so that
the original absolutive t came to be used solely with accusative nouns. When the Huichol absolutive suffix te shifted to
plural value by (17), its distribution naturally shifted to
being determined by number.

Finally, a reanalysis may have the effect of creating
conditions that trigger another reanalysis. (More generally,
one syntactic change may have the effect of creating conditions that trigger another syntactic change.) For instance,
the semantic shift in (15), which extended the Southern
Paiute locative reflexive na'noo to emphatic reflexive sense,
led to the loss of the meaning component 'with' (which had
only figurative value in the new sense); this in turn led to
the boundary loss in (7) and ultimately the incorporation of
a new postposition for oblique uses of the pronoun. The
boundary creation in (11) gave rise to double marking of the
passive in Huichol, since either -ri or -ya was considered
sufficient to indicate passiveness, and as a result both came
to be used independently as passive suffixes. The P-UA change
in (21), yielding possessive locutions of the form 'He has
his N', made possible the elimination of the possessor prefix,
which resulted in the simpler locution 'He has a N'.

It is precisely because language change is essentially
local in nature that one syntactic change often leads to another. Occasionally, as in the examples of constructional
reanalysis given in the previous section, one specific change
occurs as part of a more comprehensive restructuring of a
clause or sentence, but more commonly changes are localized
to a fairly restricted domain, and even when they are not

they remain local in a broader sense of the term. Specifically, a reanalysis occurs in response to a particular set of
factors present in a particular class of expressions; it resolves certain structural pressures or exploits the structural
potential of those expressions. Speakers do not however re-
design their entire language or check the implications of a
modification for all other aspects of the linguistic system
before adopting the modification. A change which resolves
certain structural pressures may therefore create new ones
and lead to further changes.

Consider (21), for example. The P-UA existential possessive locution in question was modified in response to the
abnormality of a situation in which a meaningless element (the
possessed suffix (*-wa) occurred in conjunction with a unit of
meaning lacking overt manifestation ('be'). Reanalysis (21)
brought about the more straightforward situation of a one-to-
one correspondence between units of meaning and overt units
of form. However, this modification, which resolved one
source of structural pressure for change, gave rise to another
one, since it changed locutions of the form 'His N is' to locutions of the form 'He has his N'. The former are common
cross-linguistically and non-redundant; the latter are less
common cross-linguistically and do incorporate a certain a-
mount of redundancy.[17] The more highly marked locutions of
the form 'He has his N' arising from (21) were therefore susceptible to a further change, which did indeed occur, eliminating the redundant possessor prefix and resulting in unmarked locutions of the form 'He has a N'.

These changes also illustrate the interaction of reanalysis with substantive language universals. Briefly stated,

the output of a reanalysis tends to conform with the expectations of universal grammar. On the one hand this may mean
that a reanalysis is facilitated if the construction affected
has the potential of an alternate interpretation in accordance with universal tendencies. On the other hand it may
mean that the output of a reanalysis undergoes further modifications to bring it in line with such tendencies. The
change in the P-UA possessive locutions with *-wa just discussed illustrates both points. Both changes, from 'His N is'
to 'He has his N', and from the latter to 'He has a N', are
changes from one universal type of possessive locution to another, as all three kinds of locution are found in many languages of the world. I think it not unreasonable to suggest
that reanalysis (21) was greatly facilitated by the existence
of an alternative, universally specified possessive locution
that could plausibly be expressed by the same surface sequence that the change affected. The second change, from 'He
has his N' to 'He has a N', was similarly facilitated and also traded a relatively marked construction for an unmarked
one.[18] The two reanalyses of *na-w(i) as a simple postposition, (5) and (19), also illustrate the second point. The resegmentation by itself resulted (or would have resulted) in a
postposition standing as an independent word. While this
sometimes happens (cf. (13)), it is more in accordance with
universal tendencies for prepositions to stand as independent
words and for postpositions to be suffixed to their object.
In both Cahuilla-Cupeno and Numic the new postposition created
by the reanalysis was attached to nominals and was not allowed
to remain as an independent word. This subsequent change
therefore eliminated a discrepancy between the output of the
reanalysis and universal tendencies.

Causes of Reanalysis

I hardly need emphasize that any discussion of the
causes of syntactic change must be offered and accepted with
great caution and with full understanding of the limitations
of the claims that are made. It is presently beyond our ability -- and may remain ever so -- to predict with any certainty
when a construction or expression will undergo syntactic
change or what precise form such a change will take. Given
two languages with a comparable construction, one of them may
modify it and the other not, or the two may modify it differently. For example, the P-UA sequence *-t-a has remained in
Tubatulabal as an absolutive-accusative sequence to this day;
in Luiseno, however, it has been reanalyzed as an absolutive
suffix -ta (change (2)), while it has been reanalyzed as an
accusative suffix -ta in Yaqui (change (4)).

Despite this uncertainty, it remains true that syntactic
change occurs and that there are factors subject to rational
discovery and explication that permit, facilitate, instigate,
or influence change. I will refer to these as the "causes"
of syntactic change with the admonition that this term must
be taken in the loose and rather weak sense in which I offer
it. A term like "contributing factors" might be more indicative of what I intend, and I will use such terms also; but
"cause" provides greater economy of expression and suggests
the more ambitious goal -- which I would not like to abandon
prematurely -- of isolating those factors most directly responsible for syntactic change and without which it might not
occur.

I reject the position that we cannot speak of a factor
being a cause of syntactic change because the change does not
occur every time the factor is present. The fallacy in this
position is that it presupposes that the causes of change can
only be absolute. I suggest, on the contrary, that it is perfectly reasonable to talk of factors or conditions that facilitate or encourage change with varying degrees of force (just
as I find it reasonable to recognize universal tendencies of
language structure having varying degrees of strength). Likewise I reject the position that we cannot speak of a factor
being a cause of syntactic change because the change may occur without that factor being present. The fallacy in this
position is that it presupposes that the causes of change
must be unique. I suggest, on the contrary, that different
factors may trigger the same type of change, and that several
different factors may converge in instigating and determining
the direction of a given change.

To talk sensibly about the causes of syntactic change,
then, we must reject the implicit assumptions that would
force us to look for a single determining factor that will
always be associated with a given type of change and will un-
failingly trigger it. Language and speech are highly complex
entities in which a multiplicity of factors interact in very
complex ways. Some of these factors are structural, some are
psychological, and some are social. Two or more factors may
converge to favor the occurrence of a change, or they may conflict and tend to cancel each other out. Factors no doubt
differ greatly in strength and are in any case ultimately subject to the whims and vagaries of individual speakers and the
accidents of the social history of language use. Consequently,

any syntactic change will represent the vector sum of a variety of different pressures, some of which we may be able to isolate and some of which may remain forever beyond our grasp. This may make it very difficult to demonstrate conclusively the validity of proposals concerning the causes of syntactic change, but it does not in itself remove the matter from the domain of rational inquiry and empirical verification. It does mean that our methods, theories, and argumentation must accommodate the complexity of the subject matter -- we will be served well neither by simplistic or grandiose claims nor by the rejection of accounts that fail to provide simple and sweeping answers to complex questions.

We are presently far from being in a position where we can formulate accurate and comprehensive hypotheses about the fundamental causes of language change (syntactic change in particular) and devise rigorous empirical tests to demonstrate the correctness of these hypotheses. We are, however, in a position to advance various hypotheses in a presystematic and exploratory way. Any linguist who works extensively with diachronic problems soon develops an informal conception of the kinds of situations that lend themselves to language change and the variety of considerations that play a role in determining its character. We will gain nothing by shutting our eyes to these conceptions because of their informality and intuitive character. Rather we should work to enlarge the pool of well-grounded and accessible empirical data available for discussions of syntactic change; to translate informal and intuitive notions of the nature and causes of change into explicit proposals that can be scrutinized for their adequacy; and ultimately to devise methods to evaluate alternative proposals on empirical grounds.

In the remainder of this section I will attempt to make explicit some notions concerning the causes of syntactic reanalysis (and other changes) as they emerge from the body of examples I have collected, in particular as illustrated in the cases presented earlier in this paper. The motivating factors I outline are certainly not new to linguists, nor are they restricted in their impact to syntactic reanalysis. Certainly they are not exhaustive of the causes of change, and those causes which are included can perfectly well be grouped in other ways. This is but one preliminary attempt to make certain ideas accessible to examination and discussion and to group them in a way that will hopefully prove illuminating.

Discussions of the causes of language change tend to center -- and often founder -- on such notions as "simplicity" or the "principle of least effort". Scholars have rightly been ambivalent about such notions. On the one hand it is obvious that the tendency to simplify things is a pervasive and undeniably relevant factor in language change. On the other hand, languages do not appear to decrease in overall complexity in the long run; changes do occur that seem to increase rather than reduce complexity; and the notion of simplicity, left unexplicated, is so vague as to be almost vacuous. A vicious circle tends to arise: X changes to Y because Y is simpler than X; we know Y must be simpler than X because X changes to Y.

To be useful for serious investigation, then, the concept of simplicity must be considerably refined and given specific content. There are different kinds of simplicity. They pertain to different aspects of language structure and language

use, and sometimes they conflict. These more specific notions of what constitutes simplicity should prove considerably more illuminating and less vacuous than a single vague
and unanalyzed one. Ultimately, of course, the circularity
noted above will reintroduce itself -- language change occurs
because speakers find some situations easier to handle or
more optimal in some sense than others, and we can only determine what these are by observing which situations are most
susceptible to change and what they tend to change to. This
need not be a vicious circle, however. As we isolate various
kinds of simplicity and establish individually on empirical
grounds their relevance in determining syntactic change, we
are in effect working toward an explicit characterization of
linguistic optimality in its various interacting dimensions.
The circle is vicious only if we fail to provide such concepts
as simplicity with substantial empirical content and invoke
them solely at our convenience without regard for the incon-
sistencies or contradictions this may entail.

I believe we can isolate a number of broad categories of
linguistic optimality. Languages will tend to change so as to
maximize optimality in each of these categories, and several
of these tendencies can reasonably be regarded as tendencies
in the direction of greater simplicity, in an obvious intuitive sense of the word. The tendencies toward these various
types of optimality will often conflict with one another. We
will be much more concerned with certain of them than with
others.

The first of these tendencies is the tendency toward
what might be called "signal simplicity". Signal simplicity
is economy in regard to production of the physical speech sig-

nal. Naturally it is very similar to the principle of least
effort when this is understood as pertaining to the more o-
vert aspects of language structure. However, it will have
considerably more explanatory value than the vague principle
of least effort if we recognize it as only one of several
competing tendencies toward optimality and further seek to
give it more precise content by enumerating the various
kinds of language change that are said to exemplify it.

Many phonological changes of course illustrate the tendency toward signal simplicity. These include assimilations,
the simplification of consonant clusters, vowel mergers such
as aw>o, reduction and elimination of unstressed vowels, and
so on. All of these kinds of changes simplify the speaker's task by shortening the signal he must produce or making
its articulation less exacting.

We are more concerned here with syntactic aspects of the
tendency toward signal simplicity. One of these is the process of selection, for instance the innovation in Huichol of
the two new passive suffixes -ri and -ya as alternatives to
the longer passive suffix -riya (cf. (11)). The reduction of
the Proto Cupan pronoun *?ičami 'we' to *čami by the selection
shown in (12) is another example.

Other syntactic aspects of signal simplicity pertain to
reduction in the status of units from relative independence
to relative dependence. Boundary reduction is one type. I
place under this rubric a continuum of processes that include
the incorporation of independent words as clitics or affixes
(i.e. reduction of word boundaries to clitic or morpheme
boundaries), the reduction of clitic boundaries to morpheme
boundaries, and the loss of morpheme boundaries. Another

type is the reduction of a clause to a phrase and of a phrase
to a word. Quite possibly these two types should be grouped
in a single broad continuum of reduction in status. Over a
long enough period of time, then, an independent clause consisting of several words may fuse into a single word or phrase
and be incorporated as part of another clause; this expression
may in turn be incorporated as a clitic, losing its status as
an independent word; the clitic may be reinterpreted as an affix and ultimately as part of a stem morpheme by further
boundary reduction and loss.

While my restricted data base does not contain any examples that illustrate this entire long development from
clausal to submorphemic status, it does contain many examples
that illustrate various parts of it. The reduction in P-UA of
a clause meaning 'He is by himself' to the status of a single-
word reflexive pronoun was discussed in conjunction with (20).
The Aztec reanalysis in (14) was prompted by the coalescence
of a two-word postpositional expression into a single word.
(9) shows the reduction of a clitic boundary to a morpheme
boundary in Hopi and Proto Takic. Many examples have been
given here of the loss of a morpheme boundary.

I think the tendency toward signal simplicity is an un-
deniable aspect of the evolution of natural language. Not
only are all these kinds of change massively attested, but also they are largely unidirectional. Boundary loss is very common, for instance, but boundary creation is quite uncommon by
comparison. Words are frequently incorporated as affixes, but
affixes show no great tendency to break away and become independent words. Established locutions clearly show an overall
trend toward erosion in their status rather than the opposite.

It has often been observed that language change reflects
a tension between convenience for the speaker and for the listener. Signal simplicity naturally benefits the speaker more
than the listener, as it limits the complexity of the task of
physically producing an utterance by reducing the number,
length, and difficulty of the units to be articulated. Obviously, though, continued erosion of the units of expression
will ultimately render the listener's task more difficult. A
second category of linguistic optimality therefore pertains
to the adequacy of sentences in their overt form to convey
the desired information to the listener. This tendency
toward perceptual optimality will of course often conflict
with that toward signal simplicity.

We will treat perceptual optimality only in passing,
since it relates only obliquely to our central topic, syntactic reanalysis. The tension between signal simplicity and
perceptual optimality does not manifest itself basically as
an ebb and flow in the erosion of established expressions; I
have noted that the processes contributing to signal simplicity are largely unidirectional. Instead the central mechanism for achieving perceptual optimality in syntax is a process
I will call "periphrastic locution", which is simply the creation by ordinary or extraordinary means of periphrastic expressions to convey the desired sense. As these new locutions
become established in a language, they too gradually fall prey
to the processes leading toward signal simplicity, and the
cycle begins again.

We have encountered various examples of periphrastic locution. The Aztec reflexive pronoun no?ma treated in (8) derives from the periphrastic locution *no-ma-ka 'from my hand',

which is regularly formed from the lexical stock and grammatical principles of the language. The Tarahumara plural pronoun *?a-binoy, discussed in (10), was less regular in its
formation, but it too originated as a periphrastic expression that was later reduced by boundary loss and phonetic
processes to ?aboy (or the variant ?aboni). The P-UA appositive construction 'that one, (the) N' considered in (18) was
a longer, periphrastic locution that quite possibly was adopted to give more phonological substance to the single-syl-
lable demonstratives *pɨ and *?a; as noted earlier, the resulting sequences *pɨma and *?ama have for the most part been
eroded in the daughter languages to simpler forms by selection or phonological developments. The P-UA locative reflexive pronoun *pɨ-nak^{W}ayɨ had a periphrastic source, as we saw
in (20); originally it was a clause which meant 'He is by
himself' quite literally and regularly.

It would not be entirely inappropriate to regard languages in their diachronic aspect as gigantic expression-com-
pacting machines. They require as input a continuous flow of
creatively produced expressions formed by lexical innovation,
by lexically and grammatically regular periphrasis, and by
the figurative use of lexical or periphrastic locutions. The
machine does whatever it can to wear down the expressions
fed into it. It fades metaphors by standardizing them and
using them over and over again. It attacks expressions of
all kinds by phonetic erosion. It bleaches lexical items of
most of their semantic content and forces them into service
as grammatical markers. It chips away at the boundaries between elements and crushes them together into smaller units.
The machine has a voracious appetite. Only the assiduous efforts

of speakers -- who salvage what they can from its output and recycle it by using their creative energies to fashion a steady flow of new expressions to feed back in -- keep the whole thing going.

The creative recycling of compacted expressions is seen clearly in the evolution of the Southern Paiute oblique reflexive pronoun na'noo-p 'for himself'. Etymologically, this pronoun contains three reflexive or reciprocal pronouns (two occurrences of *na- and na'noo) and three postpositions (*-w(i) 'to, with', *-noo 'with', and -p(a) 'at, for'). The original periphrastic locution *na-w(i) 'with one another, together' was compacted phonologically in Proto Numic to *noo, which triggered the reanalysis shown in (19) that makes *noo a simple postposition meaning 'with'. This new postposition was then combined again with *na-, which in Proto Southern Numic was reflexive as well as reciprocal. The locative reflexive *na-noo 'by oneself' so obtained was extended to emphatic reflexive use by (15). Since the postpositional sense was only figurative in this use, the boundary between *na- and 'noo was lost by (7), yielding in Southern Paiute the emphatic reflexive pronoun na'noo. The postposition -p(a) was then attached to this for oblique uses in yet another regular periphrastic locution.

Another type of optimality toward which languages tend is what I will call "constructional simplicity". This is the analog, for more abstract domains, of signal simplicity. It is reflected syntactically in the tendency for marked categories to be replaced by relatively unmarked ones; for marked constructions to give way to more commonplace ones; and for the intrinsic complexity of constructions to be reduced. I

realize that concepts like markedness and the "intrinsic complexity of constructions" are problematic in various ways,
but it is not my intent to elaborate on them here. For the
moment I will simply appeal to the presystematic conception
of these notions that all linguists develop -- and hopefully
share in large measure -- through their experience with various languages.

Reanalysis (16), loss of the Hopi unspecified argument
prefix tɨɨ- as a separate morpheme, exemplifies the elimination of a marked category. Verbal affixes indicating explicitly that a subject or object is unspecified are much less
common linguistically than, say, pronominal affixes specifying the person or number of subjects or objects. Not only
are unspecified argument affixes susceptible to reanalysis as
part of the verb stem (more susceptible than pronominal affixes, I suggest), but also they are susceptible to complete
loss from a language. Uto-Aztecan is a case in point. P-UA
had three unspecified argument verb prefixes, and all three
have been lost in a substantial majority of the daughter languages. Absolutive suffixes have also shown a tendency in
Uto-Aztecan to be lost, reanalyzed as part of noun stems, or
adopted for other uses (cf. (17)), in accordance with their
somewhat marked status. The possessed suffix *-wa of P-UA
has also tended strongly to be eliminated, as in (21), in distinct contrast to the unmarked possessor affixes, for example.

The distinction between the markedness of grammatical
constructions and their complexity is conceptually clear (a
fairly complex construction, like a relative clause, may be
virtually universal), but in practice the two are closely associated. Change (18), which derived simple P-UA demonstra-

tive-noun sequences from an earlier appositive construction, certainly had the effect of trading a relatively marked demonstrative construction for an unmarked one. The complexity of the rules and underlying representations responsible for the construction were also no doubt reduced. The change in P-UA possessive locutions subsequent to (21), from 'He has his N' to 'He has a N', also achieves greater constructional simplicity by providing a construction that is both less complicated and more common. In a number of examples, including (13), (14), and (19), it can be argued that syntactic change has simplified a construction although it is at best debatable whether a less marked construction has resulted. (13) and (14) both eliminate (in Yaqui and Aztec respectively) the pronoun copy construction for postpositional phrases, and presumably the operation which introduces the pronoun copy; the number of morphemes that figure in the surface sequences is reduced, and possibly also the number of operations involved in their derivation. However, in Yaqui this yields the somewhat unusual situation in which postpositions can follow their objects as independent words, and in Aztec it produces the marked situation in which a connective is inserted between nouns and certain postpositions. In the case of (19), Numic expressions of the form 'N_1 and N_2 V with one another' gave way to expressions of the form 'N_1 V with N_2', which are undeniably simpler, but it is not obvious which of these types of locution should be considered less marked. It should be apparent from examples like these that the various facets of constructional simplicity may conflict with one another on occasion.

The last type of linguistic optimality I will consider

in detail might be termed "transparency". It is based on the
notion that the ideal or optimal linguistic code, other things
being equal, will be one in which every surface unit (typically a morpheme) will have associated with it a clear, salient, and reasonably consistent meaning or function, and every
semantic element in a sentence will be associated with a distinct and recognizable surface form.[19] Languages are thus
optimal along this parameter to the extent that they show a
one-to-one correspondence between units of expression and u-
nits of form, and languages should therefore tend to change
toward this situation rather than away from it. Obviously,
though, natural languages routinely and massively fail to
achieve this state, a problem I will discuss below.

First, however, let me indicate the kinds of tendencies
I would consider as contributing to transparency. For one
thing, languages should show a tendency to eliminate morphemes
with no obvious meaning or syntactic function -- by incorporating them in other morphemes through boundary loss, by assigning them new meaning or function, or by omitting them entirely; we have seen numerous instances of this, for example (2),
(4), (5), (6), (7), (8), and (17). By the same token, language change should tend to minimize or eliminate cases where
a unit of meaning has no surface realization; we observed
this with respect to 'be' in (21). Reanalysis (19), in which
two semantic elements (reciprocal and 'with') were lexicalized
by a syncretistic expression with no non-arbitrary boundary,
eliminated the reciprocal value of the expression and restored
the one-to-one correspondence between semantic and surface u-
nits.

Two other tendencies that I take as contributing to

transparency are those leading toward "boundary coincidence"
and the elimination of allomorphic variation. By boundary coincidence, I simply mean the tendency for different kinds of
boundaries to occur in the same position in a string rather
than in conflicting positions. One such case is the tendency
for morpheme boundaries to occur at syllable boundaries rather than in the middle of a syllable; word boundaries are virtually always morpheme boundaries as well; constituent boundaries are usually (but not always) located at word boundaries.
I hardly need comment on the tendency for allomorphic variation to be minimized or eliminated, i.e. the tendency for one
shape of a morpheme to be generalized to all environments.
This tendency is naturally included under the rubric of transparency as I have defined the term, and transparency may
therefore be responsible for a substantial proportion of analogical changes in language. Both boundary coincidence and
the elimination of allomorphic variation were seen to figure
in reanalysis (3).

We must go back now to the question of why natural languages never achieve anything very closely approaching the
one-to-one correspondence between expressive and grammatical
or semantic units that transparency predicts. The reason, of
course, is that transparency is only one type of linguistic
optimality, and to a certain degree it conflicts with other
types. The extent to which languages achieve transparency
appears consistent with what we might expect as the compromise
resolving several competing forces. Conflicting with transparency are both signal simplicity and what I will call "code
simplicity".

Signal simplicity, which favors fewer and shorter units

of expression, will of course conflict with the tendency of
transparency for every semantic unit to be associated with a
distinct and recognizable surface form. There is a natural
way to partially resolve this inherent conflict, however, and
languages uniformly show a reasonably high degree of success
in resolving things along these lines. Specifically, units
of meaning vary enormously along a gradient of information
content, and the salience of the corresponding units of expression varies accordingly. A minimal semantic unit, one
that is redundant or contrasts with only a small set of alternative units, can be marked overtly in a relatively subtle
way. On the other hand, a semantic unit that is non-redundant and contrasts with a large class of potential alternatives must be marked overtly in a relatively distinctive way.
This correlation between the gradients of semantic content and
expressive salience has long been noted and makes languages
highly "efficient" given the conflicting design specifications they must meet.

Many well-known facts about language make sense when
viewed against this backdrop. It is expected, for example,
that repeated constituents, being semantically redundant, will
be deleted or realized by a pro form. Zero can play a contrastive role under certain conditions, since the absence of
an element contrasts with the presence of one, especially in
a paradigmatic set such as a set of pronominal forms; signal
simplicity predicts that languages will often exploit this
potential and use zero for one member (usually the least
marked or most frequent) of a paradigm. The correlation between the gradients of semantic content and expressive salience also predicts that the "heavier" an overt element is

semantically the more likely it is to stand alone as an independent surface form or represent a major category. Noun incorporation, for example, usually affects only indefinite, un-
quantified, and unmodified nouns; to the extent that a noun
is elaborated by semantic content contributed by modifiers
and determiners, it tends not to be incorporated as part of a
verb but rather to stand overtly as a separate constituent.
Noun incorporation is also more likely to affect generic
nouns or those with very general significance (e.g. 'man')
than more specific ones (e.g. 'toddler').[20] The members of
major categories, such as noun, verb, and adjective stems,
are nearly always segmental in character and usually serve as
"heads" or defining elements of constituents (e.g. stems are
the central elements of words, a noun is the pivotal element
of a nominal or noun phrase, and a verb or other predicate is
the basic element of a clause); this can be related to the
fact that noun, verb, or adjective stems number in the hun-
dreds or thousands, so that the choice of one rather than another contributes very substantial semantic content. When
fewer distinctions have to be made, less substantial surface
signals are typically used. The handful of basic speech act
types can therefore be marked by subtle means such as intonation, word order, particles, clitics, or zero. Tense, aspect,
and modality are typically indicated by particles, clitics,
affixes, other inflection, or auxiliary verbs. Other categories with restricted membership that are often marked by
means less substantial than typical noun or verb stems include
pronouns, conjunctions, prepositions or postpositions, grammatical case, articles and demonstratives, quantifiers, negation, and subordinators. There are of course individual exceptions to the correlation between the two gradients, but

the overall pattern is quite evident.[21]

A second type of linguistic optimality conflicting with
transparency is code simplicity. Code simplicity pertains to
the number of different fixed expressions, patterns, and locutions that a speaker must master, remember, and manipulate in
language use. The impracticality of having a separate lexical item for every conceivable object, event, or situation a
speaker is likely to encounter is of course a truism. Languages never provide a lexical inventory that is vast enough
to label with uniqueness and precision the elements of every
conceivable contingency; rather they depend on the speaker to
use creatively a more restricted inventory of lexical units
in conjunction with the resources of the grammatical system.

This creativity has several facets. One facet is the
construction of grammatically regular expressions to describe
entities for which no established lexical expression exists;
a simple example is the elaboration of a noun by means of a
relative clause. A second facet is determining reasonable and
appropriate use for established lexical expressions whose
sense is general to a greater or lesser degree. Even a concrete noun like rabbit is fairly general and not at all mechanical in the determination of its applicability. We apply
this term to a large, open-ended (and rapidly multiplying)
class of entities rather than to a single, unique entity (as
with a proper name). We also apply it to distinguishable
species, to pictures of members of any of these species, to
dead rabbits, to rabbits with a leg or foot missing, to dolls
or mechanical devices in the shape of rabbits or any reasonable facsimile thereof, and so on. Determining whether or
not something is properly called a rabbit is a creative act

on the part of the speaker. It calls for his knowledge of
the prototype and the conventional range of non-proto typical
cases generally covered by the term, his estimation of where
the object in question falls in relation to this range, his
assessment of the context and likelihood that the listener
will grasp his intent, and his judgment of the expressive potential of the term in relation to other alternatives. Here
we are touching on figurative language, which is yet another
facet of the creative use of a limited lexical inventory.
When no pre-existing lexical item is fully appropriate, the
speaker may convey the desired notion figuratively rather
than creating a new periphrastic locution for it. Besides
its intrinsic expressive and esthetic value, then, figurative
language serves the purposes of code simplicity, enabling
speakers to adapt limited lexical resources to an essentially
unlimited range of circumstances.

In all these ways a balance is struck between transparency and code simplicity. These devices maximize the
utility of the stock of lexical expressions present in a
language, obviating the necessity for an essentially unlimited set of such expressions but yet allowing them to handle
the unlimited range of potential circumstances to be described. Working against transparency are the related problems of possible ambiguity between the literal and the figurative sense of an expression, possible indeterminacy due
to the broad range of literal and extended uses to which most
common lexical items are put, and the vagueness of generic
terms. In many cases however, linguistic or extra-linguistic
context allows speakers to eliminate potential ambiguity

or uncertainty. In many others only a general statement is
intended or appropriate, so that a vague or generic term is
much more useful than a series of more specific ones. If the
concept of transparency is made relative to the kinds of notions speakers want to express, transparency and code simplicity will be very compatible in this type of case.

Conclusion

In this paper I have tried to discuss, in a preliminary
yet reasonably comprehensive way, a type of grammatical
change that I have called reanalysis. Reanalysis was defined
as change in the structure of an expression or class of expressions that does not involve any immediate or intrinsic
modification of its surface manifestation. I have given a
representative group of examples from Uto-Aztecan and presented an informal notation that is useful for showing the
essentials of at least simpler examples of the process. A
distinction was made between the types of reanalysis, its
causes, and its effects. These were discussed at some length
in conjunction with other selected aspects of language change.

For purposes of discussing syntactic reanalysis, the surface level of representation -- that level which by definition
remains unchanged -- can be characterized roughly as the phonemic level together with indications of word boundaries. Typically it is necessary to consider at least two other levels,
one relatively superficial and one relatively abstract, because reanalysis normally hinges on the interplay between
form on the one hand and function or meaning on the other. A
reanalysis can effect change at either one of these levels a-
lone or at both.

I have divided syntactic reanalysis into two broad types, resegmentation and reformulation; a given reanalysis may involve either one or both. Resegmentation pertains to the occurrence and placement of morpheme boundaries, while reformulation pertains to more abstract aspects of semantic and syntactic structure. All three of the expected types of resegmentation occur: boundary loss, boundary creation, and boundary shift. Reformulation was classified with respect to the effect of the reanalysis on semantic representations. Some reformulations affect only elements that have purely syntactic function or are semantically redundant; it is possible to argue that they have no effect on semantic representations. For those instances of reformulation that do affect semantic structure, we can distinguish between their effect on particular elements, such as lexical expressions, and their effects on the overall structure of a clause or sentence. With respect to lexical expressions, reanalysis may involve the loss of semantic units, their addition, or a change in their value. When these changes in the semantic value of lexical expressions occur as an integral part of an overall reshaping of the structure of a clause or sentence, the change is called constructional reformulation.

The question naturally arises whether some of these types of reanalysis are more basic than others. Certainly some complex examples can be broken down into a group (possibly simultaneous) of simpler changes. Beyond that, however, is the issue of whether some of the basic types described earlier can be reduced to others. I believe they probably can, though it is too soon to make a definite determination. Let us abstract away from the complexities of specific examples (including linear order) and briefly examine, in abstract terms, the types of reanalysis that have been exemplified here.

An abstract characterization of boundary shift is given in (22).

$$(22) \quad \begin{matrix} A & & B & & A & & B \\ | & & | & > & | & & | \\ XY & - & Z & & X & - & YZ \end{matrix}$$

Change (3) was of this type. We explored earlier, and left unresolved, the question of whether boundary shift can be eliminated as an independent kind of change in favor of a combination of boundary creation and boundary loss.

Boundary loss, when not accompanied by semantic loss, has the abstract form shown in (23).

$$(23) \quad \begin{matrix} A & \emptyset & & A \\ | & | & > & | \\ X & - & Y & & XY \end{matrix}$$

Changes (2), (4), and (5) are precisely of this type (ignoring linear order). We will see, however, that this schema can be regarded as a basic component of other kinds of reanalysis, including of course boundary shift (cf. (3')).

Three types of boundary creation are depicted in (24) - (26).

$$(24) \quad \begin{bmatrix} A \\ B \end{bmatrix} > \begin{bmatrix} A \\ B \end{bmatrix} \qquad (25) \quad \begin{matrix} A & A & A \\ | & > | & | \\ XY & X & - Y \end{matrix} \qquad (26) \quad \begin{matrix} A & A & \emptyset \\ | & > | & | \\ XY & X & - Y \end{matrix}$$

$$\begin{matrix} | & & & \diagup\diagdown \\ XY & & A & B \\ & & | & | \\ & & X & - Y \end{matrix}$$

These are exemplified in (10) - (12) respectively. The three varieties represent the three basic logical possibilities. In

(24), the content of a semantically complex unit is divided
between the two new units derived by the boundary creation.
In (25), each new unit inherits the full meaning of the original. In (26), the content is localized in one unit, the
other being left with no apparent function. All three kinds
of boundary creation are the same at the lower level, reducing to the common schema XY > X-Y   they differ only in how
the original semantic content is distributed over the new u-
nits.

These, then, are the basic kinds of resegmentation, with
(22), boundary shift, possibly eliminable and the three kinds
of boundary creation, (24) - (26), all special cases of the
schema XY > X-Y. Let us now outline the basic types of reformulation as they affect the semantic value of lexical units.
Then we can try to determine to what extent more complex reanalyses can be decomposed into these simpler ones.

Semantic loss, addition, and shift are schematized in
(27) - (29) respectively.

$$
(27) \quad \begin{matrix} A \\ | \\ X \end{matrix} > \begin{matrix} \emptyset \\ | \\ X \end{matrix} \qquad (28) \quad \begin{matrix} \emptyset \\ | \\ X \end{matrix} > \begin{matrix} A \\ | \\ X \end{matrix} \qquad (29) \quad \begin{matrix} A \\ | \\ X \end{matrix} > \begin{matrix} B \\ | \\ A \\ | \\ X \end{matrix}
$$

We happen not to have examined any cases in which semantic
loss occurs and nothing else, but (27) can easily be seen to
figure in various more elaborate reanalyses, for example (16)
and (18). (17) is a straightforward example of semantic addition, exactly the same in form as (28). (29) embodies a
claim about the nature of semantic shift. While I do not
wish to deny the possibility that a morpheme X might simply
shift from sense A to sense B, I suggest that semantic shift

more commonly originates in semantic extension, where an element with basic sense A, without losing that sense, is used
-- often figuratively -- to convey the extended meaning B.[22]
(29) is a simplified version of the type of change exemplified in (15).

Before going on to complex cases, we must note some principles of equivalence that can be defined over representations of the kind we are using. First, the representation on
the left-hand side of (30) can clearly be regarded as equivalent to that on the right-hand side, and the same is true of
(31).

$$
(30) \quad \begin{array}{c} A \\ | \\ \emptyset \\ | \\ X \end{array} = \begin{array}{c} A \\ | \\ X \end{array} \qquad (31) \quad \begin{array}{c} A \\ | \\ A \\ | \\ X \end{array} = \begin{array}{c} A \\ | \\ X \end{array} \qquad (32) \quad \begin{array}{c} \begin{bmatrix} A \\ B \end{bmatrix} \\ | \\ A \\ | \\ X \end{array} = \begin{array}{c} \begin{bmatrix} A \\ B \end{bmatrix} \\ | \\ X \end{array}
$$

Situation (30) can arise through reanalysis, as we will see,
and (31) presumably can, though I have no examples. (32),
which is very much akin to (31), also arises through reanalysis. The equivalence in (32) is perhaps less obvious than
the other two. It hinges on X containing no morpheme boundary. In such a situation, (32) claims, X cannot simultaneously retain its literal sense A and be used figuratively to express another meaning containing A as a component. This is
said to be equivalent to X having the new, extended sense [A,
B], and indeed, it is hard to see what the difference would
be between X, meaning A, being used figuratively to mean [A,B]
and X having the alternative meanings A and, by extension,
[A,B].

Once these equivalence principles are recognized, it is
immediately apparent that certain complex reanalyses can be
reduced to more basic ones. Both (6) and (7), for example,
can be broken down into the two-part reanalysis shown in (33).

(33)

$$
\begin{bmatrix} A \\ B \end{bmatrix} \quad > \quad \begin{bmatrix} A \\ B \end{bmatrix} \quad = \quad \begin{bmatrix} A \\ B \end{bmatrix}
$$

As depicted earlier in (6)(b) and (7)(b), the changes were
given as leading directly from the left-most representation
in (33) to the right-most. We can see, however, that the
first step in (33) is identical to the basic boundary loss
schema (23), while the second step is simply the equivalence
(32). By the same token, (8) can be reduced to boundary loss
plus equivalence (30), as shown (in simplified form) in (34).

(34)

The first step is simply the special case of boundary loss
(23) in which the element labeled A in (23) happens to be zero.

 By now it is obvious that boundary loss is an extremely
common type of change that tends to eliminate elements with
no obvious semantic content or syntactic function. (23),
which eliminates a zero element, however, represents only a
special case of a more general process in which boundary loss
eliminates an element with only limited or marginal semantic

or syntactic value. This general process is represented in
(35), where (B) can be a substantial semantic unit rendered
superfluous by virtue of a broader constructional reformulation, a pro form or other highly restricted semantic unit, a
redundant semantic unit, a dispensable syntactic marker, or
-- as a special case -- zero.

$$(35) \quad \begin{matrix} A \\ | \\ X \end{matrix} - \begin{matrix} (B) \\ | \\ Y \end{matrix} \quad > \quad \begin{matrix} A \\ | \\ XY \end{matrix}$$

When generalized in this way, simple boundary loss accounts
for several more of our examples of reanalysis, including
(13), (14), (16), and (18).

    Further reductions can be made but begin to appear more
speculative. The essentials of (9), for example, are given
in (36).

$$(36) \quad \begin{matrix} A \\ | \\ X \end{matrix} = \begin{matrix} (B) \\ | \\ Y \end{matrix} \quad > \quad \begin{matrix} A \\ | \\ X \end{matrix} - \begin{matrix} (B) \\ | \\ Y \end{matrix}$$

(9) involves the downgrading of a clitic boundary to a morpheme boundary. In the example at hand, the status of (B) in
the output is not clear, since B duplicates part of the semantic content of A (the first person plural pronoun) but is
still probably recognizable and analyzable as a (plural) morpheme. If it can be argued that the status of (B) is more
marginal in the output of (36) than in the input, it would be
reasonable to collapse (35) and (36) in a still broader category of boundary downgrading, in which morpheme boundary loss
and full loss of (B) are but endpoints in the scale of possible reductions. The incorporation of words as clitics (i.e.
the downgrading of a word boundary to a clitic boundary)

could also be included in this category.

The only reanalyses we have not yet considered are (19)
- (21). (19), reformulated here (with linear order reversed)
as (37), can be related to schema (35), but it is questionable
whether it can be fully assimilated to (35).

(37)   A   (B)   >   A
                                 |
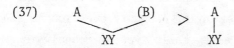
           XY   XY

The two facets of (35) are elimination of a morpheme boundary,
resulting in the single-morpheme sequence XY, and elimination
of the marginal semantic or syntactic element (B). These can
be conceived of as simultaneous developments, though in various examples there was reason to believe that full loss of
(B) (i.e. reduction of (B) to zero, the endpoint on its scale
of possible values) was temporally or functionally prior to
loss of the boundary. In (19)/(37), on the other hand, phonological merger (*na-w > *noo) appears to be temporally and
functionally prior. This merger eliminated any non-arbitrary
morpheme boundary in the XY sequence, thus triggering the
loss of the reciprocal element (B), which was rendered expend-
able through constructional reformulation. It appears, then,
that (35) can be collapsed with (37) only if its domain is ex-
panded to allow inclusion of a prior phonological change. This
can perhaps be done if we distinguish between the merger as a
phonological event and the boundary disappearance that it entails. However, we still might want to separate cases where
loss of the boundary triggers the semantic reformulation from
those where the converse situation obtains.

(20) and (21) are complex reanalyses that involve extensive constructional reformulation that includes shifts in the

alignment of units of form and units of meaning. This redistribution of semantic content to the overt units of form presents us with a choice. Either we can try to assimilate this
redistribution of semantic wealth to the broader problem of
constructional reformulation (which may be less susceptible
to a reductionist approach), perhaps doing the same for the
semantic redistribution accompanying boundary creation in (24)
- (26), or we can introduce a new basic type of reanalysis
called "realignment", which is given schematically in (38).

$$(38) \quad \begin{matrix} A \\ | \\ \emptyset \end{matrix} \quad - \quad \begin{matrix} (B) \\ | \\ X \end{matrix} \quad > \quad \begin{matrix} A \\ | \\ X \end{matrix}$$

One thing in favor of this second approach is that the operation of realignment can probably be reduced to schema (35),
boundary loss. The left-hand side of (38) is just a special
case of the left-hand side of (35), in which the X of (35)
happens to be zero. If we further recognize the obvious e-
quivalence between $\emptyset X$ and X, (38) can be restated as (39),
which consists of boundary loss (35) plus this equivalence.

$$(39) \quad \begin{matrix} A \\ | \\ \emptyset \end{matrix} \quad - \quad \begin{matrix} (B) \\ | \\ X \end{matrix} \quad > \quad \begin{matrix} A \\ | \\ \emptyset X \end{matrix} \quad = \quad \begin{matrix} A \\ | \\ X \end{matrix}$$

Let us now examine (20) and (21) with (39) in mind.

Reanalysis (20) can be broken down into three components,
two instances of simple boundary loss, as given in (35), and
one instance of realignment, as given in (39), which in turn
is reducible to boundary loss. The overall change is given ab-
stractly in (20)(b). One component, the loss of D and the
boundary between Y and Z, is represented in (40).

(40)   (A)   B   C   (D)   (A)   B   C
         | | | | > | | |
         W - X - Y - Z   W - X - YZ .

Our concern now is with the transition between the output of
(40) and the ultimate result, in which W realizes B and XYZ
realizes C. Examination seems to reveal that the conditions
for neither (35) nor (39) are met. For (35) to apply, eliminating the boundary between X and YZ, B would have to be
zero or at least marginal in content, and (35) would eliminate B. For (39) to apply, aligning B with W, X would have
to be zero.

The key to the solution is the realization that the two
processes must apply simultaneously. If B is to be realigned
with W, B is marginal and eliminable as the unit realized by
X, hence the conditions for (35) are met. If X is to be reanalyzed as part of the morpheme realizing C, the realization
of B can be regarded as zero, hence B is free to be realigned
with W through (39). If we conceive of the two operations as
sequentially ordered, therefore, they are not applicable; the
complex operation can be broken down into more basic ones only if the latter are regarded as simultaneous, mutually feed-
ing facets of the overall reanalysis. As a notational device, we can invoke the equivalence between B and BØ and between X and ØX, since B functions as Ø with respect to the
boundary loss involving following elements while X functions
as Ø with respect to the realignment affecting preceding elements. (20), partially treated in (40), can now be completed
as in (41).

(41)   (A)   B   C _ (A)   BØ   C   B   C _   B   C
         | | | = | | | >| | = | |
         W - X - YZ   W - ØX - YZ WØ - XYZ   W - XYZ

(21) is much easier to deal with. Only the last two elements (POSSD and BE) undergo change with respect to the form
and content of morphemes, though this change is part of a constructional reformulation that the present notation is not
meant to accommodate. The change affecting these two elements
can be given as in (42).

$$(42) \quad (A) \qquad B \quad > \quad C$$
$$\quad \mid \qquad\quad \mid \qquad\qquad \mid$$
$$\quad X \;-\; \emptyset \qquad X$$

The marginal element A, with only redundant syntactic function, was eliminated, and the overt unit X was realigned with
the meaning component B, which however assumed the new value
C (specifically HAVE). Pushing reductionism to its limits,
we can represent the change as in (43).

$$(43) \quad (A) \qquad B \quad > \quad B \quad = \quad B \quad > \quad C \quad > \quad C \quad = \quad C$$
$$\quad \mid \qquad\quad \mid \qquad\quad \mid \qquad\quad \mid \qquad\quad \mid \qquad\quad \mid \qquad\quad \mid$$
$$\quad X \;-\; \emptyset \qquad X\emptyset \qquad X \qquad B \qquad \emptyset \qquad X$$
$$\qquad\qquad\qquad\qquad\qquad\qquad\qquad\qquad \mid \qquad\quad \mid$$
$$\qquad\qquad\qquad\qquad\qquad\qquad\qquad\qquad X \qquad X$$

All of the changes and equivalences are well-established ones
that we have previously considered. The only question that
arises is whether X goes through the intermediate
which it retains the meaning B that is used by extension for
C, as in (29), or whether this should be considered a case
where X simply changes in sense directly from B to C. In
this particular example the latter may be more likely.

Let us summarize the results of this exploratory discussion of the reductionist approach to the types of reanalysis.
The limitations of this approach are self-evident. For one
thing, the discussion has attempted to handle only surface
units and their semantic or categorial value, not the more

elaborate aspects of constructional reformulation. There is also the question of when the reductionist program ceases to reveal something about language change and becomes an empty game.

Be that as it may, it is evident that a broad array of superficially different reanalyses can be reduced to the boundary loss schema shown in (35), possibly to be generalized to a schema that will include other kinds of boundary down-grading. The boundary creation subtypes shown in (24) - (26) all involve the basic development XY > X-Y and differ only in how the original semantic content of XY is distributed over the two new morphemes; essentially (24) - (26) represent the three logical possibilities. Boundary shift, sketched in (22), can be reduced to boundary creation plus boundary loss. Other basic types of changes are semantic loss (27), which is one component of the general boundary loss schema (35); semantic shift, schematized in (29); and semantic addition, shown in (28).[23] We found ways, speculative to varying degrees, to re-duce all of the other, apparently more complex types of reanal-ysis, to some combination of these basic types.

The types of reanalysis therefore present a complex pic-ture. The effects of reanalysis are also complex, but are much less amenable to classification or broad generalizations. The basic generalization that can be made is that elements af-fected by reanalysis change their subsequent behavior in those ways one would predict given their new value. The output of a reanalysis tends to conform to substantive language univer-sals, and to the extent that it does not, further change in the direction of universal expectations is a common result. Since reanalysis by definition leaves surface representations unchanged, it is by the subsequent effects of a reanalysis that we can tell most unambiguously that it has occurred.

The causes of reanalysis cannot be sharply distinguished from the causes of syntactic change in general. These causes are neither unique nor absolute, and any given syntactic change can be regarded as the vector sum of a variety of possibly conflicting pressures and tendencies. Language is highly complex, both in terms of structure and in terms of use. Language change reflects the pressure to achieve linguistic optimality, but linguistic optimality has numerous dimensions reflecting the multi-faceted character of language, and the tendencies to achieve these different kinds of optimality are often in opposition to one another.

One kind of linguistic optimality is signal simplicity, which is economy in regard to production of the physical speech signal. Many phonological changes serve the purpose of signal simplicity. Grammatical changes contributing to this goal include selection, defined as the process whereby one portion of a sequence with a given syntactic or semantic role is singled out and comes to stand alone in that role; boundary reduction and loss; the incorporation of words as clitics or affixes; and the reduction of clauses to the status of words or phrases and their incorporation as part of another clause.

Signal simplicity inherently conflicts with perceptual optimality. The central mechanism of perceptual optimality, at least as it relates to phenomena of concern here, is periphrastic locution, the creation of new periphrastic expressions. As these become established in a language they are subject to the various kinds of erosion subsumed under the

heading of signal simplicity. The cycle of periphrastic locution and consequent erosion is a continuous one in   language.

A third type of optimality is constructional simplicity.
One aspect of the tendency toward constructional simplicity
is the replacement of marked categories by less marked ones,
and a second is the replacement of marked constructions by
more common ones. Another aspect, related to the previous
two, is a tendency for the intrinsic complexity of constructions to be reduced.

Transparency is another kind of linguistic optimality.
It is the optimality inherent in a code in which every surface unit has associated with it a clear, salient, and consistent meaning or function, and in which every semantic element is realized by a distinct and recognizable surface form.
The loss of marginal semantic or syntactic elements, as schematized in (35), is a primary type of change contributing to
transparency. A second type is the elimination of semantic
units with no surface realization. Other contributing factors are the tendencies toward boundary coincidence and the
elimination of allomorphic variation.

Transparency conflicts with signal simplicity. The result is a far-reaching compromise whereby the degree of semantic content tends to correlate with the degree of expressive
salience. Numerous facts about natural language can be related directly to this compromise. Transparency also conflicts with code simplicity, a type of optimality which pertains to the number of distinct patterns and expressions that
must be learned, recalled, and manipulated. This conflict is
largely resolved through the use of generic terms, periphras-

tic locutions, and figurative expressions.

This account of syntactic reanalysis is preliminary and exploratory in numerous respects. While I have tried to present a fairly wide array of cases, there is no assurance that they are fully representative of the phenomenon in general. Alternate treatments of individual reanalyses can easily be conceived, and the different ways we have considered for classifying reanalyses are certainly not the only possibilities. My discussion of the causes of reanalysis is to be noted in particular for its preliminary character. It should be regarded as an initial attempt to bring out in the open, for the purposes of more systematic discussion and investigation, the intuitions and tacit knowledge about the causes of syntactic change that students of diachronic syntax all develop.

Notes

1. Here is a conservative sketch of the genetic relationships of the major Uto-Aztecan languages:

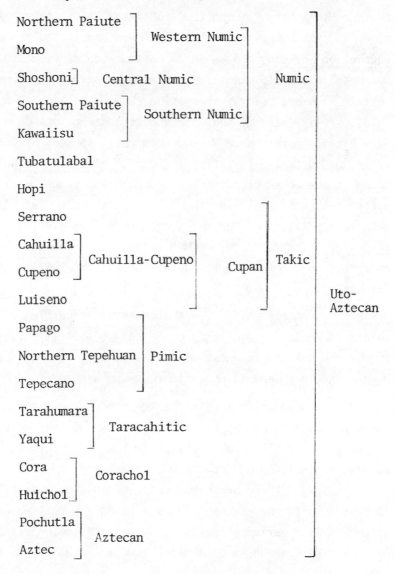

2. These include the following: <u>Non-Distinct Arguments in Uto-Aztecan</u>, Berkeley and Los Angeles, University of California Press, <u>UCPL</u> 82, 1976; 'The Syntax of Postpositions in Uto-Aztecan', <u>IJAL</u> 42, 1976; 'A Note on Consonant Gradation in Uto-Aztecan', submitted to <u>IJAL</u>; 'Semantic Representations and the Linguistic Relativity Hypothesis', to appear in <u>Foundations of Language</u>; and 'Reconstruction of Pronominal Elements in Takic', manuscript (presented before the Southwestern Anthropological Association, San Francisco, 19 April 1973). I will give my analyses and reconstructions only very briefly here; basic Uto-Aztecan data, sources of information, and detailed justification of the analyses can be found in the works cited above. I think the reader will be better served by my presenting a fairly wide array of cases than by repetition of the documentation and motivation of a few, since I have presented this information elsewhere. I hope this does not detract unduly from the credibility of the discussion.

3. Daughters vary as to the phonetic properties of the reflex of lenis /t/, so it is not clear whether [1], [d], or [r] is the best representation of the lenis allophone for the P-UA stage, nor can dialect uniformity be assumed.

4. An absolutive suffix in Uto-Aztecan, very roughly speaking, is one that appears on a noun that is not otherwise inflected; in P-UA the absolutive did however occur with the accusative suffix, and details vary considerably in the daughter languages. There are three pairs of absolutive suffixes in Luiseno: -<u>ta</u> and -<u>t</u>; -<u>la</u> and -<u>l</u>; -<u>ča</u> and -<u>š</u>. All descend from *-<u>ti</u>. The variants ending in <u>a</u> result from the reanalysis under discussion, and parallel remarks hold for all three

sets. The forms beginning in -l derive from lenition and the
phonological reanalysis shown in (1). -ča and -š result from
assimilation to a preceding i (č—→š is regular in syllable-
final position).

Pamela Munro has plausibly suggested that the absolut-
ives without a may derive through final-vowel loss from -ta,
not by retention of nominative -t; the discussion in the text
is basically compatible with this alternative and is not meant
to foreclose it.

5. This was also a factor in change (2), which happened
independently in Luiseno and Proto Aztecan.

6. This is the situation in Shoshoni, and it can be posited with fair confidence for earlier stages of Mono. Nasalization has subsequently been lost as an active process in
Mono, merging with gemination.

7. This account of ? is admittedly speculative. This
situation is further complicated by the existence of the variant   -no?ma-t(i)-ka, with the connective -ti- and the postposition -ka; I take this to be a relexicalization of the
'from' sense after the reduction of the original -ka to ?
left it unrecognizable, and before the literal sense of the
expression was completely forgotten. I am reasonably sure
that the text explanation is a correct characterization of
the development of this expression with respect to loss of
the boundary between no and ma (and that is sufficient for
present purposes), but other hypotheses can be entertained
about the postposition. I should note that close analogs of
*no-ma-ka 'from my hand' can be found in Cupan.

8. I have no deep principled reason for including this

downgrading from clitic to morpheme boundary under reanalysis
while excluding the downgrading from word to clitic boundary
-- the choice for now is more a matter of convenience than a
substantive claim. Some rationale for the decision was however offered earlier.

 9. Though sporadic, vowel harmonization is an extremely
common process in historical Uto-Aztecan grammar.

 10. The French word <u>licorne</u> 'unicorn' has a transparent
and interesting history, including an instance of boundary
creation prompted by analogy. For sake of discussion, I will
take 'unicorn' as consisting semantically of the components
MYTH-AN (for "mythical animal"), ONE, and HORN -- this is obviously a crude decomposition and should not be taken seriously outside the context of this note. Here is my conception
of the evolution of <u>licorne</u>:

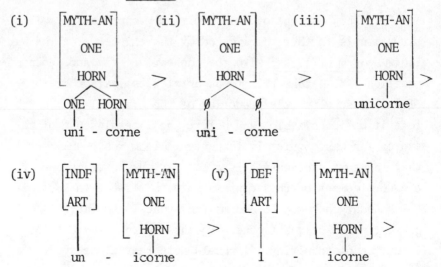

(vi)
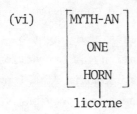

licorne

At stage (i), the two-morpheme sequence ONE-HORN was used to
stand for the entire conceptual complex of a mythical one-horn-
ed animal. As speakers gradually lost consciousness of the
semantic value of uni and corne (stage (ii)), the expression
became liable to reanalysis, specifically boundary loss, resulting in stage (iii). The boundary creation lies in the
transition between stages (iii) and (iv). The motivating factor of this resegmentation was clearly the existence of the
indefinite article un(e), identical in shape to the initial
portion of unicorne. The boundary was thus inserted by analogy to numerous expressions of the form un-N, where N stands
for a noun beginning in a vowel. Once icorne was segmented
as the noun, it could of course combine with the definite article (stage (v)), and the resulting sequence licorne was subsequently reanalyzed as a single morpheme (stage (vi)) through
a second instance of boundary loss.

11. Huichol has at least six passive suffixes, five of
which derive from *-liwa. Besides -rie, -ri, and -ya, they
include -ki (with another source), riwa (< *-riwa), and -wa
(from *-liwa by another instance of selection, this one possibly dating back to P-UA).

This step might be considered simultaneous with a further
development by which either element, ri or ya, comes to lose
its value and is treated as a functionless morpheme subject
to elimination; I owe this observation to Pamela Munro. Simul-

taneous changes are considered further in the conclusion.

12. I mention only in passing a process that might be
called "attraction". This is the localization, or attraction,
of a component of meaning to one particular subunit of a longer sequence with which that meaning component was previously
associated as a whole. This process, in conjunction with
boundary creation (as in (12)), is the first step in selection,
which is completed when the newly independently meaningful
subsequence comes to be used alone. Attraction also occurs
with boundary creation (10) with respect to the ?a of Tarahumara ?anagu, which attracts the semantic component PL. From
its definition, and from the definition of the notion "morpheme", it can be seen that attraction will often be associated with boundary creation and will always involve a boundary,
newly created or pre-existing. Strictly speaking, attraction
is not semantic reformulation, since semantic representations
are not altered. Rather it pertains to how semantic components are distributed among surface elements.

13. Exactly parallel changes affected the sequence
*?a-ma, with the demonstrative *?a and *ma 'one'. The dif-
ference between *pɨ and *?a was probably human/non-human or
animate/inanimate.

14. All of the reconstructions are non-speculative and
straightforward and are reinforced by the analysis of the parallel reciprocal pronoun *?a-nak^{W}ayɨ. There is reason to believe that this reciprocal expression was historically prior
and that *pɨ-nak^{W}ayɨ was formed on the model of it. Thus *na,
clearly reciprocal in origin, was fully appropriate semantically for the reciprocal pronoun, but was extended to reflexive
use in *pɨ-nak^{W}ayɨ. Similarly *k^{W}a probably meant 'to' origi-

nally, and this would be appropriate for certain reciprocal sentences, but in *pi-nak^{W}ayi we must attribute it general locative value rather than the specific directional sense 'to'. *?a-nak^{W}ayi was literally 'It is to one another', fully appropriate for complex sentences such as 'They are talking, (and) it is to one another'. Presumably this was but one of a whole series of periphrastic reciprocal locutions with different postpositions appropriate to the sense of the preceding verb. Eventually *?a-nak^{W}ayi was singled out for more general use, and as it gradually froze into a fixed unit the sense attributable to *k^{W}a became less precise, finally achieving very general locative sense. It was then a simple matter to form *pi-nak^{W}ayi on the model of *?a-nak^{W}ayi to obtain a locative reflexive pronoun; it was merely necessary to generalize *na from reciprocal to reflexive value in this one expression.

15. Even this boundary has most likely been lost in Tarahumara. There is a possibility that na is still recognized as a separate morpheme in Kawaiisu, though other modifications have occurred.

16. This possessed suffix *-wa almost certainly derives ultimately (with consonant lenition) from the pro form *ma 'one' discussed earlier in conjunction with (18).

17. For discussion of this redundancy, see my paper 'Functional Stratigraphy', in Robin E. Grossman et al. (eds.), Papers from the Parasession on Functionalism, Chicago, Chicago Linguistic Society, 1975, pp.351-397.

18. The interaction of (21) with universal tendencies is even stronger than the text discussion indicates. Given

the input to (21), the simplest reanalysis that would eliminate the skewed relationship between units of meaning and u-
nits of form would clearly be for *-wa to be reinterpreted
as meaning 'be'. This did not happen; rather it was interpreted as meaning 'have'. I suggest that the shift to 'have'
is due to the fact that it is more common in universal terms
for nouns to take derivational suffixes meaning 'have' than
existential suffixes meaning 'be'.

19. Transparency obviously overlaps to some degree with
what I referred to before as "perceptual optimality". I distinguish the two because I feel that transparency counts as
optimality for both the speaker and the listener. At this
preliminary stage of investigation, however, the relation between two such vague notions hardly constitutes a significant
empirical issue, and I wish to leave the whole matter open.

20. This has obvious diachronic analogs. For example,
there is evidence that the P-UA unspecified subject prefix
*ta- and unspecified object prefix *ti- derive historically
from incorporated nouns meaning 'person' and 'thing' respectively.

21. For related discussion, see my paper 'Movement
Rules in Functional Perspective', Language 50.630-664, 1974.

22. We have seen that semantic loss is particularly
likely to affect an element in the position of A in the output of (29); invoking equivalence (30), discussed below, we
can thus portray the shift of X from meaning A to meaning B
as follows:

$$\begin{array}{c} A \\ | \\ X \end{array} > \begin{array}{c} B \\ | \\ A \\ | \\ X \end{array} > \begin{array}{c} B \\ | \\ \emptyset \\ | \\ X \end{array} = \begin{array}{c} B \\ | \\ X \end{array}$$

A possible case where A shifts directly to B, without the intermediate stage, is touched on later.

23. Semantic addition could be reduced to shift and loss, as follows:

$$\begin{array}{c} \emptyset \\ | \\ X \end{array} > \begin{array}{c} A \\ | \\ \emptyset \\ | \\ X \end{array} = \begin{array}{c} A \\ | \\ X \end{array}$$

However, it is not obvious that it is meaningful to speak of the semantic extension of a zero element.

3 Reanalysis and Actualization in Syntactic Change

Alan Timberlake

1. Introduction

In this paper I will examine two syntactic changes in order to develop a model of syntactic change, concentrating on two general claims. The first claim is that is it instructive to distinguish between two types of change in syntax, as in other components of grammar: reanalysis -- the formulation of a novel set of underlying relationships and rules -- and actualization -- the gradual mapping out of the consequences of the reanalysis. This distinction is perhaps not controversial and I will illustrate it in passing while arguing for the second claim, which concerns the actualization of change. The second claim is that the actualization of change is systematic, in that it is governed by a number of linguistic parameters, which can be formalized as hierarchies. These hierarchies may be different for different changes and may be quite heterogeneous even for a single change, but I will suggest that they all obey one general principle: a change will be actualized earlier in contexts which are unmarked (or more natural) with respect to the change and later in contexts which are marked (or less natural) with respect to the change.[1]

2. Reanalysis and actualization

The model of syntactic change I will elaborate here is perhaps used by many people, but I know it from the explicit

formulation of Andersen (1973), who I will follow in most respects. I will also follow Coseriu (1962) in assuming that
the grammar is composed of two parts, the system -- the productive principles of the grammar -- and the norms -- all the
actual regularities of usage (with a possible distinction between individual and socially codified norms). I will assume
further that universals or subuniversals mediate between the
system and the norm and determine the extent to which given
norms are compatible or incompatible with a given system.

If the grammar is composed of the system and the norms,
the grammar determines the output, as in (1). New learners
of a language have to formulate the grammar that will determine their usage on the basis of the output produced from the
grammars of older speakers, but not directly from the grammars of these speakers. Given a certain output learners have
to formulate a grammar which produces the same output (or a
reasonable approximation of it), but they do not have to formulate the same grammar as that of the older generations. The
mode of inference that learners use in formulating a grammar
from output (abduction) is therefore different from that used
by speakers in producing output from a grammar (deduction).
While a grammar necessarily determines output (assuming the
norms describe stylistic variation), learners of a language
only have to formulate a grammar which is sufficient to produce a given output.

In some instances a given output is amenable to two or
more analyses and could conceivably be produced by two substantively different grammars. As in (1), the output could
potentially be produced from either grammar I or grammar II
(solid lines) and learners of the language are to a certain

extent free to formulate either grammar I or grammar II on
the basis of the output (broken lines).

(1)

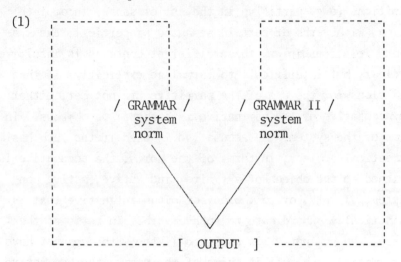

/ GRAMMAR /   / GRAMMAR II /
system   system
norm   norm

[OUTPUT]

Since the relationship between the norms and the output is
direct -- the norms are simply regularities of usage -- it is
likely that a substantive difference between grammars will
appear in the system rather than the norms. If grammar I is
substantively different from grammar II in system, and if
successive generations of speakers maintain grammar II and
eventually change their norms and output, one may speak of a
reanalysis having taken place. The concrete changes in norms
and output are the actualization of the reanalysis.

An illustration of this model of syntactic change is provided by the history of subject-to-object raising in Finnish.
Before considering this change, it will be helpful to give a
brief outline of case assignment in Finnish.[2] While a true
grammatical subject of a finite verb can only be expressed in
the nominative, various cases are used for other grammatical
constituents (objects and so-called subjects of existential

sentences). The norms specify that the partitive is used for objects under certain syntactic (e.g. negation) and semantic conditions (e.g. partitive in the strict sense, incomplete action, with verbs of certain semantic properties); the systemic relationship of these different contexts is intuitively clear, but is difficult to formalize explicitly. If the conditions for the use of the partitive are not met, either the accusative or the nominative is assigned to objects. In terms of the system, the accusative is used if the verb has a grammatical subject; in terms of the norms, the accusative is assigned to the object of a finite, indicative, active non-existential verb, or to the object of an infinitive that is syntactically subordinate to such a verb. In terms of the system, the nominative is assigned if the verb does not have a grammatical subject; in terms of the norms, the nominative is assigned to the object of an impersonal passive or imperative and to the so-called subject of an existential sentence, or to the object of an infinitive syntactically subordinate to such a verb. The genitive is basically not an object case, but is used to specify the underlying subject of certain adverbial nonfinite constructions, in addition to adnominal or possessive uses.

After verbs expressing cognition and related activities (e.g. uskoa 'think, believe', kertoa 'relate', huomata 'notice, observe'), Finnish used to and still does allow a choice between an explicit finite clause introduced by the complementizer että 'that' and a nonfinite (participial) clause. In older Finnish (as first attested in the writings of Agricola, studied by Ojansuu 1909, from whom the following data is taken) the underlying subject of the että clause

could be expressed in various cases; it was expressed in the
partitive when the matrix verb was negated (2), in the accusative when the matrix verb was active and had a subject (3),
or in the nominative when the matrix verb was an imperative
or passive (4) and lacked a subject:

(2)   eike   lwle   site   syndi oleuan
       not   think this   sin   being
                      (part)
       'does one not think this to be a sin'

(3)   seurakunnan hen lupasi pysyueisen oleuan
       congregation he   promised long-lasting being
       (acc)
       'he promised the congregation would be long-lasting'

(4)   ...homaitan se   tauara ia Jumalan Lahia poiseleua
          observed   goods and God   gift lacking
                         (nom)   (nom)
       'it is observed that the goods and the gift of God
        are lacking'

The distribution of partitive, accusative, and nominative in
this construction is exactly the distribution found for objects in general in Finnish. It suggests that the underlying
subject of the participial clause originally functioned as
the surface object of the matrix verb; that is, there was a
rule of subject-to-object raising in the older stage of Finnish.

In modern Finnish, however, the underlying subject of
the participial clause is always in the genitive, regardless
of whether the matrix clause is negated (5), has a subject
(6), or does not have a subject (7):

(5)   En   sanota lapsen tulevan
       not say   child   coming
                    (gen)
       'I did not say the child would come'

(6)   Näin lapsen panevan kirjeen taskuunsa
      saw   child   putting letter   pocket
            (gen)
      'I saw the child putting the letter in his pocket'

(7)   Lapsen huomattiin varastavan parhaan hevosen
      child   observed   stealing   best   horse
      (gen)
      'the child was observed stealing the best horse'

The fact that the underlying subject of the participial clause
is invariantly in the genitive suggests that it is not an object of the matrix clause, since it does not behave as an object for the purposes of case assignment. Aside from adnominal (possessive) constructions, the genitive is used in Finnish basically to express the underlying subject of nonfinite
clauses, such as adverbial clauses formed with participles,
reduced relative clauses formed with infinitive III, and purpose clauses formed with the translative case of infinitive I.
Further, when the underlying subject of the participle is i-
dentical to the subject of the matrix verb, the participle is
inflected with a possessive suffix, the kind of inflection
used for subject-verb agreement in the nonfinite clauses just
mentioned. Finally, the underlying subject behaves like a
subject in its own clause for the purposes of accusative case
assignment; as in (7) above, the subject of the participle
(lapsen) forces the object (hevosen) to be accusative even
though the matrix verb is passive and has no subject. For
these reasons it is clear that participial constructions no
longer involve subject-to-object raising in modern Finnish
(see A. Hakulinen 1973, Timberlake 1976).

The reanalysis that led to this difference between older
Finnish and modern Finnish can be sketched in the following
way (Anttila 1972:103-4). The original accusative desinence

*-m and the genitive desinence *-n of singular nouns became
syncretized through a phonological merger of nasals in word-
final position (pronouns and plural nouns had different des-
inences and continued to distinguish accusative from genitive,
as discussed below). As a consequence of this syncretism, at
least certain instances of the participial construction were
ambiguous. When the matrix verb was active and the underlying subject of the participial clause was a singular noun, it
would be expressed in a form with the desinence [-n] (as would
the participle, which originally agreed with the noun in case
and number). A singular noun with the desinence [-n] (the
output in (8)) could be analyzed as the product of either of
two equally natural grammars. Under one analysis (grammar I
in (8)), the noun could be viewed as an accusative object of
the matrix verb in a system with a rule of subject-to-object
raising. Under an alternative analysis (grammar II in (8)),
the noun could be viewed as the genitive subject of the participial clause in a system without subject-to-object raising.[3]

(8)
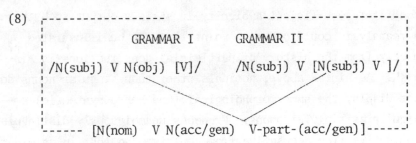

GRAMMAR I   GRAMMAR II

/N(subj) V N(obj) [V]/   /N(subj) V [N(subj) V]/

[N(nom) V N(acc/gen) V-part-(acc/gen)]

Comparative evidence and the evidence of older texts (as in (2-
4)) indicate that the original situation was that represented
by grammar I. It is clear that participial constructions in
modern Finnish are now derived by grammar II, so that a reanalysis must have taken place. The reanalysis can be seen
indirectly through various particular changes that have been

actualized in a gradual fashion: (i) all nominals -- not just
singular nouns -- have come to be expressed in the genitive;
(ii) the participle no longer agrees like an adjective in
case and number with its underlying subject, but has adopted
the invariant [-n] form; (iii) instead, the participle has
innovated a limited kind of subject-verb agreement, so that
when the matrix subject and the subject of the participle are
identical, the participle is inflected with a possessive affix agreeing in person and number with its subject.

3. Causation of reanalysis

It is difficult to discuss the causation of reanalysis
in precise terms, but in attempting to do so, it is useful to
distinguish between weak (necessary) and strong (sufficient)
causes.

A necessary precondition for reanalysis, I would claim,
is an ambiguity in the output, as schematized in (1) above.
Unfortunately it is difficult to define a priori exactly what
constitutes sufficient ambiguity in surface output such that
a reanalysis could occur, a point that can be illustrated
nicely from the history of participial constructions in Finnish. As hinted above, nominals other than singular nouns do
not display the same morphological (and hence syntactic) ambiguity as singular nouns. Pronouns unambiguously distinguish
nominative from accusative from genitive, so that in an older
Finnish participial construction like (9) the underlying subject of the participial clause (meidhet) is unambiguously an
accusative object of the matrix verb:

(9)   coska me lulema meidhet oleuan . . . ystewein
       since we think   us   being   friends
                          (acc)

       seasa
       among

'since we think we are among friends'

Also, although plural nouns and numerals syncretize nominative
and accusative, they keep both of these cases distinct from
the genitive, so that in (10) the plural noun -- the underlying subject of the participial clause -- is unambiguously not
a genitive and can be identified as an accusative object of
the matrix verb:

(10)   coska me näem ne Jumalattomat hyuesti
       since we see   godless   well
                           (acc)

       menestyuen
       going

'since we see the godless ones faring well'

Further, even a singular noun would not be ambiguous with a
matrix negated verb since it would be in the partitive, as in
(2), and a singular noun would not be ambiguous with a matrix
impersonal passive or imperative since it would be in the suf-
fixless nominative form, as in (4) above. Remarkably enough,
the reanalysis of participial constructions in Finnish occurred although the ambiguity which allowed it to occur was
found only in a subset of these constructions. One might argue that the reanalysis was based on the most unmarked (and
apparently statistically most frequent) variant of the construction, but still it is surprising that the ambiguity inherent in only one variant of the construction could be taken
as representative of the whole construction. This example
shows how difficult it is to define what constitutes suffi-

cient surface ambiguity for a reanalysis, but at the same
time it shows how a significant reanalysis is possible: a giv-
en surface output does not automatically lead to the formulation of the same grammar from which the output was derived.

Given the difficulty of defining surface ambiguity, one
might want to look for stronger (sufficient) causes for reanalysis. It sometimes appears that a series of reanalyses
(and actualizations) over a period of time are part of a high
level tendency in the system. And sometimes it appears that
a particular reanalysis is forced to occur, or to take one
form as opposed to another, by some systemic principle operating in the language. In still other instances it appears
that a reanalysis follows from some universal principle, such
as the tendency to decrease opacity (Chung, this volume) or
to increase iconicity (Langacker, this volume). In all these
cases, to the extent that they can be documented, the reanalysis can be viewed as the actualization of the given structural
principle or universal; the reanalysis is caused in a strong
(sufficient) sense in the same way that any actualization is
caused (see below).

In many cases, however, it does not seem possible to
show that a reanalysis is predictable from any structural principle or universal, at least not in an obvious way. For the
Finnish participial constructions, it could be suggested that
the reanalysis is just the actualization of some systemic
principle, conceivably the principle that subjects of nonfinite clauses are expressed in the genitive. If direct evidence could be found for this principle, it would be a strong
(sufficient) cause for the reanalysis. Even so, it can be
safely assumed that this principle would not have been opera-

tive in participial constructions without the ambiguity in surface output. In other words, it is still necessary to reckon with ambiguity in surface output as the weak (neces-sary) cause for reanalysis.[4]

4. Causation of actualization

A hypothesis about what causes actualization depends on an assumption about whether reanalysis precedes actualization or vice versa. Some generative work on change seems to sup-pose that reanalysis occurs only after a long series of more or less unrelated changes which lead to such complications in the grammar that a restructuring is inevitable (King 1969, Klima 1964). Such a view leaves unexplained how the compli-cations could have arisen in the first place. Given that grammar determines output, it is not clear how a grammar could change to become increasingly complex over a period of time. An analysis along these lines for Finnish might claim that the reanalysis occurred only recently, after several cen-turies of confusion during which pronouns and plural nouns were increasingly used in the genitive, although for no appar-ent reason. This analysis, if proposed, would leave unex-plained how the genitive came to be used for pronouns and plu-ral nouns in the first place, and why they were used more and more consistently over time. Clearly, in order for pronouns and plural nouns to be used in the genitive in this construc-tion, it must already have been reanalyzed as containing -- systemically -- a genitive subject, on the basis of the ap-parent genitive of singular nouns. In the Finnish case, and presumably in general, the actualization must have followed the reanalysis and must have been caused by the reanalysis.

If reanalysis preceded and caused the actualization in
the Finnish participial constructions, it is still not clear
how the actualization was able to maintain its directionality,
so that pronouns and plural nouns were increasingly used in
the genitive. Shortly after the reanalysis, new learners had
to formulate a grammar that would produce output commensurate
with the output of the teaching generations, some of which is
given schematically in (11) (it is assumed here that the accusative of singular nouns has already been reanalyzed as a
genitive in (11b)):

(11) a. N   neg   V   N-sg   V-participle
          (nom)   (part)

      b. N   V   N-sg   V-participle
          (nom)   (gen)

      c. --   V-passive   N-sg   V-participle
                                    (nom)

      d. N   V   Pro   V-participle
          (nom)   (acc)

      e. N   V   N-pl   V-participle
          (nom)   (acc)

The output in (11b) was of course no problem; because of the
syncretism of accusative and genitive, it could be produced
equally well by grammar I or grammar II. But the output in
(11a, 11c-e) posed a problem for grammar II. At the systemic
level subjects of participial clauses (like subjects of other
nonfinite clauses) should in principle be assigned genitive;
yet in order to produce the output in (11) the norms would
have to include a complicated and detailed list of subrules,
which matched specific contexts with specific cases. Within
a grammar that tried in principle to assign genitive to parti-

cipial subjects, the subrule responsible for producing (11b) would be motivated, but the other subrules responsible for (11a, 11c-e) would be unmotivated and exceptional. Hence succeeding generations of speakers, once they have arrived at grammar II and the systemic principle of assigning genitive to participial subjects, would try to formulate their norms with fewer and fewer of these unmotivated subrules. To the extent that they could succeed in doing this without producing radically different and unacceptable output, they would be actualizing the change. The directionality of the change is thus ensured as the consequence of the reanalysis, through the mechanism of eliminating exceptional and unmotivated norms.[5]

5. Constraints on actualization

In this paper I am primarily interested in the form that actualization takes. It seems that typically the actualization of a reanalysis occurs earlier in some contexts, or for some elements, than others. This point can be illustrated by considering again Finnish participial constructions and a related change involving infinitives.

In modern Finnish as described by slightly conservative manuals (e.g. Fromm and Sadeniemi 1956, L. Hakulinen 1960), it is still possible to find examples of participial constructions in which the underlying subject of the clause is expressed in the nominative or accusative, not the genitive. All the examples I have seen involve plural nouns, usually inanimate, but never pronouns. This suggests that the actualization of the change took place earlier for pronouns than for (plural) nouns.[6] This conclusion can be supported weakly from the language of Agricola. It is apparent that the actualiza-

tion had already begun before Agricola's time, since there
are a number of instances where agreement for case and number
between participle and noun has broken down. In his study
Ojansuu (1909) found exactly one example where the underlying
subject of the participial clause was expressed in the genitive, not in one of the object cases. It is perhaps significant that this example involves a pronoun, rather than a
plural noun.

The tentative hierarchy of pronouns/(plural) nouns (or
even pronouns/animate nouns/inanimate nouns) can be confirmed
by looking at a related change involving the small and closed
class of verbs antaa 'give, let', sallia 'permit', and käskeä
'order'. These verbs govern object complement clauses, but
they do not seem to involve equi (A. Hakulinen 1973, Timberlake 1976). Originally in Finnish verbs of this class allowed the underlying subject to be expressed as the object of
the matrix clause, where it was subject to the regular case
assignment rules for objects. For example, if the matrix verb
was negated, the underlying subject was partitive (12):

(12)   Ele ama meite coolla
        not let us   assemble
                 (part)
        'do not let us assemble'

If the underlying subject was a pronoun and the matrix verb
was not negated, it was unambiguously in the accusative (13):

(13)   ia annoit Heiet mene
        let   them go
                  (acc)
        'and you let them go'

And a singular noun with a matrix passive or imperative verb
was in the nominative (14):

(14)   anna se walkeus ... alati sytytte
        let this light   always shine
              (nom)
        'let this light always shine'

Thus, the distribution of case suggests that this construction
also used to involve subject-to-object raising. Obviously,
an accusative singular object in this construction was ambiguous in the same way as an accusative singular object in the
participial construction. As part of the same change, these
constructions with infinitive I were reanalyzed as having a
genitive expressing the underlying subject.[7]

In this construction in modern Finnish the genitive is
obligatory for pronouns:

(15)   Hän antoi meidän mennä
        he let us   go
              (gen)
        'he let us go'

But for plural nouns, T. Itkonen (1974) reports that both genitive and accusative are possible, although with a slight semantic difference. When the underlying subject is relatively
agentive, the genitive must be used:

(16)   Annoin niiden miesten jäädä reserviksi
        let those men   stay reserves
                      (gen)
        'I let those men stay in the reserves (as they
            wished)'

The accusative can occasionally still be used, but only when
the subject is nonagentive:

(17)   Annoin ne miehet jäädä reserviksi
                      (acc)
        'I let those men stay in the reserves (without re-
            gard for their desires)'

Although it might appear that the contrast of (16-17) represents a contrast of two separate constructions, this contrast
has arisen only as a transitional stage in the change from the
assignment of an object case (partitive, accusative, or nominative) to the assignment of genitive for the underlying subject in this construction. One speaker I consulted found the
accusative in (17) extremely archaic even with a nonagentive
meaning, while a younger speaker could not accept (17) at all.
And as mentioned above, pronouns obligatorily use the genitive
here. The contrast in (16-17), then, is the remnant of a
long gradual process in the actualization of the reanalysis.
Little by little, the old exceptions to the general rule that
the genitive is assigned to the subject in this construction
have been eliminated. The elimination of these exceptional
subrules in the norm has followed the hierarchy in (18):

    (18) pronouns / (plural) agentive nouns / (plural) non-
        agentive nouns

    To the extent that syntactic change is now recognized as
gradual, the existence of such a hierarchy is not surprising.
But it is interesting that this hierarchy is not arbitrary,
but is predictable from the type of change which it constrains.
The change here and in the participial construction involves
treating underlying subjects of nonfinite clauses as subjects
expressed in the genitive, rather than as objects of the matrix verb. It stands to reason that the change would be actualized earlier for constituents which are relatively more subjectlike. Pronouns, and secondarily animate agentive nouns,
are more subjectlike than inanimate or nonagentive nouns, and
accordingly rank higher on the hierarchy and receive genitive
assignment earlier.[8]

This example is fairly straightforward, but it suggests a more general principle governing the actualization of change. It suggests that the actualization of change is systematic in the sense that it is governed by linguistic hierarchies. Further, the hierarchies are motivated, in the following sense: the change will be actualized earlier for terms in the hierarchy which are unmarked, or more natural, contexts for the change and later for terms which are marked, or less natural, contexts for the change.

6. More constraints on actualization

I would like now to consider a complex example of actualization, involving the historical replacement of the genitive by the accusative for objects in Russian. In Russian the genitive has many recognizably distinct uses, which may be classified into (i) adnominal (possessive), (ii) adverbal, (iii) prepositional, and (iv) adverbial. Adverbal uses may be further classified into objective and subjective (for the subject of an existential intransitive verb). The objective adverbal genitive includes the use of the genitive for the object of negated verbs, for objects with a partitive sense, and for objects governed by certain verbs, both reflexive (bojat'sja 'fear', slušat'sja 'obey') and nonreflexive (ždat' 'wait for', izbežat' 'avoid', dostignut' 'achieve'). Here I will discuss only the genitive of negation and the governed genitive.

Even limiting our attention to objective adverbal genitives, it appears that the uses of the genitive are rather heterogeneous and it is difficult to write a single, unified transformational rule which will produce these genitives. In order to formalize the use of the genitive for objects, it is necessary to write separate subrules for each context: (18a)

assigns genitive to the object in the syntactic presence of
negation, (18b) assigns genitive to objects of certain verbs,
and (18c) assigns genitive to objects with a partitive sense.
There appears to be no obvious formal device that would allow
the conflation of these subrules into a single rule.

(18)   a.   NP → [gen] / neg V _____
       b.   NP → [gen] / V _____
                        [+F]
       c.   NP → [gen] / V _____
                             [+part]

Although it is a trivial exercise to formalize rules for the
assignment of genitive in this way, it is not an instructive
formalization, since it does not explain how the various uses
of the genitive are related to each other. Nevertheless, it
appears that they are related. Since the sixteenth century
there has been a general tendency to use the accusative instead of the genitive for objects and, although the change has
proceeded at different rates for different types of genitives,
it has by now encompassed all types of objective genitives at
least partially. Moreover, as I will show below, this change
obeys basically the same hierarchies even for different uses
of the genitive. Given their diachronic unity, and the close
typological parallel in Finnish, the different uses of the objective adverbal genitive must be related in some way.

Jakobson (1936) has argued that all varieties of the genitive express a single value in the system: for objects, the
genitive expresses a limitation on the extent to which an object participates in the event. Under negation, the event
does not take place and the object is excluded from participation. With a partitive sense only a limited quantity of the
object participates in the event. And in the case of governed

genitives, the lexical meaning of the verb dictates that the
object is not included in the action, but is a limit to the
action, whether the limit is positive (žd̲a̲t̲'̲ 'wait for'), neutral (d̲o̲s̲t̲i̲g̲n̲u̲t̲'̲ 'achieve'), or negative (i̲z̲b̲e̲ž̲a̲t̲'̲ 'avoid').
In the sense that the genitive signals a quantitative limitation on participation, it involves a kind of quantification
(and probably for this reason is tied up both with explicit
quantifiers and with existential quantification). If the heterogeneous subrules of (18) are viewed as part of the norm,
they are related as expressions of the systemic principle that
the genitive expresses a limitation of participation.

The reanalysis which led to the replacement of the objective adverbal genitive by the accusative is not striking. Given
data which exclusively used the genitive for objects in the
contexts of (18), learners were free to formulate either of
two grammars: in one grammar, quantitative limitation of participation by the object would be an essential systemic principle and specific subrules would assign the genitive to objects in contexts of quantification -- negation, lexical government, etc.; in another grammar, quantitative limitation of
participation would not be an essential systemic principle, so
that in principle only the accusative would be assigned to objects, except that for a period of time the norms would continue to assign the genitive to objects in accordance with a
set of complicated and unmotivated subrules. Apparently at
some point learners of Russian chose the second option and, as
a practical consequence of this reanalysis, the accusative has
begun to appear in contexts where only the genitive was possible before. It could be that the decision to devalue quantification of objects is related to other changes in the case

system of Russian, but at the moment this is not clear.

While the reanalysis itself is not interesting, the actualization of this reanalysis is quite complex and interesting. In the following I will discuss and compare the hierarchies that govern the loss of the genitive of negation to those that govern the loss of the governed genitive. The hierarchies basically are of four types, the first of which includes a number of subhierarchies.[9]

First, the loss of the genitive of negation refers to a general hierarchy of individuation, the extent to which the object is conceptualized as an individual. The more the object is individuated, the more likely it is to use the innovating accusative, while the less the object is individuated, the more likely it is to use the conservative genitive. In the examples below the accusative form will be given before the genitive. Relative acceptability will be indicated by an absolute scale of [√] (acceptable, preferred),[°] (acceptable, not preferred), [?] (marginal), and [*] (unacceptable).

Proper names have an inherently unique reference while common nouns do not, so that proper nouns are more individuated than common nouns. In modern Russian proper nouns almost obligatorily use the accusative under negation:

(19)   Ja ešče ne čitala √Cement/*Cementa
       I   still not read
       'I still haven't read Cement'

(20)   Ja ešče ne čitala √roman/°romana Gladkova
                          novel
       'I still haven't read Gladkov's novel'

Animate nouns are likely to be viewed as individuals more than inanimate nouns and animate nouns are used in the accusative

more than inanimate nouns, even under emphatic negation, as
in (21-22):

(21)   ?Nikakuju ženščinu/√ nikakoj ženščiny ja ne vižu
             any woman   I not see
        'I don't see any woman'

(22)   *Nikakuju mašinu/ √nikakoj mašiny ja ne vižu
          any   car   I not see
        'I don't see any car'

Abstract nouns refer to concepts which inherently cannot be
individuated, while concrete nouns may be more or less individuated. Accordingly, concrete nouns (23) tend to use the accusative more than abstract nouns (24):

(23)   On ne prodast tebe √xorošee plat'c/°xorošego plat'ja
        he not sell   you   good   dress
        'he won't sell you a good dress'

(24)   On ne dast tebe °xorošij sovet/√xorošego soveta
        he not give you   good   advice
        'he won't give you good advice'

In an obvious sense a singular object is individuated while a
plural object is not, so that singular objects (25) are more
likely to use the accusative than plural objects (26):

(25)   Ja ne našel √cvetok/?cvetka
        I   not find   flower
        'I didn't find a flower'

(26)   Ja ne našel °cvety/√cvetov
                         flowers
        'I didn't find flowers'

Finally, a definite participant is understood as a uniquely defined individual within a set of individuals which might conceivably be involved in the event. A definite object is therefore more individuated than an indefinite object, and is more
likely to use the accusative; compare the definite object in

(27) with the indefinite object in (26) immediately above:

(27)   Ja ne našel √cvety/°cvetov

'I didn't find the flowers'

The hierarchies of individuation which constrain the loss
of the genitive of negation are listed in (28):

(28)   individuated / nonindividuated

proper   / common
human / animate / inanimate
concrete   / abstract
singular   / plural
definite   / indefinite

For each hierarchy the term which is relatively more individuated is more likely to use the accusative than the nondividu-
ated term.

The hierarchies listed in (28) can be used to argue for
two points about the actualization of the change replacing genitive by accusative. First, the hierarchies are consistent
with the general claim outlined above in Section 5 that a
change is actualized earlier in contexts which are unmarked
for the change and later in contexts which are marked for the
change. In an obvious sense, individuation is the inverse of
quantification. The more an object is conceptualized as an
individual, the less it can be quantified and, specifically,
the less it is possible to express limited participation
through the use of the genitive of negation. Conversely, the
less an object is individuated, the easier it can be quantified, and the easier it is to express limited participation
through the use of the genitive of negation. Contexts in which
the object is individuated are therefore marked contexts for
the use of the genitive and unmarked contexts for the use of

the accusative. Hence the genitive is replaced by the accusative earlier in contexts of individuation.

Second, the concept of markedness (or naturalness) has to be applied relative to the particular change involved. For example, one would probably assume that -- in general terms, not relative to any particular rule or context -- singular is unmarked with respect to plural and concrete with respect to abstract. On the other hand, one would probably assume that proper is marked with respect to common, and -- at least in object function -- animate is marked with respect to inanimate and definite with respect to indefinite. So in terms of markedness values defined in general terms, or even with respect to object function in particular, the hierarchies in (28) are mutually contradictory. They only become consistent when they are evaluated in terms of a generic property like individuation and when this property is correlated with the specific change of genitive to accusative.

It can easily be documented that the same hierarchies of individuation constrain the replacement of the genitive by accusative for lexically governed objects.[10] Thus, proper nouns take the accusative more readily than common:

(29)   Oj, čto ty! √Lenu/°Leny pugaeš'sja?
           what you   terrified
        'what's your problem -- terrified of Lena?'

(30)   Oj, čto ty!   °Ženu/√ženy pugaeš'sja?
                      wife
        'what's your problem -- terrified of your wife?'

Human nouns take the accusative more readily than nonhuman animate nouns, which in turn take the accusative more readily than inanimate nouns:

(31)   Vse bojalis' √djadju/*djadi, a ja bolee vsex
       all feared   uncle   I more all
       'everyone was afraid of my uncle, but I was more
           afraid than everybody'

(32)   Vse bojalis' √medvedicu/?medvedicy, a ja bolee vsex
                        bear
       'everyone was afraid of the bear, but I was more
           afraid than everybody'

(33)   Vse bojalis' √ètu mašinu/°ètoj mašiny, a ja bolee
                        that car

       vsex
       'everyone was afraid of that car, but I was more
           afraid than everybody'

Concrete nouns take the accusative earlier than abstract
nouns:

(34)   Ja ožidala √tvoe pis'mo/°tvoego pis'ma v konce
       I expect   your letter   at end

           avgusta, a polučila 15ogo sentjabrja
                       received
       'I expected your letter at the end of August, but I
           got it only on the 15th of September'

(35)   On ždal ego °uxod/√ uxoda, čtoby pogovorit'   s
       he wait his exit   to   talk   with

           Lenoj, uznat', čem ona rasstroena
                  learn   what she upset
       'he waited for his departure in order to talk with
           Lena, to find out why she was upset'

Singular nouns are more likely to use the accusative than plural nouns as objects of verbs that originally governed the
genitive:

(36)   Vmesto togo, čtoby naladit' socialističeskoe sorev-
       instead that to   resolve socialist   compe-

           novanie, my iščem √legkij put'/°legkogo puti
           tition   we seek   easy   way
       'instead of dealing productively with socialist

competitiveness, we are looking for an easy way out'

(37)   ... my iščem   ?legkie puti/√legkix putej
                           ways
       '...we are looking for easy ways out'

Finally, definite nouns are more likely to take the accusative
than indefinite nouns:

(38)   I ej stalo uže ne dosadno, čto tak dolgo
       and her became   annoying   that so long

            ždala √pis'mo/?pis'ma
                  letter
       'and it was already less annoying to her that she
            had waited so long for the letter'

(39)   Mat' ždala xot' ᵘpis'mo/√pis'ma ot syna, čtoby
       mother wait just letter   from son   to

            uznat', čto on naxoditsja v živyx
            know   that he located   in living
       'the mother waited if only for a letter from her
            son in order to know that he was still among the
            living'

Thus, the hierarchies of individuation behave exactly the
same both for the loss of the genitive of negation and for the
loss of the governed genitive. This is the first set of hierarchies.

    A second set of hierarchies that constrain the loss of
the genitive of negation involve verbal categories. For these
verbal categories it appears that the force or scope of negation is attenuated. For example, a negative imperative presupposes that the positive event might be about to happen,
whereas a negated indicative does not. Also, a negated question presupposes the possibility that the positive version of
the event could occur, whereas a negated declarative does not
necessarily. In the imperative and interrogative, then, the

force of negation is attenuated, at least in comparison to an
indicative declarative. It turns out that the accusative appears more readily in place of the genitive of negation in an
imperative (40) and an interrogative (41) than in an indicative declarative sentence (42):

(40)   Smotri ne poterjaj √očki/?očkov
      watch not lose   glasses
      'watch out you don't lose your glasses!'

(41)   Ty poterjal √očki/?očkov?
      you lose   glasses
      'did you lose your glasses?'

(42)   Net, ja ne poterjal √očki/°očkov, u menja
      no   I   not lose   glasses   I have

      kontaktnye linzy
      contact   lenses
      'no, I didn't lose my glasses, I have contacts on'

Three points follow from the interaction of the imperative and interrogative with the genitive of negation. First,
it supports the claim that the replacement of genitive by accusative takes place earlier in environments which are unmarked for the change. It stands to reason that in contexts where
the force of negation is attenuated, the negative quantification is less, and hence that the genitive would be less likely
to be used in these contexts.

Second, this interaction again shows the importance of
considering markedness relative to the particular change involved. Presumably in the most general terms the interrogative is marked with respect to the declarative and the imperative is marked with respect to the indicative. Yet in terms
of negation the interrogative and imperative involve attenuation and therefore are unmarked contexts for the replacement

of the genitive of negation by the accusative.

   Third, since the property of attenuation of negation in
the imperative and interrogative deals specifically with negation, it could be expected that the verbal categories would
not play a significant role in the loss of the governed genitive, in which the limitation of participation derives from
the inherent semantic properties of the verbs, not from negation. In fact, with verbs that originally governed genitive
objects, the accusative is equally likely with the imperative (43) as with the indicative (44):

   (43)   Ždi √otvet/°otveta, a potom reši!
          wait answer   then   decide
          'wait for an answer and then decide!'

   (44)   Ona ždala √otvet/°otveta, a potom rešila
          she
          'she waited for an answer and then decided'

And the accusative is as normal in the interrogative (45) as
in the declarative (46):

   (45)   Pet'ka boitsja ?mašinu/√mašiny
                  fears   car
          'Pet'ka is afraid of the car'

   (46)   Ty boiš'sja ?mašinu/ √mašiny?
          you
          'are you afraid of the car?'

The sense in which the semantics of these verbs treat the object as a goal, and hence limited in participation, does not
vary with the imperative or interrogative, although the force
of negation does vary. For this reason, as the examples show,
these verbal categories are not a relevant hierarchy for the
replacement of the governed genitive by the accusative. Thus,
while it is true in this case that the loss of the genitive

of negation and the loss of the governed genitive do not obey
the same hierarchies, this difference is predicted by the difference between quantification through negation and quantification by means of lexical government.

Verbal categories are the second set of hierarchies that
constrain the loss of the genitive of negation. The two other
types of hierarchies that constrain the loss of the genitive
of negation, and the loss of the governed genitive as well,
are radically different and do not require special comment.
One is a purely morphological hierarchy; the other is stylistic, such that for any context where the accusative and genitive are both acceptable, the accusative will be relatively
informal (substandard to colloquial to neutral) compared to
the genitive, which will be relatively formal (neutral to formal to archaic). The stylistic hierarchy is related in part
to the social standing and the age of the speaker. The existence of these two hierarchies show, among other things, just
how far a change will go in order to be actualized gradually.

7. Conclusion

In the preceding I have argued for a series of related
points concerning syntactic change. It is important to distinguish between reanalysis and actualization. Reanalysis is
made possible by the potentially ambiguous character of surface output, while actualization occurs as the consequence of
reanalysis. Actualization takes place through the elimination of rules or subrules in the norm that are evaluated as
unmotivated with respect to the productive systemic principle
established by the reanalysis. Actualization, which proceeds
gradually, is accomplished earlier in contexts that are unmarked for the innovation and later in contexts that are

marked for the innovation. The concept of markedness, or naturalness, must be understood with reference to the particular change involved.

Notes

1. I would like to thank the participants of the conference in general and Arthur Schwartz, Georgia Green, Jean Mulder, and Allen Munro in particular for helpful discussion.

2. See Runeberg (1951:45), Siro (1964:85), Moreau (1972),
Wiik (1972), and Timberlake (1975a).

3. This change can be described as a shift in constituency of the noun phrase from object of the matrix clause to
subject of the participial clause; changes of this type are
identified as metaanalyses by Andersen (1974) and as boundary
shifts by Langacker (this volume). However, although a shift
in constituency is clearly involved, I suspect that it is not
the primary reanalysis here. In order to see this it is necessary to mention at least three kinds of nonfinite clauses in
Finnish: (i) participial constructions; (ii) object-controlled equi clauses formed with infinitive III and governed by
the open class of verbs like pytää 'ask', neuvoa 'advise',
estää 'prevent', and kieltää 'forbid'; and (iii) other object
clauses formed with infinitive I and governed by a small
closed class of verbs, the most representative of which is
antaa 'give, let' -- this construction is discussed in Section
5.

Except for differences in the form of the nonfinite verb,
all three types of construction had identical surface structures in older Finnish (Ojansuu 1909). All had a surface noun
phrase that was the object of the matrix clause (and case assigned partitive, accusative, or nominative) and that represented directly or indirectly the underlying subject of the
nonfinite clause. Yet only participial constructions and

antaa constructions underwent the reanalysis; object-controlled equi constructions did not.

An explanation for this depends on the proper analysis of antaa constructions. They allow the embedding of impersonal sentences (namely, existential sentences); therefore, they cannot be derived by equi, which requires that there be a noun phrase in the matrix clause that controls deletion of a coreferential subject in the embedded clause (A. Hakulinen 1973). Since the reanalysis affected participial and antaa constructions but not equi constructions, it apparently differentiated constructions with one noun phrase in underlying structure (e.g. [N V [N V]]) from constructions with two noun phrases in underlying structure (e.g. [N V N_i [N_i V]]).

The fact that a reanalysis could differentiate among these constructions even though they have identical surface structures is interesting, since it suggests that the reanalysis referred simultaneously to underlying structure and surface structure, but I will leave that for another investigation. The point I want to mention concerns a difference between participial and antaa constructions. Syntactic tests show that now in modern Finnish the underlying subject of a participial clause (expressed in the genitive) is the surface subject of the participial clause, but the same syntactic tests -- case assignment, reflexivization, nonfinite subject-verb agreement -- show that the underlying subject of an antaa clause does not remain the subject of that clause, but is apparently raised to some oblique status in the matrix clause. This fact suggests that the reanalysis in its most general form simply identified the ambiguous noun phrase in [-n] as genitive, not necessarily as the surface subject of the non-

finite clause. Accordingly, it appears that the shift in
constituency in participial clauses is a secondary consequence
of the reanalysis, a consequence that is particular to participial clauses (see Anttila 1972:103).

4. As mentioned in fn. 3, the antaa constructions discussed in Section 5 underwent the same reanalysis, but the
underlying subject in these constructions does not remain a
surface subject of the nonfinite clause. For this reason the
reanalysis cannot be explained simply in terms of a general
tendency to express subjects of nonfinite verbs in the genitive.

5. I have departed here from Andersen (1973), who would
presumably describe the transitional stages of development by
means of (i) a motivated and productive core rule that universally assigns genitive to subjects of participial clauses
and (ii) a set of unmotivated and unproductive adaptive rules
that reassign other cases in the specific contexts of (11).
A third possible way of describing the transitional stages is
implied by Hankamer (this volume) and discussed by Chung (this
volume). In this approach there are two competing grammars;
presumably for Finnish there would be one grammar, corresponding to the original grammar, that universally assigns normal object cases (partitive, accusative, or nominative) to underlying subjects of participles, while a second grammar, the innovating one, universally assigns genitives. Without further
modification, this approach of multiple analysis cannot adequately describe the numerous transitional stages of development; it cannot describe the fact that during Agricola's time
the innovating grammar with the genitive applied very rarely
and only for pronouns, while in the early twentieth century it

applied with only occasional exceptions of plural nouns, etc.
This approach requires a metastatement characterizing the relationship between the two grammars in particular contexts.
With the addition of this metastatement, the three approaches
mentioned here -- my approach with system and norm, Andersen's
approach with core and adaptive rules, and the approach of
multiple analysis -- may well be notational variants of each
other.

6. Only plural nouns are relevant here, since singular
nouns syncretize accusative and genitive. One would expect to
be able to remove the specification of plural for other
changes, for example, in the elimination of the partitive in
favor of the genitive in this construction.

7. However, in this construction the genitive does not
seem to be the surface subject of the nonfinite verb, as it is
in participial clauses (fn. 3).

8. The assumption that pronouns are always conservative
is naive. Although pronouns are usually conservative morphologically, they are not necessarily conservative in syntactic
changes that involve the innovation of subjects. As parallels
to Finnish I can think of two cases where pronouns innovate
subject properties earlier than nouns, one involving case and
the other agreement. Munro (this volume) has argued that copular sentences in contemporary Yuman languages derive historically from structures in which the copular expression functioned as a sentential subject to a matrix existential verb;
the original subject of the embedded copular expression has
come to function as the subject of the matrix clause. In
Tolkapaya pronouns but apparently not nouns have acquired the
subject case marking [-č]. Kuz'mina and Nemčenko (1971) have

examined the historical development of passive constructions
in North Russian dialects; in this change impersonal passives,
with the underlying object in an object case and no agreement
in the predicate, are becoming personal passives, with the underlying object in the nominative and agreement in the predicate. From the data they cite it is clear that pronouns develop agreement earlier than nouns.

   9. The data and analysis here are taken from Timberlake
(1975b), where further references for the documentation of
these hierarchies can be found.

   10. On the loss of the governed genitive in general see
Straková (1961), who lists the hierarchies of count/mass,
concrete/abstract, and feminine animate/other nouns (a conflation of animacy with the morphological hierarchy). On the
loss of the governed genitive with reflexive verbs in particular see Butorin (1966), where the examples suggest the hierarchies human/nonhuman, proper/common, and definite/indefinite.
For exact parallels in Czech, where the loss of the adverbal
objective genitive is virtually complete, see Hausenblaus
(1958).

References

Andersen, H.   1973.   Abductive and deductive change.   Lg. 49.
     765-93.

Andersen, H.   1974.   Towards a typology of change: bifur-
     cating changes and binary relations.   Historical lin-
     guistics, 2, ed. by J. Anderson and C. Jones, 17-60.   Am-
     sterdam: North Holland.

Anttila, R.   1972.   An introduction to historical and compar-
     ative linguistics.   New York: Macmillan.

Butorin, D. I. 1966.   Ob osobyx slučajax upotreblenija
     vinitel'nogo prjamogo ob''ekta v sovremennom russkom liter-
     aturnom jazyke.   Normy sovremennogo russkogo literaturnogo
     slovoupotreblenija, ed. by G. A. Kačevskaja and K. S.
     Gorbačevič, 125-36.   Moscow-Leningrad: Nauka.

Coseriu, Eugenio.   1962.   Sistema, norma y habla.   Teoria del
     lenguaje y lingüistica general, 13-113.   Madrid: Gredos.

Fromm, H. and M. Sadeniemi.   1956.   Finnisches Elementarbuch.
     Heidelberg: Carl Winter.

Hakulinen, A.   1973.   Semanttisia huomiotia lauseenvastik-
     keista. Sananjalka 15.38-68.

Hakulinen, L.   1960.   Handbuch der finnischen Sprache, 2.
     Wiesbaden: Otto Harrassowitz.

Hausenblaus, K.   1958.   Vývoj předmětnového genitivu v
     češtině.   Prague: ČAV.

Itkonen, T.   1974.   Ergatiivisuutta suomessa.   Virittäjä 78.
     379-98.

Jakobson, R. 1936. Beitrag zur allgemeinen Kasuslehre. TCLP 6.240-88.

King, R. 1969. Historical linguistics and generative grammar. Englewood Cliffs, N.J.: Prentice-Hall.

Klima, E. 1964. Studies in diachronic transformational syntax. Ph.D. dissertation, Harvard University.

Kuz'mina, I. B. and E. V. Nemčenko. 1971. Sintaksis pričastnyx form v russkix govorax. Moscow: Nauka.

Moreau, J.-L. 1972. La corrélation du sujet et de l'objet en finnois. Mélanges offertes à Aurélien Sauvageot pour son soixante-quinzième anniversaire, ed. by J. Gergely et al., 193-202. Budapest: Akadémiai Kiadó.

Ojansuu, H. 1909. Mikael Agricolan kielestä. Helsinki: Suomalaisen kirjallisuuden seura.

Runeberg, A. 1951. Some observations on linguistic patterns in a bilingual society, 1. (Societas Scientiarum Fennica, Commentationes hymanarum litterarum, 17.4)

Siro, P. 1964. Suomen kielen lauseoppi. Helsinki: Oy.

Straková, V. 1961. Genitivní slovesná rekce. Kapitoly ze srovnávací mluvnice ruské a české, 2: Studie syntaktické, 261-97. Prague.

Timberlake, A. 1975a. The nominative object in Finnish. Lingua 35.201-30.

Timberlake, A. 1975b. Hierarchies in the genitive of negation. SEEJ 19.123-38.

Timberlake, A. 1976. Nonfiniteness in Finnish. Texas Linguistic Forum, 5. (Transatlantic conference on Finnish.)

Wiik, K. 1972. Suomen akkusatiiviobjektin muoto. (Turun
    Yliopiston fonetiikan laitoksen julkaisuja, 12.) Turku.

II Word Order Change

4 The Drift from VSO to SVO in Biblical Hebrew: The Pragmatics of Tense-Aspect

Talmy Givón

1. Introduction: Pragmatic hierarchies

I would like at the outset to summarize the findings of an earlier paper (Givón, 1976a) as background for this study. In that paper I investigated a certain typological continuum which may be termed "the VS/SV to SV continuum". At its one end one finds languages such as Spanish, Swahili, Russian, probably German and many others which show a high incidence -- in terms of both grammar and text distribution -- of VS syntax[1]. In languages of this type the subject's position relative to the verb is highly flexible and most commonly determined by __pragmatic__ considerations such as __relative topicality__[2] of the subject vis-à-vis the predicate. These considerations are discussed in detail by Bolinger (1952, 1954). Somewhere in the middle of this typological continuum one finds Israeli Hebrew, in which the frequency of VS syntax in both grammar and text is on the wane (as compared to Spanish), and in a number of environments SV syntax has already grammaticalized. Finally, close to the other end of the continuum one finds English, in which SV syntax has grammaticalized almost completely in most environments and is the prevalent order in text, though a few 'relic' environments, such as existentials, 'surprise subject'[3] and a number of other 'frozen' attestations of VS syntax still remain.

Unlike a number of studies (e.g., Lehmann, 1973) which
tend to downgrade the difference between VS and SV languages
(and thus consider the OV-VO dichotomy the most significant
typological parameter), my own findings suggest that the drift
along the "VS/SV to SV continuum" represents a profound typological change in the discourse-pragmatic strategies used by
the language. Whereas languages at the Spanish "free-word-or-
der" extreme tend to express topic-focus relations of the subject vis-à-vis the verb largely in terms of relative word-order (with the more topical old information tending to come
first), languages at the SV extreme, such as English, tend to
express the very same pragmatic contrast via stress-focus or
other intonational devices.

In a detailed competence-type study[4] of Israeli Hebrew
(Givón, 1976a), which stands roughly in the middle of the
drift continuum, I have shown that largely pragmatic considerations determine the order by which the various grammatical
environments in the language will gravitate toward SV syntax.
The environments may be ordered in a number of independent im
plicational hierarchies, the first of which involves the degree
of subject's topicality:

(1)   EXISTENTIAL > INDEFINITE > DEFINITE > ANAPHORIC-PRONOUN

The anaphoric-pronoun subject in Israeli Hebrew requires obligatorily SV syntax. The existential construction requires obligatory VS syntax. And the indefinite and definite subjects allow the VS/SV variation which is pragmatically controlled.
However, the 'normal' tendency in text is for sentences with
definite subjects to show more SV syntax, and those with indefinite ones to show more VS syntax. That the hierarchy in (1)
is essentially one of relative topicality seems rather trans-

parent, but extensive justification may be found in Bolinger (1952, 1954) and Givón (1976a).

Since the VS/SV variation involves the relative topicality of the subject vis-à-vis the verb, it is not altogether surprising that in addition to subject type, predicate type is also important in determining the distribution of VS vs. SV syntax. This may be first expressed as:

(2) SPECIFIC > GENERIC

In general, more generic (habitual tenses, adjectival and nominal predicates) predicates will drift _earlier_ toward SV syntax. While not immediately obvious, this hierarchy is again traceable to relative topicality relations. When a predicate is generic -- and thus _low in referentiality_ -- chances are higher that the subject -- which is the most referential-topical constituent of propositions (Keenan, 1975, Givón, 1975a) -- is more topical than the predicate. Thus, for example, _copular_ constructions in both Spanish and Hebrew tend on the whole to have predominantly SV (SP) syntax.

A third implicational hierarchy, derived initially by inference from (2), involves verb type:

(3) ACTIVE > STATIVE

If (3) holds, then it is predicted that in the drift from VS/SV to SV stative verbs or constructions will grammaticalize the SV order earlier. The rationale behind this inferential leap is as follows: States/qualities are more likely to represent stable, inherent properties of the subject, while actions tend to represent events which took place at specific -- referential -- times. The latter are more likely to have higher referential properties than the former, and thus compete more

vigorously with the subject for the top reference-topicality
slot in the sentence.[5]

A somewhat muddier implicational hierarchy, one which
presents a number of complications, involves the modality of
the predication. It may be given as:

(4)   IRREALIS › REALIS

(4) suggests that -- all other things being equal -- SV syntax will grammaticalize earlier in more presuppositional
('factive') modal environments, while the VS/SV variation will
persist longer in hypothetical, IRREALIS environments. In Israeli Hebrew, for example, presupposed WHEN-clauses ('When he
came, I left') show a strong tendency toward SV syntax, while
structurally identical irrealis clauses ('When he'll come,
I'll leave') retain the VS/SV variation longer. The rationale
behind adducing a pragmatic interpretation for these facts is:
The more presuppositional a clause is, the more likely it is
that the subject would be known to both hearer and speaker and
thus high in topicality.

A number of -- ultimately again pragmatic -- factors intervene with the clear application of hierarchy (4). For examples, while object relative clauses are typically presuppositional, they tend to exhibit in languages along the drift continuum more consersative VS syntax. This turns out to involve
the fact -- discussed extensively in Givón (1976a, 1976c)[6]
and originally noted in Schachter (1975) -- that the head of a
relative construction is in some sense high in topicality vis-
à-vis other arguments of the embedded clause. Thus, by making
a non-subject argument higher in topicality, the relative topicality of the subject is downgraded. The very same phenomen-

is observed when a non-subject is topic-shifted to the left.

The hierarchy in (4) also explains, I believe, another implicational hierarchy found in Givón (1976a):

(5) AFFIRMATIVE > NEGATIVE

If (5) holds, then one would expect -- all other things being equal -- that negative sentences would grammaticalize SV syntax earlier than corresponding affirmatives, in languages drifting along our typological continuum.[7] The pragmatic rationale behind this is similar to that motivating the hierarchy in (4), and has to do with the more presuppositional nature of negative sentences as compared to affirmatives in discourse (see Givón, 1975b).

A seeming counter-example to hierarchy (4), in Biblical Hebrew and elsewhere, are IRREALIS clauses embedded in V-COMP or ADV-clause environments. But here again a combination of pragmatic factors is involved: (i) V-COMP environments are on the whole more presuppositional than main clauses. Topic-shift rules are most commonly barred from them (see Hooper and Thompson, 1973). But as will be shown below, marked topic-shift rules are the major driving force toward SV syntax in Biblical Hebrew. (ii) V-COMP clauses in Biblical Hebrew are historically derived from adverbial clauses, which are in turn -- both semantically and diachronically -- akin to object relative clauses. And the pragmatic motivation for the conservative VS syntax of the latter has been mentioned above (see also fn. 6). This also explains the conservative VS syntax of adverbial clauses in general, in addition to the fact that many of them are highly presuppositional to begin with.[8]

In searching for typological correlates to the position

of a language along the VS/SV-to SV continuum, one feature
emerges as the best candidate. This feature is the viability
of the subject-agreement conjugation of the verb as a subject-
anaphora device. The facts are surprisingly straightforward:
Within Romance one finds Spanish, Portuguese, Italian and Romanian grouping together against French. The former all show
the VS/SV characteristics of Spanish, and all have a viable
use of the subject agreement on the verb in subject anaphora.
The latter is much closer to English on the continuum, i.e.,
the grammaticalization of SV syntax in it has progressed much
further, and it is also the one modern member to lose the
agreement conjugation almost entirely (in the spoken language).
The same observation may be made within Germanic: While English and the Scandinavian languages are both further along in
terms of fixed SV syntax and erosion of the verb-agreement as
a viable subject-anaphora device, German -- while not using
the subject agreement anaphorically any more -- shows a much
less eroded agreement conjugation (suggesting later survival
of its anaphoric function) and is also much less advanced in
grammaticalizing SV syntax.[9] Why this correlation? As noted
in the implicational hierarchy (1) above, the independent anaphoric pronouns are the spearhead (in terms of subject type)
in the change from VS to SV. The same is seen in Biblical Hebrew. Therefore if a language -- such as Spanish -- uses the
verb-agreement as its subject anaphora device, and given that
anaphoric subjects are a highly prevalent feature in discourse
(see Keenan, 1975, Givón, 1975a), anaphoric expression in a
language such as Spanish is likely to be V-first clauses. On
the other hand, in a language with no agreement-anaphora but
with independent subject-anaphoric pronouns (English), subject-anaphora clauses will appear as SV clauses.[10]

In summary, then, discourse-pragmatic factors are already singled out as the major <u>driving force</u> for typological change along the drift continuum VS-to-SV. What I will contend is that the drift from VS to SV syntax is motivated by the fact that (a) the subject is the most topical element in the sentence, and (b) that at least for some language types -- probably most -- Bolinger's (1952) principle holds by which older or more-topical information tends to be presented first. One must not, however, confuse explanatory <u>principles</u> with actual <u>mechanisms</u> via which natural change takes place. In the present study, based on text counts in various stages of Biblical Hebrew, it turns out that there exists a crucial link between the VS-to-SV drift and an equally profound change in the typology of the tense-aspect system of the language. These changes take place simultaneously, and to characterize the interaction between them one may resort to the following metaphor:

"The complex interaction under investigation may be likened to a <u>journey</u>, whereby the VS-to-SV drift is the <u>cargo</u>, the pragmatic principles of discourse-topicality are the <u>driver</u>, and the change in the tense-aspect system is <u>the vehicle</u>".

While the <u>driver</u> may indeed be universal, the <u>vehicle</u> may often not. And while the driver may easily be detected via competence-grammaticality studies (as in Givón, 1976a), the vehicle is often totally obscure to such traditional generative methodology, and may only be identified via text-distribution and text-frequency studies. To this extent, this paper is also an exercise in the interaction between these two methodologies.

2. Some notes on the data base

The Old Testament is by no means the ideal text to run a

time-lag diachronic study on. While the chronology of codification (last editorial interference) may indeed be ascertain-
ed, it does not necessarily correspond to the actual chronology of contiguous diachronic stages in the natural drift of
Biblical Hebrew. In an earlier study (Givón, 1974b), using
variables which are easier to control such as morpho-syntactic and phonological parameters, I was able to pin down at
least four points along a diachronic drift continuum. The
first, referred to as Early Biblical Hebrew (henceforth EBH),
is represented by the language of Genesis, Joshua and Judges.
Given the criteria used in the previous study, no categorical
change occurs until the very late books, beginning with Esther. From there a great leap occurs toward the next identifiable point on the continuum, that of Ecclesiastes. For the
diachronic change studied in the earlier work, Ecclesiastes
represented the midpoint of the shift, in terms of frequency
of both the phonological and morpho-syntactic changes studied.
Finally, the endpoint of the change, identified as the most
progressive Hebrew dialect-level evident in the Old Testament,
was the book Song of Solomon.

   In the present study I have capitalized on those earlier
findings, but added two more points, one at the very end of
what I had previously considered EBH. The texts represent
the following points:

(a) Genesis -- first 12 chapters

(b) Kings II -- first 12 chapters

(c) Esther -- the entire text

(d) Lamentations -- the entire text

(e) Ecclesiastes -- the entire text

(f) Song of Solomon -- the entire text

It is of course unfortunate that out of the six texts, the
three most crucial for this study -- Lamentations, Ecclesiastes and Song of Solomon -- are of a radically different stylistic and topical register. I will deal with the difficulties
raised by this fact at the appropriate sections. I have briefly entertained the notion of adding Mishnaic Hebrew as the
endpoint of this study but discarded the idea after further
reflection. While largely SVO in syntax and representing the
later stage of the tense-aspect system, the text presents
special problems. First it was probably NOT the language of
native speakers, but rather of fluent scholars whose native
tongue was most likely Aramaic. Second, it is heavily impact-
ed in terms of vocabulary at least by both Aramaic and Greek.
Finally, the style-register is so restricted (codex and reports of rabinical arguments pertaining to it), and the major
tense-aspect is the habitual, so that a reasonable distributional profile of the language is just about impossible to obtain. Besides, as it turned out, the change from VSO to SVO
-- at least in main clauses -- had been largely complete by
Late Biblical Hebrew (Song of Solomon, henceforth SOS), and
the same holds true with respect to the change in the tense-
aspect system. Mishnaic Hebrew, therefore, is not a critical
dialect point for this purpose. And at least with respect to
the morpho-syntactic and phonological parameters studied earlier (Givón, 1974b), it falls roughly within the range of the
LBH-SOS dialect.

3. The syntax of subject position in EBH-Genesis

In Table 1. below the distribution of VS and SV syntax

in the various grammatical environments in the EBH-GENESIS
text is given. The data is divided according to the three verbal aspects plus a separate category for copular predicate expressions. For the latter, no attempt was made to separate
out instances in which the verb 'be' -- in whatever aspect --
is present, though one may as well note that the majority of
copular constructions in Biblical Hebrew in general appear
without 'be'.

The environments listed in Table 1. on the left are illustrated as follows. The main-clause continuity category belongs overwhelmingly to the imperfect aspect, and its functional characterization will be analyzed in Section 4. below. It
almost always appears with the conjunction va- 'and', one
which carries other vocal patterns when it precedes other aspects of the verb. As an example consider:[11]

(6)   va-yiqra? ?elohim la-yabaša   ?erec (IMPERF; Gen. 1.10)
       and-called God to-the-dry   land
       'And God named the dry portion "land"'

The effect of a pronominal object, be it dative or accusative,
is to defer the post-verbal subject even further, again illustrating the general pragmatic principle that more topical old-
information material goes to the left:

(7)   va-yiten ?otam ?elohim bi-rqia' ha-šamayim
       and-gave ACC-them God in-sphere-of the-sky
       And God put them in the sky's sphere'
                                        (IMPERF; Gen. 1.17)

Though the main-clause order in the imperfect is overwhelmingly VS, independent pronominal subjects precipitate an
obligatory SV order even in this aspect, as in:

(8)   hu? yišuf-xa ro?š   (Imperf; Gen. 3.15)
      he will-smite-you head
      'He will smite you on the head'

TABLE I.: Subject position in EBH-Genesis

MAIN CLAUSE	IMPERFECT		PERFECT		PARTICIPLE		COPULAR	
	VS	SV	VS	SV	VS	SV	VS	SV
continuity	168	0	1	21	0	4	5	72
pro-OBJ	9	0	0	0	0	0	0	0
pro-SUBJ	/	/	0	4	0	6	2	15
fronted ADV/OBJ	/	/	13	0	0	1	2	15
NEG	/	/	1	0	0	0	1	2
ADV-CL/V-COMP	/	/	13	0	2	0	10	1
OBJ-REL	2	0	12	0	0	0	/	/
OBJ-WH	2	0	1	0	0	0	/	/
IRREALIS	8	7	3	0	/	/	/	/
neg	4	0	/	/	/	/	/	/
adv-clause	2	0	/	/	/	/	/	/
pro-SUBJ	0	5	/	/	/	/	/	/
fronted ADV/OBJ	1	0	/	/	/	/	/	/
total IRREALIS	15	12						
total	195	12	54	25	2	11	20	105

One must note, further, that the categories NEG, ADV-CLAUSE,
pro-SUBJ and fronted-ADV/OBJ in the _imperfect_ always occur in
the IRREALIS function rather than in the _continuity_ function.
Thus (8) above is embedded within a direct-quote context as a
probabilistic, future-directed expression. In fact, a strong
characteristic of the irrealis category in BH in general is
this type of embedding. The story-teller himself never uses
the prerogative of IRREALIS.

The next topicality-related effect is shown in the PER-
FECT and PARTICIPLE aspects as well as in copular expressions.
All three already show an overwhelming preference for SV syntax in main clauses. But the left-fronting (topic-shifting)
of a non-subject constituent, be it an object or adverb
phrase, precipitates VS syntax, which should be viewed as a
consequence of LOWERING the relative topicality of the subject via making another constituent more topical (see discussion in section 1. above). Thus consider the contrast:

(9)   ve-ha-?adam yada' ?et ḥava ?išto
       and-the-man knew ACC Eve wife-his
       'And Adam knew his wife Eve'
                       (PERF; Gen. 4.1) (SV) (SUBJ-topic)

(10)   bi-re?šit bara? ?elohim ?et ha-šamayim...
       in-beginning-of created God ACC the-heaven
       'In the beginning God created the heaven...'
                       (PERF; Gen. 1.1) (VS) (ADV-topic)

(11)   u-me-?eleh nafca ha-?arec
       and-from-these dispersed the-land
       'And from these the whole earth originated'
                       (PERF; Gen. 9.19) (VS) (OBJ-topic)

A similar effect toward VS syntax is exerted by ADV-
clauses and V-complements, two environments which for a number of reasons cannot be separated (see Givón, 1974b). The
subordinator ki- is used in EBH for both 'because' clauses
and indirect-quote V-complements. Thus consider:

(12)   ki   šat li ?adonay
       because listened to-me lord-my
       '...because the Lord has listened to me...'
                       (PERF; Gen. 4.25) BECAUSE-clause

(13)   va-yeda' Noah ki qalu ha-mayim
       and-knew Noah that ended the-water
       'And Noah knew that the water had sank down'
                       (IMPERF; Gen. 8.11) V-COMP

The two structures may occasionally blur and produce
clauses which are open to either interpretation, as in:

(14)   va-yar? ?elohim ?et ha-?arec ve-hineh nišhata,
         and-saw God   ACC the-earth and-lo it-had-spoilt
         'And God saw that the earth had become corrupted,

              ki   hišhit kol   ha-basar ?et dark-o
              that   corrupted all the-flesh ACC way-his
              because/that all the flesh had corrupted its
                   ways...'

Since both 'because' clauses and verb-complements of
these types are largely presuppositional and therefore REALIS,
the conservative VS syntax in them flies in the fact of the
hierarchy prediction (4) above. Here one must admit the obvious, namely that the diachronic source of a construction
may exert syntactic influence beyond its synchronic pragmatic scope. To begin with, BECAUSE-clauses as well as other
adverbial clauses are semantically ADV/OBJ-relative clauses.
And if it is true, as discussed above, that there is a strong
connection between topicalization and relativization, then
one would expect (a) conservative VS syntax in adverbial
clauses, and (b) similarly conservative syntax in clauses
which diachronically arise from (or still blend with) adverbial clauses. As to the second V-COMP subordinator, ve-hine
'lo', .lit. 'and-there-be', one may view it historically as
a fronted adverb of place/time, in which case the same pragmatic factor is ultimately responsible for VS syntax following this subordinator.[12] The effect of the ve-hineh 'lo'
subordinator by itself may be seen in:

(15)   va-yar?   ve-hineh harvu pney   he-?adama
         and-he-saw and-lo dried face-of the-earth
         'And he saw that the earth had dried up'
                   (PERF; Gen. 8.13)

The verb in the complement clause in (15) is in the PERFECT,
but never-the-less appears with VS syntax.

The effect of negative context on the syntax of EBH can-
not be gauged accurately due to the slimness of the sample.
At least in one instance it seems to induce VS syntax in the
PERFECT:

(16)   ve-lo? mac?a ha-yona manoaḥ (PERF; Gen. 8.9)
       and-not found the-dove rest
       'And the dove didn't find resting place'

Another environment which induces VS syntax in the
PERFECT is that of OBJ/ADV relative clauses, including
OBJ/ADV WH-questions. The discourse-pragmatic background for
this behavior has already been discussed (see Schachter, 1975
and discussion in Givón, 1976a, 1976c). Thus consider:

(17)   kol ha-ḥaya   ha-romeset   ?ašer šarcu   ha-mayim
       all the-animal the-crawling that spawned the-water
       'All the crawling animals which the water had
          spawned'
                        (PERF; Gen. 1.21)

The same effect may be seen for a WH question:

(18)   ve-lamah naflu paney-xa (PERF; Gen. 4.6)
       and-why fell face-your
       'And why has your face sunk?'

In EBH the IRREALIS function of the imperfect is already
well established, though dwarfed in terms of frequency by
its main function, that of narrative-continuity (see discussion in section 4. below). The 8/7 ratio in simple irrealis
clauses in the IMPERFECT of VS/SV syntax certainly does not
bear out the prediction of hierarchy (4) concerning the more
conservative VS syntax expected in IRREALIS clauses. One
may of course argue that all these IRREALIS clauses are in a

verb-complement environment. However, it is a <u>direct</u> quote
environment and thus immune from both the effect of various
subordinators (there are none for direct-quote in BH), as
well as from the pragmatics of presupposed-complement clauses
and the restriction on topicality operations in those (see
Hooper and Thompson, 1974). One finds VS syntax in these
subjunctive-type complements, as in:

(19)   va-yo?mer ?elohim: "Yiqavu ha-mayim..."
        and-said God: "shall-gather the-water..."
        'And God said: "May the water gather..."'
            (IMPERF; Gen. 1.9)

But one also finds the opposite SV syntax, <u>viz</u> the switch in:

(20)   va-yo?mer ?elohim: "Yišricu ha-mayim.....
        and-said God: "will-spawn the-water.....
        'And God said: "May the water spawn...

        vi 'of yi'ofef 'al ha-?arec   (IMPERF; Gen. 1.20)
        and-bird will-fly on the-earth
        ...and may birds fly over the earth..."'

What it all boils down to is that while the <u>continuity</u> function of the imperfect is used overwhelmingly to carry on the
narrative <u>with the same topic/subject</u>, in the irrealis category one already finds a considerable number of instances of
topic switching, as in the second line in (20). And, as will
be shown below, the topic/subject shifting function in BH is
the main driving force on the way from VS to SV syntax. The
gist of all this is that one cannot assess the effect of the
IRREALIS modality separately in the present data, because of
the intruding effect of topic/subject switching in this category.[13]

There are several facts about the distribution of VS and
SV word order in <u>Table 1.</u> which are rather striking.

(a) Copular sentences: The are overwhelmingly SV (SUBJ-PRED) even at this early stage of BH, not only in main clauses but already also in clauses with fronted adverbials. This clearly validates hierarchy (2) discussed earlier.

(b) Pronominal subjects: In conformity with hierarchy (1), pronominal subject -- even in the most conservative aspect, the imperfect -- exhibit 100% SV order. However, since in both the IMPERFECT and PERFECT the function of simple anaphora is carried out by the subject-agreement on the verb, what motivates SV syntax for these pronouns? A look at their functional distribution in EBH/Genesis reveals the following facts: Out of a total of 17 instances of third-person independent pronouns found in the text, 7 or 41% are involved in marked topic-shifting, as in:

(21)   va-yo?mer ha-?adam: "ha-?iša ?ašer natata 'imadi
        and-said the-man: "The woman that you-gave with-me

        hi? natna li min ha-'ec va?oxel   (Gen. 3.12)
        she gave to-me from-the-tree and-I-ate"

        'So Adam said: "The woman that you have given me,
        she gave me from the tree, so I ate"'

Another 8 instances or 47% are emphatic-cleft contexts semantically, as in:

(22)   Šem ha-?eḥad Pišon, hu? ha-sovev ?et kol...
        name-of the-one Pishon, he-is-the-one the-circling
        ACC all...

        'The name of the first one was Pishon, and that was
        the one that circled the entire...'
                                                      (Gen. 2.11)

In addition to the emphatic-cleft function of sentences such as (22), one must also note that they also involve subject/topic shifting. Next, one instance was found of contrastive topic shift, as in:[14]

(23)   vɨ-ʔeyva ʔašit   beyn-xa   uveyn   ha-ʔiša,
        and-hate I-will-put between-you and-between the-wom-

            beyn   zarʼa-xa u-veyn zarʼ-a
            an, between seed-your and-between seed-her

            huʔ yɨšuf-xa roʔš, vɨ-ʔata tišuf-eno ʼaqev
            he will-smite-you head, and-you will smite-him
            heel

        'And I will put hatred between you and the woman, be-
        tween her children and your children, they will
        smash you on the head, and you will bite them
        in the heel.'
                                        (Gen. 3.15)

Only one instance out of the seventeen can be categorized as
simple anaphoric, and that one involves a parenthetic pause
and a non-verbal (i.e., non-agreeing) clause:

(24)   bɨ-ʼecem   ha-yom ha-ze baʔ Noah vɨ-... ?el
        in-self-of the-day the-this came Noah and-... into

            ha-teva; hema vɨ-xol ha-ḥaya ... (Gen. 7.13-14)
            the-ark they and-all the-animal

        'On that very day Noah and... came into the ark;
        they and all the animals...'

One must thus conclude that it is not the simple/anaphoric topicality of the independent subject pronouns which makes them
so prone to SV syntax, but rather the marked, topic-shifting
function which is involved. Thus while hierarchy (1) stands,
the actual vehicle for placing the independent subject pronouns
at the top of the hierarchy (in terms of innovative SV syntax)
must be reassessed. As we shall see below, topic-shifting is
indeed a prime mover in the diachronic change involved here.

(c) The PARTICIPLE and PERFECT aspects: A quick look at the
main-clause syntax of EBH (Table 1.) shows that the syntax of
verbs in these aspects is already overwhelmingly SV. All the
instances to the contrary, such as topicalized non-subjects,

adverbial or complement clauses and non-subject relative
clauses, may be shown to involve increased topicality of a
non-subject and thus suppressed topicality of the subject.
Since the facts concerning the progressive SV syntax of both
the PERFECT and PARTICIPLE are so unexpected, a study of their
function in EBH is called for.

4. Verb aspects and their functions in EBH-Genesis

4.1. The Universal Creole aspectual system

The most striking feature of the BH aspectual system is
that it corresponds, in major details, to the Universal Creole
Aspectual system described recently by Bickerton (1975a, 1975-
b).[15] The central matrix of such an aspectual system is one
binary feature which controls the flow of the story: The opposition between unmarked or sequential narration as against coun-
ter-sequential narration. Bickerton's terminology for these
are 'simple' vs. 'anterior'. In this paper I will use the
terms 'continuity' vs. 'anterior', respectively. Schematically put, these two narrative strategies are as follows:

(25)   (i)   CONTINUITY:
               time-sequence of events: A,B,C,D,...
               sequence of narration: A,B,C,D,...

        (ii)   ANTERIOR:
               time-sequence of events: A,B,C,D,...
               sequence of narration: A,C,B,D,...

The continuity aspect is thus one which relates the narrative in
the same order in which it occurred in real time: All the verbs
in (25i) above will be given in the 'continuity' aspect. In
(25ii), however, the order of event B and C has been reversed
in narration, and thus event B appears later in the narrative

than in real time, and thus violates the sequentiality rule
(event C does not violate it, since in real time it did precede D and did come after A). The verb of event B will be marked in this system by the 'anterior' aspect. One may thus view
the ANTERIOR aspect as a look-back system, used when later in
the narrative you project backward over events which in real
time should have followed, i.e.:

    (26)   A, C, B, D,.....

While this aspectual feature takes under its scope the 'classical' perfect ('I have already done it') and plu-perfect ('At
that time I had already done it') it does not directly correspond to them, since (a) the system is purely aspectual and
does not involve the notion central to TENSE systems, that of
time of speech; and (b) a great number of instances in which
the ANTERIOR is used in this system may not be all covered by
either the perfective or plu-perfect in 'classical' tense-ori-
ented systems.

    In EBH/Genesis, the continuity function is carried al-
most entirely by the IMPERFECT, most commonly with the conjunction va- 'and'. Thus consider the following illustration:

    (27)   va-yo?mer ?elohim: "Yihi ?or". va-yhi ?or;
            and-said God   : "shall-be light". and-was light;

            va-yar? ?elohim ki tov, va-yavdel ?elohim beyn
            and-saw God that good, and-divided God between

            ha-?or u-veyn ha-hošex;   va-yiqra? ?elohim
            the-light and-between the-dark; and-called God

            la-?or yom...
            to-the-light "day"...

        'And God said: "There shall be light", and there
        was light; and God saw that it was good, and
        God separated the light from the dark; and God
        called the light "day"...' (Gen. 1.3-5)

The events in (27) are narrated in the order of their actual
occurrence in time. In terms of a TENSE system, all the instances of the imperfect here denote PAST tense. However, our
'past' may be equally well denoted by the PERFECT/ANTERIOR, if
it 'looks back', as in the relative clause in:

> (28)   va-yar? ?elohim ?et kol ?ašer 'asah   (Gen. 1.31)
>   and-saw God   ACC all that he-had-done
>   'And God surveyed all that he had done...'

One may also find the <u>anterior</u> in V-COMP environments, as in:

> (29)   va-yo?mer ?elohim: "hineh natati   laxem ?et kol
>   and-said God: "lo I-have-given to-you ACC all
>
>   ha-'esev..."
>   the-grass
>
>   "And God said: "Lo, I have given you all the grass-
>   es...""   (Gen. 1.29)

The use of the ANTERIOR may also be found when an event
<u>has no preceding event at all</u>, and thus 'does not follow in or-
der of continuity'. This is obvisouly the case in the first
line of Genesis:

> (30)   bɨ-re?šit   bara? ?elohim ?et ha-šamayim...
>   in-beginning created God ACC the-heaven...
>   "In the beginning God created the heaven...'
>   (Gen. 1.1)

The ANTERIOR vs. CONTINUITY feature of the PERFECT/IMPER-
FECT contrast in EBH shades into a parallel contrast which
must be considered <u>derived</u>. IMPERFECT or 'continuity' aspect
is used to relate the events in the actual order of occurrence
and to <u>maintain the same topic/subject</u>.[16] The PERFECT (and
to a lesser extent the PARTICIPLE), on the other hand, is used
to both 'look back' in discourse as well as to <u>switch topic</u>.
This is first illustrated in the first lines of Genesis, al-

though there the use of the PERFECT in the second line and
PARTICIPLE in the third may also denote a break in the discourse continuity, something like a parenthetical description:

(31)   bɨ-re?šɨt   bara? ?elohim ?et ha-šamayim vɨ-et
         in-beginning created God ACC the-heaven and-ACC

         ha-?arec;
         the-earth;

         'In the beginning God created the heaven and the
             earth;   (Gen. 1.1) PERF.

         vɨ-ha-?arec   hayta tohu va-vohu,   (Gen. 1.2) PERF.
         and-the-earth was   chaos and-confusion
         'And the earth was chaos and confusion,

         vɨ-ruaḥ   ?elohim mɨraḥefet 'al pney ha-mayim;
         and-spirit-of God   hovering on face-of the-water
         'And the spirit of God was hovering over the water;
                                        (Gen. 1.2) PARTICIPLE

         va-yo?mer ?elohim: "Yɨhi ?or"... (Gen 1.3) IMPERF
         and-said God   : "will-be light"
         and God said: "There shall be light:...'

The second and third line in the narrative in (31) both shift
the topic/subject and in addition do not advance the narrative.
The fourth line comes back to the topic -- God, and also to
the continuity of the narrative.

Topic switching, however, is not necessarily confined to
subject-switching. Thus consider:

(32)   va-yivra? ?elohim ?et ha-?adam,
         and-created God   ACC the-man
         'And God created man,
                   (Gen. 1.27) IMPERF/CONTINUITY

         bɨ-celem ?elohim bara?   ?otam,
         in-image-of God he-created them
         in the image of God he created them,
                   (Gen. 1.27) PERF/NON-CONTINUITY

zaxar u-nɨqeyva <u>bara?</u>   ?otam,
male and-female <u>he-created</u> them
male and female <u>he created</u> them...'
        (Gen. 1.27) PERF/NON-CONTINUITY

The first line in (32) maintains the discourse continuity and
is in the IMPERFECT. In both the second and third lines, a
grammatical <u>object</u> is topicalized, and in addition the continuity is broken and something like a <u>parenthetic</u> addition occurs. The grammatical subject remains the same -- God; but
the object has been left-shifted (or 'made topic') and this
again shows up via the use of the PERFECT.

One of the nicest examples of a whole chain of topic
switching occurs in the following passage:

(33) u-lɨ-šem   <u>yulad</u>   gam hu?...
      and-to-Shem <u>was-born</u> also he...
      'And to Shem also was born (children)...
                (PERF, PASSIVE)

      vɨ?arpašxad   <u>yalad</u> ?et šelah
      and-Arpashchad <u>sired</u> ACC Shelach
      and Arpashchad sired Shelach,
                (PERF, ACTIVE)

      vɨ-šelah   <u>yalad</u> ?et 'ever
      and-Shelach <u>sired</u> ACC Ever,
      and Shelach sired Ever,
                (PERF, ACTIVE)

      u-l-'ever   <u>yulad</u>   šney banim
      and-to-Ever <u>was-born</u> two sons
      and to Ever two sons were born...'
                (PERF, PASSIVE) (Gen. 10.21-25)

The <u>topic</u> is shifted in each line in (33), but in the first
and fourth line the topic is the <u>dative-benefactive</u> of a passive, while in the second and third line it is the grammatical
<u>subject</u> of the active (of the same verb). This again under-

scores the fact that the use of the ANTERIOR aspect (and later
also the PARTICIPLE) for topic-switching is oriented toward
the TOPIC rather than strictly speaking the grammatical subject.

Passages such as (33) above are also the very few where
it seems that the PERFECT is used in a non-anterior capacity,
i.e., to advance the narrative in the actual order of events
(though with the topic switching). However, the passage represents a digression after the genealogy had already been discussed, then later events were related, then the narrative
goes back to further elaborate on the genealogy. In other
words, while topic switching, the anterior rule is never really unambiguously broken in the Genesis/EBH narrative. This
complete overlap of the two functions of the PERFECT furnishes
the clue as to their naturalness:

(34)   "Shifting to a new topic in the EBH narrative is
        done overwhelmingly by looking back in time into
        events already discussed previously, and 'fishing
        the new topic' out of there".

This is an extremely coherent strategy, since in it narrative
participants are first introduced in non-topical capacity,
then when the narrator wishes to make them topical, he simply
goes back to an event already established earlier in time --
and thus known to the hearer -- and pulls the topic out of
that event. Automatically he must then use ANTERIOR/PERFECT
for that purpose, since he has not only broken the topic-con-
tinuity of the discourse, but also its sequence-continuity.
The two are thus coupled in EBH.

Two more aspectual features are common to the Universal
Creole and EBH: The non-punctual or 'continuous' aspect, and

the _irrealis_ modality. The first function, quite minor in Gen-
esis/EBH though on the ascendance in later texts of BH, is carried exclusively by the PARTICIPLE and will be discussed in
the appropriate sub-section below. The second shows an interesting split between the PERFECT and IMPERFECT in EBH, though
by Late Biblical Hebrew (LBH) it shifts entirely to the IMPER-
FECT. It will be discussed in the appropriate sub-sections below.

4.2. The distribution of IMPERFECT functions in EBH-Genesis

Table 2. below shows the frequency distribution of the
various functions performed by the IMPERFECT aspect in the EBH-
Genesis text.

TABLE 2.:   Functions of the IMPERFECT in EBH-Genesis

	score	%
continuity	379	79%
irrealis	85	16%
imperative	9	3%
neg-imperative	7	2%
total	476	100%

The major function, at 79% of all occurrences, is that of narrative _continuity_. The second large category, at 16%, is that
of _irrealis_. It is found always in direct-quote complements,
with the speaker most commonly being God; the situation is always future-oriented subjunctive, command or prediction. As
an example of the subjunctive function of IMPERFECT-IRREALIS,
consider:

> (34)   va-yo?mer ?elohim: "Yɨ-hi   ?or"   (Gen. 1.3)
>   and-said   God : "shall-be light"
>   'And God said: "There shall be light:...'

The somewhat expected hypothetical-conditional irrealis within
this category plays only a minor function, partly because many
adverbial clauses of this type are still given in a non-finite,
nominal form (see Givón, 1974b), and partly for a competition
with the PERFECT, see below. But instances of this usage are
found in Genesis, as in:

(35)   halo? ?im   teyṭiv   s?et   vɨ-?im lo? teyṭiv
        since if you-will-be-good bearing and-if not you-

            ...
        will-be-good...
        'Since whether you do well in persisting or if you
           will not do well..." (Gen. 4.7)

The 'imperative' category is minor, and is not distinguishable
from the subjunctive. The only way of singling it out is by
the second-person form of the imperfect verb. It is in competition in EBH-Genesis with the proper IMPERATIVE form -- 9 to
24 IMPERFECT vs. IMPERATIVE in this function. The IMPERFECT
thus fulfills only 27% of the affirmative-imperative function
at this point, as is on the wane from here onward. On the other hand, the 7 occurrences of neg-imperative represent this entire function, which the proper-imperative form in BH never
fulfills.

4.3 The distribution of PERFECT functions in EBH-Genesis

    In Table 3. below the distribution of the various func-
tions of the PERFECT aspect in EBH-Genesis are given. As one
may see, the ANTERIOR function is dominant, covering 82.3% of
all occurrences. But in more than half of those, as can be
seen from Table 3., the ANTERIOR and TOPIC-SHIFT functions are
in total overlap.

    The most baffling category in the IMPERFECT in EBH is

the irrealis. It is baffling particularly because the ANTERIOR
function is the realis par excellence category, the most presuppositional of the aspects, and (a) involves retrieving topics mentioned earlier, and (b) the one which eventually develops into a PAST tense, the most presuppositional within a
tense-system. Further, historically the Semitic-PERFECT is a
stative, resultative, nominal conjugation, and by that virtue
even more REALIS.[17]

TABLE 3.: Functions of the PERFECT in EBH/Genesis

ANTERIOR	score	%	% of ANTERIOR
TOP-shift-SUBJ	40		27.2%
TOP-shift-OBJ	38		25.6%
RELATIVE CL.	38		25.6%
ADV-CL/V-COMP	24		16.2%
WH-QUESTIONS	9		6.6%
total ANTERIOR	149	82.3%	100%
IRREALIS	32	17.7%	
total PERFECT	181	100%	

The clue to the naturalness of this phenomenon again comes
from Bickerton's work on the aspectual system of Creoles. In
the system, counter-fact-conditionals, i.e., negative-presup-
positional clauses -- are always marked by the ANTERIOR marker,
while hypothesis/future-probability clauses are either unmarked (i.e., are given by the 'continuity' form) or are marked by
a special IRREALIS marker. When one looks at the use of the
PERFECT as an irrealis modality in EBH, one is struck by the
fact that (a) It is always found in complements of direct-
quote type, largely with God as the quoted speaker, and (b) it
is usually related to secure-promises given by God or dire in-

junctions against a disasterous course of action. As an example consider the following passage:

(36)   va-yo?mer ?elohim: "Zo?t ha-brit ?ašer ?ani noten...
         and-said   God   : "This the-pact that I am-giving...
         'And God said: This is the covenant that I am estab-
               lishing...   (PARTIC)

         ?et qašti natati   be-'anan,
         ACC how-my I-have-given/I-will-give in-cloud
         Lo, I have given/am putting my bow in the cloud,
                                   (PERF-ANTERIOR)

         ve-hayta   li-?ot   brit beyn-i   u-veyn
         and-it-shall-be as-sign-of pact between-me and-be-

                     ha-?arec
               tween the earth

         and it shall be a sign of the pact between me and
               the earth,
                           (PERF-IRREALIS)

         vi-haya   bi-'anin-i   'anan 'al ha-?arec
         and-be-it at-clouding-my cloud on the-earth
         and whenever I bring clouds upon the earth
                           (PERF-IRREALIS)

         vi-nir?ata   ha-qešet be-'anan,
         and-will-be-seen the-bow in-cloud
         then the rainbow will be seen in the cloud,
                           (PERF-IRREALIS)

         vi-zaxarti   ?et brit-i...
         and-I-shall-remember ACC pact-my...
         and then I shall remember my covenant...'"
                     (PERF-IRREALIS) (Gen. 9.12-15)

Out of the 32 irrealis instances of the PERFECT in the Genesis
text counted, 23 involve hypothetical conditionals with extremely strong injunctions. Thus consider the following passage, given in the context where God is contemplating the dire
consequences to ensue if Man would ever eat from the tree of
life:

(37)   ...pen yišlaḥ yad-o   (IMPERF-IRREALIS)
         lest he-send hand-his
        '"...lest he had extended his hand

        vɨ-laqaḥ   me-'ec   he-ḥayim   (PERF-IRREALIS)
        and-he-took from-tree-of the-life
        and took (fruit) from the tree of life

        vɨ-ʔaxal vɨ-hay   lɨ-'olam
        and-he-ate and-he-lived for-world
        and he would then eat (the fruit) and live forever...
                (PERF-IRREALIS) (Gen. 3.22)

In normal logic-based analysis, currently in vogue among sem-
anticists dealing with language, the categories CERTAIN vs.
POSSIBLE represent an absolute dichotomy. However, there is a
growing body of evidence suggesting that in language the category of certainty is actually scalar, a matter of degree rather than a simple binary choice. What characterizes the seeming IRREALIS usage of the PERFECT in EBH is that the majority
of occurrences denote a situation of extremely low probability
(23 of a total of 32, or 72%), which thus approach the REALIS
character of a counterfact conditional. Given this, one is en-
titled to suggest that this usage first developed as the normal Creole use of the ANTERIOR to mark counterfact conditionals. And that later it was extended gradually -- down the
probability scale -- toward 'less realis' clauses, and there
entered into competition with the IMPERFECT, which covers normally the lower probability end of the irrealis scale. As we
shall see later on, this usage of the PERFECT -- except for
true counter-fact clauses -- dies out in LBH.

4.4 The distribution of PARTICIPLE functions in EBH-Genesis

    The distribution of the various functions of the PARTIC-
IPLE aspect in EBH-Genesis is given in Table 4. below. The

participle in Hebrew arose from a NOMINAL conjugation, and
68% of its occurrences in EBH-Genesis are still non-sentential.
The 28.2% which are sentential are all non-punctual in Bickerton's terms, either 'continuous' or 'habitual'. In fact, there
is no clear way of distinguishing between the nominal-genitive
form and the habitual, since semantically they shade naturally
into each other. Thus consider:

(38)   ...deše?   'esev mazria'   zera' 'ec   pri
          lawn-of grass seeding-of seed tree-of fruit

                 'oseh pri...
                 doer-of fruit...

         '...grasses which spread their seeds, and trees
               which give fruit...'

         '...seed-making grasses, and fruit-bearing trees...'
                                      (Gen. 1.11)

Whenever a genitival structure was involved, I have counted
the instance as one of NOMINAL (non-sentential) function, admittedly in a somewhat arbitrary fashion.

TABLE 4.:   Functions of the PARTICIPLE in EBH/Genesis

	score	%
CONTINUITY		
TOP-shift-SUBJ	5	
TOP-shift-SUBJ-PRO	3	
continuity alone	0	
total TOP-shift	8	28.2%
ADV-CL/V-COMP	1	
total sentential	9	32.0%
NOMINAL-GENITIVE	19	68.0%
total	28	100.0%

The overwhelming majority of the sentential occurrences
of the participle in EBH-Genesis text involve topic-shifting,
with or without a pronoun. All of them are SUBJECT-topic
cases. Examples cited earlier ((31), Gen. 1.2 and (22), Gen.
2.11) serve to illustrate this. In terms of the total cover-
age of topic-switching functions in EBH/Genesis, we thus have
the ratio of 8/78 PARTICIPLE vs. PERFECT. The overwhelming
strategy is still the 'look-back' or 'anterior' strategy described above. But the sentential use of the PARTICIPLE at
this early point of the drift continuum is largely that of
topic shifting, in addition carrying the non-punctual semantic load, while the PERFECT-ANTERIOR carries the punctual load.
While small, the place of the participle in the topic-shift
functional area is nevertheless significant, since it does
furnish the only clear instances of separation between the
TOPIC-SHIFT and ANTERIOR function. As we shall see further
below, that separation eventually penetrates the PERFECT as
well and ultimately divorces the two functions from each other
altogether.

4.5 Summary: Topic shifting and SV syntax in EBH

At this point one may make the following generalizations:

(a) The two verbal aspects -- PERFECT and PARTICIPLE -- which
show the earliest tendency toward SV syntax in EBH are those
used for TOPIC-SHIFTING;

(b) The verbal aspect used primarily for TOPIC CONTINUITY --
the IMPERFECT -- shows a preponderance of VS syntax;

(c) Therefore it is not primarily the unmarked-topicality of
subjects which puts them at the vanguard of the VS-to-SV drift,
but rather the more marked function of topic-switching. This

obviously requires reassessment of the generalizations made
in Givón (1976a) and summarized in section 1. above;

(d) Similarly with pronominal subjects, their pioneering SV
syntax in EBH must be ascribed to their overwhelming function
in marked topic-switching operations, rather than unmarked
continuity-type anaphora;

(e) Finally, as we shall see below, the PARTICIPLE advances
more rapidly toward SV syntax than the PERFECT, and although
this may be viewed as an instance of hierarchy (3) above
since the PARTICIPLE is both synchronically and diachronically 'more stative'), one must at the same time note that the
PARTICIPLE has no viable subject-agreement conjugation in anaphora, and that in anaphoric contexts it requires independent
subject pronouns, those which show the earliest drift toward
SV syntax. Thus, a complex interaction between both marked
and unmarked topicalization/thematization may be involved in
rendering the participle aspect of EBH the most progressive
in the drift toward SV syntax.

In the following sections I shall document, to the extent permissible by the text, the way in which the continuing
shift in functional distribution of the three aspects brings
about the almost complete VS-to-SV word-order shift in Biblical Hebrew.

5. Subject position and aspectual functions in EBH-Kings II

In terms of the syntax of the subject position in the
Kings II data, as compared to Genesis, very little categorial
change can be found. The facts are given in Table 5. below.
The few slight changes are all of interest. In the Genesis
text there were no instances of indefinite subjects, but in

this text there are 3, and in spite of the relatively LOW
topicality of indefinite subjects, 2 of those show SV syntax,
both in the perfect (Kings II, 1.6, 2.7). The one instance
of VS syntax follows the subordinator ve-hineh 'and-there-be'
(Kings II, 1.14) which ordinarily induces VS syntax. One also
finds one instance of SV syntax in the perfect when an object is fronted:

(39)   ...davar gadol ha-navi? diber ?eley-xa
           thing big the-prophet told to-you
       '...The prophet has told you a great thing...'
                    (PERF) (Kings II, 5.13)

One also finds two instances of SV syntax in the PERFECT in
a conservative environment, ADV-CL/V-COMP (Kings II, 2.2,
2.4), both following the subordinator ki- 'because'. The
2/11 ratio of VS/SV syntax in the PARTICIPLE is even more
striking, as well as the 0/5 ratio in the environment of
fronted-OBJ/ADV, and a 4/2 ratio in OBJ-relative clauses. The
participle again proves to be more progressive along the VS-
to-SV continuum.

TABLE 5.:   Subject position in EBH-Kings II

MAIN CLAUSE	IMPERFECT		PERFECT		PARTICIPLE		COPULAR	
	VS	SV	VS	SV	VS	SV	VS	SV
continuity	172	0	2	41	0	12	3	20
pro-OBJ	13	0	4	0	0	0	/	/
indef-SUBJ	0	0	1	2	0	0	0	0
pro-SUBJ	/	/	0	8	0	21	4	4
fronted OBJ/ADV	/	/	22	1	0	5	/	/
NEG	/	/	3	4	0	0	/	/
ADV-CL/V-COMP	/	/	14	2	2	11	4	2

(Table 5. continues on next page)

	IMPERFECT		PERFECT		PARTICIPLE		COPULAR	
	VS	SV	VS	SV	VS	SV	VS	SV
OBJ-REL	2	0	14	0	4	2	/	/
WH-REL	1	0	2	0	1	0	/	/
IRREALIS	7	10	5	0	/	/	/	/
neg	0	0	/	/	/	/	/	/
adv/clause	3	0	/	/	/	/	/	/
pro-SUBJ	1	3	/	/	/	/	/	/
fronted-OBJ/ADV	4	0	/	/	/	/	/	/
total IRREALIS	15	13						
total	203	13	67	58	7	51	11	36

Some frequency shift is also evident in the IRREALIS (non-continuity) category of the IMPERFECT, where the 8/7 VS/SV ratio in Genesis has shifted to 7/10 in Kings II. Whether this is a significant change, given the low counts, is not clear, but the direction is certainly suggestive. What is also striking is that the bulwark of the IMPERFECT -- the main-clause <u>continuity</u> category -- remains as staunchly VS as in Genesis. The 'topical-to-left' principle is illustrated in the PERFECT with 4 instances where a pronominal object appears before the subject and induces VS syntax, as in:

(40)   vɨ-natnu šama̱ ha-kohanim...?et kol ha kesef
        and-gave the̱re the-priests...ACC all the-money
        'And the pri̱ests put there all the money...'
                            (PERF, Kings II, 12.10)

More striking -- though not by any means categorial -- changes begin to appear in the functional distribution of the tense aspects. In Table 6. below the distribution of the various functions of the IMPERFECT in Kings II is given.

TABLE 6.:   Functions of the IMPERFECT in EBH-Kings II

	score	%
continuity	753	82.6%
irrealis	138	15.0%
imperative	4	0.4%
neg-imperative	17	2.0%
total	912	100.0%

The only shift here is the virtual disappearance of the imperative function.   In Genesis 9 out of the total of 33 instances of this function (or 17%) were performed by the IMPERFECT, the rest by the 'proper' imperative form. In Kings II it is 4 out of 132, or roughly 3%.   The proper imperative form, in the affirmative, has thus taken over this function completely, while the IMPERFECT continues to retain the neg-imperative function as well as the irrealis-subjunctive one (with non-second person subjects-manipulees).   The functional distribution of the PERFECT is given in Table 7. below.

TABLE 7.:   Functions of the PERFECT in EBH-Kings II

	score	%	% of ANTERIOR
ANTERIOR			
ANT alone	17		9.8%
TOP-shift-SUBJ	66		38.4%
TOP-shift-OBJ	16		9.2%
RELATIVE	49		28.5%
ADV-CL/V-COMP	20		11.6%
WH-QUESTION	4		2.5%
total ANTERIOR	172	77.4%	100.0%
IRREALIS	37	16.8%	

(Table 7 continues on next page)

	score	%	% of ANTERIOR
CONTINUITY			
CONT alone	0		
TOP-shift-SUBJ	6		
TOP-shift-OBJ	7		
total CONTINUITY	13	5.8%	
total PERFECT	222	100.0%	

Apparent shifts are again small but interesting. First, there
appears the beginning of separation between the ANTERIOR ('look-
back') and topic-shift function, and 6% of the instances of
the PERFECT in this text have no ANTERIOR meaning whatever,
though all of them are involved in either subject or object
topic-switching. As an example consider the second sentence
in:

(41)   va-yismaḥ   kol 'am   ha-ʔarec, vɨ-ha-'ir
        and-rejoiced all people-of the-earth and-the-city

        šaqṭa,   vɨ-ʔet 'atalyahu hemitu be-ḥerev
        quieted and-ACC Ataliah they-killed by-sword

        'And the people of the country rejoiced, and the
        city quieted down, and Atalia was put to the
        sword'   (IMPERF) (Kings II, 11.20)

The second frequency-shift of interest is the ratio of
subject to object in the use of the PERFECT for topic shifting.
In the Genesis text this ratio was 40/38 or almost identical.
In the Kings II text it is 72/23 SUBJ/OBJ topic-switching. As
we shall see below, a similarly high subject-topicalization
ratio holds for the participle. This is crucial for the following reason: Since toward the end of Biblical Hebrew the PER-
FECT and PARTICIPLE take the CONTINUITY function away from the
IMPERFECT altogether, and since in EBH they are (a) the pio-

neers of SV syntax and (b) are used in main clause for TOPIC-
SWITCHING, then a high preponderance of SUBJECT -topic-shift-
ing in EBH automatically insures that the language will eventually gravitate toward SVO rather than TVX[18] (Topic-V-X, or
'verb-second', as is the custom of characterizing the early
Germanic dialects, see extensive discussion in Canale, 1976).

   In Table 8. below the distribution of the various functions of the PARTICIPLE in EBH-Kings II is given. The major
shift here is in the ratio of NOMINAL to SENTENTIAL function
of the participle. In Genesis its 'free' sentential function
was only 32% while in Kings II it is 91% of the total instances
counted. Within this elapsing period (quite impossible to
actually ascertain) of internal development of EBH, the PARTI-
CIPLE has moved from a largely nominal to a largely sentential-
aspectual role, i.e., the marker of non-punctual aspects ('continuous' and 'habitual').

TABLE 8.:   Functions of the PARTICIPLE in EBH-Kings II

	score	%
CONTINUITY		
TOP-shift-SUBJ	28	
TOP-shift-PRO-SUBJ	25	
TOP-shift-OBJ	5	
total TOP-shift	58	59.0%
continuity alone	4	4.1%
total CONTINUITY	62	63.1%
RELATIVE	15	
WH-QUESTION	3	
ADV-CL/V-COMP	9	
total sentential	89	91.0%
NOMINAL-GENITIVE	9	9.0%
total	98	100.0%

Further, just as in the PERFECT above, a small category has
developed of CONTINUITY use of the participle withou any topic-
shifting function. One may find it within a subjunctive-com-
plement clause, as in:

(42)   vi-?et ?izevel yo?xlu ha-klavim biḥeleq   Yizra'el
        and-ACC Jezebel will-eat the dogs in-part-of Yizrael
        'And as to Jezebel, the dogs will eat her in Yiz-
            rael's fields   (IMPERF)

        vi-?eyn kover   (PARTIC) (Kings II, 9.10)
        and-neg burying
        and no one will bury her...'

But this usage may be still interpreted as a nominal one. However, one also finds the following past-narrative continuity
use of the PARTICIPLE:

(43)   vi-xol ha-'am   seameaḥ vi-toqea' ba-ḥacocrot
        and-all the-people happy and-blowing at-trumpets
        'And the whole people was happy and blowing their
            trumpets'   (Kings II, 11.14)

The third, quite radical, change from Genesis involves
the function of TOPIC-switch within the participle. In the Genesis text 28.2% of the participle was used for this function.
In Kings II it is 59.0%. The rise of the participle as a sentential aspect thus goes via a stage where its prime function
is in topic-switching. And within that function, again the
overwhelming majority of instances (53 out of the total of 58)
are SUBJECT-topic instances.

The evolution of the EBH aspectual system through the
dialect-layer of Kings II may be summarized the following way:

(a) The PERFECT and PARTICIPLE are invading slowly the CONTIN-
UITY function, though still primarily in TOPIC-SWITCHING capacity;

(b)   TOPIC-SWITCHING becomes primarily that of SUBJECT;

(c)   The non-topic-change function of CONTINUITY remains largely vested in the IMPERFECT;

(d)   The IMPERFECT loses its role in affirmative imperatives
(to the proper IMPERATIVE form);

(e)   Within the PERFECT, the category IRREALIS hovers around
16-17% with no change from Genesis to Kings II.

(f)   The PERFECT and PARTICIPLE seem to split the TOPIC-SHIFT
function along purely semantic lines of PUNCTUAL vs. NON-PUNC-
TUAL.

6.   Subject position and aspectual function in EBH-Esther

The book of Esther was earlier[19] identified as a swing
point in the dialect progression of Biblical Hebrew, a point
where changes in the morphology and phonology have just begun
to appear. While the grounds for a discrete decision are admittedly arbitrary, the book should be still considered as
part -- perhaps terminal -- of the EBH continuum. This is
born out by the fact that in terms of the syntax of subject
potition, as seen in Table 9. below, the distribution remains
rather similar to that observed for Kings II. The trends noted earlier continue here. One added change, in the main-ir-
realis IMPERFECT, is a further shift toward SV (when other
conservative factors do not intervene), from the VS/SV ratio
of 7/10 in Kings II to a ratio of 2/8 here. The continuity
function of the IMPERFECT, on the other hand, remains as con-
servatively VS as before.

The frequency-distribution shifts in the functions of
the three aspects continue in Esther along the same lines seen
above. Table 10. below gives the distributions for the IMPER-
FECT, Table 11. for the PERFECT and Table 12. for the PARTI-

CIPLE.

The continuing trends may be summarized as follows:

(a) Perfect: Irrealis drops further, down to 5.7% of PER-
              FECT count;
              Continuity use within the perfect rises drama-
              tically to 38.1% of PERFECT count;

TABLE 9.: Subject position in EBH-Esther

	IMPERFECT		PERFECT		PARTICIPLE		COPULAR	
	VS	SV	VS	SV	VS	SV	VS	SV
MAIN CLAUSE								
continuity	95	0	4	25	0	11	0	6
PRO-subject	/	/	0	1	0	0	0	2
fronted-OBJ/ADV	/	/	12	0	0	6	2	0
NEG	0	1	1	1	0	0	0	0
ADV-CL/V-COMP	/	/	10	2	3	5	1	2
REL-OBJ	0	0	18	0	0	7	/	/
WH-OBJ	0	0	0	2	0	1	/	/
IRREALIS	2	8	0	0	/	/	/	/
neg	1	2	/	/	/	/	/	/
pro-SUBJ	0	0	/	/	/	/	/	/
ADV-CL/V-COMP	3	0	/	/	/	/	/	/
fronted-OBJ/ADV	3	0	/	/	/	/	/	/
REL-OBJ	1	0	/	/	/	/	/	/
total IRREALIS	10	10						
total	105	11	45	31	4	30	3	10

TABLE 10.: Functions of the IMPERFECT in EBH-Esther

	score	%
continuity	162	71.3%
irrealis	60	26.3%
imperative	0	0.0%
neg-imperative	5	2.4%
total	227	100.0%

TABLE 11.: Functions of the PERFECT in EBH-Esther

	score	%	% of ANTERIOR
ANTERIOR			
ANT alone	5		6.5%
TOP-shift-SUBJ	3		4.8%
TOP-shift-OBJ	12		13.2%
RELATIVE	50		62.0%
ADV-CL/V-COMP	20		23.5%
total ANTERIOR	90	56.2%	100.0%
IRREALIS	9	5.7%	
CONTINUITY			
CONT alone	18		
TOP-shift-SUBJ	25		
TOP-shift-OBJ	18		
total CONTINUITY	61	38.1%	
total PERFECT	160	100.0%	

Topic-switching divorces itself almost entirely from the 'look-back' anterior strategy,
and rather moves into the continuity category.
That is, the dialect now prefers, when switching topic, not to disrupt the narrative's con-

tinuity but rather to maintain it, even when
the hearer must adjust to a new topic; Within the topic-switch category, the SUBJECT
loses its primacy at this point;
<u>Anterior</u>: within this function of the per-
fect, topic-switching appears to be receding
now (from 47.6% in Kings II to 18.0% in Esther); the bulk of the ANTERIOR now is represented in overwhelmingly presupposed, past-
oriented clauses such as relative clauses,
adverb clauses and V-complements.

<u>TABLE 12.</u>:   <u>Functions of the PARTICIPLE in EBH-Esther</u>

	score	%
CONTINUITY		
TOP-shift-SUBJ	17	
TOP-shift-PRO SUBJ	8	
TOP-shift-OBJ	0	
total TOP-shift	25	43.5%
continuity alone	0	
total CONTINUITY	25	43.5%
RELATIVE	14	25.0%
ADV-CL/V-COMP	13	23.0%
total sentential	52	91.5%
NOMINAL-GENITIVE	5	8.5%
total	57	100.0%

(b) <u>Imperfect</u>: The <u>Imperative</u> function disappears altogether. All 8 instances of this function in
the affirmative are represented by the 'proper' imperative form;

The percent of irrealis in the IMPERFECT
goes up (20% in Kings II to 30% in Esther, if
one includes both the Subjunctive and neg-Imperative.)

(c)   Participle: The frozen, nominal instances remain around
8.5%, a slight but probably insignificant
drop. This may represent a bottom-line lexical use, subject to contents rather than gram-
mar-dependent variation.

The continuity function drops in favor of presupposed clauses. This may represent further
'lateralization' of this aspect from main to
subordinate clauses.

There is still a complete overlap in the PAR-
TICIPLE between the continuity and topic-shift
functions, and therefore also a drop in the
percent of topic-shift within this category.

7.   Subject position and aspectual functions in Late Biblical
          Hebrew

While the three texts used to investigate the drift continuum in EBH were roughly of the same discourse type (historical narrative), the available texts for any study of LBH present vexing problems. There are three texts that should be
considered in this category: Lamentations, Ecclesiastes and
Song of Solomon. The earlier study[19] clearly tagged the latter as the most progressive point on the Biblical Hebrew continuum, and the second as a mid-point in the shifts investigated there. Lamentations was not included in the earlier investigation due to extremely low counts of the variables stud

ied then. In terms of the phonological change investigated,
it represents a slightly earlier point than that of Ecclesiastes: 9 instances of the subordinator ?ašer as against 4 of
its reduced form še-. In terms of the grammatical shift, Ecclesiastes also represents a midway point (about half verb
complementizers are še-/?ašer the rest the older ki-/vehineh);
but Lamentations attests not a single occurrence of either
še- or ?ašer as V-COMP subordinators. The counts of the others, most ki-, are too small to judge whether the omission is
significant or not. One is thus justified in placing Lamentations earlier on the continuum than Ecclesiastes.

In terms of contents and style, all three LBH books present major headaches. Lamentations is cast in a choppy poet-
ic style addressed mostly to God, with various historical a-
sides. Ecclesiastes is a book of wisdom couched almost entirely in the HABITUAL aspect, but with occasional historical
asides. Song of Solomon, though presumably a popular love
song in origin, has somewhat more continuous narrative, but
portions are dialogue, addressed from one lover to the other,
mostly from the woman (who is responsible for most of the narrative as well).

With respect to at least one book, Ecclesiastes, there
are grounds for suspecting some sort of interference or dis-
continuity in the grammar, but nothing that is categorically
absolute. There are three features of its grammar that might
suggest this:
(a) An overwhelming use of the IMPERFECT as the HABITUAL aspect rather than the PARTICIPLE as in EBH. This usage is perfectly natural from a semantic point of view, as may be demonstrated from the equally plausible glossing of:

(44)   ?im yiškvu šnayim, vɨ-ḥam   lahem   (Ecc. 4.11)
         if will-be two   and-warm to-them
         'If two people will lie down together, they'll be
             warm' (CONDITIONAL)

         'Whenever two people lie down together, they are
             warm' (HABITUAL)

While one may find rare instances of such usage of the IMPER-
FECT in other books, an overwhelming use as in Ecclesiastes
is certainly unprecedented. And the use of the PARTICIPIAL
for this function, as occasionally found in Ecclesiastes as
well (cf. (45) below), is certainly more characteristic of
the entire BH continuum:

(45)   dor   holex vɨ-dor   ba? vɨ-ha?arec
         generation goes and-generation comes and-the-earth

         lɨ-'olam 'omedet (Ecc. 1.4)
         to-world stands

         'One generation goes, another comes, but the earth
             remains forever'

(b) A highly exceptional feature, with neither explanation
nor precedent before or after Ecclesiastes, is the use of VS
syntax with pronoun subjects, as in:

(46)   vɨ-šavti   ?ani va-?er?eh ?et kol ha-'ašuqim
         and-returned I   and-saw   ACC all the-oppressed
         'And again and again I saw all the oppressed...'
                                                (Ecc. 4.1)

This use is with the verb in the PERFECT in a main-continuity
clause, a truly bizarre style. This is also coupled with a
high VS/SV ratio in main-clause PERFECT (7/3), again rather
exceptional.

(c) Finally, there is an unexplained wealth of OV syntax in
Ecclesiastes, and although some of it may be ascribed to OBJ-
TOPIC-shifting, some clearly cannot. Thus consider:

(47)   ?im 'óšeq   raš vɨ-gézel   mišpaṭ va-cedeq
       if oppression-of poor and theft-of justice and-right
          tir?eh...
          you-will-see...
       'If you see oppression of the poor and misapplica-
          tion of justice...'   (Ecc. 5.7)

This feature is found also to some extent in Lamentations, a-
gain in many instances in paragraph initial context which do
not characterize topic-shift of objects:

(48)   ?et kol nɨ?ot   Ya'aqov haras   bi-'evrat-o
       ACC all oases-of Jacob he-destroyed in-wrath-his
       'He has destroyed all the oases of Israel in his
          wrath...'   (Lam. 2.2)

Also, to some extent one finds a higher proportion of VS syntax
in main clause PERFECT in Lamentations than in non-poetic text
as early as Genesis. Nevertheless, in terms of the development of the aspectual system into a tense-aspect system, both
Lamentations and Ecclesiastes are indispensible points on the
BH drift continuum, though both are very close in this respect
to the end-point as represented by the Song of Solomon. Since
historical-narrative texts from this dialect stage are simply
not available, one has no choice but to use what is there.

The syntax of subject position (for the three VERBAL aspects only) in Lamentations is given in Table 13. below.

The functions of the IMPERFECT in the book of Lamentations are given in Table 14. below, those of the PERFECT in
Table 15. and those of the PARTICIPLE in Table 16..

The tense-aspect sitatuion in the book of Lamentations
may be summarized as follows:
(a) IMPERFECT: A complete reversal has occurred in the major
functional distribution of this aspect, with the CONTINUITY

function going from 71.3% in Esther to 26.5% here, while the
IRREALIS function going from 26.3% in Esther to 67.5% here;
(b) PERFECT: A corresponding reversal is almost completed
here, with the CONTINUITY function rising from 38.1% in the
book of Esther to 83.0% here. Further, while in the book of
Esther 43 out of the total CONTINUITY count of 61, or 70%, was
involved in TOPIC-SHIFTING, in the book of Lamentations 72 out
of the total of 215 count of CONTINUITY -- or 33.5% -- was involved in TOPIC-SHIFTING. The major function of the PERFECT
has just shifted to carrying on the 'continuity' or past-e-
vents narrative.

TABLE 13.: Subject position in LBH-Lamentations

	IMPERFECT		PERFECT		PARTICIPLE	
	VS	SV	VS	SV	VS	SV
MAIN CLAUSE						
continuity	3	0	31	29	0	6
pro-OBJ	/	/	7	0	0	0
pro-SUBJ	/	/	0	5	0	1
fronted-OBJ/ADV	/	/	15	2	0	0
NEG	/	/	1	1	0	0
ADV-CL/V-COMP	/	/	5	2	1	0
REL-OBJ	/	/	1	0	0	0
WH-OBJ	/	/	1	0	0	0
IRREALIS	2	1	/	/	/	/
neg	1	1	/	/	/	/
ADV-CL/V-COMP	6	0	/	/	/	/
fronted-OBJ/ADV	3	0	/	/	/	/
WH-OBJ	4	0	/	/	/	/
total IRREALIS	16	2				
total	19	2	51	39	1	7

TABLE 14.:   Functions of the IMPERFECT in LBH-Lamentations

	score	%
continuity	31	26.5%
irrealis	78	67.5%
neg-imperative	7	6.0%
total	116	100.0%

TABLE 15.:   Functions of the PERFECT in LBH-Lamentations

	score	%
ANTERIOR		
ANT alone	0	
RELATIVE	14	
WH-question	5	
ADV-CL/V-COMP	24	
total ANTERIOR	43	17.0%
IRREALIS	0	
CONTINUITY		
CONT alone	143	
TOP-shift-SUBJ	34	
TOP-shift-PRO-SUBJ	7	
TOP-shift-OBJ	31	
total CONTINUITY	215	83.0%
total PERFECT	258	100.0%

Correspondingly, the IRREALIS function of the PERFECT has altogether disappeared by this point of the continuum. Finally,
the ANTERIOR function is entirely concentrated in presupposed
clauses, thus separating completely from the CONTINUITY and
TOPIC-SHIFT categories.

    With the exception of the residual use of some IMPERFECT

for continuity (out of a total continuity score of 246, 31 instances or 12.6% are in the IMPERFECT, the rest in the PER-
FECT), the system has become the Mishnaic and Modern Hebrew
tense-aspect system, with the PERFECT used for past-narrative,
the IMPERFECT for future and conditional, and the PARTICIPLE
as a non-punctual 'continuous' aspect, used for 'present' or
'habitual'.

TABLE 16.: Functions of the PARTICIPLE in LBH-Lamentations

	score	%
CONTINUITY		
TOP-shift-SUBJ	6	
TOP-shift-PRO-SUBJ	2	
total TOPIC-shift	8	29.6%
CONT alone	2	
total CONTINUITY	10	37.0%
RELATIVE	7	
ADV-CL/V-COMP	2	
total sentential	19	70.4%
NOMINAL-GENITIVE	8	29.6%
total	27	100.0%

As can be seen below, this system remains in the books of
Ecclesiastes and Song of Solomon.[20]

The syntax of subject position in Ecclesiastes is given
in Table 17., and the functional distribution of the tense-
aspects in Tables 18., 19. and 20. below.

The syntax of the subject position in Song of Solomon,
the last text to be studied and the most progressive dialect
level on the BH continuum, is given in Table 21. below, and

the function distribution within the tense-aspects is given
in Tables 22., 23. and 24.

TABLE 17.:   Subject position in LBH-Ecclesiastes

	IMPERFECT		PERFECT		PARTICIPLE		COPULAR	
	VS	SV	VS	SV	VS	SV	VS	SV
MAIN CLAUSE[21]	4	25	7	3	0	13	5	36
pro-SUBJ	0	2	14	3	1	1	2	20
fronted-OBJ/ADV	11	1	8	0	3	2	/	/
NEG	7	8	1	1	0	5	0	3
ADV-CL/V-COMP	20	7	6	0	1	2	3	6
REL-OBJ	4	0	13	0	0	5	/	/
WH-OBJ	1	0	1	0	0	2	/	/
IRREALIS[21]	/	/	2	0	/	/	/	/
total	47	43	53	7	5	30	10	67

TABLE 18.:   Functions of the IMPERFECT in LBH-Ecclesiastes

	score	%
continuity	4	1.9%
irrealis	187	89.0%
imperative	1	0.4%
neg-imperative	17	8.7%
total	209	100.0%

TABLE 19.:   Functions of the PERFECT in LBH-Ecclesiastes

	score	%
ANTERIOR		
ANT alone	7	
ANT + REL	60	
ANT + WH	1	
ADN-CL/V-COMP	0	
total ANTERIOR	68	36.0%
CONTINUITY		
CONT alone	64	33.9%
TOP-shift-SUBJ	7	
TOP-shift-OBJ	26	
total CONTINUITY	97	51.0%
IRREALIS	24	13.0%
total	189	100.0%

TABLE 20.:   Functions of the PARTICIPLE in LBH-Ecclesiastes

	score	%
CONTINUITY		
TOP-shift-SUBJ	20	
TOP-shift-PRO-SUBJ	3	
TOP-shift-OBJ	6	
CONT alone	11	10.1%
total CONTINUITY	40	37.0%
RELATIVE	44	40.7%
ADV-CL/V-COMP	8	7.4%
total sentential	92	85.1%
NOMINAL-GEN	16	14.9%
total	108	100.0%

TABLE 21.: Subject position in LBH-SOS

	IMPERFECT		PERFECT		PARTICIPLE		COPULAR	
	VS	SV	VS	SV	VS	SV	VS	SV
MAIN CLAUSE[21]	4	3	2	18	0	6	14	57
pro-SUBJ	0	0	2	0	0	2	2	8
fronted-OBJ/ADV	1	0	4	0	0	0	/	/
NEG	0	2	0	0	0	0	/	/
PRO-OBJ	0	0	3	0	0	0	/	/
ADV-CL/V-COMP	0	0	7	2	0	0	6	4
REL-OBJ	0	0	8	0	0	0	/	/
WH-OBJ	0	0	2	0	0	0	0	1
IRREALIS[21]	/	/	0	0	/	/	/	/
total	5	5	28	20	0	8	22	70

TABLE 22.: Functions of the IMPERFECT in LBH-SOS

	score	%
continuity	3	4.6%
irrealis	61	94.0%
neg-imperative	1	1.4%
total	65	100.0%

TABLE 23.: Functions of the PERFECT in LBH-SOS

	score	%
ANTERIOR		
ANT alone	0	
RELATIVE	13	
ADV-CL/V-COMP	11	
WH-QUESTION	2	
total ANTERIOR	26	28.9%
CONTINUITY		
CONT alone	22	24.4%
TOPIC-shift-SUBJ	26	
TOPIC-shift-OBJ	14	
total CONTINUITY	62	69.0%
IRREALIS	2	2.1%
total	90	100.0%

TABLE 24.: Functions of the Participle in LBH-SOS

	score	%
CONTINUITY		
TOP-shift-SUBJ	10	
TOP-shift-PRO-SUBJ	1	
CONT alone	14	30.0%
total CONTINUITY	25	53.0%
RELATIVE	20	42.5%
total sentential	45	95.5%
NOMINAL-GEN	2	4.5%
total	47	100.0%

As one can see from the tabulations above, the functional shift in the various aspects has been completed at this
end-point of the available BH text. This point can no longer
be characterized as a Creole-type ANTERIOR-based aspectual
system, but rather as a <u>tense</u>-aspect system, where the following functional distributions obtain:

(a) The IMPERFECT has become the IRREALIS aspect, covering
     SUBJUNCTIVES, CONDITIONALS and the FUTURE tense in main
     clauses;

(b) The PERFECT has become the main <u>past</u>-narrative <u>tense</u>,
     covering both continuity and anterior functions;

(c) The PARTICIPLE has become the sentential non-punctual/
     continuous/habitual aspect.

While it was not possible to document this with precision, I suspect topic-shifting has invaded the IMPERFECT-IR-
REALIS paradigm at some point, and this could explain the in-
creasing shift to SV syntax in this portion of the IMPERFECT
paradigm. The CONTINUITY-IMPERFECT, while gradually receding
to ultimate extinction, retained VS syntax to the very end.

8. Summary of the shifts

At the available end-point of Song of Solomon, Biblical
Hebrew cannot be characterized as having completed the VS·SV
shift, although it has certainly completed it in MAIN CLAUSES
which have no other pragmatic-related retarding effects (PRO-
OBJ, NEG, topicalized-non-subject, RELATIVIZED non-subject
and ADV-CLAUSE/V-COMP environments). The shift in those categories is more advanced in the PARTICIPLE, less so in the
PERFECT. In order to characterize the VS-to-SV rate of shift
across the available dialect continuum points, I have chosen
to combine the counts for <u>main clause only</u> of the three verbal

aspects.[22] Table 25. below summarizes the data.

TABLE 25.: Shift in main-clause syntax in BH

book	VS	SV	total	% SV
Genesis	169	25	194	12.9%
Kings II	174	53	227	23.2%
Esther	99	36	135	26.7%
Lam.	36	36	72	50.0%
Eccl.	11	41	52	79.0%
SOS	2	26	28	92.0%

In Table 26. below the functional shift in the distribution of the CONTINUITY function among the three verbal tense-aspects across the dialect continuum of BH is recorded.

TABLE 26.: Aspect-distribution of the CONTINUITY function in BH

book	PERFECT		PARTICIPLE		IMPERFECT		TOTAL
	score	%	score	%	score	%	score
Genesis	0	0.0%	8	2.0%	379	98.0%	387
Kings II	13	1.5%	62	3.4%	753	91.1%	828
Esther	61	24.6%	25	10.0%	162	65.4%	248
Lam.	215	84.0%	10	3.9%	31	12.1%	256
Eccl.	97	68.5%	40	28.4%	4	3.1%	141
SOS	62	69.0%	25	27.8%	3	3.2%	90

When the percentages of SV syntax in Table 25. are correlated with the % share of the IMPERFECT in the function of CONTINU-

ITY, one obtains the correlation as expressed in Figure 1. below.

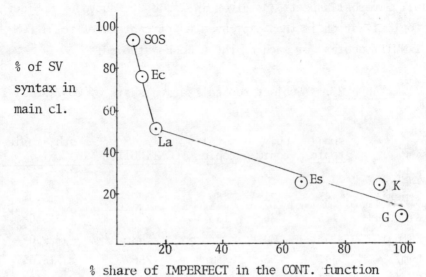

% of SV
syntax in
main cl.

% share of IMPERFECT in the CONT. function

Figure 1.: Syntactic change and functional shift

While a correlation between the functional shift in the tense-
aspect system and the overall SV syntax in main clauses does
obtain, the curve shows two distinct phases: (a) From Genesis
to Lamentations the rate of dependency of the syntactic change
upon the functional change is weaker; (b) from Lamentations to
Song of Solomon the rate is much stronger. At the moment I'm
not sure how to interpret this differential rate, though perhaps some type of 'critical mass' effect may be here at work.
In this connection, it is of interest to note that the main-
clause syntax in Lamentations is 50% SV/VS, i.e., the point
above which the new categorial generalisation can be made by
the speakers.[23]

In Table 27. below the scores of SUBJECT-topic-shift and

OBJECT-topic-shift combined for the PERFECT and PARTICIPLE
are given, together with the scores for total CONTINUITY in
all 3 verbal aspects (as given in Table 26. above). Subject
topicalization is then expressed as percentage of total CON-
TINUITY scores for each of the 6 books studied.

TABLE 27.: Subject topicalization share of CONTINUITY
in BH

book	subj topic	obj topic	total topic	CONTINUITY	% subj-topic in CONT
Genesis	45	41	86	387	11.0%
Kings II	125	28	153	828	15.0%
Esther	53	30	83	248	21.0%
Lam.	47	33	80	256	18.0%
Eccl.	30	32	62	141	21.0%
SOS	37	14	51	90	41.0%

There are two ways of interpreting the data in Table 27. (a-
side from dismissing it as irrelevant). One may first suggest that there is a strong dependency between subject-topicalization in Old Biblical Hebrew (Genesis, Kings II, Esther),
during the stage in which non-categorial frequency shift in
word-order is observed. Then there is a second period of rap-
id shift in word-order but no further increase in subject-topicalization. This characterizes the period between Esther and
Ecclesiastes, the portion of the continuum during which virtually all the parameters studied, both within the tense-aspect functions and word-order, undergo a fast leap toward the
new categorial state. The third phase, between Ecclesiastes
and Song of Solomon, may represent discourse re-alignment with-

in the new <u>categorial</u> grammar of LBH, or it may represent
some stylistic fluke that is text-specific and cannot be
gauged here.

    As always when the data is not selected with idealized
care under well controlled conditions, there is another way
of interpreting it.   One may simply dismiss the texts of Lamentations and Ecclesiastes as representing a totally different discourse type, that of non-continuous, non-narrative
fragmented dialogue.   Then one could presumably claim that
the curve should be extrapolated from Genesis, Kings II and
Esther <u>directly</u> to Song of Solomon, ignoring the other two.
When this is done, a reasonably close correlation between the
percent of subject-topicalization out of the CONTINUITY score
and the word-order shift from VS to SV in main, verbal clauses can be asserted.   I have represented both interpretations
in Figure 2. below, and at the moment see no grounds for pre-
ferring one over the other.

FIGURE 2.:   The shift from VS to SV as a function of
                    subject topicalization in BH

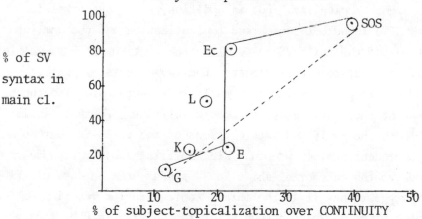

9. Discussion

9.1. Pragmatics and the change from VS to SV

In an earlier study of the later portions of the VS-to-SV continuum (Givón, 1976a), it seemed that one principle of unmarked thematization (i.e., one which does not involve topic shifting or contrastive-topic) could account for all the hierarchies that predict which environments will undergo the change first and which will be 'conservative'. That principle was labeled 'relative topicality', and it was found that all other things being equal, environments in which the subject is of low relative topicality will tend to remain VS longer, and thus exhibit more conservative syntax along this continuum.

In the present study a very clear correlation was found between both marked and unmarked topicality and word-order shift from VS to SV. First with respect to unmarked topicality, the 'conservative' environments found here were on the whole the same ones reported earlier, i.e., in which the subject topicality is lower, while a non-subject lays claim to higher topicality. But in addition, a strong correlation was also found between marked topicalization and the earlier stages of the shift VS-to-SV along the continuum. For example, with respect to verbal aspects, the two aspects -- perfect and participle -- which show earlier SV syntax are also those used at that early stage for topic-shifting. Further, while in both the early and late portions of the VS-to-SV continuum independent subject pronouns are the first subject type to undergo the categorial shift to SV syntax, the BH data clearly suggest that it is the marked topicalization function of these pronouns which accounts for the shift. In EBH, thus, the verb agreement (in the IMPERFECT and PERFECT) is used for unmarked anaphora (i.e., when the topic remains unchanged), and the independent pronouns are used in these aspects only for marked topicalization. While the two principles are not in conflict, it is nevertheless clear that in terms of the early impetus for the VS-to-SV shift, marked topicalization plays the predominant role in main-clauses, while unmarked topicalization explains the conservative nature of many other environments.

9.2 The pragmatics of conservative subordinate environments

At least for the shift from VS to SV syntax, I think one must concede that the principle that "subordinate environments are syntactically more conservative than main-clauses" must be re-evaluated and perhaps relegated to the status of a derived universal.[24] For all of these environments, (relative-object, WH-object, adverbial clauses and V-complements), there exist, at least for Biblical Hebrew, good arguments that their conservative tendency to preserve VS syntax longer merely reflects the fact that the topicality of the subject is lower in those environments than in the main clause. Whether similar arguments will account for the conservative nature of the very same environments in the shift from SOV to SVO, as in Germanic,[25] remains to be seen. But at least for the VS-to-SV shift, one must concede that a 'purely structural' principle is not necessary, and that the pragmatics of relative topicality, coupled with the principle of "more topical goes first", explain all the data adequately.

9.3 The role of grammatical agreement

While I have argued that factors of relative topicality

explain the more progressive SV syntax of both the PARTICI-
PIAL verbal aspect (more stative) and the COPULAR construction (more generic), one may as well note that in Biblical
Hebrew both have weak or no anaphoric-function of subject a-
greement. Thus even in unmarked theme/anaphora, these two
constructions must use independent pronouns. And it may well
be true that their more progressive tendency toward SV syntax
may be also influenced by the --ultimately pragmatic too --
factor of weak grammatical agreement (see discussion in section 1. above as well as Givón, 1976a).

9.4 Tense-aspect shift and word-order change

One of the most striking facts about the VS-to-SV shift
in BH is that it was driven from the beginning to the end by
the functional-distribution shift in the aspectual system. At
the earliest point available, the IMPERFECT was the main continuity aspect used for advancing the narrative, while the
PERFECT (and to a lesser degree the PARTICIPLE) were used for
marked topic shifting. The SV syntax of the latter may be
seen as a direct result of their marked topic-switching function. The syntax of the IMPERFECT-CONTINUITY never changed
from VS to SV. What did change, though, was the role alloca-
tion of the aspects: While the IMPERFECT ceded its continuity function and specialized in IRREALIS, the PERFECT and PAR-
TICIPIAL gradually enhanced their share of the main-clause,
continuity-function narrative pie. And they brought along their
SV syntax with them. This is very reminiscent of the diachronic change paradigm suggested by Ard (1975), whereby word-order
of various constructions does not change directly. Rather,
functional re-analysis of two constructions which exhibit opposite word-order results in the emergence of one as the dom-

inant.

9.5 The VS-to-SV shift in the wider typological-change
          context

One must first note that a VSO language is 'pragmatically
schizophrenic', since the new information portion of the sentence is scattered on both sides of the topic/subject. Such a
conflict has been known to resolve in either one of two ways:
(a) A language may choose to emphasize the "topic to the left"
principle in its unmarked thematization (i.e., in normal, neutral word-order) and shift from VSO to SVO. This is what
seems to have happened in Biblical Hebrew, other Semitic Dialects, Luo of the Nilotic group, Indonesian of the Western-
Austronesian group and probably many others.[26]   (b) A language may choose the opposite unmarked-theme principle of
"topic to the right" and resolve the conflict into VOS. In
a recent paper Chet Creider (1976) brings strong evidence that
this is happening in several Nilotic languages (Nandi, Kipsigis), Celtic (Irish, Welsh), Austronesian (Tongan, Fijian, Samoan, Malagasy, at least incipiently in the Philippine languages). Creider further observes that in all these VOS-tend-
ing V-first languages, while unmarked thematization obeys the
new principle, marked topicalization always adheres to the
"topic to left" principle. This raised the possibility that
while VOS languages solved their unmarked-thematization dilem-
ma, they have introduced another, potentially more thorny pragmatic conflict into the language, since in those languages
marked and unmarked thematization obey opposite ordering principles. On the other hand, the resolution toward SVO results
in pragmatic consistency in the language.

Another implication of Creider's finding is this: V-first

syntax seems to be in many cases a rather transitory stage
on a continuum from SOV to SVO. But if a language adopts the
"topic to right" principle in unmarked thematization, and
thus drifts toward VOS, it stands an excellent chance of stab-
ilizing and prolonging -- perhaps indefinitely -- this V-
first stage. Thus, languages such as Malagasy, Tagalog, Ton-
gam, Fijian (Austronesian), Nandi, Kipsigis (Nilotic) and
Irish and Welsh (Celtic) seem to have adopted this typological path. While Indonesian and Oceanic (Austronesian[27]), Romance, Germanic[28] and Semitic, seem to have opted for the
other pragmatic alternative. Whether one could predict from
other typological factors that a language will adopt one or
the other pragmatic word-order in unmarked thematization remains to be seen.

With the possible exception of Austronesian[27], it seems
that natural word-order drift follows the paradigm: SOV --->
VSO ---> SVO as a major typological continuum. To my knowledge all documented shifts to SOV from VO (Akkadia, Ethiop-
ian-Semitic, New-Guinea Austronesian) can be shown to be contact induced, with the exception of Chinese which has acquired certain OV characteristics and constructions through internal reanalysis (see Li & Thompson, 1974 and Li, 1975). To
my best knowledge a serious claim of SVO to VSO shift has
been only made for Austronesian, and I think even there the
jury is not yet in. What I have attempted to do here and in
the preceding paper (see section 1.) is to show that there
exists a pragmatic motivation for the second stage of the
drift. While Hyman (1975) has raised the possibility that
pragmatic processes, such as afterthought-topic (right-dis-
location), may be involved in the OV to VO shift, the seeming-
ly incipient recurrence of VS syntax as a stable, grammatical-

ized stage (Semitic, Celtic, Nilotic, perhaps Austronesian too) or as a probabilistic phenomenon at the phase when an SOV language becomes 'grammatically unstuck', remains to be explained. I hope to show at some future date that this shift too -- SOV to V-first -- may have some functional, discourse-related explanation.

* This work was supported in part by the NSF-Stanford Language Universals project. I am indebted to my colleagues on the project for their patience and support, moral and otherwise. I would also like to record my debt to Derek Bickerton, who has watched over the beginning of this work and contributed many hours of stimulating discussion and a great many important comments. I retain full responsibility for the final contents of this paper.

Notes

1. By VS syntax here I will simply mean "the verb preceding the subject", regardless of what other constituents
are involved and what their position is.

2. "Relative topicality" should be equated, roughly,
with the degree to which a constituent of a proposition is or
is not the focus of new information. "More topical" is then
"less new information". In a number of earlier studies (see
e.g., Givón, 1974a; Givón, 1976a; Givón, 1976b) I have shown
that the division of topic vs. focus or old vs. new information, respectively, is not a simple discrete binary division,
but is clearly a matter of relative degree. In the discussion
below I will simply take these points for granted. A good example for 'relative topicality' at work may be cited from Bolinger (1954), where in Spanish the WH-question focusing on
the identity of the subject: 'Quien canta?' ('Who sings?')
will elicit the VS response 'Canta Juan' ('John sings'), while
the focusing on the predicate as in 'Que hace Juan?' (What
does John do?') will elicit the SV response 'Juan canta'
('John sings').

3. 'Surprise subject' in English is something like:
"And there, lo-and-behold, stood my arch enemy, the Duke of
Gore". For further discussion see Gary (1975). The TV show
titled "And then came Bronson" may or may not be another instance of this construction type.

4. By 'competence type study' I refer to the normal
study of grammatical environments and grammaticality/accept-
ability judgements, be they 'absolute binary' ones or the
more realistic 'scaled' ones. I consider this methodology at

best suggestive, one which must be complemented by -- or rather validated through -- text-frequency studies.

5. Put another way, 'always' is less likely to be topical than 'at that time'.

6. Briefly, the facts boil down to a persistent connection between object relativization and object topicalization. Somehow, within a relative clause the argument coreferential with the head is more topical. In object relative clauses this will automatically downgrade the relative topicality of the subject, and thus in languages along the VS/SV continuum will tend to induce 'more conservative' VS syntax in these embedded clauses.

7. This constitutes a clear counterexample to generalizations made in Givón (1975b) to the effect that on the whole negative sentences tend to be diachronically more conservative. The question of diachronic-conservatism will be repeatedly re-opened here, since one of the by-products of this study is a very strong suggestion that pragmatic rather than syntactic considerations determine the diachronic conservatism of constructions.

8. Thus 'because John didn't come' is paraphraseable as: 'because of the reason for which John didn't come'; and 'When John came' may be paraphrased as: 'at the time when John came'.

9. There are indications that Old English, right after the breakdown of the older SOV syntax, was typologically at the same point as German is roughly now. The continuum must have been exhibited diachronically via the various stages of the history of English, much as it will be shown to have operated via the diachronic development of Biblical Hebrew.

10.   Tweed (1975) has counted the frequency of subjectless (i.e., anaphorically used) verbs in the surrogate language spoken around Spanish children around the age of 18-24
months. Out of 250 tokens, less than 10 -- i.e., less than
4% -- had overt subjects. In other words, over 95% of verbal
clauses input to the Spanish child at this critical age of
language acquisition were verb-first clauses. In terms of
text frequency at acquisition time, then, a viable subject-
agreement paradigm must surely act as a retardant in the
drift along our continuum toward grammaticalized SV syntax.

11.   A brief word about the transcriptions used here. I
have attempted to render all consonantal distinctions made in
BH, but have disregarded gemination and in other ways have
elected to give the Israeli Hebrew pronunciation of the text,
especially with respect to the vowels. If this was a phonological or morpho-phonemic study, such a practice would be obviously inadequate. However, for the purpose of the present
study, I have elected to forego puristic transcriptions, and
humbly hope that this practice will not offend scholars more
exacting than myself.

12.   One could of course take refuge in the time-honored
observation that 'in general subordinate clauses change their
syntax more slowly'. While I have supported this position in
ths past (Givón, 1974a), it seems to me that it is incumbent
upon the linguist to find reasons for such generalizations,
not merely invoke them. And one surprising upshot of this paper is that it is possible to find functional-pragmatic explanation for the conservative behavior of all major types of
embedded clauses in the change from VS to SV syntax.

13.   Of the 7 instances of irrealis clauses with SV syn-

tax (Gen. 1.20, 4.14, 4.15, 6.17, 9.2, 9.3, 9.6), not a single one is a <u>continuity</u> subject, but all are new subjects,
i.e., mentioned in that particular narrative for the first
time (although they are all definite, as is the general rule
for subjects in BH).

14.   For details of the notion 'topic shifting' and
'contrastive topic' as universal discourse categories, see
Kuno (1972, 1973) and Givón (1975c).

15.   I would like at this point to record my great debt
to Derek Bickerton for hours of stimulating conversation on
aspectual-tense systems in general and the Creole aspectual
system in particular.   It was the fortunate accident of working in Hawaii on Derek's Creole data when this investigation
was just beginning, which helped me appreciate the striking
similarity of the BH and Universal Creole aspectual systems.

16.   While the basic notion here is 'topic' or 'what one
is talking about' rather than the strict grammatical subject,
the 'continuity' function of the imperfect quite often gives
long equi-subject narrative chains.   Thus, for example, of
the 5 verbal events related in (27) above in the IMPERFECT,
the subject of 4 is God, while the subject of one is 'light'.
However, while 'light' is the grammatical subject in that one
occurrence, the discourse-narrative is not <u>about</u> 'light', but
continues to be about God and what he was up to.   Hence the
IMPERFECT is maintained and subject-shifting is not equivalent here to topic-shifting.   On the other hand, as will be
shown below, the frequency of subject-shifting coinciding
with topic-shifting is naturally high, being that subjects
are the <u>most topical</u> participants in events, all other things
being equal (see extensive discussion in Keenan, 1975; Li and

Thompson, 1975; and Givón, 1975a).

17. See Haupt (1978), Hudson (1974) and discussion in
Givón (1976d).

18. The term TVX is originally due to Vennemann (1973),
where a suggestion that languages change from SXV to SVX via
TVX (or TOPIC-VERB-X) syntax. While early Germanic dialects
exhibit the so-called TVX word order (or 'verb-second'), that
stage may be less than universal, and further it may be hard
to decide whether 'verb second' or X-VS-Y is the significant
generalization. My own observation at this point is simply
that somewhere between SOV and SVO as stable, grammaticized
word-order strategies, a high frequency of ...VS... syntax
seems to crop up, sometimes fully grammaticized as VSO or VOS,
sometimes as 'verb-second', 'TVX' or what have you.

19. Givón (1974b).

20. One adjustment Israeli Hebrew has made to this system is the virtual abolition, in the spoken dialect, of the
proper-IMPERATIVE form in favor of use of the IMPERFECT-future-
irrealis form. This unifies all the IRREALIS functions except
for the HABITUAL under one formal category, a situation reminiscent of Early Biblical Hebrew.

21. All the instances of the IMPERFECT recorded here are
IRREALIS or HABITUAL, so that the CONTINUITY category is not
any more relevant for the imperfect, and the IRREALIS category
is redundant.

22. The syntax of copular constructions is fairly stable
-- and tending toward SV -- from the earliest text of BH.

23. I am not familiar with the psychological and psycho-

linguistic literature on rule-generalization, but it seems reasonable to assume that somewhere beyond the 50% point one should expect to obtain, in addition to the dependency on the factors which originally drove the change in a particular direction, also some sort of 'avalanche effect' of rule generalization, as speakers begin to perceive the mounting frequency of an event as a categorial change.

24.   I have earlier suggested (Givón, 1974a) other functional explanations for the conservative nature of subordinate clauses, functions which were related to discourse structure and thus ultimately to topicality. However, the data discussed here are much more specific in this respect.

25.   For the more conservative nature of dependent clauses in the SOV-to-SVO shift in Old English, see Canale (1976). Modern German is an obviously parallel example.

26.   I think there is an excellent possibility that Romance has gone through a stage of ...VS... syntax, the strong mark of which remains to this day in Spanish, Portuguese, Italian and Romanian. Further, while the Germanic intermediate word-order -- between SOV and SVO -- is often characterized as 'verb second' or TVX (Vennemann, 1973), there are grounds for suspecting that one could characterize that stage just as well as '...VS...', at least in the sense of "a period of high probability in text of the finite verb appearing before the subject". For data supporting this I am indebted to Michael Canale (in personal communication). Similar conclusions have been independently drawn by Rybarkiewicz (1976) and Carter (1970).

27.   I would like hereby to challenge Clark's (1974) and Foley's (1976) reconstruction of Proto-Austronesian

as SVO. I think the data could be better explained by VSO reconstruction, and I hope to demonstrate this eventually.

28.   See footnote 26 above.

References

Ard, J.   (1975) "Raisings and Word order in diachronic syn-
    tax" Ph.D. Thesis, UCLA.

Bickerton, D.   (1975a) "Creolization, linguistic universals,
    natural semantax and the brain", paper read at the Con-
    ference on Pidgins and Creoles, University of Hawaii, Hon-
    olulu, January 1975.

_____ (1975b) "Creoles and natural semantax", UCLA lec-
    ture, April 1975.

Bolinger, D.   (1952) "Linear modification", reprinted in his
    Forms of English, Harvard University Press (1965).

_____ (1954) "Meaningful word-order in Spanish", Boletín
    de Filología, Universidad de Chile, tomo VIII.

Canale, M.   (1976) "Implicational hierarchies of word order
    relationships", paper read at the Second International
    Congress on Historical Linguistics, Tucson, January 1976.

Carlton, C.   (1970) Descriptive Syntax of the Old English
    Charters, The Hague: Mouton.

Clark, R.   (1974) "Transitivity and case in Eastern Oceanic
    languages", paper read at the First International Confer-
    ence on Comparative Linguistics, Honolulu, Hawaii.

Creider, C.   (1976) "Thematization and word order", Univer-
    sity of Western Ontario, Dept. of Anthropology (ms).

Foley, W.   (1976) "Comparative Syntax in Austronesia" Ph.D.
    Thesis, UCB.

Gary, N.   (1975) "A discourse analysis of certain root trans-
    formations in English", UCLA (ms).

Givón, T.   (1974a) "Toward a discourse definition of syntax",
    UCLA (ms).

_____   (1974b) "Relative clauses and verb complements in
    Biblical Hebrew", Afroasiatic Linguistics, vol. 1.

_____   (1975a) "Topic, pronoun and grammatical agreement",
    in C. Li (ed.) Subject and Topic.

_____   (1975b) "Negation in language: Pragmatics, func-
    tion, ontology", Working Papers on Language Universals,
    18, Stanford University.

_____   (1975c) "Universal grammar, lexical structure and
    translatability", in M. Guenthner-Reutter and F. Guenth-
    ner (eds) Meaning and Translation: Philosophical and Lin-
    guistic Approaches, London, Duckworth.

_____   (1976a) "On the VS word-order in Israeli Hebrew:
    Pragmatics and typological change", in P. Cole (ed.) Pa-
    pers in Hebrew Syntax, Amsterdam: North Holland.

_____   (1976b) "The development of the numeral 'one' as
    an indefinite marker in Israeli Hebrew", in S. Bolotzky
    and M. Barkai (eds) Generative Studies in Hebrew Linguis-
    tics, Tel Aviv: Tel Aviv University Press.

_____   (1976c) "Promotion, accessibility and case-mark-
    ing: Toward understanding grammars", Working Papers in
    Language Universals, 19, Stanford University.

_____   (1976d) "On the SOV origins of the suffixal agree-
    ment conjugation in Indo-European and Semitic", in A.
    Juilland (ed.) Studies Presented to Joseph Greenberg on

the Occasion of his 60th Birthday, Stanford: Stanford
University Press.

Haupt, P. (1878) "The oldest Semitic verb", Journal of the
Royal Asiatic Society of Great Britain and Ireland,
10:244-251.

Hooper, J. and S. Thompson (1973) "On the application or root
transformations: Linguistic Inquiry, 4.

Hudson, C. (1974) "Amharic postposition embedding and relative clause history", paper read at the Conference on
word-order and word-order change, UC Santa Barbara, Janu-
ary 1974 (ms).

Hyman, L. (1974) "On the change from SOV to SVO: Evidence
from Niger-Congo", in C. Li (ed.) Word Order and Word
Order Change, Austin: University of Texas Press.

Keenan, E. (1975) "Toward a universal definition of 'subject'", in C. Li (ed.) Subject and Topic.

Kuno, S. (1972) "Functional sentence perspective: A case
study from Japanese and English", Linguistic Inquiry 3:
269-320.

_____ (1973) The Structure of the Japanese Language, Cambridge: MIT Press.

Lehmann, W. (1973) "A structural principle of language and
its implications:, Language 49:47-66.

Li, C. (1975) "Synchrony vs. diachrony in language structure. Language 51.4:873-886.

Li, C. (1976) (ed.) Subject and Topic, New York: Academic
Press.

Li, C. and S. Thompson (1974) "An explanation of word order
    change SVO → SOV", Foundations of Language 12:201-214.

Li, C. and S. Thompson (1976) "Subject and topic: A new typo-
    logy of language", in C. Li (ed.) Subject and Topic.

Pawley, A.   (1974) "Some problems in Proto-Oceanic grammar",
    U of Hawaii (ms).

Rybarkiewicz, W. (1975) "Word Order in Old English Prose",
    MA Thesis, English Language Dept., University of Lodz.

Schachter, P.   (1975) "The subject in Philippine languages:
    Topic, actor, topic-actor, or none of the above?", in C.
    Li (ed.) Subject and Topic.

Tweed, L.   (1976) "Parent input and language acquisition"
    UCLA (ms).

Vennemann, T.   (1973) "Topics, subjects and word-order: From
    SXV to SVX via TVX", paper read at the First Internation-
    al Conference on Historical Linguistics, Edinburgh, Sep-
    tember 1973 (ms).

5 Syntactic Change and SOV Structure: The Yuman Case

Margaret Langdon

There has been much talk lately about universals of word
order and word order change, and with good reason. The results of this particular type of research spurred by the pioneering work of Greenberg (1963) are already impressive (see
in particular, Li 1975) and have made possible the statement
of generalizations not hitherto recognized. While Greenberg's
original proposal was commendably tentative and extremely carefully worded not to claim more than the initial survey justified, there has been more recently a tendency, as a number of
generalizations received broader confirmation, to relax the
wording of some claims and to assume that the magic line between hypothesis and proven fact has been crossed. As long
as only synchronic inferences are made on that basis, I believe that not too much damage will be done since we may hope
that we will eventually have a sample of descriptive material
sufficiently representative of the languages of the world to
bring about needed corrections under empirical pressure. More
disturbing, however, is the temptation to apply the tentative
findings of word order typologies in a categorical manner to
less empirically verifiable fields, such as historical reconstruction, especially for those language families where no
earlier documents exist. A hypothetical example of the kind
of argumentation I have in mind would go like this: "Language
X has present-day word order SVO and postpositions. Postpos-

itions are typological characteristics of SOV languages,
therefore language X used to be SOV. Furthermore, since language X used to be SOV, it must have had at one time all other SOV characteristics, even some for which no direct evidence
has been preserved, e.g. the genitive preceded the governing
noun, etc." This would be the prelude to a complex and elegant argument demonstrating how such change could have taken
place, etc. thus reinforcing the strength of the initial generalization. While I welcome the use of word order generalizations as a much-needed new tool for diachronic investigation, I also feel that it must be used with extreme caution
and only if its results are compatible with other syntactic
properties of the languages in question, as well as with their
phonological constraints.

These remarks are prompted by my current efforts to reconstruct aspects of the syntax of Yuman languages, a family
of American Indian languages spoken in Southern and Baja California as well as Arizona,[1] which in turn is believed to belong to the Hokan stock, one of the most difficult and problematic of the genetic groupings proposed for the New World
(see Langdon 1974 for a survey of the field). It seems to me
that the application of this type of argumentation to problems
of Yuman syntactic reconstruction could give results which
are not supported by the structure of these languages or at
the very least would create totally unnecessary complications.
The intent of this paper, therefore, is to demonstrate the extent to which the use of word order typology both assists and
hinders the job of syntactic reconstruction. In the course
of the discussion, I will propose some slight emendations to
some proposed universals, some additional justification for

others. Since Yuman languages are all of the SOV type, the
suggestions made in this paper are meant to apply to SOV languages only, although some of our concerns may have implications for other types as well. In addition, some specific reconstructions will be proposed and justified.

The basic synchronic SOV character of Yuman languages
leaves no doubt, as can be seen from the following characteristics: the basic unmarked word order in a sentence with two
nominal arguments is SOV; insofar as they can be said to have
such categories, they have postpositions; subordinate clauses
normally precede main clauses, adverbial modifiers precede
the verb, question particles are postclitics, inflected auxiliaries follow the verb, there is a case system marked by suffixes. On the other hand, all Yuman languages also share the
following traits not usually associated with SOV typology: the
adjective follows the noun it modifies; relative clauses do
not precede their heads; prefixes predominate over suffixes.

In view of the above, it might be tempting to propose
that the non-SOV traits found in Yuman languages, particularly
the elaborate prefix system which is clearly quite old, point
to an earlier period when these languages were not SOV, but
possibly SVO, or maybe even verb initial. One might look for
confirmation of such hypothesis in other branches of the proposed Hokan stock and note with satisfaction that some of the
Chumash languages have the preferred order VOS (Beeler, 1972;
Applegate 1972). I propose to demonstrate that these conclusions are erroneous and totally unwarranted given the particular structure of Yuman languages. In fact, I will demonstrate
that the apparently aberrant features noted above are themselves a natural consequence of the SOV order, and that they

are, in fact, shared by a number of SOV languages of North
America which are not genetically related to each other in
terms of the most commonly accepted classifications.

1. The Noun + Adjective construction

The standard form of noun phrases in Yuman languages is
            Head noun + modifiers + case marker

Modifiers include the typical array of semantic modification
normally subsumed under the labels adjective, quantifier, etc.
These immediately follow the head noun. More than one modifier may be present in a single NP, but this is not overly frequent. A demonstrative element, either an independent word
or a suffix, may follow the last modifier and it, in turn may
be followed by a suffixed case marker which determines the
function of the whole NP in the matrix sentence. In other
words, an NP may be marked for case only once. Examples illustrating a variety of possibilities follow (in full sentences
the NP is underlined):

(1)   nyayuu lay-tan-ts
        thing bad-very-subj
        'bad things' (Yu-NOR)[2]

(2)   ?ava vatay-ts
        house big-sub
        'a big house' (Yu-NOR)

(3)   ?itskuruuw xamaaly-nya nyuwits-tum
        car white-dem=obj own-always
        'He owns a white car.' (Yu-NOR)

(4)   piipaa lamee-nyin-ts avesh-sh
        man tall-dem-subj run-evid
        'The tall man is running.' (Yu-LAN)

(5)   ?-ahvay havasu:-c idu:-k
      1-dress green-subj be-tns
      'My dress is green, i.e. I have a green dress.'
                              (Mo-MUN-DIS)

(6)   ?ah?a: vl^{y}tay-c
      cottonwood big-subj
      'a big cottonwood' (Mo-CRA-YT)

(7)   n^{y}awi· l^{y}cas̆
      thing little
      'a little thing' (Co-CRA-DIS)

(8)   ska· ptay
      bow big
      'a big bow' (Co-CRA-DIS)

(9)   pan milmil s̆it
      bread long=round one
      'one long and round loaf of bread' (Co-CRA-DIS)

(10) ?i·k^{w}ic peya·-c
      man this-subj
      'this man' (DiMG-LAN)

(11) nya·-c xat nyiɫy-a ?-c̆ap
      I-subj dog black-dem 1-hit
      'I hit the black dog' (DiLH-HIN)

(12) ?i?i· l^{y}ap-c mat i·ya·k
      wood burnt-subj ground lies
      'The burnt stick is on the ground.' (DiCA-LAN)

(13) kxo kak-ha
      p̃inon open-dem
      'the open p̃inon cone' (Pa-JOE)

(14) mh^{w}ata ?k^{w}aθa
      bear yellow
      'grizzly bear' (Ya-SHA-P)

(15) kwe tavsa
      thing flower
      'flower' (Ha-KOZ-DIS)

(16)   pa tai
       man old
       'old man'   (Wa-RED-M)

It should be noted immediately that the terms adjective and
quantifier are not the most appropriate characterization of
the Yuman items in question. All adjectives and quantifiers,
as well as a large number of nouns, are of verbal origin, so
that perhaps demonstratives and pronouns are the only genuine-
ly nominal elements in these languages. Nevertheless, the
constructions illustrated above definitely function as NPs in
surface structure in Yuman since they can be modified by demonstratives and marked for case. In the examples above therefore we will assume that the "adjectives" and "quantifiers"
are nominal derivatives of verb stems which are overtly marked by a variety of nominalizing morphemes which might be said
to constitute a hierarchy of more and more nominally marked
items. These will not be included in the discussion for the
sake of simplicity. On the other hand, there are many situations in which the "adjectives" and "quantifiers" illustrated above are ambiguous between verbal and nominal status, i.e.
when no demonstratives or case markers are present, so that
examples (7), (8), (9), (16) could also be interpreted as complete predications with meanings such as 'the thing is little',
etc. since the subject case marker may be omitted when no ambiguity in case function results. This observation should
make clear that these "adjectives" and "quantifiers" are genuine predicates synchronically. The can also take the overt
morphological markers of verbs, such as personal prefixes,
and various other predicating suffixes, auxiliaries, etc.
Since Yuman languages are basically SOV, it is clear that
there is a direct relation between the Noun + Adjective con-

struction and the Subject + Verb construction, that the former is derived from the latter without any change in the order of the constituents, and often without any change at all
in the form of the constituents as well, although the more normal situation is for some overt morphological marking of the
nominal structure, e.g. for case. The verbal origin of adjectives and quantifiers should come as no surprise since just
such an analysis has been proposed for many languages which
have distinct adjectival categories (e.g. English). The Yuman case, seen in this context, is simply one where the relationship is more immediately verifiable and synchronically apparent, and the placement of the adjective after its head
noun is nothing more than the retention in surface structure
of the Subject + Verb order demanded by SOV languages. It is
therefore completely consistent with SOV structure.

In addition, there is no evidence whatsoever that a different order is to be assumed for earlier stages. These languages all exhibit profuse evidence of compound nominals where
the order of elements is invariably Noun + Predicate. Some
of them are of the same type as the examples above but forming
a single "word", with reduced stress on the first element,
others have other underlying structures, such as Object +
Predicate. Some are recent and very productive. In fact,
many new cultural items introduced since European contact are
of this type. Others are obviously much older, and very old
items show signs of being this type, though some parts are no
longer independently in use as free forms. Some examples
will illustrate a variety of compound formations:[3]

   (17)   šal^{y}mak
            i·ša·ly 'hand, arm' + amak 'be behind'
            'back (body part)' (Yu-HAL-Y)

(18) ʔavu·spo
      ʔava 'house' + ?
      'abandoned house'   (Yu-HAL-Y)

(19) xi·ko·taxan
      white man + real
      'Mexican'   (Yu-LAN)

(20) humarapa:ve
      humar 'baby' u:pa: 'lie down'
      'baby cradle, lit. where the baby lies'
                           (MO-CRA-YT)

(21) <u>tadi:c-havaso m-ama:-ly-i</u>
      corn-blue 2-eat-mod-aug
      'You will eat "blue corn"'   (Mo-MUN-YT)

(22) šał^y-ckxa·p
      hand surround
      'ring'   (Co-CRA-DIS)

(23) n^{y}i·ya· cax^{w}a·t
      mouth redden
      'lipstick'   (Co-CRA-DIS)

(24) šał^y tekxap
      arm surround
      'bracelet'   (DiJ-LAN)

(25) yay u·šac
      heart stabber
      'pin, broach'   (DiJ-LAN)

(26) wi-ñmšap
      rock-white
      'a type of rock'   (Pa-JOE)

(27) qwa:q-tmar
      deer-bury
      'barbecue'   (Pa-JOE)

(28) ʔmat xca·pu
      earth split
      'tractor'   (Ki-MIX)

(29)   sal sc?irpu
        hand bunched=up
        'knuckles'   (Ki-MIX)

(30)   ?i:-tvk^{y}ala
        (wood- ?)
        'branch'   (Ya-SHA-P)

(31)   myala myula
        bread sweet
        'cake'   (Ya-SHA-P)

(32)   mat-Өuvliw
        ground- ?
        'hole'   (Ha-KOZ-DIS)

(33)   ha-kiam
        water-flow
        'river'   (Wa-RED-M)

(34)   ha-kie
        water-cross
        'bridge'   (Wa-RED-M)

(35)   ha-tu-i
        water-pull-inst
        'pump'   (Wa-RED-M)

It is safe to assume that Proto-Yuman had constructions of
this type and that no change in the order of elements is to be
postulated, since they remain in the position required by the
SOV structure, which is therefore also reconstructed for Proto-Yuman.

There are, however, some constructions that deviate from
the normal ones described above. There are, for example, NPs
with more than one demonstrative and even more than one case
marker. This is particularly common in Paipai, where sentences of the following type are found.

(36)   ñ̓e?nii muvšii-ha-Y sa-Y ya:m-i-k
        my-sister woman-dem-subj dem-subj went-also-ss
        'My sister went also.'   (Pa-JOE)

(37)   muviyay-ha-Y sa-Y rab-i-k
        (deceased-dem-subj dem-subj sick-also-ss
        'The deceased also got sick.'   (Pa-JOE)

(38)   xëma:ñlĕčkas-ha ñi?sa-? qwa:qñimay pa:-kuwi:c
        small=children-dem dem-obj milk pl.=obj-distribute=
               pl
        'For the little children they distributed milk.'
                        (Pa-JOE-OM)

This seems to be a topicalization mechanism. Thus, sentence
(36) probably really means 'As to my sister (who is the topic
of this discourse), she went also' so that the two subject
markers denote two clauses and not just one. The same interpretation would account for (37). (38) on the other hand,
might be derived from a predicate nominal construction such as
xëma:ñlĕčkas-ha ni?sa 'little children are these, these are
little children' which is then in turn used as an NP in the
matrix sentence. Note that predicate nominal[4] constructions
of just this type are found in the language, e.g.

(39)   paxmi-ha kisye
        man-dem doctor
        'The man is a doctor.'   (Pa-JOE)

The same analysis might be proposed for some Upland Yuman sentences illustrating what appears to be a similar construction,
but with the demonstrative word preceding the noun, as in

(40)   ñiθa pa-ha-c
        this-one man-dem-subj
        'this man' (Ha-KOZ-DIS)

This can be derived from a predicate nominal of the type
found for example in

(41)   ñiθa Ed
        this-one Ed
        'This one is Ed.'   (Ha-KOZ-DIS)

Because these constructions are complex and seem to be attested only in the Pai sub-group, I assume they are fairly recent innovations. Note that the Upland Yuman construction
might be evidence for a mechanism whereby the order Noun +
Modifier can be changed to Modifier + Noun in an SOV language.

2. Relative Clauses (RC)

    Yuman relative clause constructions have been discussed
in detail by Gorbet (1974), Munro (1974), Kendall (1974),
Couro and Langdon (1975), and Sundheim (1976). I will not
deal here with the question of the best analysis for these
constructions. The reader is referred to Gorbet (1974) for
a full treatment of this very interesting problem. I wish
here only to present the facts in as concise a fashion as possible. It should be noted first of all that there is no special element in Yuman that can be called a "relative marker"
as such (except for the prefix k^w- which marks some relative
clause constructions, but only when the relativized noun is
the subject of the relative clause), so that the analysis of
a sentence as containing a relative clause is based essentially on semantics, since the shape of the elements need not differ in any way from what may be other types of constructions.[5]
In addition, the item corresponding to what is traditionally
called the 'head' of the relative clause may not, except under extremely marked conditions, follow the rest of the clause,
even though this is supposed to be the standard order for SOV
languages.   In terms of word order, relative clause formation

in Yuman does not require any statement of movement at all. A
relative clause is basically a nominalized sentence, with the
internal order of elements parallelling exactly the basic order of main clauses, namely SOV. This nominalized sentence,
now acting as an NP, then appears in the matrix clause in precisely the position required by its syntactic function in
that clause. So if the RC is the subject of the main clause,
the order will be RC O V, if it is the object, it will be S
RC V. The nominal character of the RC is indicated by its
being marked with either demonstrative element or case marker
or both, these being suffixed to the last element of the
clause (i.e. the verb) as well as by some morphological modification of the verb itself, although the latter is not always required. This construction is found in all Yuman languages as the following examples will demonstrate. For clar-
ity of exposition, the RC in each sentence is underlined.

(42)   John-ts vii uutap-in-ts ava-nya tav-sh
        John-subj rock throw[nom]-dem-subj house-dem hit-
            evid

        'The rock John threw hit the house.'
                        (Yu-LAN) RC(S) O V

(43)   iipaa ava vadeny kw-tsow-nyin-ts in^y'ayts
        man house this Rel-make-dem-subj is=my=father
        'The man who built the house is my father.'
                        (Yu-LAN) RC (S) V

(44)   Mary-c John mal^{y}ki: hutav-ən^y hidaw-m
        Mary-subj John ball hit[nom]-dem catch-tns
        'Mary caught the ball John hit.'
                        (Mo-MUN) S RC (O) V

(45)   hatcoq pos̆ k^w-taver ?-iyu:-pc
        dog cat Rel-chase 1-see-tns
        'I saw the dog that chased the cat.'
                        (Mo-MUN-DIS) RC(O) V

(46) ʔin^yep ʔ-nakut ʔava: u:co:-n^y-c val^ytay-pc
me 1-father house make[nom]-dem-subj big-tns
'The house my father built is big.'
(Mo-MUN-DIS) RC(S) V

(47) ʔapa k^w-ʔas-pi-c n^yway=pit
man Rel-say[nom]-dem-subj crazy
'The man who said it is crazy'.
(Co-CRA) RC(S) V

(48) n^ymca· uyus-pin^y an^yca
mountain=lion be(=do)[nom]-dem do=too
'He did what the mountain lion did.'
(Co-CRA) RC(O) V

(49) n^yawi· yu·-ṣin^y 1-urar-m lax
thing 1=do-dem[past] neg-do-neg neg
'I don't do what I used to do.'
(Co-CRA) RC(O) V

(50) n^yaʔta·t ʔəwa· əcuw-və-c ʔəmtətay təpur-vi əwa·-s
my=father house built[nom]-dem-subj mountain top-
at is-indeed

'The house my father built is on the hill.'
(DiMG-LAN) RC(S) Loc V

(51) ʔən^ya·-c n^yaʔta·t ʔəwa· əcuw-vu ʔə-pəṣuw-s
I-subj my=father house built[nom]-dem 1-take=care=
of-indeed

'I take care of the house my father built.'
(DiMG-LAN) S RC(O) V

(52) ʔən^ya·-c ʔi·k^wic va·k n^yə-ku-ṣu·xu·-vu ʔə-məxəyay-s
I-subj man cow me-Rel-steal-dem 1-fear-indeed
'I am afraid of the man who stole a cow from me.'
(DiMG-LAN) S RC(O) V

(53) tiñur-ya qwaaq k-wii-ha-? m-ʔe:-k ʔi-k
letter-dem cattle Rel-have-dem-obj 2-give-k say-k
'Give the letter to the one who has cattle, he said.'
(Pa-JOE) O RC(IO) V

(54) kumšray sey ku-wa-ha kunaab
chief there Rel-live-dem talk
'He spoke to the chief there.' (Pa-MIX) RC(O) V

(55) naku· txpha? ?-wi?u-t pa·
      girl letter 1-give[nom]-subj leave
      'The girl I gave the letter to left.'
                  (Ki-MIX) RC(S) V

(56) pa· t-k^W-spu·w wi?t
      man things-Rel-know be
      'He is a wizard.'
                  (Ki-MIX) RC(predicate nominal V

(57) kiθarqwara qoleyawa k-ne·-ha-c ñieki+θo wa·-k
      coyote chicken Rel-kill-dem-subj tomorrow come-ss

          ono·-kəm
          will-imp

      'The coyote that killed the chicken will return to-
          morrow.' (Ya-KEN-DIS) RC(S) adverb V

(58) ña·cə Ruby k^Weta?ole ñə-?e·-wa-l ?a?a cəwo-k-uwum
      I-subj Ruby pot me-give-dem-in cactus put-ss-do
      'I put the cactus in the pot Ruby gave me.'
                  (Ya-CHU) S RC(loc) OV

(59) ña·cə m-iyure me-chenal-a ?-yo
      I-subj 2-dress 2-lose-dem 1-find
      'I found the dress you lost.'
                  (Ya-CHU) S RC(O) V

(60) ?n^Ya-c waa-n^Yə mi-yoo-va tukwe
      I-subj house-dem 2-have-dem burn=do
      'I burned your house (the house you have)'
                  (Ha-HIN) S RC(O) V

(61) olo k-ña ña ñuhatvcyu
      horse Rel-black my pet=is
      'The black horse is mine.'
                  (Ha-KOZ-DIS) RC(first NP of predicate
                      nominal) NP be

(62) kwe k-wal-wa-c...va:k
      thing Rel-feathered-dem-subj arrive
      'The feathered one arrived' (Wa-WIN-T) RC(S) V

(63)   many-a ha-k wa:-h nyituvkwanyikiny
        child-dem there-at live-dem they=killed=him
        'They killed the child living there.'
                    (Wa-WIN-T)   RC(O) V

The examples above show that this type of RC formation is
attested in all Yuman languages and therefore, I reconstruct
it for Proto-Yuman. Since it requires no movement of any of
the constituents I assume it to be the basic relative clause
construction in Proto-Yuman. I further conclude that it is
totally compatible with SOV structure. In addition to its
simplicity, this analysis also allows an easy statement of
divergent word orders which are also common and fall into the
following general categories.

1) topicalization of the relativized noun by placing it at
the beginning of the RC.   Since in many cases this is the
position it has already (e.g. sentences (43), (45), (47), (52),
(54), (55), etc.), this applies only to RCs containing both
subject and object NPs and where the object is relativized.
This process thus often has the effect of placing the relativized noun first in the sentence as well since the matrix sentence need not have an NP subject or object as the case may
be.

(64)   qwaak xatalwe uudaw-nya ?-asoo-sh
        deer coyote catch[nom]-dem 1-eat-evid
        'I ate the deer that the coyote caught.'
                    (Yu-SUN-W)

(65)   ?ava: k^{W}aθə?ide: wa:v-θ ?-iman^y-k
        house doctor be=in-dem 1-come=from-tns
        'I came from the house the doctor lives in'
                    (Mo-MUN-DIS)

(66)   nya·-c wa· ma·-pa m-ta·t caw-h-i man=?= yiw
        I-subj house you-dem 2-Fa make-dem-at come=from
        'I came from the house your father built.'
                    (DiLH-HIN)

(67)   i·pa·-si ʔña̓ʔp-t ʔ-ñu·uʔ-m ʔmat=ya·q-i yu·=qhaw
        man-a I-subj 1-kill[nom]-obj desert-in stumble
        'He stumbled on a man I killed in the desert.'
                    (Ki-MIX)

(68)   qoleyawa kiθar=qwara ne·h-a ʔ-ma·-k ʔ-ono·-kem
        chicken coyote kill-dem 1-eat-ss 1-fut-incompl
        'I am going to eat the chicken the coyote killed.'
                    (Ya-KEN-RT)

2) movement of the entire RC either to the very beginning or
to the very end of the sentence. This may or may not be accompanied by topicalization of the relativized noun as in 1). Note
that this type of structure avoids center embedding and thus
resolves a number of ambiguities and difficulties in processing for which center embedding is notorious. Thus

(69)   John-ts piilot uukwit-nya Mary-ts adaw-sh
        John-subj ball hit[nom]-dem Mary-subj catch-evid
        'The ball John hit, Mary caught it.' (Yu-SUN-W)

(70)   Mary-ts adaw-sh John-ts piilot uukwit-nya
        Mary-subj catch-evid John-subj ball hit[nom]-dem
        'Mary caught it, the ball John hit.'   (Yu-SUN-W)

(71)   ʔipa m-u:yu:m-n^y ʔin^{y}ec ʔ-iyu:-pc-m
        man 2-see=neg-dem I 1-see-tns-tns
        'The man you didn't see, I saw him.'   (Mo-MUN-DIS)

(72)   ʔ-su:paw-k-e hatcoq m-ətav-n^y
        1-know-tns-aug dog 2-hit-dem
        'I know which dog you hit.' (Mo-MUN-DIS)

(73)   xat ku-mespac-bo ma·-c mə-ţim-bə-cu
        dog Rel-dead[nom]-dem you-subj 2-shoot-dem-Q
        'Is that the dead dog you shot?' (DiCa-LAN)

(74)   ʔen^{y}a·-c ʔ-u·ya·w ʔi·k^{w}ic nyə-ku-x^{w}ic-vu
        I-subj 1-know man me-Rel-hate[nom]-dem
        'I know the man who hates me.'   (DiMG-LAN)

(75)   k^{W}aq=matuyak ?-nax ?i?i· pa nal-u-ha-m
       deer 1-kill stick bullet fall-nom-dem-with
       'I killed the deer with the stick the bullet struck.'
                              (Pa-MIX)

3) the "head" may be separated from the rest of the RC
which then appears sentence final, as an afterthought, in
which case both the "head" and the rest of the clause are likely to be marked separately as NPs by either demonstratives or
case or both.

(76)   ?avu:ya-n^y ?-talaθ-m m-su:pet-m-n^y
       door-dem 1-bump-tns 2-close-neg-dem
       'I bumped into the door you didn't close.'
                              (Mo-MUN-DIS)

(77)   mashxay-en-ts anyoor=nyiinyaytum Florida kwi-teemp-
       girl-dem-subj write=to=us Florida Rel-move-

            en-ts
            dem-sub

       'The girl writes to us, who moved to Florida.'
                              (Yu-SUN-W)

(78)   nya·-c ?i·pac ?-u·ya·w siny kw-atra·p
       I-subj man 1-know woman Rel-beat
       'I know the man who beats his wife.'   (DiBL-LAN)

(79)   ñi-bok-m ?paa-ha-Y šu?uuy-uli-v qwaaq k-wii-ha-Y
       when-rain-ds people-dem-subject happy-very-pl cattle-
            Rel-have-dem-subj

       'When it rains, the people are very happy who have
            cattle.'   (Pa-JOE)

It should be pointed out that the three variant orders can be
accounted for quite easily as long as the constructions illustrated in (42)-(63) are considered basic, the first two as facilitating interpretation and avoiding center embedding, the
third as after-thoughts, which incidentally, also avoid center embedding. If any other construction were considered basic, accounting for the common RC types in (42)-(63) would

be difficult and counter-intuitive. This should conclusively
prove the primacy of the RC type with no movement. Since
the variant orders are attested in each of the major subgroups,
their existence in Proto-Yuman can also be proposed, although
it is likely that such movements are of a completely general
character and thus not restricted to RCs. A word of caution
is in order on what is meant by proposing the existence of certain reconstructed sentence types. The abundance of examples
of RCs illustrated above might be interpreted to mean that
these sentence types are very common in Yuman. In point of
fact, the only instances of RCs which are very common in texts
are those where the RC is the only overt NP in the sentence,
and has itself no more than one overt NP argument, often none
at all. The reasons for this are not far to seek. Contexts
in which all the arguments are overtly specified as separate
NPs are not easy to imagine, since pronominal reference (overt
or covert) on the verb is all that is required in Yuman. Fully
specified arguments then would be appropriate only where none
of them have been previously introduced in the discourse and
for some reason they must be introduced all at once. Most sentences cited above are in a sense unnatural, as they were elicited by linguists for the express purpose of obtaining instances
of RCs in Yuman. Speakers of these languages differ considerably with respect to the ease with which they comply, since
other constructions besides RCs are available to convey essentially the same semantic content. The proposed reconstruction thus assumes only that the mechanisms underlying the formation of RCs were a part of the productive processes of Proto-
Yuman, and not that sentences containing the full complexities
of the cited examples were in common use.

One negative observation is also worth making. Of all
the possible movements the one most conspicuous by its absence
is that which would produce the kind of RC which has been assumed to be most likely for SOV languages, namely where the
head follows the RC.   The only construction which shows anything that could conceivably be interpreted as a following
head is illustrated below.

(80)   i·pac a·k wi·-m tuc-pu a·k-pu sin^y-c wyaw
         man bone rock-with hit[nom]-dem bone-dem woman-subj
         find

         'The woman found the bone that the man hit the rock
         with.'   (DiIV-GOR-DIS)

Not only is this the only genuine example of this type I am
aware of, but the second instance of the word 'bone'   a·k
clearly must be a repetition of real head (note that both it
and the preceding RC are marked by a demonstrative suffix
so that they represent two separate NPs) necessitated by the
ambiguity of the sentence as a whole, since the woman could
have found either the bone or the rock. The example is, however, instructive since it points to a possible mechanism
whereby Yuman languages could develop an RC with following
head.   I would like to suggest that Yuman languages provide
evidence for the fact that not only are non-final heads in
compatible with SOV structure, they can be seen to be a very
natural consequence of the SOV order.   To make things more interesting, I would like to suggest that RCs of the Yuman type
are in fact the most normal type of RC to be expected in SOV
languages and that these are probably the earliest kinds of
RCs these languages develop.   In support of this claim which
is subject to empirical refutation, I would like to mention
the great frequency of this type of RC in North American lan-

guages with SOV order, namely Navajo (Athapaskan) (Platero, 1974), Lakota (Siouan) (Taylor and Rood, to appear), Tunica (Macro-Algonkian) (Haas, 1941), where the following head RC is either not attested or very marginal at best (to my knowledge, only Navajo among these languages has some trace of it). I also would like to point out that Kuroda (1974) has demonstrated the existence of the Yuman-type of RCs in Classical Japanese, where they coexist with the better known type. He has also demonstrated (Kuroda, 1976) that head-internal RCs still exist in present-day Japanese, but in more restricted contexts and with more specialized meanings than the head-final type, which seems to indicate that they are losing their productivity in present-day Japanese. Whether they are the older construction remains of course unproven at this point.

One last point needs to be made in connection with RCs. It was noted above that only those RCs where the subject is relativized are unambiguously marked as such by a prefix k^w-. Not only are these RCs more common than all others, they are also obviously extremely old, since many Yuman nouns seem to be old $\underline{k}^w$- forms for which no synchronically remaining verb source can be found. It is therefore suggested that these represent the most unambiguous case of RC in Yuman. This confirms the observation that cross-linguistically, subjects relativize with greater ease than any other arguments, and that relativization may be limited to subjects in some languages.[6] Non-$\underline{k}^w$- marked RCs could then be interpreted as special cases of the more general process of nominalization from which they are indistinguishable formally. A few examples from Diegueño will demonstrate the formal similarity.

(81)   ?ə-suw-x-və-c nyuk pam-cu
        1-cat[pl]-irr-dem-subj already arrive-Q
        'Is it time to eat yet? (lit. our future eating, has
            it arrived already?)'   (DiMG-LAN)

(82)   mə-mic-pu kə-pəṣkwi?
        2-cry[nom]-dem imper-stop
        'Stop your crying!'   (DiBL-LAN)

(83)   ?nya·-c ?-u·ya·w ma·-c nyəm-a·rap-x-bo
        I-subj 1-know you-subj you/me-hit-irr-dem
        'I know that you are going to hit me.'
                                (DiBL-LAN)

Note that these can with various degrees of felicity be translated by the equivalent of a headless relative clause; thus
(81) could be paraphrased 'that which we will eat, ...', (82)
'...the fact that you are crying', (83) '...the fact that you
are going to hit me.' Sentences like (81)-(83) are totally
natural and are spontaneous utterances by native speakers
with no prompting by the linguist. It is in fact suggested
that the complex RCs illustrated earlier in this paper are
modelled on these constructions are are essentially the same
with the only difference that more of the nominal arguments
are overtly present as nouns.

    To summarize the first part of this paper, it is clear
that in Yuman languages, the order of elements in the Noun +
Adjective construction and in the head internal relative
clause are a direct consequence of their basic structure as
both constructions are derived directly from underlying sentences with no change in the order of elements. Not only is
this compatible with SOV structure, but it seems to be the
most natural and, I propose, the first type of adjectives and
RCs that such languages develop. Again, Yuman is not uniqu-
in this respect and the parallels between the two construc-

tions hold for Navajo, Lakota, and Tunica.

3. Possessive Constructions

We might now consider whether other constructions of Yuman are equally well motivated by their SOV structure. One
construction which at first sight does not seem so obviously
motivated, though it does follow the normally observed order
in SOV languages is the possessive, where the order is <u>Posses-
sor noun + Item possessed</u>. The possessor is typically unmarked,
and the possessed takes personal prefixes, so that a phrase
meaning, say 'the man's hat', is more literally translated
'the man his-hat'. Once more, there is evidence in Yuman
that some possessed items at least are verbal elements. Thus,
Halpern (1942) has demonstrated conclusively that the kinship
terms of Yuma are true verbs, so that the concept "father" is
more correctly interpreted in Yuma as 'to call someone father'
or 'to have as a father'. The use of a kinship term in its
true verbal function is illustrated by

(84)   mak^{y}e-c n^y-ašuc-mə-k
        anyone-subj he/me-call=younger=brother-privative-tns
        'Nobody calls me younger brother.' (Yu-HAL-KT)

The noun is then derived from the verb in the same manner as
adjectives are so derived and ašuc, normally translated 'his
younger brother' more literally means 'whom he calls younger
brother' and the possessor noun when present precedes because
it is the underlying subject of the sentence, e.g. 'whom <u>the
boy</u> calls younger brother'. I believe there is some less obvious evidence for analyzing all possessed constructions in
the same manner. The demonstration of this claim would be
too complex and lengthy and will be presented in a separate
paper.

4. Verbal Prefixes

Yuman verb prefix morphology may be summarized as follows.
A verb stem consists of a root often preceded by one or more
"instrumental" prefixes, which denote such things as the shape
of the object or instrument involved in the action, the body
part used as instrument, and various other less easily defined
notions. These are derivational prefixes. Their phonological shape is typically a single segment, most commonly a consonant. They are also quite old and several are reconstructible for Proto-Yuman (Langdon, 1968). Verb stems are then inflected for person by the use of person prefixes denoting subject and object. Langdon and Hinton (1976) have shown
that the order of prefixes is essentially Object-Subject and
that they are historically the result of the incorporation of
pronominal forms into the verb prefix structure in reduced destressed form. The object-subject order is a result of two
waves of pronoun incorporation, and can be accounted for once
more by the basic SOV order of the languages. The first wave
is one of subject pronoun incorporation in constructions where
only a subject pronoun was present (i.e. all intransitive
verbs and also the most common use of transitive verbs where
a third person object is known and unstated since there are
basically no third person pronouns), and therefore the subject
immediately precedes the verb. Once subject-marked verbs are
established as word units, the stage is set for the next wave
of incorporation, that of object pronouns which by virtue of
the OV order now come to stand directly before the verb inflected for subject and then become prefixed to it in unstressed form. This explanation for the order of person prefixes
on verbs in SOV languages may be valid for other languages as

well, e.g. Navajo, and Lakota Sioux, which exhibit the same
order of pronominal prefixes.

There is ample evidence that the process of incorporation
of a nominal element into a verb stem as a prefix has been an
active process in the history of Yuman languages. Following
the incorporation of personal pronouns, additional waves of
nominal incorporation produced in Yuman languages a number of
discontinuous verb stems consisting of a prefix deriving from
such a source plus an ordinary verb stem. The personal pronominal prefixes are infixed between the nominal prefix and the
stem. In some cases, the nominal prefix can no longer be omitted.[7] Once more this prefixation is a direct result of the
OV structure since these stems derive from constructions where
the nominal to be incorporated functioned as some sort of object and therefore appeared in the sentence directly before
the inflected verb. Most common as incorporated nominals are
various demonstratives, indefinites, and some body parts. Examples:

<u>Demonstratives:</u>

va...adu 'be thus', va...awi 'do thus', va...aʔi 'say thus',
sa...awi 'do thus', sa...adi· 'come thus' (Yu-HAL-Y)
v...aʔwi: 'do this way', v...idu: 'be this way', v...iʔi·
'say this way' (Mo-MUN-DIS)
pa...wa 'be located here', pu...wa 'be located there' sa...
yi· 'come along there' (Co-CRA-DIS)
pa...wi· 'do that', pa...i·'say that', pa...wa· 'be located
here' (Di-LAN-GR)
ñuv...ʔi· 'say thus', ñuv...wi 'do thus', ñuv...yu 'come
along thus' (Pa-JOE-DIS)
ñuva...ʔi 'say it' (Ya-SHA-P)

Indefinites:

av...ado 'do whatever', av...a?i· 'say whatever', ka...awi
'do what', ka...l^{y}avi· 'resemble what' (Yu-HAL-Y)
k..idu: 'be how', k..i?i: 'say how', k..a?wi: 'do how'
(Mo-MUN-DIS)
ka..yu 'perhaps', kt̲..?i 'be how' (Co-CRA-DIS)
m..yu· 'be how, mawi· 'do what' (this has become a true
stem and takes personal prefixes before the indefinite) (Di-
LAN-GR)
kav...?i 'say what', kav..wi 'do what', kav..yu 'get along
how' (Pa-JOE-DIS)
kav..yu 'be how' (Ha-KOZ-DIS), ka..yu 'be how' (Wa-RED-M)

Unspecified object:

?ac..kana·v 'tell about things', ?ac...tapuy 'kill things'
(Yu-HAL-Y)
?ic..ma 'eat things' (Mo-MUN-DIS) ?ǝc...yu·w 'sing' (Di-
LAN-GR),
?ic..ma: 'eat things', ?ic..ñe: 'hunt things' (Pa-JOE-DIS),
?c..ñe 'hunt things' (Ya-SHA-P),
kwe..ñe 'hunt things' (Wa-WIN-WS), kwe..θo 'eat hard
things' (Ya-SHA-P)

Body part:

do...alaw 'turn one's head', do..atar 'be blind', do..n^{y}ame·
'be dizzy' (cf. i·do 'eye') ya..kapet̲ 'be crazy', ya..ša·l
'to crave' (cf. i·ya· 'mouth'), wa..ada· 'be excited',
wa..kavar 'to desire' (cf. i·wa· 'heart') (Yu-HAL-Y)
wa...apet 'to forget', ya..a?a·v 'to understand', ya..kapet
'be drunk' (Mo-MUN-DIS)
wa...ši·v 'to think', wa..yi·v 'to hurry', wa..yaw 'to

fool', way..pem 'be drunk', šal..i·kwis 'to shake hands'
(cf. šal 'hand') (Pa-JOE-DIS), wa..si·v 'to think' (Ya-
SHA-P)

More interesting yet are nominal elements incorporated into
the verb stem with full case markers.

n^{y}i-k..adi· (dem-loc-come), 'come from there', ?ac-k..u·va
'stay at places', n^{y}a-m..axav 'enter thereby', da-m..ayu·v
(eye-by means of..see) 'be plain, evident', xa-1^y..ašuc
(water-in..?) 'to sweat' (Yu-HAL-Y)
xa-1..skwil (water-in..?) 'to wash head' (Pa-JOE-DIS)

Finally, there are stems of this type where the incorporated
element is a bare case marker:

al^y..adi (in..lie) 'to lie in it', al^y..tadu·n 'to dip it
into' (Yu-HAL-Y)
m..xavik (with..be two) 'be together with' (Yu-NOR)
1^y..n^{y}avay 'live in it', el^y..u·nu 'be around in there'
(Mo-MUN)
m..xu:wa:k 'be two with' (Pa-JOE)

Much of this appears to be fairly recent as attested by the
fact that the formations are not comparable point for point
across the languages, and also in some cases have been recorded only in recent work. This affords an opportunity to gain
insight into the mechanics of this incorporation and its syntactic consequences. Halpern (1947), who was first to note
these prefixes for Yuma, states that they occur on a verb only
if no overt noun bearing the case marker is present, so that
the incorporation is due to a stranded case marker with no
overt noun to be suffixed to being attracted to the only other
possible full form, namely the following verb. It is very

likely that this was indeed the only initial possibility, but
since then examples have been recorded of the case prefix on
the verb even if a full NP is present to carry the case, and
even some with the case marker both on the NP and on the verb.
The most peculiar of these cases is that where the case marker
appears on the verb and not on the preceding noun where it
presumably belongs. Some aspects of this are discussed in
Munro (1975) in connection with the comitative construction.

   (85)   Tri:ni šwaar-uli-k Sa:m mə-xu:wa:k ʔapa:šwaarč
           Trini sing-much-tns Sam with-be=two old=song
           'Trini sang a lot of old-style songs with Sam.'
               (Pa-MUN-CC)

   (86)   ʔava m-u:co:-n^y 1^y-ʔ-n^{y}avay-k
           house 2-make-dem in-1-live-tns
           'I live in the house you built.'   (Mo-MUN-CC)

   (87)   John ʔ-ma-xvik Yuma ʔ-eniyem-š
           John 1-with-be=two Yuma 1-go=pl-evid
           'John and I went to Yuma, i.e. I, being two with
             John, we went to Yuma.'   (Yu-NOR)

Note that in (87), instead of the person prefix appearing between the case marker and the stem, it is now prefixed to the
whole thing. This is obviously an analogical formation which
makes the new stem behave like ordinary verb stems, with the
person markers prefixed. Such fluctuation is attested in other instances of this type of stem, and may give a clue to the
manner in which additional prefixes get to be added to a stem.
The ease with which speakers of these languages produce such
forms suggests that the process has occurred also in earlier
times.

    The syntactic result of this kind of resegmentation is
that new verb stems are developed incorporating semantically
the content of the case marker and thus behaving syntactically

as new transitive verbs. The NP which previously required a
case marker is now unmarked, in the object case, and the case
system is changed. The synchronic state where both structures
cooccur presents some serious problems of analysis.

While the order of elements in the sentence reveals the
manner in which these resegmentations have occurred, it does
not give a motivated reason for why this should have happened
at all. The answer lies in some phonological properties of
Yuman languages which combine with the word order to produce
these new verb stems. Yuman words typically have stress on
the last syllable, more precisely the root, and suffixes occur only as syntactic markers. The processes described above
are clearly ways the languages use to keep the word-final
stress whenever possible by reanalyzing suffixed material as
belonging phonologically to the next word, where one more prefix is completely tolerable.

At first sight, this may appear counter-intuitive, since
this resegmentation occurs at a major syntactic boundary, between an oblique complement and the verb. This situation is,
however, attested in other languages as well. Note that the
well-known cliticization of English auxiliaries in sentences
such as 'I've done it.', 'He'll sing.' is exactly like the Yuman case except in the other direction. It is interesting to
note in this connection that instrumental studies performed
on English sentences (Lea, 1976) reveal that there are intonational correlates to major syntactic constituents, but that
their boundaries cannot be identified on the basis of the physical signal. The Yuman facts suggest that this is the case
in Yuman as well. Investigators of Yuman languages have often
noted the difficulty of determining word boundaries in connect-

ed discourse. More interesting yet is the fact that native speakers, even linguistically sophisticated ones, have difficulties making this kind of judgment as well.

We may therefore conclude that nominal incorporation in various forms was and still is an important process of syntactic change in Yuman and can be accounted for by the combined pressures of the SOV order and the partciular stress patterns of the languages. The question can therefore be asked whether the complex prefix systems of Yuman verb stems are also the result of such incorporation, at a greater time depth. I am concerned in particular with the previously mentioned "instrumental prefixes", a number of which are clearly reconstructible as already being prefixes in Proto-Yuman, so that their antiquity leaves no doubt. This is a difficult question. As mentioned earlier, these elements typically consist of only a single segment and attempts to relate these to some overtly nominal elements are of rather dubious validity. There are, however, some clues that point to such connection, though much more work needs to be done in this area. For example, there is a morpheme associated with plurality which is either prefixed to the verb stem or infixed into the prefix structure, which has a shape that can be reconstructed as *č (~*t in some specifiable phonological environments) and which Munro (1976, 3.331) has related to the "unspecified object" prefix ʔič illustrated above. She has suggested also (Munro, 1976, 3.54) that the same origin may be arguable for the causative prefixes *č and *t. In addition, it should be noted that the so-called "instrumental" prefixes usually involve some semantic notion of causation as well, and represent a device for producing transitive verbs from intransitive roots. The parallelism to the recent developments described above is strik-

ing. It should be noted also that these prefixes represent
the only general process for producing causatives in Yuman
languages. The possible nominal origin of at least some of
them may in fact provide an explanation for the fact that Yuman languages produce causatives by prefixation rather than
by suffixation as is more normal for SOV languages where causatives may be formed by predicate raising and should therefore appear as suffixes, a position which all other auxiliary
elements take in Yuman.

The basic simplicity of the processes needed to explain
the aspects of Yuman structure described above coupled with
the naturalness of these processes both from a syntactic and
a phonological point of view are obviously totally compatible
with an ancient SOV structure. The widespread occurrence of
features of this type in SOV languages of North America suggests at the very least an important areal generalization,
and probably widespread applicability to other SOV languages
as well.

In general outline, the processes described for Yuman
languages confirm much of current thought concerning syntactic change. It is particularly compatible with the point of
view most succinctly expressed by Givón (1971), namely that
today's morphology is yesterday's syntax. Within that view,
it seems to me that the most important task to be undertaken
for specific language families is the determination of how
much of today's morphology is still today's syntax and, conversely, how much of yesterday's morphology is still yesterday's morphology.

Notes

1. My work on comparative Yuman syntax is supported by NSF grant SOC74-18043 "Yuman languages of the Southwest". I wish to thank Pamela Munro, Susan Norwood, Don Crook, Sandra Chung, and Yuki Kuroda for many interesting discussions on Yuman and other syntactic problems, and to acknowledge my ever more deeply-felt intellectual indebtedness to Mary Haas, especially on matters dealing with the history of American Indian languages. Yuman languages still spoken are as follows. The most commonly accepted sub-grouping is indicated. Abbreviations of language names as shown will be used throughout to identify the language in example sentences.

   a. River group: Yuma (Yu), Mojave (Mo), Maricopa (Ma)

   b. Delta-California group: Cocopa (Co), Diegueño (Di)

   c. Pai group: i. Upland: Walapai (Wa), Yavapai (Ya), Havasupai (Ha)

                ii. Paipai (Pa)

   d. Kiliwa (Ki)

2. Abbreviations used in the morpheme-by-morpheme analysis should be obvious to any linguist. Those that may not be so immediately evident are: ss = same subject marker, ds = different subject marker, nom = special nominalized form of a verb stem, evid = evidential. The coded abbreviations following each cited sentence are to be interpreted as follows. First comes the language abbreviation using the first two letters of the language name. Next come the first three letters of the author of the source, then a conventional abbreviation of the work the sentence is specifically quoted from (the absence of the last item in the code indicates that the source consists of unpublished field notes). The full reference is

found in the reference section where the code is repeated for
easy identification.

3. The forms exemplified here are defined as compounds
on rather loose grounds; either they are so identified by the
source, or they are written as one word, or they have a meaning which is more than the sum of the parts. No special significance should be attached to the fact that some are written
as one word, some as two.

4. See Pamela Munro's contribution to this volume for a
discussion of predicate nominal constructions in Yuman.

5. A similar problem is discussed by Hale (1976) for
several Australian languages.

6. As discussed in particular in Keenan and Comrie
(1972).

7. Such stems thus represent an exception to Greenberg's
(1963) Universal 28, which states that if both inflection and
derivation are marked before the root, the derivation is always between the inflection and the root. The tendency for Yuman languages to reshape such stems to fit the more common
pattern does, however, support the generality of Greenberg's
observation. Note that Yuman languages are also a counterexample to Universal 38 which states that the only case that
ever has only zero allomorphs is the one which includes among
its meanings that of the subject of the intransitive verb. In
Yuman, these subjects are marked by the ordinary subject morpheme -č, and only objects are always zero marked.

References

Applegate, Richard B. Ineseño Chumash Grammar. Ph.D. dissert-
    ation (UC Berkeley) 1972.

Beeler, Madison S. "Word order in Barbareño Chumash" paper
    read at AAA meeting 1972.

Chung, Sandra. Unpublished field notes on Yavapai. (Ya-CHU)

Couro, Ted and Margaret Langdon. Let's Talk 'Iipay Aa. Ball-
    ena Press and Malki Museum Press. 1975.

Crawford, James. The Cocopa Language. Ph.D. dissertation (UC
    Berkeley) 1966. (Co-CRA-DIS)

_____ Unpublished data on Cocopa. (Cro-CRA)

Crawford, Judith. "Seven Mohave Texts", in Yuman Texts IJAL-
    NATS. 1(3).31-42 (1976). (Mo-CRA-YT)

Givón, Talmy. "Historical Syntax and Synchronic Morphology:
    An Archaeologist's Field Trip." CLS 7.394-415 (1971).

Gorbet, Larry. Relativization and Complementation in Diegueño:
    Noun Phrases as Nouns. Ph.D. dissertation (UCSD) 1974.
    (Di-GOR-DIS)

Greenberg, Joseph. "Some Universals of Grammar with Particu-
    lar Reference to the Order of Meaningful Elements." In
    Universals of Language, Greenberg, ed., MIT Press. 1963.

Haas, Mary. Tunica. Handbook of American Indian Languages,
    Vol. IV. J. J. Augustin, New York. 1941.

Hale, Kenneth. "The adjoined relative clause in Australia."
    in Grammatical Categories in Australian Languages (P.M.W.
    Dixon, ed.), Canberra, Australian Institute of Aboriginal

Studies. 1976.

Halpern, A. M. "Yuma Kinship Terms." AA 44.425-441 (1942).
     (Yu-HAL-KT)

_____ "Yuma." IJAL 12 (1946), 13 (1947). (Yu-HAL-
     Y)

Hinton, Leanne. Unpublished data on La Huerta Diegueño (DiLH-
     HIN) and Havasupai (Ha-HIN).

Joel, Judith. Paipai Phonology and Morphology. Ph.D. dis-
     sertation (UCLA), 1966.

_____ "Some Notes on Paipai Object Order and Object-
     Marking," Proceedings of the First Yuman Workshop. James
     E. Redden (Ed), 7:142-148 (1976). (Pa-JOE-W)

_____ Unpublished field notes on Paipai. (Pa-JOE)

Keenan, Edward and Bernard Comrie. "Noun phrase accessibility
     and universal grammar." 1972 unpublished ms.

Kendall, Martha. Selected problems in Yavapai Syntax. Ph.D.
     dissertation (Indiana) 1972. (Ya-KEN-DIS)

_____ "Relative clause formation and topicalization
     in Yavapai," IJAL 40.89-101 (1974). (Ya-KEN-RT)

Kozlowski, Edwin. Havasupai simple sentences. Ph.D. dissert-
     ation (Indiana) 1970. (Ha-KOZ-DIS)

Kuroda, S.-Y. "Pivot-independent relativization in Japanese
     (I)", Papers in Japanese Linguistics 3.59-93 (1974).

_____ "Headless relative clauses in Modern Japanese
     and the relevancy condition", to appear in the proceed-
     ings of the second meeting of the Berkeley Linguistic
     Society, 1976.

Langdon, Margaret. A Grammar of Diegueño: The Mesa Grande
    Dialect. UCPL 66 (1970). (Di-LAN-GR)

_____ "Proto-Yuman verb morphology", paper read
    at AAA meeting, 1968.

_____ Comparative Hokan-Coahuiltecan Studies: A
    Survey and Appraisal. Janua Linguarum, Series Critica 4
    (1974).

_____ Unpublished field notes on Yuma (Yu), Mesa
    Grande Diegueño (DiMG), Baron Long Diegueño (DiBL), Jamul
    Diegueño (DiJ), Campo Diegueño (DiCA).

Langdon Margaret and Leanne Hinton. "Object-subject pronominal
    prefixes in La Huerta Diegueño", in Hokan Studies, Janua
    Linguarum, Series Practica 181.113-128 (1976).

Lea, Wayne. "Acoustic correlates of stress and juncture: a
    systematic testing of alternative hypotheses", paper pre-
    sented at the Symposium on Stress and Accent, 1976.

Li, Charles. Word Order and Word Order Change. Texas 1975.

Mixco, Mauricio. Unpublished data on Kiliwa. (Ki-MIX)

Munro, Pamela. Mojave Syntax. Garland Publishing, 1976.
    (Mo-MUN-DIS)

_____ "Comitative conjunction: a syntactic reinter-
    pretation in Yuman", paper read at LSA Winter 1975.   (Mo-
    MUN-CC)

_____ "Two stories by Nellie Brown", Yuman Texts
    IJAL-NATS 1(3).43-50 (1976). (Mo-MUN-YT)

Norwood, Susan. Unpublished field notes on Yuma. (Yu-NOR)

Platero, Paul R. "The Navajo relative clause", IJAL 40.202-

246 (1974).

Redden, James. "Walapai II: morphology", IJAL 32.141-163.
(Wa-RED-M)

Shaterian, Alan. Yavapai Phonology. Unpublished ms. (Ya-
SHA-P)

Sundheim, Beth. "Internal and external heads in Kwtsaan relative clauses". Proceedings of the First Yuman Workshop.
James E. Redden (Ed.), 7:88-92 (1976). (Yu-SUN-W)

Taylor, Allan and David Rood. "Lakhóta", to appear in Volume
XV of North American Indians, Smithsonian Institution.

Winter, Werner. "Yuman Languages II -- Wolf's Son -- A Walapai Text", IJAL 32.17-40 (1966). (Wa-WIN-WS)

_____ Walapai Texts, transcribed by Christel Jarr
Butcher, unpublished ms. (Wa-WIN-T)

6 Motivations for Extraciation in Old English

Robert P. Stockwell

The earliest Germanic documentation (the early Runic In-scriptions) indicate that Proto-Germanic was SOV in main clauses. This has been the 'received position' since the time of the Neo-Grammarians (see, e.g., McKnight 1893). What has not been documented is the transitional sequence between Gmc. SOV order and MnE (X)SVO order (V-3rd; i.e., in an unmarked statement V is preceded at least by subject and optionally by another constituent such as adverb). An appealing hypothesis about these intermediate steps, but one which may not be sus-ceptible to complete verification in the existing documenta-tion, is the following sequence of stages (a) through (e):

(a) FIRST STAGE: vSO(V) variants arise by a rule that I shall call COMMENT FOCUSING.[1] The rule may have been inherited from IE, since VSO variants must have existed (they are the early norm in Celtic and, to a lesser extent, in Slavic); or in Gmc. it may have been extended from a narrower function such as the imperative or presentative. This rule would code some semantic content such as 'vivid-ness' of action: i.e., the action, not the partici-pants, would be primary in the expression. Heusler (1931:168) speaks of VSO order in OIc. as the 'mov-ing' order ('bewegt' as distinct from 'ruhend'). McKnight (138) speaks of it as 'dramatic' or 'pa-

thetic' (= inducing feeling). Both Haiman 1974
(for Icelandic) and Givón 1976a,b (for Hebrew,
Spanish, and several Bantu languages) assume VSO
as intermediate between SOV and SVO.[2] It is not
clear that McKnight assumed VSO as the first stage,
but the subsequent stages are reasonably clear in
his exposition of SOV → SVO. We can summarize this
first step by the formula:

$$\text{SO(V)v} \xrightarrow{\text{COM FOC}} \text{vSO(V)}$$

where v = modal, have, be/become, finite V (prob-
         ably a restricted set of V, such as V of
         motion)
       S = subject
       O = object/verb complements
       (V)= optional non-finite verb

(b)   SECOND STAGE: The heightened vividness -- the al-
       most exclamatory character -- of vSOV sentences is
       contextualized by explicit LINKING words (then,
       there):

$$\text{vSO(V)} \xrightarrow{\text{LINK}} \text{xvSO(V)}$$

where x = then, there, etc.

    I take it that this linking construction is
the origin of V-2nd sentences in OE. If we assume
also a rule of TOPICALIZATION, by which NP's as
well as adverbs are moved into this initial slot,
we produce the TVX structure discussed by Vennemann 1974b; it is also the V-2nd structure of

Haiman; and it is the 'indirect' order of McKnight.
The latter's discussion of topicalization is in-
sightful -- though, like everyone who has looked
at the question, he finds the rise in several Gmc.
dialects, and ultimate stabilization in German, of
the V-2nd constraint 'difficult of explanation'
(214). About topicalization, he writes:

> 'This general subjective order in the progres-
> sion of ideas is from the known to the un-
> known. Of a thing known, something new, un-
> known, is predicated. That the new idea may
> be connected with ideas already in mind, the
> speaker begins with something known.' (138)

But later, explaining why V follows the topic immediately (producing V-2nd), he argues much less
persuasively about motivation for V-2nd:

> 'The verb is closely connected in thought
> with the initial word or phrase, and is ac-
> cordingly placed next to it. That such con-
> nection is the determining principle is proved
> by... [the fact] ... that inversion is rela-
> tively more frequent after an initial predi-
> cate word than after an object.' (215)

Haiman throws up his hands on this matter. Starting from Wackernagel, whose claim that V-2nd was
found in PGmc. and originated in PIE to differentiate main from subordinate clauses is vigorously
disputed by McKnight (217), Haiman first rejects
the Wackernagel claim that V-2nd developed from

the 2nd-position enclisis rule for clitics in IE
(Wackernagel's Law) on the grounds that precisely
those languages which had this clitic rule <u>never</u>
<u>became</u> V-2nd languages (Sanskrit, Greek). He then
concludes:

> 'If there are any general structure features
> or principles which determined these ... [V-
> 2nd] developments, they elude me.' (148)

Vennemann argues that TVX (of which, according to
him, there are two types, only one of which has
the V-2nd constraint; but only this type is discussed further so that one may as well read TVX =
V-2nd) is the stage intermediate between SOV and
SVO, but he does not speculate about how the finite verb came to appear in second position -- he
assumes that it functions to set off the topic, and
that no further explanation is needed: presumably,
he assumes it was moved into that position by some
rule. This is, however, not a trivial gap in his
explanation: it is one thing to speculate about
the need to mark off a topic, another to show how
and why a particular device comes to be used for
that purpose. He explicitly claims that VSO is a
possible subsequent, but <u>not</u> prior, stage relative to TVX:

> 'An SXV language whose substantive S-O mark-
> ing is affected in this way [i.e. partially
> destroyed by sound change], will first devel-
> op into a TVX language, where the finite verb
> is used to mark off the topic(s) T, then fur-

ther into an SVX language by specializing T
to the primary topic case, S. The language
may change further into a VSX language, under
conditions which I have not yet investigated.'
(1974a:15)

(c)   THIRD STAGE: Among the V-2nd sentences with topic-
      alization or linkage, two sub-types occur with suf-
      ficient frequency to provide a basis for abduction
      of a new word-order rule:

      (i)   Those in which, as Vennemann notes above,
            topic is specialized to the primary topic
            case, namely the subject: i.e. TVX = SVO.

      (ii) Those in which the finite verb is simple so
            that there is no remnant of a complex verb in
            the final position: i.e. SvO(V) = SVO.

(d)   FOURTH STAGE: Verb-final variants of the SvOV var-
      iety are destroyed by exbraciation (Vennemann's
      term [1974b], though the concept, in a weaker form,
      goes far back in the tradition of German syntactic
      studies). That is, rightward movement takes place
      to eliminate nominal and adverbial elements from
      within the brace [v...V], thus reunifying the aux-
      iliaries and main verbs:

$$SvO(V) \rightarrow Sv(V)O$$

(e)   FINAL STAGE: If there is a differentiation be-
      tween main and subordinate-clause order (which was
      never fully implemented in OE), it is destroyed by
      analogical spread (generalization) of main-clause
      order into non-main clauses. (This turns out to be

factually dubious: according to Bean 1976, the
SVO word order of subordinate clauses was fully
grammaticized before matters had settled down in
main clauses. It is at least possible that the
analogy went the other way, therefore. In any
case, with the exception of þa clauses (then vs.
when), the correlation between clause type and
word order was not a simple matter of main vs. subordinate.)

Summarizing this account we have

(a) SO(V)v → vSO(V) by Comment Focusing
(b) vSO(V) → xvSO(V) by Linkage or Topicalization
(c) TvX(V) → SvX(V) by Subject = Topic
(d) SvX(V) → SvVX by Exbraciation
(e) Subordinate Order → Main Order by Generalization
     (or, at least, elimination of whatever differences
     existed)

The first stage is only weakly supported by the available evidence, since there is already linkage in most of the
examples (figures are given below). The SOV proto-stage is
supported by data studies from the end of the 19th century
(in particular McKnight) to quite recently and still on-going
(Smith 1971, Lehmann 1974, Canale in progress, Bean 1976). We
would like to find evidence that there really was a V-1st alternate co-existing with SOV, however. There is evidence that
other IE languages had such an alternate (Celtic, Slavic --
see Ard 1975), but the Gmc. evidence is very slender. From
the documents alone, one can almost conclude that after SOV,
the V-2nd sentence type with linkage (though not the topicalized type) sprang from the head of Thor full-grown into the

language. All the documentation after about 600 A.D., according to Smith, is fairly strongly V-2nd (except Gothic, where the documentation does not provide independent word-order evidence because of the way it came into being as an almost word-for-word Greek translation). The early documentation is perhaps more strongly V-2nd than Smith's figures indicate, since he counts as separate independent clauses all subjectless 2nd-conjunct verb phrases, which increases his V-1st count and reduces the proportion of V-2nd. Where his figures for the Anglo-Saxon Chronicle (ASC) show 45% V-2nd and 9.5% V-1st, my figures show 69% V-2nd and 3% V-1st. Some OE figures are even worse relative to the expectations set up by the above hypothetical reconstruction: Of the 13 V-1st clauses in the Parker MS of the ASC up to the year 900, 10 are after 892, at which date we know there to have been a new scribe anyway; and even within his total output up to 900, these 10 constitute only 10/92 (or 11%) of his main clauses. This is a substantial increase, but the increase seems to be innovative, not archaic! In that same period (892-900) there are only 9 SOV main clauses (10%) as compared with 73 V-2nd (79%). A word-order pattern that can only be described as 'strange' for OE, namely OSVX (i.e. topicalized object, followed by normal SVO order -- it ought to be OVSX, at worst) is exactly as frequent as absolute V-1st in the 832-900 ASC, namely 3% of the total set of main clauses. Strictly speaking, both V-1st and OSV must be considered 'rare'. Why, therefore, should we bother at all with the first-stage speculation, given so little apparent support? Answer: we assume that the V-1st paucity is only superficial -- that many (even most) of the V-2nd sentences are really V-1st. They begin, overwhelmingly, with þā, þonne, or þǣr ('then', 'then', 'there'), or they are

SVO (i.e., the preverbal constituent is the subject). If we
remove these two classes of examples from the data, the number of V-2nd sentences becomes negligible. Put another way,
we have lots of vSO(V) examples if we can count the transitional adverbs as linkage (thus agreeing with Rybarkiewicz,
except we claim that vSO(V) is typologically different from
VSO, being really a variant of SOV). If we do not make this
assumption, we are left with no explanation at all for the
startling increase of V-2nd sentences in OE.

The other questionable matter in this hypothetical reconstruction is the role played by the syntactic rules of exbraciation in reuniyfing the finite and non-finite verbs. The
standard wisdom here goes back to McKnight, who originated
the view that a principal motivation in the rise of post-verbal complementation was by way of 'afterthoughts':

'To the apparently finished sentence are added a number
of explanatory details, afterthoughts; or some element,
by reason of close connection with the following clause,
may be put after the verb. To motives like these the
analytic order probably owes its origin.' (217)

Hyman 1974 reaches a similar conclusion:

'The fourth and last approach to word order change I
term afterthought ... the grammatical elements between
the S and the V move out in accordance with the likelihood of their serving as afterthoughts.' (119, 121)

'Afterthoughts' is a motivational term; 'exbraciation' is a
description of a process. I shall devote some effort below to
characterizing specifically OE motivations for the process of
exbraciation, since while the 'afterthought' notion draws

some explanatory force from the plausible psychological motivation it suggests, I think there are a number of structural
motivations within the syntax of OE that considerably
strengthen the tendency to exbraciate, and in general I find
more persuasive than psychological generalizations any explanation that depends on the prior existence of syntactic patterns as a basis for analogical extension. Many of these,
as I shall acknowledge in detail later, have already been
pointed out for MnGer. by Vennemann (1974 lecture).

But before looking at these rightward-movement processes in OE, I want to characterize briefly my notion of how
syntactic change might operate, given such processes. I am
not concerned about the question of dispersion/spread of a
change, nor the social reasons why an individual might prefer one of a set of alternatives that are available in the
language around him: I am concerned, at this point, only
with the question of how a new pattern, or a new interpretation of an old pattern, may be innovated at all, because
the way I understand the answer to that question will determine both what I look for and whether what I find will count
as evidence in anyone else's view. In essence, what I claim
is that an innovation starts life as an error: either a misunderstanding (perception error) or a misuse of the received
grammar (production error). By misunderstanding I do not
mean a simple mishearing, though that certainly occurs (as
in the transmission of proper names, especially), but rather
a misanalysis, a faulty processing, of the linguistic code.
I do not believe this process of abduction is confined to
the childhood stage of language acquisition: indeed, I
think only adult innovations commonly survive and spread;

most of the childhood analogs, though much more frequent, die
under correction during maturation. I summarize below four
well-known and, to my mind, persuasively explained examples
of such errors that produced changes in the grammar/lexicon:

(1)   start naked → stark naked
       ['tail',
       as in
       'Redstart']

       Note that this cannot be explained phonetically,
       since the natural assimilation is in fact contravened.
       It can only be an instance of abducing that the unfam-
       iliar word <u>start</u> must be the familiar word <u>stark</u>.

(2)   hydrangea → high geranium

       This example, though non-standard, is documented with-
       in my own family; the explanation is clearly abduc-
       tive misanalysis of the morphemic identity of the pho-
       neme sequence [hay-].

(3)   me thinks ... → I think ...

       This famous example could, when it originated, only
       have been a rather gross-sounding error to the ears
       of cultivated speakers, much like <u>he</u> <u>don't</u> ... today,
       or <u>they</u> <u>was</u> ..., both of which are exceedingly wide-
       spread non-standard forms. The obvious, and oft-re-
       peated, explanation hardly bears further discussion
       here.

(4)   [It is necessary them] [to leave]
                      [DAT]
       → [It is necessary to them] [to leave]
       → [It is necessary for them] [(for) to leave]
       → [It is necessary] [for them (for) to leave]

This instance of re-analysis of constituent boundaries, carefully documented by Visser (1966:968 et
passim), must have occurred many times independently
under the obvious pressure to assign subjects and
predicates one-on-one, as it were; and the re-analysis was totally forced for all speakers/learners when
examples with passives and non-animate or impersonal
subjects appeared in the erstwhile benefactive dative
slot:

> It is important for him to be assassinated.
> [hardly interpretable as a benefactive dative]

> It is good for it to rain.
> [hardly 'good for it']

To make a case for change in which such faulty analysis
is explanatory (and I agree with Andersen 1973 that it plays a
central role in all linguistic change except low-level phonetic reduction/assimilation -- and even there, at the next stage,
abduction plays a role when the reduction/assimilation is reanalyzed, e.g. by Vennemann's rule inversion (1972), as the
'base' or 'canonical' form), it is obviously necessary to show
some sentence patterns and syntactic processes that might reasonably be supposed to provide the basis for error. To put it
in plain English, they might show why someone made a mistake,
then made it again, and why many someones found it an easy mistake to make, so that the time came when no one knew it was a
mistake.

What are some of the patterns that led OE speakers, increasingly as time went on, to believe that it was perfectly
all right to put any object or adverbial constituent out to the
right of the final verb, although this had earlier been rare

and heavily constrained, or even totally ungrammatical?
(All examples are from the ASC 832-900, in the Smith edition
of the Parker MS.)

1. Many V-2nd sentences have simple verbs; all
   Obj/Adv material naturally appears to be post-verbal in such sentences.

   900.4.   ond he heold þæt rice oþrum healfum læs
            þe xxx wintra.

            and he held the kingdom the-other-half-
            year less than 30 winters.

   900.2.   Se wæs cyning ofer eall Ongelcyn butan
            þæm dæle þe under Dena onwalde wæs.

            That-one was king over all the-English-
            race except-for the part that under
            Danish control was.

   896.29. ond þreo stodon æt ufeweardum þæm muþan
            on drygum.

            and three stood at the inner mouth on dry
            land.

   896.20. þa wæron ægþer ge swiftran ge unwealtran
            ge eac hieran þonne þa oþru.

            those were both swifter and steadier and
            also higher than the others.

Of 223 clauses in the ASC 892-900, 83% contain sin-
gle-unit verbs, i.e. single finite verbs without
auxiliaries, and only 37 (17%) contain two-unit
verbs of any type (MOD + INF, COP + PP, V_{intent} +
INF, have + PP, become + PP). This eight-year period covers the 'lively' section of the Chronicle,
namely the vivid, possibly even eye-witness, accounts of the successful defensive strategies of
Alfred against the Danes: it is the section of

greatest complexity in sentence structure and the
most distinctive individual style. Before this
period, relatively complex sentences are much
rarer, especially before 885 (when there appears,
on internal evidence, to be another scribal discon-
tinuity). Of these 37 two-unit verb sentences, 9
are contiguous V-final phrases in subordinate
clauses, irrelevant to exbraciation. Of the remaining 28, 5 are V-1st main clauses, and one is
just like MnE (i.e. AUX + V internally in sequence,
without braced object). The other 22 are true V-
2nd sentence-brace constructions (10% of the total).
Some of these contain partial exbraciations, and --
probably significant -- some of them are ambiguous
as to whether the final verb is a verbal participle
or an adjective: e.g.

893.27. Ac hi hæfdon þa heora stemn gesetenne ond
         hiora mete genotudne.

         But they had then their tour-of-duty com-
         plete [ADJ] and their food consumed
         [ADJ].

         [see p. 44, note 27, of Smith's edition
         for evidence that these are indeed ADJ,
         not V: namely, case-number agreement be-
         tween DIR OBJ and ADJ, which is ungram-
         matical with the AUX have in normal OE]

896.34. þa wurdon eac swiþe uneþelice áseten.
         Those were also extremely awkwardly
         grounded.

896.46. þa wæron hie to þæm gesargode.
         Then were they to-that-extent disabled.

Some examples, including V-1st with partial exbraciation, are these:

893.43.   þæs Hæsten þa þær cumen mid his herge.

            Was Hasten then there come with his army.

            [ADV exbraciated]

896.22.   Næron nawþer ne on Fresisc gescæpene ne
            on Denisc.

            Not-were [the ships] neither in Frisian
            [way] shaped nor in Danish [way].

            [CONJ-ADV exbraciated]

896.33.   on þæm wæron eac þa men ofslægene buton
            fifum.

            on that were also the men slain, except-
            for five. [ADV exbraciated]

893.61.   ond eft oþre siþe he wæs on hergaþ gelend
            on þæt ilce rice.

            and again another time he was on harrying
            gone in that same kingdom. [ADV ex-
            braciated]

But the 'normal' two-unit V-2nd (and V-1st) constructions have clause-final main verbs:

893.44.   ond eac se micla here wæs þa þær tocumen.

            and also the great army was then there to-
            come.

893.15.   Hæfde se cyning his fierd on tu tonumen.

            Had the king his army in two divided.

896.30.   wæron þa men uppe on londe of ágáne.

            were the men up on land off gone.

893.81.   þa wæron hie mid metelieste gewægde.

            then were they with famine troubled.

893.93.   þa ne mehte seo fird hie ná hindan
          offaran.

          Then not might the army them never from-
          behind overrun.

896.3.   Næfde se here, Godes þonces, Angelcyn
          ealles forswiþe gebrocod.

          Not-had the [Danish] army [SUBJ], thank
          God, all the-English-race [OBJ] com-
          pletely destroyed.

It is apparent, within the textual material summarized above,
that the braced construction is really quite rare even in a
text where almost 80% of all main clauses and 50% of the subordinate clauses obey the V-2nd constraint. To the extent
that this text is typical of OE spoken usage -- and nothing
in existence is known to be more typical -- the first fact
potentially dangerous to the learner's establishment behavior was simply that he did not hear the braced construction
nearly as often as he heard constructions, predominantly V-
2nd, in which the V was followed exclusively by complements
of various types. That is, he had very good reason to ab-
duce a rule of the following nature:

Nominal and adverbial complements follow their
head verb.

2. Apart from frequency, there were, from earliest OE,
certain rightward-movement rules which lifted constituents out of the sentence brace and destroyed
the verb-final appearance of surface clauses.

(i)   RELATIVE-CLAUSE EXTRAPOSITION (REL-EXTRA).

This rule conspires with several others to
make it possible for internal clauses to be

avoided. The extraposed relative structure
probably is a historical consequence of relative clauses having derived from conjunct
clauses of a form which still exists in OE:
roughly, The king is a fool, that-one lost the
battle (i.e. 'The king who lost the battle is
a fool.') But though it has this source, it
cannot have this synchronic analysis since the
relative clause can be introduced by nothing
more than the general subordinating particle
þe, without any trace of the relativized NP,
whether subject or object, and therefore without any trace of main-clause independence.   So
we find examples like these:

893.44.   ond eac se micla here wæs þa þær
            tocumen, þe ær on Limene muþan
            sæt æt Apuldre.

            and also the great army was then
            there to-come, that previously
            on Limen's mouth encamped at
            Apuldor.

893.96.   ond þa men ofslogon þe hie foran
            forridan mehton butan geweorce.

            and those men [DIR OBJ] slew who(m)
            they from-in-front ride-down
            might outside the-encampment.

896.50.   Ond þa men comon on East-Engle þe on
            þæm ánum scipe wæron, swiþe
            forwundode.

            And those men came into East Anglia
            who on the one ship were, ex-
            tremely wounded. [two relative
            clauses, the second being re-
            duced.]

This rule is not obligatory:

896.6.   ealles swiþost mid þæm þæt manige
            þara selestena cynges þena þe
            þær on londe wæron forþferdon
            on þæm þrim gearum.

            [they were exceedingly damaged] most
            of all by the fact that many of the
            best of-king thanes that there in
            land were died in those three years.

Equally grammatical, surely, would be:

            ... king's thanes died in those three
            years who in land were.

But REL-EXTRA is, I think, much more favored
in OE than MnE. It is quite frequent and must
provide one more model of clause-closure by
elements other than the verb, furthermore closure by an element that can optionally surface
internally to the braced construction.

(ii)   CONJUNCT-EXTRAPOSITION (CONJ-EXTRA).

Though this analysis of these constructions is
not without viable alternatives,[3] the construction certainly gives the surface appearance of
more instances of non-verbal closure:

893.50.   ond þa scipu eall oþþe tobræcon oþþe
            forbærndon oþþe to Lundenbyrig
            brohton oþþe to Hrofesceastre.

            and those ships [DIR OBJ] all either
            broke-up or to London brought
            or to Rochester.

893.57.   ond eac swa þa he þone cniht agef
            ond þæt wif.

            and also then he the boy [DIR OBJ]
            returned ['gave back'] and the woman.

878.5.   ond he lytle werede unieþelice æfter
          wudum for ond on morfæstenum.

          and he with-a-little band with-dif-
          ficulty into forest went <u>and in-
          to</u> <u>moor-strongholds</u>.

(iii)   APPOSITIVE-EXTRAPOSITION (APPOS-EXTRA).

Appositives are reduced non-restrictive relative clauses, in effect, and they obey the
same general rule: move them out to the right,
away from the focal constituents, if possible:

885.34.   ... be AElfredes bene West-Seaxna
          cyninges.

          ... by <u>Alfred's</u> request, <u>of West-
          saxons</u> <u>king</u>.

          [i.e. 'by Alfred's request, King of
          the West Saxons']

878.25.   Ond þæs ymb iii wiecan com se cyning
          to him Godrum þritiga sum þara
          monna.

          And after-this three weeks came <u>the
          king</u> to him <u>Godrum</u> with <u>some
          thirty</u> <u>of</u> <u>the</u> <u>men</u>

          [i.e. 'King Godrum with 30 men came
          to him']

(iv)   ADVERBS AND AFTERTHOUGHTS.

This category is as loose as it sounds. There
are examples that really seem to be adverbial
expansions -- further specifications of an
earlier adverb -- or real afterthoughts in the
sense that they correct something already said
or specifically expand it in a way that suggests it was not in mind earlier in the sen-

tence.   'Except' is the afterthought par excellence.

896.33.   on þæm wæron eac þa men ofslægene
                   buton fifum.

           on that were also the men slain, ex-
                   cept-for five.

Locative adverbs in general (probably universally) are sequenced from more to less specific,
or conversely, not randomly mixed: i.e. either
'in England in London in Chelsea' or 'in Chelsea in London in England'.   A locative afterthought is one in which a specific locale is
cited, and then, after the sentence is really
complete, a more general locale is added just
in case the audience's command of geographic
details is weak (or the converse order, as in
the second example):

893.45.   se micla here ... þe ær on Limene
                   muþan sæt æt Apuldre.

           the great army ... that previously on
                   Limen's mouth encamped at Apuldor.

896.3.   ond suþ ofer sæ foron to Sigene.

           and south over sea went to Sigen.

     I know the above list of types of rightward movement is
incomplete; in particular, I have omitted one category that
was always, from earliest dates, found to the right of all
verbal dominance, namely sentential subjects and objects. In
the case of sentential objects, even MnGer. requires that
they be placed to the right of the brace, and this same rule
is without exception in OE:

> Ich hatte geglaubt, dass Maria krank sei. [Venne-
> mann 1974 lecture]
>
> I had believed that Mary ill was

Vennemann (1974 lecture) has pointed to MnGer. tendencies toward exbraciation that parallel some of those noted above for
OE: REL, lists, appositives, afterthoughts, certain adverbs,
not only ... but also constructions, the 'standard of comparison' within comparative constructions, and of course the
sentential object, which is obligatorily exbraciated.

Sentential subjects are never, even through the EMnE
period, preverbal (i.e., constructions like 'That he is a
fool is obvious' are unattested), and it is not clear how to
argue that they should nonetheless be generated by rightward
movement. But in any case they provide one more body of data
to justify the learner's increasingly strong conviction, or
so it seems, that no part of the verb can follow nominal or
adverbial complements in his (OE) language.

In the face of examples such as the above, it is not at
all surprising that the OE and EME speaker found it difficult
to discover (and internalize) the brace pattern, nor is it
hard to see how he would grammaticize the surface order that
these other processes conspired to suggest was the norm,
namely, verbs precede their complements.[4]

Notes

1. As far as I know, no one else has suggested that
the rise of a syntactic rule with this content is what initi-
ated the sequence of developments in Germanic characterized
below, although Vennemann (1974b:354) speculates that sub-
ject-final languages like Tagalog may 'originate by reevalu-
ating as unmarked that structure which occurs in many other
languages as a marked sentence pattern, ... Comment before
Topic, marked for vividness or emotionality.'

2. I have seen a draft of an interesting paper by W.
Rybarkiewicz in which he finds very numerous instances of
VSO in OE; however, he counts initial single-word adverbs
such as her, þa, þonne, and negatives as non-occupants of
the first slot, like coordinating conjunctions. He conflates
VSO and V-2nd types, without presenting any argument to support the conflation of these two patterns that should be understood as typologically distinct. In languages like MnGer.
which have the V-2nd constraint, conflation with VSO produces a peculiar typology indeed: there are numerous syntactic properties that are unique to V-2nd or former V-2nd
languages (Haiman), and they are very different from the
properties of VSO languages, in general. This fact seems to
me also to create a problem for the straight SOV → VSO → SVO
proposal of Givón 1976a,b, where he persuasively argues that
the primary motivation for VS → SV is relative topicality
(with 'topic shift' being the highest degree, and the most
demanding of SV order), but where the rise of VSO from SOV
is left without explanation. In Gmc., at least, it is strik-
ingly the case that V-1st and V-2nd sentences are character-

ized by SOV correlations, to a considerable extent (ADJ-N,
V-AUX, IO-DO, V-final subordinate clauses), not by VSO correlations: the latter arise, if at all, only after the gram-
maticization of SVO.

3. Dena Abramowitz, at UCLA, is currently investigat-
ing the properties of this rule, and until she finishes, I
have no more to say about it.

4. I am particularly grateful to Theo Vennemann, Talmy
Givón, and Marian Bean for many ideas in this paper: but
responsibility for errors and interpretations are entirely
mine, since they all three disagree with me on several (non-
intersecting) points.

References

Andersen, Henning. 1973. 'Abductive and Deductive Change'.
Lg. 49.765-93.

Ard, Josh. 1975. Raising and Word Order in Diachronic
Syntax. UCLA dissertation. University Microfilms:
Ann Arbor, Mich.

Bean, Marian. 1976. Germanic Word Order Studies in Relation
to the Origins of Modern English Word Order. UCLA dissertation.

Canale, Michael. In progress. Studies in Old English Word
Order. McGill University dissertation.

Givón, Talmy. 1976a. 'On the VS word-order in Israeli
Hebrew: Pragmatics and Typological Change'. Genera-
tive Studies in Hebrew Linguistics, ed. by S. Bolotzky
& M. Barka. Tel Aviv: Tel Aviv University Press.

_____. 1976b. 'The drift from VSO to SVO in Biblical
Hebrew: Pragmatics and Tense-aspect'. (This volume.)

Haiman, John. 1974. Targets and Syntactic Change. The
Hague: Mouton. (Revised version of 1970 Harvard dissertation.)

Heusler, Andreas. 1931. Altisländisch. Heidelberg: Carl
Winter.

Hyman, Larry. 1974. 'On the Change from SOV to SVO: Evi-
dence from Niger-Congo.' Word Order and Word Order
Change, ed. by Charles N. Li. Austin: University of
Texas Press.

Lehmann, W. P. 1974. Proto-Indo-European Syntax. Austin:
    University of Texas Press.

McKnight, George. 1893. 'The Primitive Teutonic Order of
    Words'. Journal of English and Germanic Philology.
    I.136-219.

Smith, A. H. (ed.) 1935. The Parker Chronicle (832-900).
    London: Methuen.

Smith, Jesse Robert. 1971. Word Order in the Older Germanic
    Dialects. University of Illinois dissertation. Ann
    Arbor: University Microfilms.

Vennemann, Theo. 1972. 'Rule Inversion'. Lingua 29.209-42.

_____. 1974a. 'Theoretical Word Order Studies: Results
    and Problems'. Papiere zur Linguistik 7.5-25.

_____. 1974b. 'Topics, Subjects, and Word Order: from SXV
    to SVX via TVX'. Historical Linguistics, ed. by John M.
    Anderson & Charles Jones, vol. 1, 339-76. Amsterdam:
    North-Holland.

_____. 1974 lecture. 'Typological Remarks on German Word
    Order with Particular Reference to the 'Sentence Brace'
    and 'Exbraciation'. May 30, 1974. [Part of the content
    is published as Vennemann 1974b, but several of the mo-
    tivations he suggests for German exbraciation have not
    been published outside this lecture.]

Visser, F. Th. 1966. An Historical Syntax of the English
    Language, vol. II. Leiden: E. J. Brill.

III Syntactic Change and Ergativity

7 On Mechanisms by Which Languages Become Ergative

Stephen R. Anderson

Many of the traditional problems in the study of syntax can be traced to the original status of this field as a sort of "applied morphology": the conception of syntax as "the study of the meaning and function of the various inflections (cases of nouns, moods of verbs, etc.) and of the different parts of speech (especially prepositions and subordinating conjunctions)." (Householder 1972:10) A classic example of this sort is the problem of ergativity. Ever since it was first noted that in some languages, the subject of an intransitive clause (referred to below as $\underline{S}_i$) shares morphological properties with the NP in a transitive clause which corresponds to the object ($\underline{O}$) in familiar languages, rather than with the NP corresponding to the transitive subject ($\underline{S}_t$), linguists have regarded this fact as a major puzzle for grammatical analysis. It is easy to see why, in terms of the traditional conception of syntax: a morphological category which includes the functions $\underline{S}_i$ and $\underline{O}$, but excludes the function of $\underline{S}_t$, is extremely difficult to reconcile with the equally ancient tradition of subject-predicate sentence analysis. A substantial literature has grown up, therefore, around the question of whether ergative languages have a fundamentally different syntactic organization from other (especially "accusative") languages.

On this, as on so many other questions of linguistic
theory, it ought to be possible to shed some light by examining the facts of historical change. In several families
(e.g., Indo-European, Polynesian, Kartvelian) only some of
the languages which can be presumed to have a common ancestor
display ergative patterns, while others display accusative
patterns. From this it would appear to follow that languages
can change so as to become (or cease to be) ergative. We
could then propose to study instances of such change, to see
what sorts of factors in language structure it may be related
to, and whether any other changes in basic syntactic organization follow from it.

It is the intention of this paper to discuss some cases
in which a change in the ergative vs. accusative orientation
of a particular language can be presumed with some assurance
to have taken place. Such changes seem in general to be the
consequence of relatively superficial phenomena, and do not
in general (though they may: cf. the discussion of Australian
languages below) have deeper consequences for the syntactic
organization of the language. In some cases, in fact, it is
possible to derive support from such changes for the view
that ergativity is generally a rather superficial fact itself,
relating only to a low-level option in the morphological pattern of the language rather than to more fundamental aspects
of sentence structure. Before moving on to such cases, however, it is necessary to delimit at least sketchily the area
under discussion.

As noted above, ergativity is classically viewed as a
pattern of morphological categories, manifested either in
case marking or in verbal agreement pattern. An example in

which both are found is provided by the Northeast Caucasian
language Avar:

(1)   a.   emen   roq'ove v-us:ana
             father home-m m-returned
             'Father returned home'

       b.   ebel   roq'oje j̄-us:ana
             mother home-f f-returned
             'Mother returned home'

       c.   vas-as: emen   v-ec:ula
             boy-erg   father m-praises
             'The boy praises (his) father'

       d.   ins:u-c:a vas v-ec:ula
             father-erg boy m-praises
             'The father praises the boy'

       e.   vas-as: ebel j-ec:ula
             boy-erg   mother f-praises
             'The boy praises (his) mother'

In these sentences, an absolutive case (e.g. emen 'father')
serves as S_i or O, while a distinct ergative case form (e.g.
ins:u-c:a 'father (erg.)') serves as S_t. Furthermore, the verbal agreement pattern is the same: verbs (and some adverbs as
well: cf. roq'ove vs. roq'oje in 1a,b) agree in gender and
number with S_i or with O, but not at all with S_t. This is
the canonical form of an ergative morphological system: compare it, for example, with the Latin opposition of nominative (for S_i or S_t) vs. accusative (for O), and verb agreement with S_i or with S_t, but not with O.

     It is this sort of ergativity, a morphological fact,
with which we will be concerned, but we should note that the
question of whether ergative languages are fundamentally different from others involves claims about clause structure
and the operation of syntactic rules, not simply about word

forms. Those who would claim that ergativity is a fundamental
syntactic characteristic, that is, would argue that in a language like Avar not only do S_i and O have the same form, distinct from S_t, but they also represent the same grammatical
relation (perhaps "structural subject"), which S_t does not
share in. The consequence of this difference ought to be observable: just as familiar languages of the accusative type
have syntactic rules (e.g. raising, Equi-NP deletion, reflexive, conjunction reduction in some instances, and others)
which treat subject (i.e. S_i and S_t) as a unitary category,
such a language ought to have some rules which treat absolu-
tives (or "structural subjects") in the same way. We stress
here that the rules which could be relevant are only those
basic rules for which a transformational analysis seems clearly indicated and which seem to be sensitive to grammatical relations: perhaps the class of cyclic structure preserving
rules, formulable in relational terms, or the like[1]. Certain
other types of rules are irrelevant to this issue: postcyclic, non-structure-preserving rules (root and local transformations, in Emonds' terms), because they are not in general
sensitive to grammatical relations at all; lexical redundancy
relations, and rules of semantic interpretation, because
these are in general more sensitive to thematic relations of
a semantic nature such as "theme", "agent", "source", "exper-
iencer", etc. than to structural relations of a syntactic nature such as "subject" and "object". Of course, in order to
make the the claims about linguistic structure involved here
precise, it is necessary to delimit and properly constrain
the classes of rules involved here; but work such as Emonds
(1976) on the one hand, Jackendoff (1975), Wasow (1977) and
Anderson (1977) on the other, and the relational properties of

rules uncovered by Perlmutter and Postal (forthcoming) make
clear in at least a programmatic sense what is being sought.

Given the notion of ergativity in a morphological sense,
then, and the scope of syntactic processes that might be expected to display a sort of "syntactic" ergativity, it is
reasonably clear how to go about testing the claim that the
latter is a viable notion. In fact, as discussed in Anderson
(1972, 1976), investigation of morphologically ergative languages generally leads to the result that their syntax (and
thus, presumably, their basic principles of clause structure)
is fundamentally the same as that of non-ergative languages,
and thus does not reflect their morphology. In some cases,
however, including the Australian languages discussed by
Dixon (1976)[2] and perhaps the ancient Near Eastern language
Hurrian, the appropriate aspects of the syntax do seem to be
organized on an ergative pattern. From this, we can conclude
that "syntactically ergative" languages do exist, but that
this class is not to be identified as coextensive with the
class of "morphologically ergative" languages. Since we will
be concerned below primarily with changes that lead to morphological ergativity, one might question why this paper is
appropriate for a symposium on mechanisms of syntactic change:
beside the historical justification that ergativity is generally thought of as a fact about syntax, the fact is that a
consideration of the mechanisms of such morphological changes
can cast light on the relationship (or lack of it) between
syntax and morphology.

When we consider the areas of the grammar which impinge
on the morphological system, it is clear that there are many
conceivable sorts of change that might lead to a language's

becoming ergative. Even the operation of phonological rules
could conceivably have this effect. Dixon (1976) suggests
such a sequence of events: suppose a language has basic VSO
order, and marks nominatives with /-s/ and accusatives with
/-n/. Then suppose it acquires a phonological rule deleting
final consonants before end-of-clause boundaries. The result
of this would be that most $\underline{O}$'s and most $\underline{\underline{S}}_i$'s would lose their
case marking, creating a situation in which $\underline{\underline{S}}_t$ is marked by
/-s/ while a new absolutive case for $\underline{\underline{S}}_i$ and $\underline{O}$ has arisen,
marked by /∅/. Thus, a purely phonological change could (as-
suming its effects were suitably generalized and incorporated
into the morphology) have the effect of changing a nomina-
tive/accusative case marking system into an ergative/absolu-
tive one.

While such a possibility certainly exists, we do not
know of any instances (among the small number of cases where
a case system change can be shown to have occurred) in which
such a purely phonological account is available. The closest
to this ideal case is the example of the development of Chinook, as treated by Sapir (1926). In Chinook there is no case
marking on Noun Phrases, and consequently the internal structure of the verbal agreement system is responsible for indicating grammatical relations. The verb is preceded by a series
of prefixes marking person, number, and gender of the subject
and object(s), as well as various oblique or locational, benefactive, etc. relations. In most cases, the markers for these
last are directly followed by a sort of postpositional element. In general, the pronominal agreement markers are quite
similar to the determiners which appear with the corresponding noun phrases, and the result is that the verb appears to

be preceded by a sequence of clitic pronouns and pronoun+post-
position sequences. Independent pronouns for first and second
persons are generally omitted, although they can be included
if emphatic. Some representative examples from Silverstein
(1972) are given below:

(2)[3]a.   wixt á-i-u-u   i-qísis
          again pst-he-went-on det-bluegay
          'Bluejay went on again'

    b.   náika n-t-ú-k°ł-a   xi-t-íkš t-qášušin-ikš
          I(emp) I-them-carry-fut these   det-children
          'I will carry these children'

    c.   taka a-č-ł-ł-l-u-k°ł   ku ł-čq°   q°-ła
          then pst-he-it-it-to-carry to det-water that
              ł-k'asks
              det-child
          'Then he carried that child to the water'

    d.   i kanim   a-m-i-n-l-u-x
          det-canoe pst-you-it-me-for-make
          'You made the canoe for me'

    e.   a-č-i-ú-čtmt   i-qisqis   qix ł-k'asks
          pst-he-him-push det-bluejay that det-boy
          'Bluejay pushed that boy'

As noted, the pronominal prefixes are in general the same as
determiner elements in the corresponding NP; as a result, they
have the same form regardless of their function in the clause.
There are three major exceptions to this, all involving special forms for the transitive subject pronouns: a) the 3 sg.
masculine form is /-č-/ instead of expected /-i-/; b) the 3
sg. feminine form is /-k-/ instead of expected /-a-/; c) other
S_t forms except for 1 sg. and 2 sg. consist of the expected
form followed by an intrusive /-k-/. Consider the following
partial paradigm:

(3)   a.   i-m-i-uwaq
           'You (sg.) killed him'

      b.   i-mt-k-i-uwaq
           'you (dual) killed him'

      c.   i-č-i-uwaq
           'He killed him'

      d.   i-č-m-uwoq
           'He killed you'

Ergativity in Chinook, then, consists in just these special
forms for $\underline{\underline{S}}_t$, distinct from the "absolutive" forms (which
are the same as NP determiners) used for $\underline{\underline{S}}_i$ and $\underline{0}$.

At a later point, we will return to the problem of the
origin of the element /-k-/ which follows $\underline{\underline{S}}_t$ pronominal forms.
The most pronounced assymetry between the ergative and the
absolutive forms, however, is the pair /-č-/ and /-k-/ for 3
sg. masculine and feminine respectively, in place of absolutive /-i-/ and /-a-/. With the exception of these two forms,
there is no reason to set up distinct ergative and absolutive
pronoun sets, and the problem reduces to that of accounting
for the element /-k-/ which follows $\underline{\underline{S}}_t$.

Sapir (1926) makes it clear, however, that the forms
/-č-/ and /-k-/ for 3sg $\underline{\underline{S}}_t$ are the result of phonologically
motivated changes. He argues that originally Chinook had the
expected forms /-i-k-/ for 3sg masculine and /-a-k-/ for 3sg
feminine (i.e., exactly the appropriate determiner element
followed by the /-k-/ which appears with other $\underline{\underline{S}}_t$'s). The
sequence /-ik-/ underwent palatalization at an early point
in the history of the language, becoming /-ič-/. Subsequently,
unaccented vowels were lost in pronominal prefixes. The prefixes */-a-k-/ and */-i-č-/, however, were the only ones sub-

ject to this loss, since the other prefixes consist of consonants only and most instances of /-i-/ and /-a-/ represent-
ing a 3sg. masc. or fem. $\underline{S}_i$ or $\underline{0}$ would have been accented.
The result was the reduction of */-i-č-/ and */-a-k-/ repre-
senting $\underline{S}_t$ to /-č-/ and /-k-/ respectively. Thus, the most
distinctive and apparently idiosyncratic difference between
the ergative and absolutive pronoun sets in Chinook can be
seen to be the consequences of phonological change, unmotivated by morphological (or syntactic) considerations.

It would be of some interest if a case could be documented in which all aspects of an ergative morphological
pattern could be shown to have arisen by phonological change
alone. In the case of Chinook, we are left with the element
/-k/ which follows $\underline{S}_t$ pronouns yet to account for, and we are
not aware of any attested case which comes closer than this
to our aim. In fact most instances in which languages become
ergative are the consequence of a rather different sort of
change: what might be regarded as the morphological equivalent
of the lexicalization of opaque alternations in phonology.
That is, some morphological material which was originally associated with a syntactic process of essentially complete generality comes to be assigned independently of the operation of
such a process as a result of a change in the status of the
syntactic rule itself, when the derivational relation between
its inputs and its outputs become obscured.

A case of this sort is argued in considerable detail by
Chung (1976a, 1976b). She is concerned with the rise of erga-
tive morphology in the Polynesian family, also discussed by
Hohepa (1969) as the result of an unexplained "drift". In the
Polynesian ergative languages, such as Tongan, Niuean, Samoan,

etc., the S_t is generally marked with the particle e; the absolutive S_i or O is unmarked (or, in Tongan, marked with a
'a of undetermined origin in conservative speech); and the
suffix -Cia (where C represents one of a set of consonants)
appears on many transitive verbs. In the accusative Polynesian languages, on the other hand, S_i and S_t are unmarked, O
is marked by i, and there generally exists a passive rule
which adds Cia to the verb, marks the S_t with e and leaves the
original O unmarked. Chung argues convincingly that in the
original Polynesian situation, a)i was an object marker; b)
e marked an oblique NP, whose status was similar to that of
by phrases in English and other languages with a clear passive rule; and c) that Cia originally marked the verbs of
sentences that had undergone passive. Thus, in proto-Polynesian, case-marking was of the accusative type and a productive
passive rule derived sentences with oblique e-phrases for the
original agent. The situation was essentially the same as that
in modern Maori, in other words.

In the modern ergative Polynesian languages, however, the
passive has essentially disappeared as a productive rule, sentences have the same morphology as that of passive sentences
in e.g. Maori, but syntactic rules applying to the category of
'subject' apply to S_t (marked with ergative e) and S_i (unmarked or marked with absolutive 'a) and not to O. What has happened, then, is that active sentence structures have the morphology originally assigned by the passive rule, but the passive rule is no longer involved in their derivation. An original optional, general passive rule has been replaced by an
obligatory ergative case marking rule which no longer marks a
transformational aspect of a derivation.

It is fairly plausible to suggest that this syntactic re-analysis results from the fact that the Polynesian passive has rather wider scope than the passive in many other languages. In Maori, we can see that there are a number of environments in which passivization is obligatory and others in which it is by far the predominant structure (cf. Chung, 1976a and references given there). It seems likely that as a result of this, the passive is in some languages of the family the predominant sentence structure. As this sort of structure is generalized to new environments, however, it ceases to be the case that the distinctive semantic and functional properties of passive constructions are directly associated with exactly those structures that have undergone passivization. In the limiting case, passivization becomes essentially obligatory; at which point there ceases to be a relation between two types of surface structure, active and passive, which is captured by the structural change of the passive rule. The motivation for a difference between underlying and surface structures in the "derived" (passive) cases is thus weakened. The result of this is that the passive rule becomes opaque in a sense quite close to the use of this term in phonology. At that point, it seems, the opaque passive rule is lost, and the facts of surface structure are represented rather in terms of an ergative case marking rule. Surface structures do not change in form as a result: $\underline{S_t}$ continues to be marked with $\underline{e}$ as if it were a passive agent, $\underline{O}$ (and $\underline{S_i}$) are unmarked, and transitive verbs have the suffix $\underline{Cia}$. What has changed is that these structures are now syntactically basic and active, rather than derived and passive.

Such a re-analysis seems to be the primary attested mech-

anism by which a language can become ergative. It has long
been noted that the morphology of an ergative language is
highly similar to that of passive sentences in an accusative
language; on the other hand, the syntactic properties of
these languages are generally (as argued in Anderson, 1976)
those of active sentences in nominative/-accusative languages.
A natural account of this would be found if ergative morphology arose by generalizing the morphology of an original passive construction as the consequence of the loss of a passive
rule, once the basis of a productive transformational relationship but subsequently rendered opaque through the over-
generalized use of passive sentence types. A rather similar
analysis is proposed for Australian languages like Walbiri by
Hale (1970), though in different terms. Hale suggests that
Australian languages were originally nominative-accusative,
but that the passive rule came to be obligatory. Upon examination, however, it is clear that there is in fact no motivation
for saying that the passive rule as a transformational relationship exists any longer in modern Walbiri: since it applies (on Hale's account) after all other rules, there can be
no rule which depends on the structural change made by it,
and it has no consequence other than to produce the case-marking pattern. This analysis, then, is equivalent to saying that
the passive rule was effectively lost, and replaced by an obligatory ergative case marking rule applying to active structures.

Unfortunately, it is difficult to determine the details
of the original Australian situation. Hale's claims about o-
riginal accusativity for proto-Australian are based primarily
on syntactic behavior, rather than on a detailed reconstruc-

tion of the morphological situation; Dixon's (1976) opposite
claim that proto-Australian nouns were marked ergatively suf-
fers from a related sort of problem. It is clear that we can
reconstruct an agent or ergative marker for proto-Australian,[4]
but equally clear that we can reconstruct an object (accusative) marker, at least for some classes of NP. No one has yet
provided compelling arguments on the basis of which we could
determine for certain that one of these was originally secondary or oblique, on the order of Chung's demonstration for
Polynesian e, while the other was a direct-case marker (as
Polynesian i). Thus, the original situation remains obscure,
though if Hale's claim that an original passive rule was generalized in an accusative language is correct, a plausible
account can be given of the syntactic development of Australian languages as parallel to that of Polynesian. It seems at
least possible that the history of Australian languages presents us with another example of the generalization of an
originally derived morphological pattern as the result of the
reanalysis and loss of a syntactic rule.

A particularly interesting example of this sort of change
can be found within Indo European, especially in the Indic
and Iranian subgroups. As is well known, many of these languages provide examples of mixed ergative and accusative systems, of a type also attested elsewhere. There are a number
of interesting assymetries in systems of this type, most of
which we cannot go further into, but which should be provided
with explanations: a) languages can apparently display ergative case marking patterns and either ergative or nominative/
accusative verbal agreement, but there are apparently no languages in which an ergative verb-agreement rule is combined

with a nominative-accusative case marking system; b) languages
with ergative marking for full noun phrases may have accusative marking for (some or all) pronouns, but not vice versa;[5]
c) languages may have ergative marking in main clauses and
accusative marking in subordinate clauses, but apparently[6]
not vice versa; and d) languages may have ergative marking in
perfect (or past) tenses and accusative marking in imperfective (or non-past) tenses, but not vice versa. In Indic and
Iranian (as well as in Armenian, Georgian, Burushaski, and
elsewhere) this last situation commonly obtains, and in this
instance a sort of explanation does seem available. The source
of the explanation is to be found in the principles by which
perfect tenses are created.

We can examplify this situation from Hindi, as discussed
by Allen (1951). A more general treatment of the phenomenon
is given by Mathews (1953), though he is apparently misled by
the morphological facts into drawing a faulty syntactic conclusion. In any event, in modern Hindi the pattern is as follows: in imperfective tenses, the subject is unmarked and the
object (if definite and animate) is marked with the particle
-ko. The verb agrees in gender and number with the subject:

(4)　a. laṛkā kuttā dekhtā hai　　'The boy sees a dog'
　　　　boy　dog　sees　aux.

　　　b. laṛkā kutte-ko dekhtā hai　'The boy sees the dog'

　　　c. laṛkī kuttā dekhtī hai　　'The girl sees a dog'

　　　d. laṛkā kutte dekhtā hai　　'The boy sees some dogs'

　　　e. laṛke kuttā dekhte hãi　　'The boys sees a dog'

Sentences whose verbs are in perfective tenses, however, have
a different morphological pattern. Intransitive sentences are
treated the same way in either type of tense, but in transitive perfective clauses, $\underline{S}_t$ is marked with the particle -ne
and the verb agrees with the object rather than with the subject:

(5) a. laṛke-ne kuttā dekhā hai   'The boy has seen a dog'

    b. laṛkī-ne kuttā dekhā hai   'The girl has seen a dog'

    c. laṛkõ-ne kuttā dekhā hai   'The boys have seen a dog'

    d. laṛke-ne billī dekhā hai   'The boy has seen a cat'
                                             (fem.)

    e. laṛke-ne kutte dekhe haĩ   'The boy has seen some
                                                 dogs'

Thus, in perfect tenses, both case marking and agreement are
ergative in nature, while these rules are nominative-accusative in imperfect tenses.

    When we ask where these constructions came from, we are
fortunate in that the course of evolution from early Indic
through modern Hindi is well documented. A detailed discussion of this history can be found in Bloch (1965), where further morphological details will be found. In outline, the
facts are these: Sanskrit had an extensive series of inflected
verbal forms, with inherited Indo-European endings marking
person and number of the subject through several tenses, aspects, moods, and voices. In Middle Indic, however, virtually
all of these fell out of use. We can speculate on the possible
socio-linguistic motivations for this loss of personal verb
forms, but the net result was that a variety of periphrastic
constructions came to fill the function of the original in-

flected verbal forms. In the case of the perfect, the periphrastic form which was employed was that based on the verbal
adjective or participle in -ta. The adjectival sense of this
form is quite close to the sense of a perfective; thus, it
was quite natural for a sentence such as agnir upasamāhito
bhavati, originally "the fire is alight", to come to mean
"the fire has been lighted." Now in the case of the intransitive verb, the corresponding adjectival form in -ta has simply
this perfective sense: thus, mṛta- "dead" from mar- "die". In
the case of a transitive verb, the adjectival form is passive: thus, yukta- "yoked", not "having yoked", from yuj-
"yoke". Such a passive participial could be accompanied by a
complement in the instrumental (e.g. yamena dattaḥ "given by
Yama") representing the agent, from the earliest attested
period of the language. Such a form was thus the basis of a
periphrastic passive construction in Sanskrit which served as
an alternative to the primary inflectional passive forms
(forms in -ya and passive uses of middle forms), with a clear
perfective sense. More to the point is the morphology of this
construction: S_i or O appear in a case (nominative or accusative; usage here is complex) which will subsequently in later
stages of the language appear uniformly as the 'direct' or
'subject' case, while S_t appears in a case (the instrumental)
which will subsequently merge with other uses of a general
'oblique' case (often, as in Hindi, reinforced by the addition
of a postposition). The verb appears in a participial form
which agrees in nominal categories (gender and number) with
S_i or O, if anything, but not with S_t. Whether or not the copula appears in such constructions is variable at first: it is
not obligatory, and is generally absent in third person singulars.

In the construction with verbal adjectives in -ta, then, we have just the right morphological characteristics for an ergative pattern, but of course in Sanskrit the construction is a derived passive one, rather than an active ergative one. However, with the disappearance (or rather atrophy) of the active personal forms, the derivational relationship became opaque. Given a productive parallelism between the type "the man beat the horse" and "the horse was beaten by the man", the arguments for deriving the second transformationally from the first are well-known. With the disappearance of the active forms, however, this motivation disappears; and there ceases to be any reason not simply to treat the (original) passive directly as an active form, albeit with complex morphology. In the case we are considering, this tendency appears quite early: according to Bloch (1965:253) Patañjali already suggests the possibility of employing the participial forms directly as active perfects. In later Indic, as illustrated in the modern languages, this re-analysis is unmistakable.

The fact that such a re-analysis of the originally passive forms as active has taken place is shown directly in the morphology, to some extent. Thus, as we noted above, Hindi has a rule marking definite animate $\underline{O}$ with the particle -ko in imperfective forms like (4b). But this rule is not limited to the imperfective forms, where $\underline{S}_i$ and $\underline{S}_t$ appear alike in the direct case. In perfect tense forms also, the -ko-marking rule applies: thus, we have sentences like (6) to add to the paradigm in (5):

(6)   laṛke-ne kutte-ko dekhā hai
        boy-erg dog-acc   seen   aux
        'The boy has seen the dog'

This tendency is carried further in a language like Nepali (cf. Clark, 1963; Southworth, 1967). In this language, a set of tenses morphologically descended from earlier participial forms have S_t marked with the postposition -le; S_i unmarked; inanimate O unmarked; and animate O marked with the accusative postposition -lai (just as in other tenses where S_t is unmarked). In addition, the verb agrees with S_i or S_t, regardless of tense, and not with O:

(7)   a.   sita bholi aunechə
                Sita tomorrow will-come
                'Sita will come tomorrow'

        b.   sitale aluma nun haleko chə
                Sita-erg potatoes-in salt put has
                'Sita has put salt in the potatoes'

        c.   sitale ramlai cineko chə
                Sita-erg Ram-acc recognized has
                'Sita knows (=has recognized) Ram'

        d.   məyle ramlai cineko chu
                I-erg Ram-acc recognized have
                'I know Ram'

The morphology here is almost entirely 'active'; the marker -le functions simply as part of the material marking the different tense forms.

Morphology, however, is a poor guide to the syntactic structure of clauses, precisely because a morphological pattern reflecting (apparently) one construction may in fact simply be the fossilized relics of that structure, applied to a totally different one. We cannot, therefore, rely on morphological evidence to confirm the interpretation of modern Hindi or Nepali sentence types like (6,7) as structurally active. When we consider the operation of those syntactic processes that are usually found to be sensitive to grammatical relations, however, we find ready support for this position. Reflexivization, for example, is known to operate in many languages under the restriction that only <u>subjects</u> (either $\underline{S}_i$ or $\underline{S}_t$) can serve as antecedents for reflexive pronouns. When we look at Hindi, we find that such a condition obtains; and that the relevant notion of 'subject' is again '$\underline{S}_i$ or $\underline{S}_t$', despite the fact that these two are morphologically different:

(8)   a.   mẽ apne-ko   dekhtā hũ
             I   self-acc seeing I-am
             'I see myself'

        b.   mẽ-ne   apne-ko dekhā
             I-erg self-acc saw
             'I saw myself'

        c.   *apne-ne mujhe dekhā
             self-erg me-acc saw
             '(myself saw me)'

        d.   John-ne Bill-se apne bāre me bāt kī
             John-erg Bill-dat self   about spoke
             'John spoke to Bill about himself (=John)

                  (*=Bill)'

        e.   John apne bāre me bolā
             John self about   talked
             'John talked about himself'

Further investigation of rules such as Equi-NP deletion, raising, and conjunction reduction, which can be shown to be sensitive to conditions on grammatical relations, confirm the same proposal. In languages such as modern Hindi or Nepali, then, we can conclude that although the ergative morphology suggests otherwise in some tense forms, $\underline{S}_i$ and $\underline{S}_t$ (but not $\underline{O}$) are terms of the same grammatical relation <u>subject</u>, and the constructions of all of (4-8) should be treated as active.

We can now return to the point of this example. We observed above that in several languages, ergative case marking is found in sentences containing verbs in perfect tenses (or tenses derived from former perfects: in some languages, e.g., perfects generalize to become simply past). We can now account for this situation, at least in part. Passive constructions are semantically close to perfects, in that they generally present a state resulting from a completed action. When a language loses (as a consequence of other changes, either phonological or of usage) an inflected perfect, it is plausible to suggest that the scope of the original passive may expand to fill the gap. Where this becomes the main function of the (original) passive, furthermore, the fact of the loss of the simple active perfect will lead to a kind of opacity which has as its consequence the reanalysis of the construction. The result of this is that the morphology which originally marked the operation of a passive transformation comes to be the marker rather of perfective aspect. We normally think of verbal categories such as tense and aspect as marked on the verb, and not (partly) in the NP, but this is by no means necessary: the Lardil language of Australia, for example, inflects certain NP (those filling the relation $\underline{0}$, in fact) for the distinction future/non-future, where the difference relates to the time of the action and not to the identity of the NP on which it is marked. The explanation for why it should be perfects that have ergative morphology, then, is clear (at least in part): exactly perfects have a plausible historical source with just the necessary morphological properties.

Interestingly enough, there is one further construction which has been shown to be a possible source for newly-created perfects, and this alternative to the derivation from passives has essentially the same properties as far as the case marking which it might be expected to lead to. While the derivation of modern perfect forms in Indic from older passive participial constructions seems valid, the Iranian languages (or at least some of them: e.g., Pashto) also show ergative case marking in perfect tenses, but here an original passive construction is apparently not the source. In early Iranian, the same problem arose as in early Indic: inherited perfect forms (among others) fell out of use, and a substitute was required to mark this distinction. Here, however, the solution was somewhat different.

As discussed by Vendryes (1937) and Benveniste (1952), a remarkable number of languages have independently constructed perfect tense forms for transitive verbs by employing a possessive verbal form ("to have") as an auxiliary. English "I have read the book" is an obvious example; Latin habeo factum is another, completely independent of the Germanic development; in Celtic we find for example Breton gwelet am eus "I have seen", where the auxiliary am eus is a completely idiosyncratic combination of an 'inflected pre position' and an old verbal form, used to express possession; Portugese tenho falado "I have spoken" is an innovation, unrelated to French j'ai parlé; and so on. In a remarkable range of Indo-European languages from Hittite through the modern dialects, constructions expressing possession have been repeatedly employed as auxiliaries when a perfect is required. The development is by no means confined to Indo-

European, either: cf. Benveniste's (1970) discussion of parallel phenomena in Chuckchee. The development is in essence one
from a construction such as "I have ((the book)read)" to "I
have read the book." Semantically, it is not immediately obvious why this should be so natural; but there is abundant
evidence that it is, for whatever reason. We can thus add to
the passive as a possible source for perfects the use of "to
have" as an auxiliary, at least for transitive verbs, together again with a participial form of the verb.

But now let us consider the range of constructions employed by the languages of the world to express possession.
Many languages, of course, have a simple verb, such as English
"to have". Many others, however (cf. Benveniste, 1960), em-
ploy a periphrastic form such as Russian u menja kniga "I
have a book; lit. at me there is a book." Such a construction,
with a dative, locational expression, or genitive of the possessor (together with the copula if the language has an overt
copula) is found for the expression of possession in a wide
variety of languages. But now let us consider the combination
of this construction with the fact noted above, the possibility of employing a possessive expression as a perfect auxiliary. In that case, we would expect to find something like "to
me the book read is" as an expression of "I have read the
book"; and Benveniste (1952) has argued that this is exactly
what we find in some languages. In Old Persian ima tya manā
kr̥tam "That is what I have done", manā is a genitive-dative
form, just as in manā puṣa astiy "I have a son", literally
'of-me son is.'[7] The same construction can also be found in
Classical Armenian, as well as in Egyptian among others. For
our purposes, the interest of this fact is that it ultimately

leads to the same consequences as the derivation of perfects
from original passives. The construction of the perfect with
a possessive auxiliary is only applicable to transitive verbs,
for obvious reasons: 'I have ((the book)read)' requires a
'possessed' NP (the object) as well as a 'possessor'. For intransitive verbs, a simple equational construction with a
participle and the copula fills the same role: 'I am gone'
(compare, for example, French je suis allé with j'ai lu le
livre). As a result, both transitive and intransitive verbs
will be found in superficially comparable participial constructions; S_i and O will appear in (a reflex of) the nominative, since both are structurally 'subjects' of equational
constructions originally; while S_t will appear in (a reflex
of) the genitive, dative, etc. as a reflection of its original
status in the possessive construction. Just as in the case of
the history of original passives, the disappearance of basic,
active, personally inflected perfect forms will increase the
opacity of this construction, and decrease the motivation for
deriving it from a complex, non-active form; and we can predict that it will subsequently be restructured so as to reflect this. As a result, the morphology of this construction
comes to be interpreted simply as the mark of the perfect,
applied to a normal transitive active structure, and S_t (while
remaining in an oblique form) ceases to be oblique structurally; O ceases to be structurally a 'subject' and becomes an
object instead. Hence, while the new perfect tense form is
syntactically a straightforward active, it is marked with an
ergative morphology.

That the expected re-analysis does indeed take place can
be readily confirmed. Just as we found in Indic that accusa-

tive marking may subsequently come to apply (as in Hindi or
Nepali) to $\underline{O}$ NP's despite their 'nominative' case form, the
same thing can happen to the descendents of original possessive constructions. In the classical Armenian perfect, we
find the verb in the form of a participle in -eal, together
with a copula; $\underline{S_i}$ appears in the nominative, and $\underline{S_t}$ appears
in the genitive. This latter fact shows the origin of the
transitive perfect in Armenian as a possessive construction,
since possession in Armenian is expressed by a structure of
the 'of-me a book is' type. The important point is that the
object ($\underline{O}$) appears in the accusative case, as would be expected for an active transitive structure: zayn nšan arareal
er nora "He had performed that miracle" has subject $\underline{S_t}$ (nora)
in the genitive and object $\underline{O}$ (z-ayn nšan) in the accusative,
marked by the prefix z- at the beginning of the NP. The morphological criterion is confirmed by an investigation of the
syntax of Armenian or of modern Pashto (whose past tense forms
are descended from the Old Persian perfect derived from a
possessive), which reveals that $\underline{S_i}$ and $\underline{S_t}$ function here (as
well as in the tense forms to which nominative/accusative
case marking applies) as syntactically the same grammatical
relation, subject.

We discover, then, that there is good reason to expect
just the assymetry we found with respect to the correlation
between case marking and perfect/imperfect aspect. The reason
for this is that there are two quite distinct periphrastic
constructions, the passive and the possessive, which are abun-
dantly documented as potential sources for newly-created perfects; and both of these constructions have the property that
the NP filling the relation $\underline{S_t}$ will appear in an oblique case

as opposed to the direct or nominative form in which S_i or O will appear. It must be emphasized that these two are quite separate potential sources for perfects, although they ultimately lead to very similar morphological consequences after their re-analysis as simple, basic active structures.

Within the Indo-Iranian branch of Indo-European, we find both of these sources employed as perfects: the passive in Indic, and the possessive in Iranian. In individual cases, it is often quite difficult to be sure which of the two possibilities is at the root of a given language's perfect forms, on internal evidence alone. This is because the only ultimate difference between them is that S_t will appear in (the reflex of) the instrumental if the construction was originally passive, but in (the reflex of) the dative or genitive if it was originally possessive. In the course of the development of the Indic and Iranian languages, however, the distinctions among the original oblique cases are generally lost, and they merge as a single 'oblique' case. In some instances this may be re-inforced secondarily by postpositional elements: such is the case with Hindi -ne or Nepali -le, though these do not really give us a direct indicator of the original form of the construction.

Within Indo-Iranian, we generally find (as just discussed) ergative case marking confined to perfect forms, or more generally to those tense forms derived from original constructions based on the participles such as that in -ta. In just one language, however, we find ergative case marking which extends to all tense forms. This language is Shiṇā,[8] which is in fact the only 'fully' ergative language in the entire Indo-European family, apparently. Shiṇā is a member

of the 'Dardic' group, whose best-known representative is
Kashmiri; the exact place of these languages within Indo-
Iranian was for some time a subject of dispute, and they were
sometimes claimed to form a third co-ordinate sub-group with
Indic and Iranian. It is now generally accepted that the
Dardic languages are Indic, though somewhat peculiar and subject to considerable Iranian influence. They are spoken generally in rather inaccessible parts of the Himalayas, and apparently their speakers have been located in this region for
some time. As a result, the languages are not directly descended from any of the well-known prakrits, and our knowledge of their history is much more meager than in the case
of other Indo-Iranian languages.

The basic case-marking situation in Shiṇā can be illustrated in (9) below:

(9) a.   aš   ma bodi dūre žo peādal   vatus
          today I very far from walking came
          'Today I came walking from far away'

     b.   mas ēsai puçe bodu ṣidegas
          I-erg that-of son much I-beat
          'I beat his son a lot'

     c.   kēsai puç tu phatu vān
          who-of son you after is-coming
          'whose son is coming after you?'

     d.   mālus puç   pasīgu
          father-erg son he-saw
          'The father saw the son'

In (9a,c) the clauses are intransitive, and their subjects
(ma, puç) accordingly appear in the 'direct' or 'nominative'
case. The S_t NP in (9b,d) appear in the 'agent' or ergative
case, marked by the addition of -se or -sa after consonants,

-s after vowels, to the nominative. In (9b), the verb 'strike' is one of a small class whose O appears not in the 'nominative', but in an oblique form; more typical is the appearance of the O in (9d). "Ergative" morphological features include the appearance of S_t in a special 'agent' case; nominative/ accusative features include the appearance of some objects in oblique cases and the agreement of the verb with S_i or S_t, but not with O, in person and number. These features are constant through all tenses.

This pattern does not differ significantly from that of, say, Nepali, except that the ergative morphology is not confined to a few tenses. There is one unusual feature, however: this is the shape of the agent case form, which is made by attaching -s(e) to the nominative singular or plural. Significantly, this form is not built on an oblique stem (which is quite distinct in Shiṇā); furthermore, there is no obvious Indo-Iranian etymology for the ending itself. There is no original postposition, that is, which could be expected to become -s(e) in Shiṇā and to appear with the nominative (rather than with an oblique case). In the literature on Shiṇā, there has perforce been some speculation as to the origin of this form.

Observing that -s(e) has no clear native source, Sir George Grierson is said to have been the first to suggest that the suffix might be a borrowing from Tibetan. Shiṇā is spoken in the vicinity of Gilgit, in Baltistan, where a number of language families meet. Besides Indic and Iranian, the Tibetan language Balti is spoken in this general area, as is the language isolate Burushaski. Balti, like other Tibetan languages, is morphologically ergative in all tenses (Burush-

aski is ergative only in past forms, similar to the Indic and
Iranian situations); and more to the point, the ergative case
in Balti consists exactly of the nominative followed by the
ending -si. This would be a completely plausible source,
therefore, for Shina -s(e) except for the general oddity of a
language's borrowing a morphological category in this way. If
-s(e) is Balti in origin, this would imply that the entire
ergative construction with its associated morphology is borrowed; and while it is easy to suggest this possibility, documented instances of this sort are virtually impossible to
find. As Lorimer (1925) notes, the "borrowing of so important
and radical a construction with the particle accompanying it
would be a very serious affair, quite different from the pur-
loining of a mere word." We should therefore hope to find
some further explanation for the provenance of Shina -s(e).

    In fact, when we consider further data from the language,
we can find the outlines of a somewhat more satisfactory account than simply the outright borrowing of the ergative construction from Balti. The agent form -s(e) in Shina appears
in all tenses in the 'standard' language, that spoken in and
around Gilgit, but Bailey (1924) also provides us with data
on some other dialects. In the Guresi and Drasi dialects,
spoken some little ways from Gilgit, we find a more complex
situation. In this area the agent forms in -s(e) exist, but
they are confined to the non-past tenses. In past tense
forms, we find a separate form of the ergative or agent case:
this is formed by adding an ending -oi or -uei to the oblique
stem of the noun. In Guresi and Drasi, then, we have two distinct ergatives, neither of which is used for any other purpose. Furthermore, the situation in the Kohistani dialect,

spoken between the Gilgit and Gurēsi regions, provides a key
to the relation between these two situations. In Kohistani,
the -s(e) forms are always used in non-past tenses, while in
past tenses the forms in oblique +oi are regular, but the
forms in -s(e) can be used optionally. It is clear, then,
that the -s(e) forms are (or were, in the 1920's) in the
process of spreading from the non-past forms to replace the
-oi forms in the past.

On the basis of these observations, we can construct a
history for the Shiṇā ergative forms which is somewhat more
satisfying than simply borrowing. We can note first that the
non-Gilgit past tense agent forms, in oblique+oi look more
like what we might expect to find in an Indo-Iranian language
than do the -s(e) forms. We have already seen above that in
both Indic and Iranian, normal developments have led to a
situation in which perfect (or past) tense forms are accompanied by ergative case marking, in which S_t appears in the
reflex of either an instrumental or a dative/genitive, perhaps re-inforced by a postposition. We can suggest that the
same happened in Shiṇā, and that the oblique-case based agent
forms in -oi from the non-Gilgit dialects reflect this situation. We cannot be certain whether the construction originated as a passive (as in Indic generally) or as a possessive
(as in Iranian), given our lack of knowledge of the intermediate stages in the development of the Dardic languages,
but we can suggest the latter, since Shiṇā preserves a distinct form for the genitive, which is quite close (in Gurēsi
and Drāsi) or identical (in Kohistani) to the past tense
agent form.

Thus, at an earlier stage we can suggest that Shiṇā was

like other Indic or Iranian languages in having a set of perfect (or past) tenses in which ergative case marking (by
means of the genitive, or perhaps another oblique case, for
$\underline{S}_t$) appeared. At this point, however, we can suggest that the
discrepancy between ergative marking for some tenses but accusative marking for others would facilitate a change by which
case marking could come to be uniformly of one or the other
type. Against this, however, was the fact that precisely the
unusual ergative case marking accompanying the perfect tenses
was functional: it served as (part of) the morphological indication of the perfect. Thus, while it would perhaps be nice
to eliminate the discrepancy between ergative and non-ergative case marking systems within the same language, this
would entail the loss of some morphological material, if it
were done by simply extending one or the other system into
all tenses. Here we suggest Shinā found a clever solution: by
borrowing the Balti form of the agent case precisely for the
non-past tenses, they were not obliged to introduce ergative
case marking as part of the borrowing; rather, this borrowing
allowed the language to extend an existing ergative pattern
so as to make it completely general. At the same time, the
use of distinct forms for non-past and for past tense forms
allowed the language to preserve the overt morphological marking of the past/non-past distinction through the NP.

We can see therefore, that the original ergative system
limited to perfect forms, usual for an Indo-Iranian language,
provides a sort of entering wedge which makes the borrowing
of the Balti agent form more plausible. We can see, furthermore, that once such a dual, but uniformly ergative, system
as that of the Gurēsi and Drāsi dialects is established,

there is a tendency for the morphology of the less marked system (the present and other non-past tenses) to be generalized, to replace the system in the more marked (past) tenses. Such a generalization can apparently be observed in progress in Kohistani, and we can suggest that its natural outcome is the system in Gilgit. The -s(e) agent forms in Gilgit, then, are indeed borrowed from Tibetan (possibly from Balti), but the ergative construction is not: this is developed in the same way, through the formation of a new perfect, as in other Indic and Iranian languages where it is found.

Our discussion thus far has concerned only cases in which languages which originally had nominative/accusative morphology have acquired ergative patterns. One might well ask whether changes in the opposite direction are ever attested: do ergative languages ever come to be nominative/accusative? There are only two examples of this sort known to us, and both are in the Kartvelian (South Caucasian) family. If we accept the arguments of Chikobava (1948), the Kartvelian languages were all originally ergative in morphology. Insofar as we find instances of nominative/accusative morphology in these languages, then, we can assume that they are the result of linguistic change from ergative to accusative morphology.

One such instance is discussed at some length by Braithwaite (1973). As is well-known, modern Georgian is similar to the Indo-Iranian languages in that ergative case marking is confined to a series of tenses which can be described as perfective (although the traditional name for this series is 'aorist'), while nominative/accusative case marking is found with tenses from another series (traditionally called the 'present' series).[9] Braithwaite argues that the appropriate

characterization of the difference between the two series is
(at least originally; some individual tenses have shifted
their semantic domain somewhat) that the present series is a
set of progressive, or continuous tenses, while the 'aorist'
series is a set of punctual tenses. We could perhaps subsume
the latter group under 'perfect' tenses, and thus group the
Georgian phenomena together with the Indo-Iranian and related
facts. In that case, we might look for an account of Georgian
that would involve an original nominative/accusative system,
and an innovation consisting of the development of a set of
perfective tenses along one of the lines sketched for Indo-
Iranian. This would apparently, however, be contrary to what
is known about the history of Georgian: if common Kartvelian
had an ergative morphological pattern, it is the nominative/
accusative tenses of the present series that are in need of
an explanation, rather than the ergative tenses of the aorist
series.

Braithwaite suggests, as an answer to this problem, that
the progressive tenses of the present series are (at least in
origin) structurally similar to the English progressive: 'I
am reading the book', with a non-finite participial form of
the verb itself, and a copula element. On this view, the element VP in such tenses would always consist of a participle,
together perhaps with a dative element representing the $\underline{O}$ NP;
the subject ($\underline{S_i}$ or $\underline{S_t}$) would always be structurally subject
of a fundamentally intransitive predication. "I am reading
the book", that is, would be structurally 'I am at-reading
(with respect to the book)'. Given an ergative morphological
pattern, it would follow that all subjects in such structures
would appear in the nominative (or 'absolutive') case, since

all would be structurally S_i. The apparently 'accusative' form of O NP would also follow from the fact that these would always be structurally oblique, similar in Braithwaite's terms to benefactives and other indirect object NP types.

There is a certain amount of morphological support for Braithwaite's proposal. As he notes, the tenses of the present series, as distinct from those of the aorist series, involve a stem-formative element, following the verb stem itself. This stem formative is also present in the existing non-finite forms of the verb (such as the 'mazdar', filling a variety of participial and infinitival functions). Further, the pattern of verb agreement with objects in tenses of the present series shows certain similarities with the treatment of indirect objects, rather than direct object NP in tenses of the aorist series. There is no overt trace of a copula, despite the fact that Georgian has a verb 'to be', but this need not be a serious objection against Braithwaite's analysis; many languages in fact omit copula elements in some environments, and it is certainly possible that the Georgian tenses of the present series were originally of a structurally equational type. In fact, in modern Georgian there is such a structure, as Braithwaite points out: 'he is painting the wall' has an optional periphrastic form, literally 'he is at-painting (with respect to the wall)'.

Braithwaite's suggestion about the structural origins of the present tense series has definite merit, but there is an alternative to it which, while quite close in spirit, should also be considered. A great many languages exemplify a sort of indirect transitive construction, in which the object is treated as indirect rather than direct, with semantic

properties which are quite appropriate for the Georgian present series. In English, for example, we find relationships
such as those in (10) between ordinary transitive sentences
and corresponding sentence types in which the O NP appears
as object of a preposition:

(10)   a.   i.   John shot Bill.
             ii.   John shot at Bill.

        b.   i.   John read his speech.
             ii.   John read from his speech.

        c.   i.   John chewed his steak.
             ii.   John chewed on his steak.

The (i) sentences differ from the (ii) sentences in (10) in
that the (ii) sentences imply that the action described was
incompletely carried out, unsuccessful, still in progress,
etc. A wide variety of other languages also make use of a
similar distinction in syntactic terms for related semantic
purposes: Maori, Walbiri, Finnish, Navajo, etc. have rules
by which the O NP of a transitive construction can be 'demoted' to oblique status to indicate such incomplete, unsuccessful, etc. action. The properties of this construction in
English were discussed by Anderson (1971); since then it has
become clear that many other languages also make use of it
(see for example Timberlake, 1976, where closely similar
facts in Finnish and in Russian are discussed). Among the
purposes to which such a construction can be put is precisely the one which is relevant in the Georgian context: the
creation of a progressive tense series. 'Progressive' is
semantically quite close to 'incompletive', 'partitive',
etc., and could be expected to be expressed by the same
means. In fact, in at least one other language, (Mam, a

Mayan language also of the ergative type; cf. Robertson,
1976) precisely this device is employed for precisely this
purpose: when the $\underline{O}$ NP appears in an oblique phrase, rather
than in the direct case, the consequence is that the action
is interpreted as progressive, rather than simple or completed. Within the languages of the other Caucasian families,
this construction is also not unknown. Some examples are
given in Anderson (1976) from Bžedugh, a Circassian (North-
west Caucasian) language, in which the same completed vs.
incompleted/progressive distinction is marked in the same
way: by treating a structurally transitive clause as if it
were intransitive plus an oblique phrase, in which the $\underline{O}$ NP
is expressed. Similarly, Avar of the Northeast Caucasian
family (cf. Bokarev, 1949) displays a systematic relation
between ordinary transitive verbs, with ergative case marking, and a set of related verbs which behave structurally as
intransitives followed by an optional oblique complement
(for the $\underline{\underline{O}}$ NP), and which are interpreted as incompletives or
progressives. The same relation can be attested from a vari-
ety of languages: the point is that it is clearly in some
sense a universal that partitive, incompletive, progressive,
etc. forms can be derived from ordinary direct transitive
forms by 'demoting' the object to an oblique case.

Given the facts just discussed, it is clear that an explanation for the Georgian tenses of series I (the 'present'
series) is available. As Braithwaite noted, these tenses
have the property that the object is treated as oblique and
the subject (whether $\underline{S_i}$ or $\underline{S_t}$) as an intransitive subject.
It is certainly possible that Braithwaite's 'progressive'
analysis, consisting of a structure similar to that of the

English copula + present participle, can provide an account
of this; it is also possible that the correct explanation involves relating these forms to 'demoted object' partitives in
other languages. The two are clearly quite close. In any e-
vent, we can arrive at a coherent account of the Georgian system by starting from an ergative morphological pattern, as
Chikobava suggests: the nominative/accusative pattern in the
'present' series of tenses need not be treated as a relic of
an earlier (unattested) exclusively nominative/accusative
stage, nor need it be treated simply as unexplained 'borrowing' from an Indo-European language, as some would have it.
It can be accounted for quite naturally as an innovation,
starting from ergative marking in direct transitive structures, and proceeding to create progressive forms by structurally demoting the objects. As a subsequent stage, we can
suppose that the case marking originally associated with such
'demotion' of the O came to be generalized as a marker of the
new progressive aspect forms. Further research into Georgian
syntax is of course necessary (cf. Harris, 1976) to determine
the appropriate syntactic analysis of all of the Georgian
tense forms, as well as the correct historical account, but
it is reasonably clear that this instance of a correlation between case and tense/aspect marking, like those found in Indo-
Iranian, is susceptible of a straightforward explanation.

There is one further example of a shift from ergative to
nominative/accusative morphology which has apparently taken
place within the Kartvelian family. While Georgian has a system in which case marking is now associated with tense/as-
pect, as we have just discussed, and Laz has a system in
which all tenses are marked in an ergative fashion, the re-

lated language Mingrelian has yet another system: in Mingrelian, the ergative marker has been generalized so that not
only S_t but also S_i appears in the ergative. This is no longer, of course, an ergative system; by the generalization of
the ergative case, Mingrelian has become a nominative/accusa-
tive language morphologically. There is little to be said a-
bout this change, which apparently consisted exactly of the
extension of the ergative to cover intransitive as well as
transitive subjects. It is interesting to note, however, that
the analysis of Kartvelian languages (and of most other ergative languages, as well) which is supported by syntactic considerations makes this extension perfectly plausible. On syntactic grounds, it appears that S_t and S_i are to be identified as filling the same grammatical relation (subject), just
as in an accusative language. Hence, the spread of the ergative marker from S_t to S_i is perfectly plausible: both S_t and
S_i are subjects. We can compare this fact with the observation that (except in some Australian languages, and in Hurrian), S_i and Q do not form a unitary category syntactically,
though they are often (in ergative languages) morphologically
identified. On this basis, it is noteworthy that there are apparently no attested instances of the converse of the change
that gave rise to the Mingrelian system: no cases, that is,
where the accusative marker of Q spreads to encompass S_i as
well (but not S_t), thus creating an ergative system out of a
nominative/accusative one. If the grammatical relations suggested by an ergative morphological pattern were really significant, we could surely expect this change also to have taken
place somewhere in some language. The absence of such a
change, then, confirms the view taken throughout this paper
that ergative morphology is (generally) a superficial phe-

nomenon, unrelated to the basic aspects of clause structure
and grammatical relations.

We have discussed above several examples in which a
change to (or from) an ergative morphological pattern can be
accounted for in terms of the generalization of another well-
motivated construction, and the subsequent re-analysis of
that construction's morphology as basic, not derived. All of
this discussion, insofar as it has been based on the assumption that ergative and accusative morphologies correspond to
the same basic set of structures, provides implicit confirmation for the view that ergativity is not really very relevant
to syntax. There is at least one instance, however, which
seems to challenge that assumption. This is the case discussed above of Dyirbal and other similar Australian languages. If in fact Hale is correct, and the proto-Australian
language was accusative, how are we to account for the unusual syntactic properties of Dyirbal? Apparently, in this
case at least, the change that has occurred has been not simply morphological but syntactic in character.

This is not as difficult for our position as might at
first seem, however, although in our present state of knowledge of the morphology of proto-Australian, we can only speculate. We might assume with Hale that proto-Australian was an
accusative language. Let us assume further that it then underwent a change by which it became a (morphologically) ergative
language. Now linguists have long had the feeling that morphological categories are indicative of grammatical relations:
in fact, the whole problem of the analysis of ergative languages comes from the fact that the morphological categories
'absolutive' and 'ergative' do not square with the syntactic

categories 'subject' and 'object' in a straightforward way.
Let us take this as indicative of a more general tension,
therefore, between ergative and accusative systems in a single
language. As Dixon (1976) suggests, we might expect that
where such a tension exists, there is a tendency to resolve
it by reconciling the two systems. In general, the accusative
orientation of the syntactic structures is resistant to such
change, and if it occurs it consists of a reorganization of
the morphology, as in Mingrelian, along accusative lines. It
seems however that the peculiarity of Dyirbal and similar languages is that they have resolved this problem in the opposite
direction: having ergative morphology and (originally) accusative syntax, like other Australian languages such as Walbiri,
they have undergone a fundamental re-organization of their
basic syntactic structures along the lines inherent in the
traditional claim that underlying structures in ergative languages are 'passive'.

The dimensions of such a change are beyond the scope of
this paper to sketch, but its effect is to create a language
which is truly of 'syntactic ergative' type. While this result is certainly a radical one in syntactic terms, it is to
some extent "therapeutic" for the morphology which is thereby
rendered less opaque.

One further change remains to be discussed, though we
have little enough to say about it. We noted above that in
Chinook (after we have dealt with the 3 sg. masculine and
feminine prefixes), the sole remaining trace of ergativity
consists in an element /-k-/ which appears after $\underline{S}_t$ pronominal forms, except after 1sg. and 2sg. forms. This would appear to be a genuine ergative case marker, of sorts; but Sapir

suggests (cf. Sapir, 1926) that this marker, as well, has a
historical source outside of the ergative morphological pattern. He argues that this /-k-/ is actually a demonstrative
marker of some sort; and that in consequence, the ergative
morphological pattern is actually to be related to some sort
of earlier topicalization marker. In intransitive sentences,
that is, there is only one direct case NP, and hence no particular function for emphasis to fill. In a transitive structure, however, there are two; and we could imagine that it
was in an original emphatic demonstrative marker attached to
the first pronominal marker in a clause that the ergative
marker /-k-/ in Chinook is to be sought. This would be consistent with the facts of other ergative languages, such as
the New Guinea language Kâte (cf. Pilhofer, 1933), where the
ergative marker basically appears with any $\underline{S}_t$, but where its
function as a topicalizing or emphasizing demonstrative is
shown by the fact that under special emphasis, it can extend
to other functions such as $\underline{S}_i$. We have nothing in particular
to say about this circumstance; it would seem, however, that
topicalization provides another potential source for ergative
morphological patterns.

In conclusion, then, we hope to have shown that most
instances of change to (and from) ergative morphology are
perfectly consistent with our view that ergativity is a superficial aspect of morphology only, rather than a deep syntactic property (with the exception of the few really ergative languages, such as Dyirbal, whose existence demonstrates
the significance of the question, "what NPs have the properties of the subject in a language with ergative morphology?")
Such change generally takes place when a verbal form with

particular semantic value becomes derivationally opaque:
either by the loss of an opposed underived form, or through
the generalization of the form in question to new cases for
which the underived forms do not exist. The change itself
consists in the re-analysis of some morphology, formerly
connected with the operation of a transformational process,
as the basic marker of the semantic distinction itself. Such
changes are of general interest for the study of linguistic
change, but they do not in general suggest that ergative
morphology is in any interesting way connected with more
fundamental typological properties and distinctions.

Notes

1.   It is well beyond the scope of this paper to defend
the particular mixture of notions from Emonds (1976) and from
relational grammer that is implied here. Details will not be
important below, however, and the rules listed can be taken
as examples.

2.   I should like to record here my complete agreement
with Dixon's (1976) opinion of attempts such as that of George
(1975) to reduce Dyirbal to a nominative-accusative syntax.
That paper, in fact, seems an excellent reductio ad absurdum
of the proposition that all languages have such a syntactic
organization. See Dixon's paper for a summary of some of his
earlier arguments for ergative syntax in Dyirbal.

3.   For typographical convenience, I have used [ɬ] for a
voiceless lateral and C° for rounded consonants instead of the
transcriptions in my sources.

4.   In line with his analysis just described, Hale (1970)
considers this element (-ŋku~lu) to have been the marker for
agents in a passive construction. Dixon (1976) on the other
hand calls it simply "ergative" inflection.

5. Silverstein (1976) has attempted to explain this assymetry in terms of animacy and the notion of 'preferred ac-
tor', but it is not clear to me how his account applies to
the actors of transitive sentences but not to those of intransitive sentences.

6.   Hale (1970:772) suggests that Ngarluma-Yintjipaṇṭi
in Australia may be a counterexample to this claim.

7.   Cardona (1970) argues that Benveniste's interpreta-

tion of <u>ima</u> <u>tya</u> <u>manā</u> <u>kṛtam</u> is incorrect, and that the construction is actually passive (as traditionally assumed)
rather than possessive. The difficulty with this is that passive agents in OPersian generally appear in the instrumental,
or in a prepositional phrase with the ablative, rather than
in the genitive-dative. The latter, on the other hand, is
typical for possessive constructions. Cardona does exhibit
one (single) instance of a genuine passive with genitive-dative agent, but says that this form is secondary, and probably
represents a later extension of the new perfect to imperfect
passives. His argument against Benveniste's interpretation of
the perfects is quite unconvincing, and would in any case be
limited to Old Persian.

8. Data on Shiṇā are from Bailey (1924) and Lorimer
(1925).

9. We disregard here the third series of tenses in Georgian, called 'perfects', but in fact a set of reportive tenses.
These are clearly derived from passive forms from other tense
series; cf. Vogt (1971) for some discussion.

References

Allen, W. S. (1951). "A Study in the Analysis of Hindi Sentence-Structure." Acta Linguistica 6:68-86.

Anderson, Stephen R. (1971). "On the Role of Deep Structure in Semantic Interpretation." Foundations of Language 7:387-396.

Anderson, Stephen R. (1972). "On the Syntax of Ergative Languages." in Proceedings of the XIth International Congress of Linguistics, Bologna, Italy, vol 2:73-77.

Anderson, Stephen R. (1976). "On the Notion of Subject in Ergative Languages." in C. Li (ed.), Subject & Topic: 3-23. N.Y.: Academic Press.

Anderson, Stephen R. (1977). "Comments on Wasow: the Role of the 'Theme' in Lexical Relations." in A. Akmajian, et al (eds.), Formal Syntax. New York: Academic Press.

Bailey, T. Grahame (1924). Grammar of the Shina (Ṣiṇā) Language. London: Royal Asiatic Society.

Benveniste, Émile (1952). "La construction passive du parfait transitif." Bullétin de la Societé de Linguistique de Paris 48:52-62.

Benveniste, Émile (1960). "'Être' et 'avoir' dans leurs fonctions linguistiques." Bullétin de la Societé de Linguistique de Paris 55.

Benveniste, Émile (1970). "Definition d'un parfait en paleo-sibérien oriental." in Jakobson & Kawamoto (eds.), Studies in General and Oriental Linguistics:6-9.

Bloch, Jules (1965). Indo-Aryan. (English edition by A. Master). Paris: Maisonneuve.

Bokarev, A. A. (1949). Sintaksis avarskogo jazyka. Moscow: Academy of Sciences.

Braithwaite, Kim (1973). Case Shift and Verb Concord in Georgian. University of Texas doctoral dissertation.

Cardona, George (1970). "The Indo-Iranian construction mana (mama) kṛtam." Lg.46:1-12.

Chikobava, A. S. (1948). Ergaṭiuli ḳonsṭrukciis problema iber-iul-ḳavḳasiur enebši, I Tbilisi.

Chung, Sandra (1976a). Case-Marking and Syntactic Structure in Polynesian. Harvard University doctoral dissertation.

Chung, Sandra (1976b) "On the Gradual Nature of Syntactic Change." in this volume.

Clark, T. W. (1963). Introduction to Nepali. Cambridge: Heffer & Sons.

Dixon, R. M. W. (1976). "The Syntactic Development of Australian Languages." in this volume.

Emonds, Joe (1976). A Transformational Approach to English Syntax. New York: Academic Press.

George, Leland (1975). "Ergativity and Relational Grammar." in Papers from NELS 5:265-275.

Hale, Kenneth (1970). "The Passive and Ergative in Language Change: The Australian Case." in Pacific Linguistic Studies in Honor of Arthur Capell:757-783.

Harris, Alice (1976). Grammatical Relations in Modern Georgian. Harvard University doctoral dissertation.

Hohepa, Patrick (1969). "The Accusative to Ergative Drift in
    Polynesian." JPS 78:295-329.

Householder, Fred W. (1972). Syntactic Theory I. London:
    Penguin Books.

Jackendoff, Ray S. (1975). "Morphological and Semantic Regu-
    larities in the Lexicon." Language 51:639-671.

Lorimer, D. L. R. (1925). "The Forms and Nature of the Tran-
    sitive Verb in Shina (Gilgiti Dialect)." BSOAS 3:467-
    493.

Mathews, W. K. (1953). "The Ergative Construction in Modern
    Indo-Aryan." Lingua 3:391-406.

Perlmutter, David, & Paul Postal (forthcoming). Relational
    Grammar.

Pilhofer, G. (1933). Grammatik der Kâte-Sprache in Neuguinea.
    Zeitschrift für eingeborenen Sprachen, Beiheft 14.

Robertson, John (1976). The Structure of Pronoun Incorpora-
    tion in the Mayan Verbal Complex. Harvard University
    doctoral dissertation.

Sapir, Edward (1926). "A Chinookan Phonetic Law." IJAL 4:105-
    110.

Silverstein, Michael (1972). "Chinook Jargon: language con-
    tact and the problem of multi-level generative systems,
    I" Language 48:378-406.

Silverstein, Michael (1976). "Hierarchy of Features and Erga-
    tivity." in R. M. W. Dixon (eds.) Grammatical Categories
    in Australian Languages. Canberra: Australian Institute
    of Aboriginal Studies.

Southworth, Franklin (1967). Nepali Transformational Struc-
    ture. Poona: Deccan College.

Timberlake, Alan (1976). "Reanalysis and Actualization in
    Syntactic Change." in this volume.

Vendryes, J. (1937). "Sur l'emploi de l'auxiliaire 'avoir'
    pour marquer le passé." in Mélanges J. van Ginneken:
    85-92. Paris: Klincksieck.

Vogt, Hans (1971). Grammaire de la langue géorgienne. Oslo:
    Universittetsforlaget.

Wasow, Tom (1976). "Transformations and the Lexicon." in A.
    Akmajian, et al (eds.) Formal Syntax. New York: Academ-
    ic Press.

8 The Syntactic Development of Australian Languages

R. M. W. Dixon

This paper discusses how the rather different syntactic patterns of two modern Australian languages, Dyirbal and Yidin^y, may have evolved. Their syntactic development is related to the writer's reconstructions of proto-Australian nominal and pronominal morphology.

Our major thesis is that a syntactic change may be motivated and conditioned by the morphological structure of the language; and, vice versa, that a morphological paradigm may be restructured so that it will correspond more closely to the predominant syntactic pattern.

Section 1 briefly surveys some of the main points of Dyirbal and Yidin^y syntax. Section 2 provides theoretical discussion of the universal form of certain construction-types; mentions the possibility of the syntactic relation between a series of lexical words being generalised as a productive rule; comments on the interrelations between syntactic and morphological marking; and explains the semantic basis for 'split' case systems. Section 3 then outlines aspects of the morphology of proto-Australian; and Section 4 suggests reasons for the development of the syntactic systems described in 1.

1. Syntax of two modern languages

Dyirbal and Yidin^y, from north-east Queensland, are typical of Australian languages in having rather different sys-

tems of case inflections for nouns and adjectives (nominals)
and for first and second person pronouns:

	case marking	
grammatical function	NOMINALS	PRONOUNS
transitive subject (A)	ergative	
intransitive subject (S)		nominative
transitive object (O)	absolutive	accusative

That is, nouns and adjectives have a single form (marked by
absolutive case, which invariably has zero realisation) for
both intransitive subject and transitive object functions
(hereafter abbreviated: S and O); whereas transitive subject
function (A) is marked by ergative case ending (usually -ŋgu
or -lu after vowels; and -du after consonants, with assimilation of -d- to the place of articulation of the preceding segment).

Pronouns, on the other hand, have one form for the two
subject functions (S and A) and another for O. For non-singular pronouns we often find that the root is used for S and A
(so that we could in this case say that 'nominative case' on
pronouns has zero realisation) while the O form will involve
an accusative suffix -nʸa~-na~-na. Singular pronouns, however,
often have rather different forms for SA and O functions, that
are not readily segmentable into 'root' and 'affix', in terms
of a synchronic analysis.

A few languages, mostly in the eastern and south-eastern
part of Australia, have distinct forms of the singular pronouns for all three functions S, A and O. Giramay, most
southerly of the six dialects of Dyirbal, behaves in this way.
However, the remaining dialects of Dyirbal and its northerly

neighbour Yidin^y have one form for SA and one for O, for all numbers.

'Third person pronouns' in Australian languages are frequently semantically and morphologically rather different from first and second person forms. They may, for instance, have a deictic sense - perhaps involving obligatory specification of the position of the referent, 'here', 'there' or 'yonder'. In some languages (including Dyirbal) third person forms have an absolutive-ergative paradigm, like nominals; in others they may inflect on a nominative-accusative pattern, like first and second person pronouns; and in others they may have a quite different system of inflections, perhaps with different forms for S, A and O functions (Yidin^y falls into this category). Partly because of the lack of homogeneity in third person pronouns across Australian languages, we shall not include them in the discussion below.

1.1 Dyirbal

Specimen paradigms for two nouns and two pronouns are (in the central and northern dialects):

	'man'	'woman'	'I'	'we two'
A	yara+ŋgu	yibi+ŋgu	ŋad^{y}a	ŋali
S	yara	yibi	ŋad^{y}a	ŋali
O	yara	yibi	ŋayguna	ŋali+na

COORDINATION

Now Dyirbal has a very strong principle of coordination that is extensively used in conversations and narrative:

(1)   Two sentences can be coordinated if they have a common NP, and this NP is in surface S or O function in

each sentence. The occurrence of the NP in the second sentence is then usually deleted.

Such a 'topic NP' is often stated just once at the beginning of an utterance, and then commented on by a dozen or so
conjoined clauses.

Thus, from[1]

(2)   yaṛa miyandan^{y}u
       'The man laughed'

(3)   yaṛa yibiŋgu bund^{y}un
       'The woman slapped the man'

we can derive either

(4)   yaṛa miyandan^{y}u yibiŋgu bund^{y}un
       'The man laughed, and was slapped by the woman'

or, with the clauses conjoined in the opposite order:

(5)   yara yibiŋgu bund^{y}un miyandan^{y}u
       'The man was slapped by the woman, and laughed'

This is all perfectly straightforward -- a noun must be in absolutive case in both sentences for coordination (and deletion) to be possible. Note that there is no overt coordinating particle in Dyirbal (like 'and' in English). Coordination is effectively shown by the absence of an absolutive NP
from the second and later clauses (an absolutive NP must otherwise be obligatorily included in each sentence).

Dyirbal has a syntactic device for bringing an A NP into
surface S function, for purposes of coordination (amongst other things). This involves a transformation that is commonly
called (in work on 'ergative' languages) 'anti-passive'. This
is, roughly:

(6) NP_1 NP_2 V+tense

    noun+ergative   noun+absolutive
    pronoun+nominative   pronoun+accusative

$\Longrightarrow$ NP_1 NP_2 V+anti-pas-
                                                             sive+tense

    noun+absolutive   noun+dative
    pronoun+nominative   pronoun+dative

NP_1, which is the A NP in deep structure, now takes absolutive case on its nominal members and nominative on pronouns,
showing that it is in surface S function in an anti-passive
construction, and that an anti-passive is a derived intransitive sentence[2]. (There are in fact other grammatical data
supporting this conclusion -- Dixon 1972.150-1.)

Two points are worthy of note before we proceed. The
first is that a sentence, and even an individual NP, can mix
pronouns and nouns without any possibility of confusion, despite their different systems of case inflection -- the scepti-
cal reader is invited to try a few sentences for himself. The
second is that word order in Dyirbal sentences is remarkably
free, syntactic function being shown entirely by case inflection; the order in which we wrote words in (2-5), and constituents in (6), can be varied, without in any way affecting
our argumentation.

Now suppose we wish to coordinate two sentences like

(7)   yibi miyandan^{y}u
    'The woman laughed'

and (3). There is a common NP, yibi 'woman', but it is in S
function in (7) and in A in (3). We thus have to derive the
anti-passive of (3):

(8)   yibi yaragu bund^{y}ulŋan^{y}u $\langle =(3)\rangle$

Here ya$\underset{.}{r}$a bears dative inflection -gu, and the verb root
bund^{y}u-1 has the anti-passive suffix -ŋa-y followed by non-
future tense -n^{y}u (~ -n).

From (7) and (8), taken in either order, we can form:

(9)   yibi miyandan^{y}u yaragu bund^{y}ulŋan^{y}u
      'The woman laughed, and slapped the man'

(10) yibi yaragu bund^{y}ulŋan^{y}u miyandan^{y}u
      'The woman slapped the man, and laughed'

Let us now turn to pronouns. If we have two sentences
with a common NP that is in S function for each:

(11) ŋad^{y}a miyandan^{y}u
      'I laughed'

(12) ŋad^{y}a n^{y}inan^{y}u
      'I sat down'

they can be coordinated quite straightforwardly:

(13) ŋad^{y}a miyandan^{y}u n^{y}inan^{y}u
      'I laughed, and sat down'

Similarly if the common NP is in O function in the two sentences:

(14) ŋayguna yibiŋgu bund^{y}un
      'The woman slapped me'

(15) ŋayguna yaraŋgu d^{y}ilwan
      'The man kicked me'

giving:

(16) ŋayguna yibiŋgu bund^{y}un yaraŋgu d^{y}ilwan
      'I was slapped by the woman, and kicked by the man'

But suppose that the common NP is in S function in one
sentence and in A in the other. That is, we may wish to conjoin (11) with:

(17) ŋad^{y}a yibi bund^{y}un
      'I slapped the woman'

Note that the pronoun has the same form in both intransitive
(11) and transitive (17). But the coordination rule (1) applies as strictly to sentences involving pronouns as it does
to those involving nouns. That is, in order to conjoin (17)
to (11) the former must be anti-passivised:

(18) ŋad^{y}a yibigu bund^{y}ulŋan^{y}u ⟨≑(17)⟩

Here, although the pronoun has the same form as in (17) it is
in S function, within an intransitive anti-passive construction. And it can now be coordinated with (11), giving either
of:

(19) ŋad^{y}a miyandan^{y}u yibigu bund^{y}ulŋan^{y}u
      'I laughed, and slapped the woman

(20) ŋad^{y}a yibigu bund^{y}ulŋan^{y}u miyandan^{y}u
      'I slapped the woman, and laughed

   If we had, say:

(21) ŋad^{y}a miyandan^{y}u yibi bund^{y}un

it could only be taken to mean 'I laughed and someone (not me)
hit the woman'. That is, (21) would be taken to be a sequence
of two sentences -- not coordinated -- with the A NP being unspecified for the second, transitive, sentence. (Each sentence must contain an S or O NP -- unless deleted by a specific rule such as (1) -- but an A NP can be freely omitted.)

   Now consider (11) and (14). There is a common NP, with
form ŋad^{y}a in (11) and ŋayguna in (14). But constraint (1)
is satisfied, since the common NP is in S function in one sentence and in O in the other. So we can coordinate, in either
order, and delete the occurrence of the common NP in the sec-

ond sentence:

(22)   ŋad^ya miyandan^yu yibiŋgu bund^yun
        'I laughed, and the woman slapped me'

(23)   ŋayguna yibiŋgu bund^yun miyandan^yu
        'The woman slapped me, and I laughed'

This shows that the syntactic rule of <u>coordination always</u>
<u>identifies S and O functions</u>, treating them as quite separate
from A function; this is the case whether the common NP involves nouns, or pronouns, or a mixture of the two. Thus,
syntactic identification is parallel to the morphological paradigm of nominals -- where one form combines S and O function
-- and it is at odds with the morphology of pronouns, which
follow a nominative-accusative pattern.

RELATIVE CLAUSES

    A relative clause in Dyirbal must have an NP in common
with the main clause. Now the occurrence of the common NP in
the main clause can be in any function (S, A, O or indirect
object or even locative); the verb of the subordinate clause
bears a 'relative affix' and then an inflection corresponding
to the nominal case which marks this main clause function.
And the common NP must be in surface S or O function in the
subordinate clause; if it is in underlying A function then
the anti-passive transformation must be used to bring it into
S function.

    Thus, with (3) as main and (2) as subordinate clause we
derive:

(24)   yaṛa miyandaŋu yibiŋgu bund^yun
        'The woman slapped the man who was laughing'

In (24) the verb miyanda-y 'laugh' bears relative suffix -ŋu-

and then absolutive (with zero realisation), corresponding to
the function (O) of yaṛa in the main clause.

But from (3) and (7) we get:

(25)   yaṛa yibiŋgu miyandaŋuru bund^{y}un
        'The woman who was laughing slapped the man'

Here the verb has ergative inflection (the allomorph in this
case is -ru) agreeing with the case inflection on yibi in the
main clause.

Pronouns behave in exactly the same way -- that is, according to their syntactic function and quite irrespective of
their morphological shape. From (12) and (11) we get:

(26)   ŋad^{y}a miyandaŋu n^{y}inan^{y}u
        'I, who was laughing, sat down (i.e. I sat down
            while I was laughing)

From (14) and (11):

(27)   ŋayguna miyandaŋu yibiŋgu bund^{y}un
        'The woman slapped me, who was laughing (i.e. The
            woman slapped me, while I was laughing)

And from (17) and (11):

(28)   ŋad^{y}a miyandaŋuru yibi bund^{y}un
        'I, who was laughing, slapped the woman (i.e. I
            slapped the woman while I was laughing)

It will be seen that the verb of the relative clause bears
relative-plus-absolutive inflection, -ŋu+∅, when qualifying a
pronoun in S function (ŋad^{y}a) or in O function (ŋayguna); and
it bears relative-plus-ergative inflection, -ŋu+ru, when qualifying a pronoun in A function (ŋad^{y}a).

This is only a sample of the evidence showing that Dyirbal consistently identifies S with O at the syntactic level.

Other constructions provide further support -- for instance,
there is a very popular complement construction which demands
a coreferential NP that is in S/O function in both main and
subordinate clauses; and so on (see Dixon 1972.73-9, 130-5).

There is, in sum, an overwhelming array of data showing
that S and O belong together syntactically in Dyirbal, just
as do S and A in English. Thus, the arguments for providing
tree structures for English:

(29)   INTRANSITIVE   TRANSITIVE

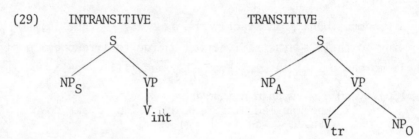

apply, mutatis mutandis, in support of a tree structure for
Dyirbal (and for other languages of this extreme 'ergative'
syntactic type):

(30)   INTRANSITIVE   TRANSITIVE

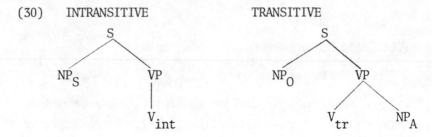

(Here the order of constituents is not an issue, merely their
hierarchical relation to each other.)

Early scholars like Uslar and Schuchardt (see Catford
1975.7) attempted to account for ergative constructions --
that is, sentences like (3) -- as 'passives'. In this inter-

pretation (3) would be 'derived' from the 'active' (8). But note that this derivation involves deletion of a derivational affix from the verb, and the conversion of a dative NP in an intransitive sentence (yaṛa+gu) into transitive object. Note also that a sentence like (8) would not normally begin a discourse in Dyirbal; anti-passive constructions are only employed under specified syntactic conditions -- as second or later clause in a coordination, or as a relative or complement clause -- in order to satisfy coreferentiality constraints such as (1). To take (8) as the unmarked, underlying construction thus goes against the most elementary principles of linguistic analysis (it leads to similar complications and difficulties as would taking the passive construction as basic in English).

Fortunately, no suggestions of this type have been put forward by serious linguists in recent years. It is accepted that structures like (3) are the norm for Dyirbal and other ergative languages, just as active sentences are for English -- cf Golab, 1969. (Leland George (1974) speaks as a voice from the past in effectively suggesting that (8) be taken as the underlying representation, with (3) being derived from it by passivisation; he shows only partial understanding of Dyirbal syntax and appears not to be familiar with the considerable literature on this general question. George is apparently motivated by a desire to fit Dyirbal into the 'relational grammar' that is being developed by Postal and Perlmutter, which -- George implies -- depends on the universal notion of 'subject' (i.e. S=A). It must be stressed, though, that George does not imply that either Postal or Perlmutter would support this facile analysis. George's 'solution' has also

been invoked by Pullum (1976) as a possible aid to reconciling Dyirbal with another proposed universal, this time concerning word order.)

Note, though, that although Dyirbal syntax is overwhelmingly in favour of an analysis like (30) -- if one is working
in terms of a theory that would specify structures like (29)
for English -- there are just two rules that identify S with
A. One is a transitivising process, described in 2.2; the
other is the imperative, where S behaves like A qua selection-
al restrictions and 'subject deletion'. It is in fact difficult on a priori grounds to see how any language could fail
to identify S and A in some way for imperatives (we return to
this point in 2.1 below).

1.2 Yidin^y

Although Yidin^y is Dyirbal's northerly neighbour it is
grammatically and lexically quite different from it (as different as almost any Australian language) while still of
course sharing typological features characteristic of the Australian language family as a whole.

Specimen paradigms follow the same pattern as for Dyirbal:

	'man'	'woman'	'I'	'we two'
A	wagud^{y}a+ŋgu	bun^{y}a+:ŋ	ŋayu	ŋali
S	wagu:d^{y}a	bun^{y}a	ŋayu	ŋali
O	wagu:d^{y}a	bun^{y}a	ŋan^{y}an^y	ŋali+:n^y

Ergative inflection is basically -ŋgu with a vowel-final
stem; a general phonological rule reduces this to -:ŋ on a
stem that has an even-number of syllables. There are also a
number of general rules which insert and delete vowel length;
the occurrence of long vowels is not germane to the syntactic

discussion which follows.

Coordination plays a relatively minor role in Yidin^y syntax (in comparison with its tremendous usage in Dyirbal) and we will first consider the important process of subordination.[3]

SUBORDINATION

Yidin^y has a stronger coreferentiality constraint for its subordinate clauses than that just described for relative clauses in Dyirbal. There must be a 'common NP' that is in S or O function in <u>both</u> main <u>and</u> subordinate clauses. Thus, from

(31)   wagu:d^{y}a maŋga:n^y
      'The man laughed'

(32)   bun^{y}a:ŋ wagu:d^{y}a wuṟa:n^y
      'The woman slapped the man'

can be derived, with (31) as main and (32) as subordinate clause:

(33)   wagu:d^{y}a maŋga:n^y bun^{y}a:ŋ wuṟan^{y}unda
      'The man, who was slapped by the woman, laughed'

Inflection -n^{y}unda on a verb marks a specific variety of subordinate clause.

With the roles of the two clauses reversed we obtain:

(34)   wagu:d^{y}a bun^{y}a:ŋ wuṟa:n^y maŋgan^{y}unda
      'The woman slapped the man who was laughing'

However, if the common NP is in A function in either clause then the 'anti-passive' transformation must be applied, placing it in surface S function. Anti-passivisation in Yidin^y is in outline identical to the corresponding process in Dyirbal:

(35)   NP$_1$ NP$_2$ V+tense
         noun+ergative   noun+absolutive
         pronoun+nominative   pronoun+accusative

$\Longrightarrow$ NP$_1$ NP$_2$ V+anti-pas-
                                                            sive+tense
         noun+absolutive   noun+dative
         pronoun+nominative   pronoun+dative

The form of the anti-passive suffix to verbs is -:d^{y}i-n.

   Thus, given

(36)   bun^{y}a maŋga:n^y
       'The woman laughed

and (32), we find that there is a common NP which is in S
function in (36) but in A for (32). Forming the anti-passive
of (32):

(37)   bun^{y}a wagud^{y}anda wuṛa:d^{y}in^{y}u $\langle$=(32)$\rangle$

enables us to derive subordinate constructions:

(38)   bun^{y}a maŋga:n^y wagud^{y}anda wuṛa:d^{y}in^{y}u:n
       'The woman, who slapped the man, laughed'

(39)   bun^{y}a wagud^{y}anda wuṛa:d^{y}in^{y}u maŋgan^{y}unda
       'The woman, who laughed, slapped the man'

Note that -nda is the dative case inflection, and that
-n^{y}unda and -n^{y}u:n are allomorphs of the subordinate inflection on verbs, as -n^{y}u and -:n^y are allomorphs of past tense.

   Exactly the same considerations apply to sentences involving pronouns. From:

(40)   ŋayu maŋga:n^y
       'I laughed'

(41)   ŋan^{y}an^y bun^{y}a:ŋ wuṛa:n^y
       'The woman slapped me'

wc can derive either of

(42)   ŋayu maŋga:n^y (ŋan^{y}an^y) bun^{y}a:ŋ wuran^{y}unda
       'I, who was slapped by the woman, laughed (i.e. I
          laughed while I was being slapped by the
          woman)'

(43)   ŋan^{y}an^y bun^{y}a:ŋ wuṛa:n^y (ŋayu) maŋgan^{y}unda
       'The woman slapped me, who was laughing (i.e. The
          woman slapped me while I was laughing)'

with the second occurrence of the pronoun optionally deleted.

   But given (40) and

(44)   ŋayu bun^{y}a wuṛa:n^y
       'I slapped the woman'

we have first to derive the anti-passive version of (44):

(45)   ŋayu bun^{y}a:nda wuṛa:d^{y}in^{y}u $\langle$=(44)$\rangle$

as a basis for

(46)   ŋayu maŋga:n^y bun^{y}a:nda wuṛa:d^{y}in^{y}u:n
       'I, who slapped the woman, laughed (i.e. I laughed
          while I was slapping the woman)'

(47)   ŋayu bun^{y}a:nda wuṛa:d^{y}in^{y}u maŋgan^{y}unda
       'I, who laughed, slapped the woman (i.e. I slapped
          the woman while I was laughing)'

   Note that although (40) and (44) both involve ŋayu 'I'
this is in S function in the first case and in A in the second.
These two sentences can _not_ simply be joined together, to
give:

(48)   ŋayu bun^{y}a wuṛa:n^y maŋgan^{y}unda

In fact (48) is an acceptable sentence in Yidin^y but it means
'I slapped the woman who was laughing', being derived from
(44) and (36).

Yidin^y has three major types of subordinate clause, marked by verbal inflections -n^{y}unda, -n^{y}um and -na respect- itvely. -n^{y}um clauses describe some completed event ('I slap- ped the woman who had laughed') while -na clauses refer to a prospective event, and have the semantic effect associated with purpose complements in English ('I hid the food so that the man should not see it'). All three types of construction have the same syntax, and all demand a common NP that is in S/O function in main and subordinate clauses.

This is, however, the only area of Yidin^y syntax in which S is consistently identified with O, rather than with A. Surveying the whole range of grammatical data in Yidin^y, the evidence appears to be balanced pretty evenly between a 'deep structure' of the traditional 'accusative' type, (29), and an 'ergative' deep structure, (30), that was found to be appropriate for Dyirbal. The 'split' nature of Yidin^y syntax is nicely exemplified by the rules for coordination.

COORDINATION

Coordination exactly follows the morphological paradigm. Just as nouns have the same forms for S and O functions, so if two clauses involve a nominal common NP then it must be in S or O function in each case to permit coordination. From (31) and (32) we can derive:

(49)　wagu:d^{y}a maŋga:n^y bun^{y}a:ŋ wura:n^y
　　　'The man laughed, and the woman slapped him'

(50)　bun^{y}a:ŋ wagu:d^{y}a wuṛa:n^y maŋga:n^y
　　　'The woman slapped the man, and he laughed'

Coordination is marked in two ways: the two clauses can make up a single intonation group; and the common NP can be delet- ed from the second clause.

If the common NP involves a <u>pronoun</u>, it must be in S or
A function in each clause (mirroring the fact that a single
pronominal form is used for S and for A functions). Thus,
from (40) and (44) we can obtain either of:

(51)   ŋayu maŋga:n^y bun^{y}a wuṛa:n^y
         'I laughed, and slapped the woman'

(52)   ŋayu bun^{y}a wuṛa:n^y maŋga:n^y
         'I slapped the woman, and laughed'

It will be noted that (52) is in fact ambiguous between 'I
slapped the woman and I laughed' and 'I slapped the woman and
she laughed'; the rules we have indicated would derive (52)
from (44) and (40), or from (44) and (36). Note, however,
that (50) is not ambiguous -- it could <u>not</u> mean 'The woman
slapped the man and then <u>she</u> laughed'. That is, identification of S and A NPs is allowed only in the case of pronouns,
never of NPs made up entirely of nouns and adjectives.

We have mentioned that coordination is not so grammatically central in Yidin^y as it is in Dyirbal. Whereas Dyirbal
may join together as many as six or twelve clauses -- with
the absolutive 'common NP' perhaps stated only once, in the
first clause -- Yidin^y seldom conjoins more than two or three
clauses at once. And while Dyirbal has a strict coreferentiality rule -- (1) above -- Yidin^y allows semantic and contextual interpretation to play a considerable role (in the
disambiguation of sentences like (52), and in a number of
other ways). But the principles of coordination just given
do illustrate the partly-accusative (i.e. S=A)/partly-erga-
tive (i.e. S=O) nature of syntactic rules in Yidin^y.

Dyirbal and Yidin^y constitute a fairly representative

sample of Australian languages. Morphologically the pattern
of a 'nominative-accusative' paradigm for pronouns and an
'absolutive-ergative' one for nouns is encountered in the
great majority of languages, though there are a few with an
absolutive-ergative case system for all parts of speech (see
4.1 below) and some with nominative-accusative throughout.

Syntactically, Dyirbal stands at one extreme in that it
treats S and O similarly (and A quite differently) in the
statement of almost every rule and constraint. There are
some languages at the other pole, identifying S and A in all
or almost all cases. But a recent symposium, devoted to the
topic 'Are Australian languages 'ergative' or 'accusative' in
underlying structure?' (see Dixon 1976.485-611) revealed that
most languages are like Yidin^y in grouping S with A in some
cases and with O in others. There appears to be a universal
continuum, rather than a strict dichotomy. Dyirbal stands
far to one end and English at the other; Yidin^y and most other Australian languages are spaced along the scale.

This, of course, suggests that the division of languages
into those for which (29) is appropriate, and those prefer-
ring (30), was misconceived. If we continue to work in terms
of a tree structure model (note that Dixon, 1977, suggests a
rather different type of syntactic representation, which we
do not have the space to go into here), then it must simply
be something like:

(53)   INTRANSITIVE   TRANSITIVE

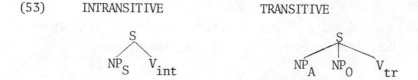

with no VP node at all.[4]

With this model, rules identifying NP_S and NP_A can involve specification

(54)   ##NP X##

that is, the leftmost NP in the sentence; and reference to NP_S or NP_O would be of the form:

(55)   ##(X) NP V##

that is, the NP immediately to the left of V. Highly ergative languages will have a preponderance of (55) while accusative languages may exclusively use (54). Languages of mixed syntactic type, 1ke Yidin^y, will make use of both types of specification.

2.   Theoretical preliminaries

2.1 Rules with universal effect

It is only within the last few years that syntacticians have fully realised that some 'ergative' languages can not be dealt with in terms of an 'accusative' base together with a late case-manipulating rule, but instead demand a rather different type of deep structure (e.g. Hale 1970, Dixon 1972). This immediately led to a flurry of activity among Australianists, counting up ways in which individual languages identify S and A, and those in which they identify S and O. It was thought that each language had, as it were, a 'syntactic personality' in terms of its preferences for grouping of syntactic functions.

Recently, Jeffrey Heath (1976) has suggested that this view is, at least in part, misconceived. Heath studied a number of recurrent construction-types and found that some do

have similar syntactic effect in every language in which they
occur (his paper gives quite detailed exemplification, which
it is unnecessary to recount here). He suggests 'it begins
to look as though the rules selecting triggering NPs are
largely predictable on the basis of the construction types to
which the transformations in question apply'. On this argument, languages show differing syntactic characters largely
as a result of which contruction-types they include (and the
inherent syntactic characters of these).

Although Heath's is an extreme view and certainly cannot
account for every aspect of syntactic identification in a language, there is without doubt a good deal of truth in it. One
of the clearest examples is imperatives. Surely every language must have imperative sentences; and the same selection-
al restrictions appear to apply to S and to A NPs, whatever
the overall syntactic type of the language. For instance,
imperative is one of the two instances of syntactic 'accusativity' known for Dyirbal. (But see Rigsby, 1975, for an account of an ergative language in which imperatives show some
'accusative' but also some 'ergative' -- i.e. S=O -- characteristics.)

We are thus suggesting that imperative constructions are
likely always to show a constant pattern, whatever changes
may affect other parts of the syntax and morphology of a language. And some other construction-types may have a more-or-
less constant form, in every language in which they occur.
(Heath's ideas have been extended by McKay, 1975, who notes
inter alia that noun incorporation appears always to involve
S or O -- never A -- NPs in Australian as in Amerindian languages; cf Sapir, 1911. It is interesting here that the re-

striction of incorporation to S and O NPs is much less intuitively 'obvious' than is the equation of S and A for imperatives.)

2.2 Semantic Conditioning

It is well for a syntactician to remind himself every
now and then that the primary role of a language is to convey
meaning from speaker to hearer, and that syntactic devices exist essentially to expedite this semantic task.

We tend to divide sentences into, say, 'transitive' and
'intransitive'. But it is important also to realise that
there are a number of quite different semantic classes of
verb involved and that these have, as it were, different syntactic expectations.

This can be exemplified from Dyirbal. There are a number of pairs of verbs which have exactly the same semantic effect save only that they differ in transitivity, e.g.

I. a. intransitive
        d^yana-y 'stand'

    b. transitive
        d^yara-l 'put standing, make stand'

II. a. intransitive
        mayi-l 'come out, emerge'

    b. transitive
        bundi-l 'take out'

III. a. intransitive
        wurba-y 'speak, talk'

     b. transitive
        buwa-y 'tell'

IV. a. intransitive
         man^{y}d^{y}a-y 'eat'

     b. transitive
         d^{y}aŋga-y 'eat (something)'

Now for those pairs which refer to motion or a position of
rest -- exemplified here by I and II -- the intransitive subject (S) corresponds to the transitive object (0). That is,

(56) a. yaṛa d^{y}anan^{y}u
          'The man stood up'

      b. yaṛa yibiŋgu d^{y}aran
          'The woman stood the man up (e.g. she assisted
           a sick man to get to his feet)'

could both describe the same event. But for verbs which are
not concerned primarily with position -- exemplified here by
III and IV -- we have S corresponding to A. Thus:

(57) a. yaṛa wurban^{y}u
          'The man is talking'

      b. yibi yaṛaŋgu buwan^{y}u
          'The man is telling the woman'

Note that there is in Dyirbal an explicit criterion for grouping these verbs into pairs. In the 'mother-in-law' or avoid-
ance style of speech there is just one transitive verb corresponding to each of the pairs I-IV (the intransitive member
being rendered in mother-in-law by the 'reflexive' form of
this verb). Details are in Dixon 1971, 1972.292-301.

There is also in Dyirbal a syntactic process for deriving a transitive stem from any intransitive verbal root; it
involves the derivational affix -ma-1. This always forms a
transitive verb whose A NP is identical to the S NP of the

underlying intransitive verb. Thus, transitive wurbayma-1
appears to be syntactically and semantically identical to
buwa-y, and man^{y}d^{y}ayma-1 to d^{y}aŋga-y. But when -ma-1 is added to an intransitive verb of the motion/rest set, the resulting form has quite different meaning from the corresponding
transitive lexical verb. That is,

(58)   a.   yugu d^{y}anan^{y}u
            'The stick is standing (e.g. a post is embedded
            in the ground)

       b.   yugu yaraŋgu d^{y}aran
            'The man stands the stick up (e.g. embeds its
            end into the ground)

could both describe a certain state-of-affairs; and a rather
different state-of-affairs could be described by either of:

(59)   a.   yaṛa d^{y}anan^{y}u
            'The man is standing'

       b.   yugu yaraŋgu d^{y}anayman
            'The man is standing with a stick (e.g. holding
            it in his hand, or wielding it)

(58b) and (59b) differ only in the substitution of d^{y}anayma-1
for d^{y}ara-1. But (58b) is related to (58a), with S=O identification, whereas (59b) corresponds to (59a), with the S=A
identification that is obligatory for the syntactic process
of 'transitivisation' (shown by the verbal affix -ma-1).

Now all languages have syntactic relations holding between transitive and intransitive pairs of verbs, as we have
illustrated above. It is quite possible that the syntactic
relation that holds between a number of important lexical
pairs could be generalised, and become the syntactic basis
for a productive grammatical rule. For instance, we could
suggest that Dyirbal has generalised the S=A identification

-- that applies to a dozen or so lexical pairs of non-motion
verbs -- to a productive grammatical process of transitivisation; note that S=A identification underlies every instance
of transitivisation, whatever the semantic type of the verb
involved. (This is the other piece of 'accusative syntax' in
Dyirbal, alluded to in 1.1.)

Our general point here is that a lexicon will always in-
vlolve relations of synonymy and partial synonymy which have
certain syntactic overtones (and it will have these whether
or not there is any syntactic process like Dyirbal 'transitivising'). When a productive derivational process does
evolve, the analogy to lexical relations must be one factor
that helps to determine the exact syntactic effect of the
process.[5]

2.3 Correlations between syntactic and morphological marking

It is important to distinguish morphological marking
(case inflections, and so on) from syntactic marking (whether
a certain NP can be pivot for subordination and coordination,
and so forth). Names such as 'ergative' and 'accusative' are
of course primarily morphological, but they have been used in
recent years also to refer to syntactic structures -- thus
(29) can be called 'accusative' (O is the marked function,
treated differently from S and A) and (30) 'ergative' (here
A is set off from S and O.)

Note that there need not be exact congruence between
morphological and syntactic marking. We demonstrated in 1.1
that although Dyirbal pronouns have the same form for S and
A functions, in the syntactic areas of coordination and relative clauses S is always identified with O, never with A. 1.2
sketched a similar situation qua subordination in Yidin[y]. As

a further example we can quote Walbiri, where nouns and free form pronouns show absolutive-ergative morphology, bound form pronouns are strictly nominative-accusative, and S=A predominates in syntactic operations.[6]

But there is never _too_ great a disparity between morphology and syntax. That is, no language is known whose case inflections consistently identify S with A, while its syntactic rules and constraints always group together S and O; or vice versa. Furthermore, we can predict that such a language would never be encountered.

A basic principle upon which discussion of this paper rests is that the morphological and syntactic systems of a language will always tend to change in order to become more congruent one with the other.[7] Morphology may remain constant and syntactic patterns realign to accord more closely with it. Or syntax may remain unchanged while morphological marking is restructured more closely to mirror the syntax. Or both levels may change simultaneously, moving towards some common target. Some illustrations of these possibilities are given in 4.1 and 4.2 in an attempt at explaining the evolution of the syntactic systems sketched in 1.1 and 1.2.

The tendency for change to promote congruence between morphological and syntactic marking is similar, in some ways, to the accepted tendency for change to eliminate paradigmatic irregularities ('cows' replacing 'kine', and so on). But just as new morphological anomalies may come into being while some old irregularities are in the process of being ironed out, so some new lack of iconicity between levels may creep in while an established syntactic-morphological non-correspondence is being eliminated. That is, languages seldom have everything

neat and symmetrical all at one time (although of course it
is conceivable that this could happen).

It is well known that morphological irregularities may
be the result of a series of phonological changes, or may be
the only partially integrated residue of a substratum. There
can be similar reasons -- formal change, within a language,
or contact with other tongues -- for lack of congruence between morphological and syntactic marking.

It is not hard to imagine ways in which this might happen. Suppose, for instance, that a certain language has fairly strict word order 'verb-subject-object', and that in addition A and S functions are marked by nominative case suffix
-n, and O function by accusative suffix -s, these being added
to stems which all end in a vowel. This could accord well
with a predominantly S=A pattern of syntactic identification.
Yet the parallelism would be lost if, say, consonants ceased
to be permitted on the last word in a sentence (at the end
of an intonation group). Transitive subject function (A)
would retain its ending -n, but S and O would both lose their
explicit marking (the fact that the marking was lost when S
and O occurred sentence-finally might be generalised to omission of these affixes in all positions). Thus, the morphology would take on an absolutive-ergative shape.

A change as radical as this would scarcely be likely if
the syntax were exclusively accusative. But suppose it were
largely in terms of S=A, with some S=O identifications. We
would still have some correspondence between syntactic and
morphological marking (so the new system should be a possible
one) but it would be nowhere nearly as good a fit as before.

Lack of congruence having thus been introduced by change external to the grammar, we would predict a tendency for syntactic and/or morphological reorientation gradually to establish a better parallelism. Such reanalysis would be -- like all grammatical change -- a slow process (and might of course be hindered by other formal changes or external pressures).

2.4 Silverstein's hierarchical explanation for morphological marking

There are a fair number of languages (Amerindian, and other) that share with most Australian languages the feature of having two systems of case-marking -- 'nominative-accusative' on some parts of speech, and 'absolutive-ergative' on others. Michael Silverstein (1976) has studied these and found that the case inflections are by no means randomly distributed amongst different types of words. He suggests a hierarchy, roughly:[8]

and suggests that for each language which mixes ergative and accusative case systems, everything to the left of a certain point on the hierarchy will show an accusative paradigm, and everything to the right an ergative system of case marking. Thus, for some languages the critical point is '3' -- pro-

nouns will then be morphologically accusative and all nouns
ergative; other languages take as their critical point '1'
or '2' or '4' or '5', and so on.

Silverstein suggests a natural explanation for this
division. Referents of pronouns are natural instigators of
actions, whereas as one moves to the right in the hierarchy,
each new class is progressively less likely to occur as transitive subject. It is thus reasonable to mark the rightmost
classes (with the ergative inflection) when they occur with
this marked function; but it is less necessary to mark the
leftmost classes when they occur in their most natural function, transitive subject. The reverse argument applies for
accusative; direct object is an unusual or 'marked' function
for the leftmost classes, so accusative marking is more natural at this end of the hierarchy.[9] We thus have, effectively, two independent parameters -- the marking of 'transitive
subject' (which extends inwards some distance from the right)
and the marking of 'transitive object' (which extends in
from the left). If the cut-off points of these two parameters coincide we get a simple split ergative/accusative system. But the parameters can overlap and we will then get
some part of the middle of the hierarchy -- say, third person
pronoun -- having three distinctive case forms: ergative
(for transitive subject), accusative (for transitive object)
with just intransitive subject function receiving the unmarked case inflection (often, zero).

Some Australian languages do, in fact, show a 'middle
area' -- between the absolutive-ergative and nominative-accusative extremes -- where there are separate forms for each
of the major syntactic functions, S, A and O. The interroga-

tive pronoun behaves in this way in Dyirbal (Dixon 1972.53) and human deictics do in Yidin^y (Dixon, 1977.187).

We thus have a principled semantic explanation for the cooccurrence within a single language of two or three different systems of case marking.

3.   The morphology of proto-Australian

We can now outline relevant aspects of the morphology of a language we refer to as 'proto-Australian', the putative ancestor of Dyirbal and Yidin^y, as of most (or all) other modern Australian tongues. The methodology and data on which these reconstructions are based have not yet been published; only the conclusions are summarised here.

Most modern Australian languages do not allow monosyllabic words; that is, for reasons partly connected with stress and rhythm, each inflected word must be of at least two syllables. Some languages do allow monosyllabic roots in some parts of speech with obligatory inflections making up (at least) a second syllable; others insist that roots, as well as words, must be polysyllabic. Now the evidence from phonotactic comparison and reconstruction, supported by the reconstruction of original systems of verbal and pronominal morphology, is that the proto-language <u>did</u> allow monosyllabic words. This is a critical claim for some of the discussion which follows.

NOUN CASE MARKING

Three non-zero cases can with certainty be reconstructed:

(a)   ergative
       *-lu (following a vowel) ~ -du (following a consonant)

(b)   locative
      *-la (following a vowel) ~-da (following a consonant)

(c)   dative-genitive
      *-gu

Modern languages have developed a more extensive repertoire
of cases from this model. Thus, although some modern languages retain -gu in both dative and genitive functions, others keep -gu for just dative function and use an augmented
form for genitive (for instance, Walbiri has dative -gu and
genitive -gulaŋu). Ablative ('motion from') may originally
have involved an increment *-ŋu.. to locative ('position
at'); but in many modern languages there is now a separate
ablative inflection, added directly to the stem (for instance,
-ŋuḻu in Walbiri, -ŋunu in Dyirbal).

We are here concerned only with the marking of the major
syntactic functions, S, A and O. Transitive subject, A, was
uniformly marked on nouns by the ergative inflection -lu~ -du
(with assimilation of the -d- in place of articulation to a
stem-final nasal or -y). Hale, 1976, has indicated how the
postvocalic allomorph -ŋgu may have developed from -lu~ -du,
through change in the phonotactic system and subsequent morphological reanalysis.

The plain stem is uniformly employed for the intransitive subject, S, and we suggest that this was so in the proto-
language (in terms of a case system we thus recognise 'absolutive', with zero realisation). Many modern languages treat
transitive object function, O, in the same way. But some show
an accusative affix -n^{y}a ~ -na (~ -na), sometimes just on proper nouns, sometimes also on common nouns with human reference, sometimes also on those with animate reference, and

sometimes on all nouns (examples are quoted in Dixon 1970.94-
7). We return to this in the discussion of pronouns.

PRONOMINAL FORMS

It is likely that proto-Australian followed the pattern
of most modern languages in having singular, dual and plural
forms of both first and second person pronouns. (An alternative possibility is a proto-system similar to that described
by Conklin, 1962, for Hanunóo). Third person forms differ
considerably from language to language, both in form and in
semantic function; we are not at present able to say anything
about their form in a common ancestor language.

Modern languages typically show a rather different paradigm for non-singular and for singular pronouns; this is exemplified in the Dyirbal and Yidin^y samples quoted in 1.1,
1.2. Non-singulars almost always have one form (that we can
take as the root) for S and A functions; the O form involves
an 'accusative' affix that derives from original *-n^{y}a ~-n̯a.
Exemplifying with the first person, ŋali, we can show the suggested proto-forms, and their reflexes in Dyirbal and Yidin^y.

NON-SINGULAR PRONOUNS e.g. ŋali 'we two'

	proto	Dyirbal	Yidin^y
SA	ŋali	ŋali	ŋali
O	ŋali+n^{y}a	ŋalina	ŋali:n^y

Singular pronouns have as a rule more complicated paradigms in individual modern languages and there are less obvious correspondences between languages. However, careful
reconstruction yields:

RECONSTRUCTION OF SINGULAR PRONOUNS

	first person	second person	
A	ŋay+d^{y}u	n^{y}un+du	ŋin+du
S	ŋay	n^{y}un	or ŋin
O	ŋay+n^{y}a	n^{y}un+n^{y}a	ŋin+n^{y}a

The root of the 2 sg pronoun is variously attested as n^{y}un, n^{y}in, ŋun and ŋin. These may have evolved out of one original form; but we prefer here to be more cautious, recognising *ŋin (which could have yielded ŋun by assimilation of vowel to preceding consonant) for a number of languages mostly close to the east coast, alternating with *n^{y}un (which could have given n^{y}in by a similar assimilation) over the rest of the continent. *ŋin and *n^{y}un forms have identical (proto-) morphology.

Leaving aside for a moment the S forms, we can compare the proto-shapes of A and O pronouns with those in present-day Dyirbal and Yidin^y.

FIRST PERSON SINGULAR PRONOUN

	proto	Dyirbal	Yidin^y
A	ŋay+d^{y}u	ŋad^{y}a	ŋayu
O	ŋay+n^{y}a	ŋayguna	ŋan^{y}an^y

(i) The development *ŋay+d^{y}u > ŋad^{y}u and *ŋay+n^{y}a > ŋan^{y}a is a natural one; many modern languages (including Yidin^y but not Dyirbal) do not permit a cluster of y followed by the palatal stop d^y or nasal n^y.

(ii) The change from *ŋad^{y}u to ŋad^{y}a is widespread, always coinciding with a change in the 2 sg pronoun *n^{y}undu > n^{y}unda or *ŋindu > ŋinda; the isogloss of pronominal *u > a almost coincides with that of *u > a for past tense *-n^{y}u.

(iii) *ŋad^{y}u > ŋayu in Yidin^y is a quite natural lenition (note that Yidin^y preserves ŋad^{y}u- as the root for oblique forms e.g. dative ŋad^{y}u:nda).

(iv) Dyirbal has plainly reformed the accusative pronoun, this being now based on the 1 sg genitive form ŋaygu (< *ŋay+gu) rather than on the original root *ŋay. -na as a reflex of *-n^{y}a is sporadically attested across the continent.

(v) For non-singular pronouns in Yidin^y the original accusative *-n^{y}a has reduced to -n^y or -:n^y (cf 1 dual ŋali:n^y < *ŋali-n^{y}a above). In order to ensure that all pronominal accusatives have the same ending, -n^y has evidently been added to *ŋan^{y}a (so that the resulting form ŋan^{y}an^y effectively includes two reflexes of *-n^{y}a).

SECOND PERSON SINGULAR PRONOUN

	proto	Dyirbal	Yidin^y
A	ŋin+du	ŋinda	
	n^{y}un+du		n^{y}undu
O	ŋin+n^{y}a	ŋinuna	
	n^{y}un+n^{y}a		n^{y}unin^y

We have already mentioned that *ŋindu > ŋinda parallels *ŋad^{y}u > ŋad^{y}a for Dyirbal. And in both languages the accusative 2 sg pronoun has been reformed, based on the modern genitives ŋinu and n^{y}uni 'your' respectively. The accusative suffixes -na and -n^y parallel those for 1 sg.

Summing up these nominal and pronominal reconstructions, it appears that we have case markings:

	non-singular pronouns	singular pronouns	nouns
A	$\emptyset$	$-d^yu \sim -du$	$-lu \sim -du$
S	$\emptyset$	$\emptyset$	$\emptyset$
O	$-n^ya$	$-n^ya$	$\emptyset \sim -n^ya$

The A inflection on singular pronouns is clearly identical with the ergative marking on nouns: -du after a consonant, with assimilation (thus, $-d^yu$ after ŋay). Accusative $-n^ya$ that occurs on <u>some</u> nouns in some modern languages is identifiable with pronominal $*-n^ya$.

   This system can conveniently be summarised in a Silversteinian diagram:

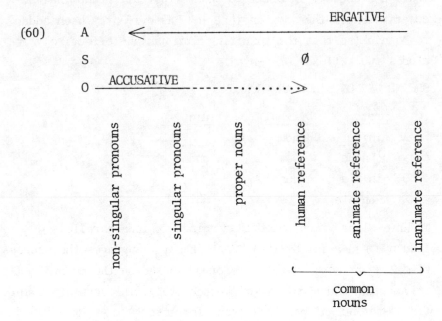

(60)

That is, ergative inflection extended in from the right, with the cut off point being to the left of singular pronouns. Accusative marking extended in from the left, covering all types of pronoun and possibly some kinds of noun. The only question we cannot answer is where exactly accusative marking ceased, in the proto-language. If we take it as extending in a minimum distance from the left, then the occurrence of $-n^y a$ on proper and some common nouns in a number of modern languages would be accounted for in terms of generalisation from pronouns. If we take it as originally extending further -- as far as, say, common nouns with human reference -- then the lack of accusative marking on any noun in some modern languages can be explained in terms of generalisation of the case-marking system shown by non-human nouns. (Third person pronouns, deictics and interrogatives would presumably have fallen between singular pronouns and proper nouns)

It remains to explain what happened to the original S forms of singular pronouns -- these were simply the monosyllabic roots ŋay and n^yun~ŋin. The solution here is in fact quite simple. At some stage after proto-Australian, monosyllabic words were proscribed in most (but not all) Australian languages. (Some of those that continued to tolerate monosyllables retained a pronominal system almost identical to that suggested for proto-Australian; Gabi in south-east Queensland is one example of this type -- see Mathew 1910.208 and Dixon 1972.7.)

There appear to have been two main ways in which a new polysyllabic S form was created for singular pronouns in those languages whose stress/rhythm/etc patterning did not permit monosyllables:

EITHER (a) the A forms were generalised to also cover S function -- ŋad^{y}u would replace 1 sg ŋay, with n^{y}undu or ŋindu taking over from n^{y}un or ŋin. OR (b) the S forms were simply made disyllabic by the addition of -ba. Thus S ŋayba is still maintained as a separate form from A ŋad^{y}u, and so on. A pronominal system like this is encountered in a number of languages in the south-east of Australia, extending as far north as Dyirbal's southerly neighbours Wargamay and Nyawaygi:

SINGULAR PRONOUNS IN WARGAMAY AND NYAWAYGI[10]

	1 sg	2 sg
A	ŋad^{y}a	ŋinda
S	ŋayba	ŋinba
O	ŋan^{y}a	ŋina

The only changes that the Wargamay/Nyawaygi forms have undergone from the suggested proto-system are (i) *u > a for A pronouns (correlating with *u > a for verbal inflection *-n^{y}u in Nyawaygi); (b) addition of -ba to S forms *ŋay and *ŋin; and (iii) simplification of the consonant cluster in 2 sg O form i.e. *ŋin+n^{y}a > ŋina.

Note that there is a great deal of evidence in modern Australian languages that -ba is regularly employed in order to (i) produce a vowel-final form, in languages which no longer allow words to end in a consonant; or (ii) produce a disyllabic form, where monosyllables are not longer tolerated. (Discussion and examples of (i) will be found in Hale, 1973b.) It is thus entirely in keeping with the general Australian pattern that -ba should be employed to form disyllabic ŋayba, ŋinba from originally monosyllabic forms *ŋay and *ŋin. (There are no examples of n^{y}unba in modern languages; note that separate S, A and O forms for singular pronouns are largely

found in the south-east, an area in which ŋin-forms predominate.)

4. Development of modern syntax

We can now consider the development of the syntactic systems described in our two case studies (1.1, 1.2) and the in-
terconnections with morphological change.

4.1 Dyirbal

In some early ancestor of Dyirbal (probably not long after the stage we are calling proto-Australian) monosyllabic
words were proscribed. The A form of singular pronouns was
generalised to cover S function, with the original S forms
(ŋay, ŋin) dropping out of use. We can suggest three main
reasons for the replacement of ŋay by ŋad^{y}a rather than by
ŋayba, which would have maintained a formal distinction between S and A varieties.

(1) Non-singular pronouns, being at the extreme left of the
hierarchy (60), lacked ergative inflections and so used the
same form (here, just the root) for S and A functions. The
replacement of ŋay by ŋad^{y}a brought the singular pronouns into
line with this pattern and could be regarded as the generalisation of a morphological paradigm from non-singular to singular pronouns.

Note that after this replacement the ergative arrow in
(60) stops at proper nouns; the new pronominal system -- and
the change which led to it -- are thus perfectly natural, in
terms of Sivlerstein's hierarchy.

(2) The language would already have imperative constructions,
that treat S and A NPs in the same way. 2 sg would be the most
common subject for an imperative; and it could be this syntac-

tic identification of S and A that led to the adoption of a
single form for 2 sg pronoun in both S and A functions (with
this then being generalised to 1 sg).

In 2.1 we quoted imperative as the prime example of a
rule with constant syntactic effect. Whatever the orientation
of the morphology and other parts of the syntax of a language,
we can predict a uniform syntax for imperatives. But, while imperatives may themselves be relatively impervious to change,
they can surely engender change in other parts of the grammar.
Other syntactic rules or, as here, morphological case assign-
ments may reorient themselves, more nearly to coincide with
the imperative pattern and so produce a greater overall homogeneity in the grammar.

(3) The inherent identification of S and A in certain lexical
pairs (outside the domain of motion and rest) may have had a
hand in determining that the A sg pronouns should be generalised to cover S function, rather than separate S forms being
maintained. (See 2.2).

It is in fact likely that the extension of ŋad^{y}a and
ŋinda to A and S marking was motivated by a mixture of two, or
all three, of these considerations. The important point to
note is that this change was triggered by something quite outside the morphological-syntactic system, that is, by a shift in
the phonotactic possibilities of the language. But once a change
became necessary for these external reasons, opportunity was taken (as it were) to restructure the case system, bringing singular pronouns into line with non-singular forms and with the syntax of imperatives.

Since that early stage, however, Dyirbal has modelled
its major syntactic rules and constraints -- those covering

coordination and subordination (1.1) -- on the morphological pattern of nominals, clearly grouping together S with O in almost every case. (S and A are treated alike only in the inevitable case of imperatives, and in transitivisation -- 2.2.)

We should surely imagine that there would now be a tendency to remodel the pronoun paradigm to conform more closely with S=O nominal morphology, and with the overwhelming S=O syntactic pattern. Such a change could involve internal restructuring -- perhaps taking the present SA (or O?) form of a pronoun as the new root, and inflecting it like a noun root (say: A $\eta ad^y a + \eta gu$, SO $\eta ad^y a$). But such a change lacks credibility in the case of words that are as frequent and important as pronouns. Pronouns are notoriously resistant to change and are often found to preserve archaic patterns (e.g. in English). The replacement of O $\eta ayguna$ by $\eta ad^y a$ (originally the A form) would be a large step, and it is difficult to imagine any simple way in which it could be accomplished.

But a change in the pronoun paradigm could well result from some factor outside the grammatical system. It appears that this is what has happened in Giramay, southernmost of the six dialects of Dyirbal. Giramay appears simply to have borrowed the pronominal system of its southern neighbours, Wargamay and Nyawaygi.[11] That is, instead of singular pronouns identifying S and A, Giramay now has different forms for all three main functions. This is a natural first step away from an S=A pronominal paradigm -- and perhaps towards eventual S=O pronominal morphology -- following the pattern of nouns:[12]

	1 sg		2 sg	
	Giramay, Wargamay, Nyawaygi	other Dyirbal dialects	Giramay, Wargamay, Nyawaygi	other Dyirbal dialects
A	ŋad^{y}a	ŋad^{y}a	ŋinda	ŋinda
S	ŋayba		ŋinba	
O	ŋan^{y}a	ŋayguna	ŋina	ŋinuna
genitive	ŋaygu	ŋaygu	ŋinu	ŋinu

Non-singular pronouns have a single SA form in Wargamay and Nyawaygi as in all dialects of Dyirbal (and in very nearly every other Australian language); there has been no possibility of change here.

4.2 Yidin^y

In Dyirbal it seems that syntactic identification is based on the morphology of nouns, and that pronominal morphology is beginning to change in order to come into line; we could describe this as syntactically-determined morphological change.

But Yidin^y, in its principles of coordination, has syntactic identification exactly mirroring morphological case assignment. The nominal and pronominal paradigms recur in other Australian languages and can be related back to the protolanguage. This suggests that it is the morphology that has determined the shape of coordination (which appears to be quite idiosyncratic to Yidin^y).

But whereas coordination in Yidin^y is a somewhat fuzzy area, partly determined by considerations of semantic and contextual plausibility, subordination in Yidin^y conforms to strict syntactic rules. And for subordination we must have identification of S and O functions for all parts of speech --

not only nominals, which show an S=O paradigm, but also pronouns, where one form covers both S and A functions. Why should subordination but not coordination be strictly S=O in Yidin^y? And why should coordination in Yidin^y mix S=O and S=A whereas in Dyirbal it is strictly S=O? We attempt answers to these two questions in the next paragraphs.

(1) The common NP in a coordination will be sometimes a noun and, at least as often, a pronoun. It is thus reasonable for the syntax of coordination to mirror the morphology of pronouns and of nouns. The common NP in a subordination, on the other hand, is very much more frequently a noun than a pronoun. In fact we found difficulty in translating subordinate constructions with a pronominal pivot into English (since sentences of this type do not occur in English). Thus (26) was glossed literally 'I, who was laughing, sat down' along the lines of 'The man who was laughing sat down', and then had to be explained in terms of an adverbial clause 'I sat down while I was laughing'.

There appear to be a number of reasons for this. Subordinate clauses in Yidin^y and Dyirbal may be 'restrictive' or 'non-restrictive', and plainly first and second person pronouns cannot be further restricted as to reference. Subordinate clauses typically qualify on O NP in the main clause, often the object of a verb of 'seeing' or 'hearing'; 'I' or 'you' or 'we' is likely to feature most often as subject of such a verb rather than as object.

Whatever the reasons for it, the simple fact to be noted is that while pronouns will be as common as nouns as the pivot for a coordination, they are many times rarer as common NP in a subordinate construction. It is, in view of this, quite

natural that the syntax of subordination should be entirely
in terms of S=O (based on nominal morphology) while the syntax of coordination gives equal weight to the case paradigm
of nouns, and to that of pronouns.

(2) Matters of style are often ignored by grammarians, but
they can be an important factor in determining syntactic preferences, which may crucially weight the balance in a choice
between different directions of grammatical change.

One important difference between Yidin^y and Dyirbal is
in the style of narrative. Dyirbal narrative style is, in
fact, quite close to that of English -- a narrator sets the
scene and refers to the characters in the third person, being sure to quote exactly any significant dialogue between
them. (The writer has never encountered a Dyirbal story --
as opposed to a reminiscence -- in which the narrator assumes
the role of the central character.)

In contrast, Yidin^y stories typically involve the principal character serving as narrator, with the whole tale being
given a 'first person' slant. There may be a few sentences
at the beginning told in the third person -- these set the
scene and introduce the main character, who thereafter takes
over the narration. If the central character changes, the
narrator will shift (still remaining in the first person);
the first narrator will introduce the arrival of the second
character and then silently relinquish his meta-role to him.
This style of first-person narrative is common to all the Yid-
in^y storytellers encountered by the writer (and note that the
two major informants belonged to different branches of the
tribe, and had never had any contact with each other).

As a result first person (and second person) pronouns are extraordinarily frequent in Yidin^y texts, occurring two to four times as often as pronouns in Dyirbal texts. This is likely to be one factor in explaining why coordination in Yidin^y depends upon identification of S=A for pronouns (following their morphology) whereas Dyirbal takes no account at all of pronominal form in its coordination rules.

Thus, whereas the grammar of Dyirbal is highly 'ergative', and appears to be moving further in that direction (although the universal nature of imperatives will ensure that it can never be as fully ergative as some European languages are accusative), Yidin^y appears to be evenly balanced -- as regards both morphology and syntax -- between the ergative and accusative poles. There is no reason to doubt that this could be a stable system, with no internal reasons for change (although of course external factors -- of a phonological or language-contact nature -- could well upset the balance).

5. Summary and conclusion

We have examined two Australian languages, both of which have nouns showing an 'absolutive-ergative' paradigm while pronouns follow a 'nominative-accusative' morphological pattern. In Dyirbal most syntactic rules treat intransitive subject (S) and transitive object (O) functions in the same way, though there are two areas in which S corresponds to transitive subject function (A). Yidin^y syntax identifies S with A about as often as it equates S and O.

We were able to trace the development of the present-day morphologies from a postulated proto-Australian system, and then to sketch some of the ways in which syntactic and morph-

ological processes of change have influenced and determined
one another, yielding the modern syntactic and morphological
patterns.

We noted that realignment of the singular pronouns was
triggered by a phonological change, with the direction of realignment being determined by a desire for congruence with
other parts of the morphology and with the syntax. External
factors also enter in with the recent 'borrowing' by a dialect
of Dyirbal of new forms for S and O singular pronouns, making
this section of the morphology accord more closely with the
predominantly 'ergative' constraints within syntax.

Coordination in Yidin^y appears to be entirely motivated
by the two types of morphological paradigm (for nouns and pronouns respectively). Subordination is based on nominal morphology because of the predominance of nominal NPs as 'pivot'
for this type of construction.

Finally, the stylistically-determined preponderance of
pronouns in Yidin^y texts may help to explain why Yidin^y syntax
reflects pronominal morphology rather more than does the syntax of Dyirbal.

Both syntactically and morphologically Yidin^y and Dyirbal
are quite typical Australian languages. It is likely that
some of the arguments we have used and lines of development we
have sketched will help to explain aspects of the development
of some of the two hundred other languages of the continent.[13]

Notes

1. In order not to introduce unnecessary complications into the presentation of Dyirbal syntax, noun markers -- article-like forms that normally accompany nouns, agree with them in case and mark their gender class -- are silently omitted. In addition, only one form of the anti-passive construction is quoted. (For further details see Dixon 1972.44-8, 65-7).

2. Compare with Langacker and Munro's (1975) suggestion that a passive construction (in non-ergative languages) is essentially intransitive.

3. Detailed discussion of the morphology and syntax of Yidin^y is in Dixon, 1977.

4. The syntactic functions of sentential constituents would be defined by their place on the tree; a convention of ordering must be chosen to facilitate this. The convention adopted -- which is oriented to showing abstract syntactic relations -- is, essentially, arbitrary, and is not tied to surface word order realisations. (But, everything else being equal, it is convenient to adopt an order of syntactic elements that corresponds roughly to the preferred word order sequence.) See Dixon 1972.149.

5. There is of course scope for Whorfian speculation on this topic. If some community pays particular attention to position and movement (as nomadic tribes of aboriginal Australians undoubtedly do) then the type of syntactic identification in this lexical area might be thought to be the most likely candidate for syntactic generalisation. But aboriginal Australians also have elaborate systems of communication, with special languages for use in the presence of taboo relatives,

at initiation ceremonies, and so on (in addition to a variety
of different song-styles, etc.). It is thus just as reasonable to suggest that the syntactic identification inherent in
the lexical domain of 'talking' should be a candidate for syntactic generalisation.

6. The writer is grateful to Ken Hale for making available data on Walbiri, and for a number of general ideas which
have been made use of throughout the paper (for instance, the
genesis of -ba in the S forms of pronouns). For information
on Walbiri see Hale 1973a.

7. This is not of course put forward as the sole motivation for change, but as just one of several factors that
can engender and direct grammatical changes.

8. Silverstein in fact suggests that the hierarchy can
read (from the left):1st person non-sg/ 1 sg/ 2 non-sg/ 2sg ...
(if number as well as person categories are relevant to split
in case-marking). We are introducing a variation of this
scheme by grouping 1st and 2nd person pronouns together, and
then distinguishing non-singular from singular forms.

9. The reader is referred to Silverstein's original exposition for reasons why non-singular forms of a pronoun occur to the left of the singular. Roughly, non-singulars are
semantically 'more marked' than singulars (and duals are more
marked than plurals, giving an order -- from the left -- 'du-
al/plural/singular').

10. The Wargamay and Nyawaygi data is from the writer's
own field work. Grammars of these languages are currently being prepared for publication in a volume of the Handbook of
Australian languages, edited by B. J. Blake and R. M. W. Dix-

on.

11. Note that Giramay is mutually intelligible with other dialects of Dyirbal, and largely unintelligible to speakers of Wargamay and Nyawaygi. Grammatical similarity to the latter is confined to pronouns.

Note also that there is nothing outrageous in the idea of an Australian language 'borrowing' pronominal forms. There is an instance within the last 25 years of the 1 sg pronoun, ŋayu, being tabooed in the Western Desert language -- because of formal similarity to the name of a recently deceased person -- and replaced by ŋangu (Miller 1971).

There is also, of course, the English example of they, their, them being borrowed from Norse (probably at least partly because of the incipient homonymy of the reflexes of the Old English third person plural forms hīe, hira, him with he, her, him); see Strang 1970.266f.

12. Pronouns can of course take on absolutive-ergative inflections for totally different reasons. In Walbiri, every sentence must involve bound-form pronouns referring to subject and object; these have one form for S and A functions and another for O function, reflecting the predominantly S=A syntax of Walbiri (cf Hale 1970). Nouns conform to the usual Australian practice with an absolutive-ergative system of inflections, and free-form pronouns follow them in this. Note that free-form pronouns are used relatively seldom in Walbiri (compared with, say, Dyirbal and Yidin^y); the major referential and syntactic load is carried by the bound pronominal affixes. So free-form pronouns have been 'regularised', presumably to simplify the grammar. The old SA forms -- 1 sg ŋad^{y}u, 2 sg n^{y}undu, 1 du ŋali, and so on -- have been taken as the roots

to which are added (with only a few exceptions) normal nominal inflections. (In fact the normal A forms of singular pronouns are ŋad^{y}u-lu-ḷu and n^{y}undu-lu-ḷu, each involving three
separate reflexes of the ergative case affix-du∼-lu∼-ḷu. Hale
mentions that only the last of these suffixes (-ḷu) has ergative force in present-day Walbiri.)

13. In revising this paper for publication I benefited
greatly from suggestions and criticisms of Barry Alpher, Barry Blake, Bernard Comrie, Warren Cowgill, Terry Crowley, John
Haiman, Ken Hale, Geoff Pullum, Alan Rumsey, Tim Shopen, Michael Silverstein, Calvert Watkins and the participants at the
1976 Santa Barbara symposium.

References

Catford, J. C. 1975. 'Ergativity in Caucasian languages'. Mimeo.

Conklin, H. C. 1962. 'Lexicographic treatment of folk taxonomies', pp 119-41 of Problems in Lexicography, ed. F. W. Householder and S. Saporta. Bloomington: Indiana University.

Dixon, R. M. W. 1970. 'Proto-Australian laminals', Oceanic Linguistics IX. 79-103.

_____. 1971. 'A method of semantic description', pp 436-71 of Semantics, an interdisciplinary reader in philosophy, linguistics and psychology, ed. D. D. Steinberg and L. A. Jakobovits. Cambridge: Cambridge University Press.

_____. 1972. The Dyirbal language of North Queensland. Cambridge: Cambridge University Press.

_____. (ed). 1976. Grammatical categories in Australian languages (Proceedings of the 1974 AIAS symposium). Canberra: Australian Institute of Aboriginal Studies.

_____. 1977. A grammar of Yidin[y]. Cambridge: Cambridge University Press.

George, L. 1974. 'Ergativity and relational grammar', pp 265-75 of Papers from the fifth annual meeting, North-Eastern Linguistic Society, ed. Ellen Kaise and Jorge Hankamer. Cambridge, Mass: Harvard University.

Golab, Z. 1969. 'Subject as a linguistic category', General Linguistics 9. 1-12.

Hale, K. L. 1970. 'The passive and ergative in language
     change: the Australian case', pp 757-81 of Pacific lin-
     guistics studies in honour of Arthur Capell, ed. S. A.
     Wurm and D. C. Laycock. Canberra: Pacific Linguistics.

_____. 1973a. 'Person marking in Walbiri', pp 308-44 of A
     Festschrift for Morris Halle, ed. S. R. Anderson and P.
     Kiparsky. New York: Holt, Rinehart and Winston.

_____. 1973b. 'Deep-surface canonical disparities in relation
     to analysis and change: an Australian example', pp 401-
     58 of Current Trends in Linguistics, Vol 11, ed. T. A.
     Sebeok. The Hague: Mouton.

_____. 1976. 'On ergative and locative suffixial alternations
     in Australian languages', pp 414-7 of Dixon (ed) 1976.

Heath, J. 1976. '"Ergative/Accusative" typologies in morphol-
     ogy and syntax', pp 599-611 of Dixon (ed) 1976.

Langacker, R. W. and Munro, P. 1975. 'Passives and their mean-
     ing', Language 51. 789-830.

Mathew, J. 1910. Two representative tribes of Queensland.
     London.

McKay, G. R. 1975. Rembarnga -- a language of central Arnhem
     Land. PhD thesis. Australian National University.

Miller, W. R. 1971. 'Dialect differentiation in the Western
     Desert', Anthropological Forum 3.61-78.

Pullum, G. K. 1976. 'Word order universals and grammatical re-
     lations' in Syntax and semantics, 8 -- grammatical rela-
     tions, ed P. Cole and J. Sadock. New York: Academic
     Press.

Rigsby, B. 1975. 'Nass-Gitksan: an analytical ergative syntax', International Journal of American Linguistics, 41.346-54.

Sapir. E. 1911. 'The problem of noun incorporation in American languages', American Anthropologist 13.250-82.

Silverstein, M. 1976. 'Hierarchy of features and ergativity', pp 112-71 of Dixon (ed) 1976.

Strang, B. M. H. 1970. A history of English. London: Methuen.

IV Development of the Copula

9 A Mechanism for the Development of Copula Morphemes

Charles N. Li and Sandra A. Thompson

0. Introduction

The aim of this paper is to show that one possible
source of the copula morpheme in predicate nominal sentences
is an anaphoric pronoun, with the mechanism of change involving a reanalysis of a topic-comment construction. In the
course of our discussion, we will present a number of other
factors which play a role in the rise and fall of copula constructions.

Our concern will be with sentences of the following
type, which we will henceforth call equational sentences:

(1) a. Frank is an attorney

     b. This is a goat

     c. That woman is the teacher

     d. That man is my uncle

That is, the term "equational sentence" will be used to refer
to all sentences in which an identificational or a member/
class relationship is expressed between two NP's. Existential
and locative constructions whose verbs are related diachronically to the copula in some languages will not be discussed
in this paper, but see Munro (this volume) for a discussion
of such constructions. Sentences containing predicate adjec-

tives will likewise not be discussed.

In many languages, equational sentences consist simply of two noun phrases.[1] But in many other languages there is a morpheme which is not a NP and whose only function in such sentences is to "link" these two NP's. We will call this morpheme a copula. This copula can be a full-fledged verb, as it is in most Indo-European, Finno-Ugric, and Altaic languages, or it can fall short of being a true verb, as in some of the languages we are about to discuss.

1. The Topic Mechanism

The role which topicalization[2] plays in the creation of a copula can be schematized essentially as follows:

(2)   Topic   Comment
      ⌒⌒⌒   ⌒⌒⌒⌒⌒⌒⌒⌒⌒⌒
      NP   that one   NP

      NP   cop.   NP
      ⌣⌣⌣   ⌣⌣⌣⌣⌣⌣⌣⌣
      Subject   Predicate

That is, the subject pronoun which is coreferential with the topic in the comment of a topic-comment construction is reanalyzed as a copula morpheme in a subject-predicate construction. We will see that Mandarin, Hebrew, Palestinian Arabic, and Wappo are among the languages that have evolved a copula via the topic mechanism.

1.1 The Chinese Connection

It is widely accepted that in Archaic Chinese (11th B.C.-3rd B.C.) equational sentences normally did not have a copula. (See Wang Li (1958a,b), Zhou fa-gao (1952, 1963)). The following examples taken from literary documents of the Archaic period illustrate this point:

(3) qí   mǔ   yù   "kǒng-zǐ   xián   rén   yě³"

his mother say: "Confucius wise man   declarative particle

'His mother says: "Confucius is a wise man."'

(Zhàn Guó Cè
5th c. B.C.)

(4) Wáng-Tái wù   zhě   yě

Wang-Tai outstanding person   declarative particle

'Wang-Tai is an outstanding person.'

(Zhuáng-zǐ 4th c. B.C.)

(5) zǐ   yù: "rǔ jì   yě"

Confucius say: "you tool   declarative particle

'Confucius say: "You are a tool."'

(Analect 5th c. B.C.)

(6) shì-gù   lǐ   zhǎng zhě,   lǐ   zhī
Therefore district chief person, district genitive
'Therefore, the district chief is the district's

rén   yě
virtuous-person   declarative particle
virtuous person.'   (Mo-zi 5th c. B.C.)

(7) "jūn-zǐ   zhí   dé   fēng; xiao-rén zhí
princely-man genitive character wind mean-man
'A princely-man's character is (like) the wind;

dé   cǎo"
genitive character grass
a common man's character is (like) the grass.'

(Analect 5th c. B.C.)

Now the modern Mandarin copula, shì, occurs regularly in
equational sentences.

(8)   nèi - ge   rén shì xuéshēng
      that - classifier man be student
      'That man is a student.'

However, the copula, shì, can be omitted and replaced with a
pause in simple equational sentences.

(9)   nèi - ge   rén, xuéshēng
      that-classifier man   student
      'That man is a student.'

If the NP's in an equational sentence are complex, the deletion of the copula is avoided.

(10) a. ?chī pingguo   de nèi-ge   rén, wǒ
          eat apple   relative that person, I
                      clause
                      marker

          xihuan de péng -you
          like relative friend
                clause
                marker

      b. chī pingguo   de nèi -ge   rén shì wǒ
          eat apple   relative   that person is I
                      clause
                      marker

          xihuan de péng -you
          like relative friend
                clause
                marker

          'The person who is eating an apple is the
          friend I like.'

This modern copula, shì, was a demonstrative in Archaic
Chinese. (See Wang Li (1958a,b); Zhou Fa-gao (1952, 1963.))
The following sentences illustrate the occurrence of shì as a
demonstrative in Archaic Chinese literature.

(11) shì ye yě   , zhaò-mèn jī zǐ-xī míng
      This night decl. , zhao-men and zi-xi ally
                particle
      'This night, Zhao-men and Zi-xi formed an alliance.'

                                    (Zhuǒ Zhuàn 6th c. B.C.)

(12)   fū-zǐ   zhì   yù shì bāng   yě
        Confucius arrive at this nation decl.
                                         particle
        'Confucius arrived at this nation.'
                                    (Analect 5th c. B.C.)

(13)   zǐ   yù shì rì kū
        Confucius at this day cry
        'Confucius cried on this day.'
                                    (Analect 5th c. B.C.)

In (11)-(13), shì occurs as a demonstrative modifying a noun.
However, shì also occurred in equational sentences in Archaic
Chinese as an anaphoric demonstrative pronoun:

(14)   zǐ   yuè: 'wǒ wú xìn ér bù   yù
        Confucius say   I not act yet not show

                  ér sān zǐ zhǐ shì   Qiu yě"
                                              decl. part.
                  you people   this Qiu (name of Confucius)

        'Confucius says: "I don't do anything that is not
            shown to you, that is I."'
                                    (Analect 5th c. B.C.)

(15)   "qióng yù jiàn,   shì rén zhǐ   sǔo
        poverty and debasement, this people genitive nomin-

                      wù   yě"
                  alizer dislike decl. particle

        'Poverty and debasement, that is what people dis-
            like.'
                                    (Analect 5th c. B.C.)

(16)   "qiān   lǐ   ér jiàn wáng shì wǒ sǔo
        thousand mile then see king, this I nominalizer

                  yù   yě"
                  desire decl. particle

        '(To travel) a thousand miles to see the king, that
            is what I wish.'
                                    (Mencius 4th c. B.C.)

(17) zhī ér shǐ zhī, shi bù rén yě
      know then use him, this not kind decl. particle
      'To use him knowing   (that he would rebel), that
            was unkind.'

                                    (Mencius 4th c. B.C.)

(18) jì   yù qí   shēng you yù qí sǐ, shi
      already wish him live also wish him die, this

            huò   yě
            indecision   decl. particle

      'Wishing him to live while wishing him to die, that
            is indecision.'

                                    (Analect 5th c. B.C.)

The important fact about sentences (14)-(18) is that
they have a topic-comment structure, the topic being the
phrase or clause in initial position, the comment being the
clause consisting of the demonstrative pronoun subject shi
and the predicate NP.

As Wang Li (1958a,b) pointed out, it was sentences like
these which gave rise to the modern copula construction. These
topic-comment constructions, then, set the stage for reanalysis: the topic-comment construction without a copula became
a subject predicate construction with the anaphoric demonstrative pronoun shi being reanalyzed as a copula.[4] Indeed, sentences (17) and (18) may very well be interpreted as subject-
predicate equational sentences with shi serving as the copula.
The reason that these sentences are given a topic-comment interpretation with shi as an anaphonic pronoun is that among
the literature of the period of Archaic Chinese, there is no
sentence where the morpheme, shi, functions unequivocally as
a copula verb.

Thus, sentences such as (17) and (18) are open to a multiple analysis, i.e. one analysis yields a topic-comment structure with <u>shi</u> functioning as an anaphonic pronoun and the other analysis provides a subject-predicate structure with <u>shi</u> functioning as a copula. In other words, it is sentences such as (17) and (18) which triggered the reanalysis.

It seems fairly clear that the use of <u>shi</u> as a copula was productive by the late Han period (1st-2nd century A.D.) (see Wang Li (1958a,b) and Zhou fa-gao (1952)). In the vernacular literature of the early A.D. centuries, for example, one can easily find convincing evidence showing <u>shi</u> used as a copula in equational sentences:

(19)   "cǐ   bái   wù   <u>shì</u> hé   děng?"
        this white thing <u>is</u> what kind
        'What kind of stuff is this white thing?'

                                (Translation of the
                                Buddha's saying in
                                late Han, 25-220 A.D.)

        dá   yuè,   "cǐ <u>shì</u> xiǎo   ér"
        answer say, "this <u>is</u> small   child"
        'Answer, "this is a small child."'

(20)   zhū kè   yuè, "cǐ <u>shì</u> Ān-shí suì jīn"
        all guest say, this <u>is</u> An-shi bit gold
        'All the guests said, "these are An-shi's bits of
                gold--(fragmentary pieces of literature
                having special excellence)"'

                                (<u>Shì Shuō Xīn Xǔ</u>
                                <u>5th c. A.D.</u>)

(21)   wèn jīn   <u>shì</u> hé   shì
        ask today <u>is</u> what world
        '(I) ask what world is today's world.'

                                (<u>Táo Huā Yuǎn Jì</u>
                                <u>4th c. A.D.</u>)

(22) yú shì   suǒ   jià fū-ren zhǐ   fù
      I be nominalizer marry woman genitive father

      yě
      decl.
      particle

'I am the father of the married woman.'

(Lùn-Héng by Wang
Chong, 1st c. A.D.)

The syntactic contexts in which the morpheme shì occurs
in sentences (19)-(22) do not permit us to analyze it as a
demonstrative; its unequivocal function in these sentences is
that of the copula. Wang Li (1958b) points out the contrast
between sentence (22), which is taken from Wang Chong's writ-
ing in the early part of the first century A.D., and sentence
(23), which is almost identical with (22), but taken from
Zhuǒ Zhuàn, a literary document of the Early Archaic period
in the 6th-7th century B.C.

(23) yú ěr   suǒ   jià fū-rén zhǐ   fù
      I your nominalizer marry woman genitive father

      yě
      decl.
      particle

'I am the father of your married woman.'

(Zhuǒ Zhuàn 6-7th
c. B.C.)

The only difference between (22) and (23) is that (23)
does not have the copula, shì. This contrast, then, provides
a convincing illustration of the fact that Archaic Chinese
had no copula in equational sentences but that shi as a copula was firmly established by the first century A.D.

By the beginning of the Tang Dynasty (6th c. A.D.),
there was no trace of the demonstrative use of shi, and it
remains the copula in modern Mandarin. To summarize the de-

velopment of the copula in Chinese described above, we note
that (i) the copula, shì, was originally a demonstrative,
(ii) the copula usage of shì developed through the reanalysis
of the topic-comment construction:

(24)   Topic   Comment   Subject   Predicate
        NP   shì   NP $\Longrightarrow$ NP   shì   NP
        this/that
        referring to
        the topic)

The topicalization mechanism as a source for copula constructions has been justified for Mandarin. Is there evidence
of such a process in other languages? We think there is. In
the following sections, we will present some facts from a
small number of other languages in which a similar development seems to be involved.

1.2 Hebrew[5]

As is well-known, the triliteral verbal copula, h-y-y,
in Hebrew is not used in the present tense; what shows up in
equational sentences is a demonstrative pronoun or a personal
pronoun (if the subject is non-sentential):

(25)   [še nitnaged   lo] ze   məguxax
        that we will oppose to him "this"   absurd
        'It would be absurd for us to oppose him.'

(26)   moše (ze)   student šeli
        Moshe that   student my
        'Moshe is a student of mine.'

(27)   ata (hu) ha-ganav
        You "he" the thief
        'You are the thief.'

According to Berman and Grosu (1976), for most speakers, the
hu morpheme is optional in sentences with pronominal subjects

and obligatory in sentences with full noun subjects:

(28)   a.   David hu ha-ganav
                  "he" the thief
            'David is the thief.'

       b.   *David ha-ganav
            David the-thief

Moreover, it is more nearly obligatory when the predicate noun
is a bare noun than when it is a modified noun:

(29)   a.   Moše hu student
            'Moshe is a student.'

       b.   ?Moše student

(30)   Moše (hu) student li rfua
                            for medicine
            'Moshe is a medical student.'

In addition, the occurrence of the pronoun morpheme in Hebrew
equational sentences is conditioned by the nature of the subject NP. If the subject NP is indefinite and non-generic, as
in (31), hu is disallowed; if the subject NP is generic, the
pronoun morpheme is obligatory, as in (32); and if the subject NP is definite but non-generic, the pronoun morpheme is
optional, as in (33). (Ruth Berman, personal communication).

(31)   *yeled hu ecli kaet
       boy   with me now
       'A boy is with me now.'

(32)   yeled hu   yicur   mufla
       boy   creature wonderful
       'A boy is a wonderful creature.'

(33)   ha-yeled (hu)   ecli   kaet
       the-boy   with me now
       'The boy is with me now.'

   The fuzzy distribution of pronouns in equational sen-

tences suggests that pronouns are being reanalyzed as copulas
in modern Hebrew, and that the mechanism involved is precisely that which produced the Mandarin copula. There are two
facts which support the claim that the change is very much
in progress at the moment:

(a) The morphemes ze and hu still function as pronouns:

(34)   ze mešune
       'That's strange.'

(35)   hu ohev et-Rivka
       he loves acc-Rivka
       'He loves Rivka.'

(b) At the same time, sentences such as (31)-(32) can be
shown to have completed the transition from topic-comment
structures to subject-predicate equational sentences. That
is, in a sentence like:

(36)   David hu ha-ganav
              "he" the-thief
       'David is the thief.'

it is no longer the case that David is the topic, and hu is
the subject of the comment hu haganav. Two pieces of evidence
brought up by Berman and Grosu show that hu is no longer the
subject in a topic sentence but is actually a copula in a
subject-predicate sentence. First, the subject of an equational sentence can be indefinite, but the topic in a topic-
comment sentence cannot be:

(37)   kol exad še   lo   gonev hu tipeš
       all one   that not steal   fool
       'Anyone who doesn't steal is a fool.'

(38)   *kol exad še   lo   gonev, hu tipeš
       all one   that not steal   fool
       *'As far as anyone who doesn't steal is concerned,
            he's a fool.'

Second, the predicate can be questioned in an equational sentence, but not in a topic-comment sentence:

(39)   a.   Moše hu   xayal
               Moshe "he" soldier
               'Moshe is a soldier.'

         b.   ma   hu   moše?
               what "he" Moshe
               'What is Moshe?'

(40)   a.   Moše, hu ohev et-Rivka
                     he love acc-
               'Moshe, He loves Rivka.'

         b.   *et-mi moše, hu ohev
               acc-who   he love
               *'Who does Moshe, he love?'

These two arguments show, then, that hu in equational sentences has definitely made the transition from pronoun subject in a topic-comment construction to copula in a subject predicate construction.

A third argument, cited in Faltz (1973), is that sentences like (39) may be pronounced with an intonation suitable for a single, simple clause, without any break after the subject.

Finally, note that hu can appear (in certain contexts) with a first person subject:

(41) ani hu ha-student   še-moše diber itxa alav
       I   cop. def.-student that Moshe spoke with-you
                     about-him
       'I'm the student that Moshe told you about.'

This fact shows that the reanalysis of the pronoun into a copula is already complete since hu cannot possibly have a third-person referent here.

In Hebrew, then, although we have oversimplified considerably, the same process of copula creation that we outlined for Mandarin seems to be taking place. Unlike Mandarin, however, which subsequently lost the pronominal function for shi, Hebrew is content for both the copular and the pronominal functions of its hu and ze to exist side-by-side.

Berman and Grosu and Faltz also show that there are several respects in which the copula hu does not behave like a verb, which suggests that having become a copula does not necessarily entail having become a verb.

1.3 Palestinian Arabic[6]

The facts for Palestinian Arabic equational sentences are nearly identical to those for modern Hebrew. Sentence (42) illustrates the 3rd personal pronoun as a subject, while (43) and (44) demonstrate its use as a copula:

(42)   hiyye le   mʕalme
        she   the teacher (f.)
        'She is the teacher.'

(43)   il bint hiyye le mʕalme
        the girl cop. the teacher (f.)
        'The girl is the teacher.'

(44)   *il bint le mʕalme
        the girl the teacher (f.)
        'The girl is the teacher.'

As in Hebrew, with a masculine subject the corresponding masculine pronoun appears:

(45)   huwwe il usta:z
        he   the teacher (m.)
        'He is the teacher.'

(46) a. il rozzal huwwe il usta:z
          the man   cop. the teacher (m.)
          'The man is the teacher.'

      b. *il rozzal il usta:z
          the man   the teacher
          'The man is the teacher.'

(47) il rozzal huwwe usta:z mni:h
      the man   teacher good
      'The man is a good teacher.'

And again, as in Hebrew, in certain contexts, huwwe can
be used with a non-third person subject:

(48) ana huwwe il usta:z alli Fari:d ʕallak ʕanno
      I   the teacher that Fari:d talked about him
      'I am the teacher that Fareed talked about.'

(49) inta huwwe il usta:z elli: Fari:d ʕallak ʕanno
      you   the teacher that Fareed talked about him
      'You are the teacher that Fareed talked about.'

In sentences (48)-(49), huwwe cannot be interpreted as the
3rd person pronoun. It has become a copula. As is the case in
Hebrew, the Palestinian Arabic copula, huwwe, is derived his
torically from the 3rd person pronoun through reanalysis of a
topic-comment construction. Sentences (46a,b) provide the crucial evidence. (46) shows that huwwe is obligatory. If the
reading of huwwe in (46) is pronominal, its obligatory presence cannot be explained. Sentences (48) and (49) demonstrate
the use of huwwe as a copula has been generalized from equational sentences with 3rd person subject to those with 1st and
2nd person subject.

In Palestinian Arabic, the generalization of huwwe as a
copula in equational sentences with 1st and 2nd person subject
is not yet complete. For example, if the predicative NP, il
usta:z 'the teacher' in (48) and (49) is not modified by a

clause, huwwe cannot occur as a copula, e.g.:

(50)   *ana huwwe il   usta:z
        I   the teacher
        'I am the teacher.'

However, a sentence such as (50) is quite acceptable in some
other Arabic dialects. Here is an example from Algerian
Arabic:[7]

(51)   inta (huwwa) 1 - muʕallim
        you   he   the teacher
        'You are the teacher.'

1.4 Wappo[8]

Wappo is a California Indian language generally believed
to be in the Yukian family. Verbs are not inflected for person or number. In Wappo the copula is the invariant, ce? (e?)
where the second syllable, e?, may be optionally dropped.

(52)   ?i ce?(e?) teme? ?eka
        I   cop.   his   child
        'I am his child.'

(53)   te ce?(e?) kanituc ma
        he cop.   chief
        'He is the chief.'
                a

(54)   mi? ce?(e?) ?i-nokh
        you cop.   my friend
        'You are my friend.'

Now, we know that this copula clearly has a demonstrative morpheme in it because the Wappo demonstrative is ce and the
Wappo sentence for 'that is his child' is

(55)   ce?(e?) teme? ?eka
        cop.   his   child
        'That is his child.'

but not

(56)   *ce ce?(e?) teme? ?eka
        that cop.   his child
        'That is his child.'

The non-existence of (56) cannot be explained unless the ce
in the copula is the demonstrative.[9] (57) shows the attribu-
tive use of ce:

(57)   ?ah ce kew hakše-lahkhi?
        I   that man like-neg.
        'I don't like that man.'

Sentence (58) shows its pronominal use:

(58)   ?ah ce hakše-lahkhi?
        I   that like -neg.
        'I don't like that.'

What we surmise is happening is this: the optional e? can be
reasonably assumed to be an older copula, which is now dis-
appearing. The obligatory part of the present-day copula ce?
is the demonstrative ce (plus the epenthetic glottal stop
which had been inserted between the vowels of ce and e?). With
the dropping of e?, ce? is now taking over the copula function.
The fact that it still functions as a demonstrative pronoun
but can also be used with first-person subjects suggests that
the language is still in the process of reanalysis. The obvious mechanism, once again, involves the topic-comment construction, just as in Mandarin, Hebrew, and Palestinian Arabic.

1.5 Zway[10]

Zway is an Ethiopian language, which, like other Semitic
languages, is rich in verbal inflectional morphology. However,
in the present tense, the copula is an invariant morpheme /u/.

In other Ethiopian Semitic languages such as Gumar, Gura, /u/
serves as the 3rd person masculine copula. Hetzron (1972) reports that the /u/ is a new element, replacing the form based
on the common copula root /n/ in South Ethiopian languages.
According to Hetzron (1972), the Zway invariable copula is
generalized from the 3rd person masculine copula. Although
the historical origin of the /u/ copula is not known, it is
significant that a very likely candidate for the origin of
this invariant /u/ is a deitic or pronominal element. In
other words, the /u/ in Zway is probably related to the 3/m
pronoun /hu/ in Hebrew and Arabic.

Thus, the Zway invariant copula for present tense is
another case of the historical development: pronominal element <u>reanalysis</u> copula. We suggest that the pathway of the
change is the reanalysis of the topic-comment construction into a subject predicate construction.

2. Summary

What we have seen, then, are several languages which
appear to have been undergoing the change from anaphoric pronoun to copula via topicalization. In the case of Mandarin
Chinese, the change is complete and documentation of the
change is possible because of several thousand years' written
literature. In the other languages discussed here, the change
is not complete and we must infer the course of the diachronic
origin of the copula from synchronic facts. Given the nature
of the synchronic facts, however, our inference of the diachronic origin of the copula appears correct. We have, therefore, provided a description of a mechanism for the diachronic origin of the copula in equational sentences.

3. Query

We hope to have shed some light on one device by which a new copula construction can develop in a language. Much more research needs to be done to determine how this generalization fits into the total picture of the rise and fall of the copula. How, for example, can we reconcile the following facts (1-4) with (5)?

1. The equational sentence without a copula is unmarked semantically, i.e. the construction

$$NP_1 + NP_{predicate}$$

is semantically complete. The copula, if it occurs, serves as a tense bearer only. Thus, although many languages have a copula in their equational sentences, the copula often does not occur if the equational sentence is in present tense. For example, Russian, Arabic, Hebrew, Bambara, Burmese, Hungarian, Luiseno, etc., all have a copula, but not in present tense. The reason is that the present tense is the neutral and unmarked tense. The equational sentence, being semantically complete, has no need for a copula in the present tense. In a non-present tense, there is a stronger semantic motivation for the occurrence of the copula in an equational sentence since the copula can signal the non-present tense.

2. In a number of the languages which have no copula in the present tense, it seems to have dropped out, but not apparently due to any obvious phonological impetus (e.g., Hebrew, Turkish, Arabic, Russian, Burmese).

3. Other languages appear to be losing their copula for what do seem to be phonological reasons. For example, the Turkish past tense copula stem is -$\underline{i}$, as in:

(59)   i-dim, I was   i-dik, we were
        i-din, thou wert   i-diniz, you were
        i-di, he was   i-dilu, they were

But in modern Turkish speech, the stem /i-/ disappears after
consonants and changes to a glide /y/ after vowels:

(60)   adam i-di   [adam di]
        man was-he   'He was the man.'

        mudur i-diniz   [murdur dunuz]
        director was-you   'You were the director.'

        asker i-dim   [askerdim]
        soldier was-I   'I was a soldier.'

        sinemada i-diniz   [sinemadaydiniz]
        cinema was-you   'You were at the cinema.'

Even the English copula is giving way to phonological pressures: the copula is typically elided when it is not stressed
and has disappeared in certain constructions in some dialects,
e.g.:

(61)   'He's a teacher.'

4. Many languages have no copula in any tense (e.g.,
many Austronesian languages and Australian languages).

5. Some languages, such as the ones we have been discussing, seem to "go out of their way" to develop a copula.
That is, given that it seems to be so easy to get rid of or
do without a copula, at least in the present tense, what motivates some languages to redevelop one? Hebrew and Palestinian Arabic are a good case in point: having just done away
with the inherited copula verb (Hebrew, h-y-y; P. Arabic, k-n)
in the present tense, they are now developing a present-tense
copula from a pronoun.

Thus, it seems that the emergence and the decline of the copula may be seen as a diachronic cycle. The cycle is clearly very complex. For instance, a language may have more than two copula verbs depending on the tense, suggesting the overlap of several diachronic processes in the emergence and decline of copula verbs. Turkish is such a language. Furthermore, variations in the status of the copula verb among closely related languages spoken in a small geographical region are not uncommon, suggesting that the copula verb may be particularly susceptible to diachronic change. The Maiduan language family (Northern California) provides a good example for this point. Within the family, Maidu has a fully inflected copula verb, whereas its two sibling languages Konkow and Nisenan do not have a copula verb. At the same time, it is also quite possible that contact might play a role; thus the Hebrew development could be at least partially explained in terms of the influence of Indo-European languages.

In this study, we have only elucidated a small section of this vastly complex diachronic cycle involving the rise and fall of the copula verb. Hopefully as more facts are uncovered regarding the diachronic origin of the copula verb, a clearer view of the cycle may be possible.

*We wish to thank James Bauman, Ruth Berman, Monica Devens, Leonard Faltz, Talmy Givón, Bonnie Glover, Amnon Gordon, Douglas Johnson, Edith Moravcsik, Pamela Munro and Russell Schuh for valuable discussion of the data and ideas in this paper.

Notes

1. Among the languages we have looked at, the following seem to be of this type:

>   Austronesian - almost all
>   Chadic - Ngizin
>   Nilo-Saharan - Kanuri
>   Dravidian - Irula
>   Telegu
>   Australian - Tiwi
>   Djingli
>   Maranungku
>   Djirbal
>   Niger-Congo-Ijo
>   Diola-Fogny
>   Luganda
>   Maidu - Nisenan
>   Uto Aztecan - Yaqui
>   Classical Nahuatl
>   Kawaiisu
>   Hokan - Diegueño
>   Otomanguean - Isthmus Zapotec
>   Algonquian - Wiyot
>   Tibeto-Burman - Naga
>   Mayan - Jacaltec

2. For a characterization of the notion of "topic," see Chafe (1976) and Li and Thompson (1976).

3. One may suspect that the so-called declarative particle, y̌ĕ in (6)-(9) is the copula. It is difficult to pinpoint the semantic content of the particle other than to say that

in certain contexts, it seems to accentuate the preceding
phrase or clause slightly. Evidence that yě was not a copula
is that it was by no means confined to equational sentences.
Sentences (9) and (10) are examples of non-equational sentences with yě. Other examples:

(i)   lái   shi bù   kě dài, wǎng   shi bù kě
        future age not can wait, past   age not can

                zhūi yě
                return declarative
                       particle

        '(We) cannot wait for the future; (we) cannot re-
        return to the past.'

                                        (Zhuāng-zi 4th c. B.C.)

(ii)   měi   zhī   zhě   yù yǐ   zè zhī   yě
        praise him   person wish to rebuke him declarative
                                                particle
        'The person who praises him wishes to rebuke him.'

                                        (Mèng-zi Zhāng-Jù)

    4. Yen (1975) has disputed the claim that the copula
shi in Mandarin developed from the anaphoric demonstrative
pronoun. His principal argument is that another Archaic Chinese demonstrative pronoun, cǐ (see examples (20), (21)), did
not turn into a copula, and that it is therefore illogical
for the demonstrative pronoun shi alone to have become a copula. We are unconvinced by this line of reasoning, and we
note that no evidence has been presented which would invali-
date the accepted derivation. Yen goes on to propose an alternative derivation for the copula. In Archaic Chinese, the
word shì was also used as a predicate meaning 'correct, right',
in opposition to the morpheme, fēi, meaning 'wrong, incorrect', e.g.:

qián-ri zhǐ bù shou shì yě, zhǐ jīn-ri
yesterday genitive not acceptance right decl. then today
                                       particle

zhǐ shòu fēi yě
genitive acceptance wrong decl.
particle   marker

'(If) yesterday's refusal to accept was right, then today's
   acceptance is wrong.'

(Mencius 4th c. B.C.)

However, the word fēi could also be used as a negative particle in an equational sentence, e.g.

(b)   zǐ fēi wǒ
you not I
'You are not me.'

(Zhuang zi, 4th c. B.C.)

There is no doubt that semantically the morpheme fēi meaning
'wrong' as it occurs in (a) is related to the morpheme fēi
signifying negation as in (b). Nonetheless, they were functionally different morphemes in Archaic Chinese. In addition,
the negative morpheme fēi in (b) was not a negative copula,
but was simply a negative particle. This is an undisputed
point accepted by all including Yen. Now, using the vague
semantic link and the homophonous relation of the negative
particle fēi and the morpheme fei meaning 'wrong' on the one
hand and the semantic opposition of the morpheme shì 'right'
with fēi 'wrong' on the other hand, Yen proposes that the copula shì is derived from the morpheme shì 'right' on analogy
with the negative particle fēi. But since the negative particle fēi was not a negative copula, Yen's analogy collapses.

5. We have cited sources for most of our modern Hebrew
data. In certain cases we have found some variation among
speakers reacting to these examples, but the variation does

not affect the main point we are making.

6.   Our source for the Palestinian Arabic data is Farid Hadad. Our thanks to him.

7.   We are grateful to Bonnie Glover and Mustafa Mebarkia for bringing this point to our attention.

8.   The Wappo data is from our consultant, Laura Somersal. We are grateful to her for working with us.

9.   This argument is strengthened by the fact that it can also be made for Hebrew. This although (41) is possible, (i) is not:

    (i) *hu hu   ha- student   še-moše diber itxa alev
        he "he" def. student that Moshe spoke with about
                                                you   him

10.   We are grateful to Robert Hetzron for bringing the Zway case to our attention.

References

Berman, R., & A. Grosu (1976). "Aspects of the Copula in
    Modern Hebrew." In Cole (1976).

Chafe, W. (1976). "Givenness, Contrastiveness, Definiteness,
    Subjects, Topics, and Point of View," in Li (1976).

Cole, P., ed. (1976). Studies in Modern Hebrew Syntax and
    Semantics. North Holland, Amsterdam.

Faltz, A. (1973). "Surrogate Copulas in Hebrew," unpublished
    manuscript.

Hetzron, R. (1972). Ethiopian Semitic Studies in Classifica-
    tion, Journal of Semitic Studies, Monograph No. 2. Man-
    chester University Press.

Li, C. N. & S. A. Thompson (1976). "Subject and Topic: A New
    Typology of Language," in Li (1976).

Li, C. N., ed. (1976). Subject and Topic. Academic Press,
    New York.

Wang, Li (1958a). Hàn-Yǔ Shǐ Lùn-Wén Jí (Collected Essays
    on Historical Chinese). Peking: Ke-xue chu-ban she.

_____(1958b). Hàn-Yǔ Shǐ-Gǎo (History of Chinese), 3 vols.
    Peking: Ke-xue Chu-ban she.

Yen, S. L. (1975). The Origin of the Copula shih in Chinese.
    Paper presented at the 8th International Conference on
    Sino-Tibetan Languages & Linguistics, Berkeley, Cal-
    ifornia, October 1975.

Zhou, Fa-gao (1952). "Jǐ ge chángyòngcí de láiyuán" [The
    source of several commonly used words]. Dalu Journal

4:7, 6-9. Also in Zhou (1963), pp. 154-57.

____ (1963). Zhōngguó Yǔwén Lùncóng [Essays on Chinese Language and Literature]. Zhengshong Shuju, Taipei.

10 From Existential to Copula: The History of Yuman BE

Pamela Munro

1. Introduction: The Yuman Predicate Nominal Construction[1]

In the Yuman languages, simple "copular" relationships may be expressed with sentences of the form

(1)   SUBJECT NP   PREDICATE NP   BE

--for example, consider the Mojave sentence

(2)   John k^{w}aθ?ide:-č ido-pč
       John doctor   be
       'John is a doctor.'

At first the pattern (1) seems highly consistent with the normal SOV word order of other sentences in these languages, but there is evidence that sentences following the pattern (1) are actually complex. In this paper I will demonstrate that the verb 'be' which appears in sentences like (2) is not a copula, but an existential, at least historically; I will further show, however, that the complex sentence type (1) is being reinterpreted by Yuman speakers as a single clause, following natural processes which, I believe, have universal implications.

Although sentences like (2) appear to follow a standard SOV word order they deviate from the normal sentence pattern in a number of ways. (2) should be compared with a typical transitive Mojave sentence like (3):

(3)   John-č   Mary iyu:-pč
       John-subj Mary see-tns
       'John saw Mary.'

In (3), the suffixes -č and -pč are glossed as 'subject' and
'tense' respectively. -č is the Mojave (and pan-Yuman) subject case marker. (Objects, like Mary in (3), are unmarked
in most Yuman languages and were not marked in Proto-Yuman.)
The -pč suffix on the Mojave verb 'see' in (3) is a perfective (present/past) marker--note that the verb is unprefixed,
the sign of a third-person subject.

   Now, when (3) is compared with (2), the unusual structure of Yuman predicate nominal sentences is quite apparent.
The -č and -pč morphemes just discussed appear in (2) as well
as in (3); as might be expected, the verb of (2) also carries
a tense marker. In (2), as in (3), one of the two nouns is
marked with the subject suffix -č. But in (2) it is the second noun which is marked with the suffix -č; the first (subject) noun is unmarked.

   The general Yuman predicate nominal sentence structure
given in (1), then, can be more fully specified as

(4) NP_1 NP_2-č BE-TNS 'NP_1 is NP_2'

where TNS is a general cover term for a number of language-
specific final tense/aspect/evidential markers (sometimes
realized simply as Ø), including Mojave -pč. This structure
is reconstructable for Proto-Yuman on the basis of comparative data like that shown in (5) below. (Proto-Yuman 'be' was
*yu; by a well-attested sound change, *y became d [ð] in the
Mojave, Maricopa, and Yuma languages. Note that the initial
y- of 'be' is sometimes absorbed by the preceding palatal č
of the subject marker.)

(5)   KILIWA: nᵞa?p Rufino xumayi-t ?-yu:-kha?
me   Rufino son-subj 1-be-tns
'I am Rufino's son.'
(Mixco FN)

PAIPAI: kitkal-ha   ?icmac ?xa(:)n-oli-c-(y)u
abalone-dem food   good-very-subj-be
'Abalone is good food.'
(Joël 1975)

DIEGUEÑO (MESA GRANDE):[2] ?i:kᵂic kusəya:y-č-(y)i-s
man   doctor-subj-be-emph
'The man is a doctor.'
(Langdon 1976)

DIEGUEÑO (IÑAJA):   pəya: t-xatəpa:-č-(y)i-s
this emph-coyote-subj-be-emph
'This is a coyote.'
(Jacobs FN)

DIEGUEÑO (IMPERIAL VALLEY):   nᵞip puš-č-(y)u
that cat-subj-be
'That's a cat.'
(Gorbet FN)

YUMA: enci:n   ?anᵞa:-c ?-ado-t-k
older=brother me-subj 1-be-assert-tns

adu-tya
be-comp

'I (myself) am your older brother.'
(Halpern FN)

MOJAVE: John kᵂaθ?ide:-č ido-pč
John doctor-subj be-tns
'John is a doctor.'

WALAPAI: nᵞa ?apa-v-č   yu
me person-dem-subj be
'I am a human being'
(Redden 1966)

HAVASUPAI: qəsaq ?čaa-v-č-yu
crow bird-dem-subj-be
'A crow is a bird'
(Hinton 1975)

YAVAPAI: John hime-v-č-yu-m
            John boy-dem-subj-be-tns
            'John is a boy'
                                    (Chung, personal com-
                                        munication)

Most languages exhibit a number of possible variations
for the structure shown in (4) and exemplified in (5). For
instance, in context an understood subject noun may be omitted, as in the examples in (6). In these sentences, the first
noun, NP_1, of (4), does not appear; the predicate noun, NP_2,
still marked with the subject-case suffix -č, remains before
'be'. This construction is presumably possible in all languages, since zero-pronominalization of understood subjects
is always an option with other types of sentences.

(6) DIEGUEÑO: kusəya:y-č-(y)i-s
                  doctor-subj-be-emph
                  'He's a doctor.'
                                    (Ted Couro, personal
                                        communication)

     COCOPA: n^{y}a:-c   yu-c   pawa-c   yu-s
                me-subj be-same=subj loc-same=subj be-evid
                'It's me here.'
                                    (Crawford 1969)

     MOJAVE: k^{w}aθ?ide:-č ido-pč
                doctor-subj be-tns
                'He is a doctor.'

     HAVASUPAI: havasu pa-v-č   yu
                   blue   person-dem-subj be
                   'He is a Havasupai.'
                                    (Kozlowski 1972)

A second variant possible in some languages (presumably
only those in which 'be' does not normally cliticize to the
subject-marked predicate noun) is for the verb 'be' to be
omitted from the pattern (4). (7) illustrates sentences of

this type, consisting only of two nouns, the second of which
is subject-marked:

(7)   YUMA: n^ya: sin^y?ak-c
                me   woman-subj
                'I am a woman.'
                                        (Langdon FN)

      MARICOPA: dan^y či=k^wtat-š
                  this catfish-subj
                  'This is a catfish.'
                                        (Alpher FN)

      MOJAVE: John k^waθ?ide:-č
                 John doctor-subj
                 'John is a doctor.'

Still a third common variant represents a further simplification of the pattern: a sentence with neither an overt
subject nor the verb 'be', consisting solely of the subject-
marked predicate noun, as in (8):

(8)   PAIPAI: n^ye-Y
               me-subj
               'It's me.'
                                        (Joël FN)

      YUMA: makxa:v-c
               Mojave-subj
               'He is a Mojave.'
                                        (Lange FN)

      MARICOPA: n^yap xumay-š
                  my   son-subj
                  'It's my son'
                                        (Alpher FN)

      MOJAVE: k^waθ?ide:-č
                 doctor-subj
                 'He's a doctor.'

Probably these three variant constructions were all allowed in Proto-Yuman, in addition to the basic structure set

forth in (4), so that the reconstructed predicate nominal
sentence pattern may be fully specified as

(9) (NP_1) NP_2-$\check{c}$ (BE-TNS)   'NP_1 is NP_2'

(with deletable elements enclosed in parentheses.) Other
variants are possible in various languages; these will be
described below.

2.   The Underlying Structure of Predicate Nominal Sentences

The predicate nominal structure of (4) and (9) is unusual, compared to ordinary simple sentences, for a number of
reasons. Predicate nominals are the only sentences in which
the logical subject is not marked with the subject -$\check{c}$, for
instance, and they are also the only sentences in which another noun in the sentence is unexpectedly marked with the
subject -$\check{c}$. The explanation for these facts, as well as for
certain other phenomena about predicate nominal sentences, is
that strings like (4) are actually complex sentences. The
structure of a sentence like the Mojave John k^waθ?ide:-$\check{c}$ ido-p$\check{c}$
'John is a doctor' should be represented not as a simple sen-
tence, like

(10)

```
                              S
                 ┌────────────┼────────────┐
                NP           NP            V
                 │            │            │
               JOHN        DOCTOR         BE
```

but rather as

(11)

```
                                    S
                    ┌───────────────────────────────┐
                   NP                                V
                    │                                │
                    S                                BE
            ┌───────┴───────┐
           NP              NP
            │               │
          JOHN            DOCTOR
```

in which the highest verb, 'be', takes a sentential subject
complement which consists simply of two nouns, the subject
and the predicate nominals.

This structure makes clearer a lot of the mysteries associated with the predicate nominal construction. For one
thing, if the subject noun (John in the example under consideration) is actually the subject of an embedded clause, it
is no longer remarkable that it is not marked with the subject-case marker -č.[3] The subjects of many types of nominalized clauses are not č-marked in Mojave (or Yuman generally),
as (12) illustrates:

(12)   MOJAVE: ?-nakut ?ava u:čo:-1^y ?-navay-k
                 1-father house make-in 1-live-tns
                 'I live in the house father built.'

Here, the subject noun ?-nakut 'my father' of the relative
clause ?-nakut ?ava u:čo: 'the house my father built'[4] is not
marked with the subject suffix -č. This lack of č-marking is
typical of the subjects of many nominalized (e.g., case-mark-
ed) clauses.

Secondly, the appearance of the subject-marker -č on
the predicate noun of the predicate nominal construction is
no longer so remarkable. The subject case marker follows the
predicate noun simply because that noun is the last element
of the embedded sentential NP in (11). It is a standard rule
of Yuman for any case marker applying to an NP to follow the
last element of that NP--as shown by the appearance of the
locative case marker -1^y on the verb (the last element) of
the relative NP in (12), for instance.

Positing a structure like (11) for Yuman predicate nominal sentences also explains certain other facts about these

constructions.

In Mojave, for instance, subject-verb agreement in predicate nominal constructions can be quite complicated. In sentences where either the subject or the predicate noun is non-
third-person, the verb 'be' may be marked to agree with that
non-third-person noun, or may remain unmarked. (In Yuman languages a ?- prefix regularly marks a first-person subject and
an m- prefix regularly marks a second-person subject. In Proto-Yuman verbs with third-person subjects were unmarked --
this is still the situation in Mojave and most other Yuman
languages, but a few languages have innovated third-person
subject markers.) Consider (13) and (14):

(13)   MOJAVE: ?in^{y}ep k^{w}aθ?ide:-č ?-ido-pč
                 me   doctor-subj 1-be-tns

                                                        'I'm a
                                                         doctor.'

                 ?in^{y}ep k^{w}aθ?ide:-č ido-pč

(14)   MOJAVE: k^{w}aθ?ide:-n^y ?in^{y}eč ?-ido-pč
                 doctor-dem   I   1-be-tns

                                                        'The doctor
                                                         is me.'

                 k^{w}aθ?ide:-n^y ?in^{y}ec ido-pč

In (13), the first (subject) noun is first-person, and a first-
person prefix may optionally appear on the verb 'be'. (The
first-person singular subject pronoun is ?in^{y}eč (note the
final -č); the unmarked (object) form is ?in^{y}ep.) In (14), the
predicate noun is first person, and, again, the verb may optionally be marked first-person. These sentences both contain
a third-person noun, k^{w}aθ?ide: 'doctor', so we might say that
the verb 'be' of a Mojave predicate nominal sentence can agree
with the person of either the subject or the predicate noun.

But consider a sentence like

(15)   MOJAVE: ʔin^{y}eč ʔ-ido-pč ⎤
                   I   1-be-tns ⎬
                                       ⎬   'I'm me.'
                   ʔin^{y}eč ido-pč   ⎦

(15) follows the pattern illustrated in (6) above, whereby
the unmarked subject NP may be deleted if it is readily infer-
able in context. Given the meaning of (15) (which might be
used as a mild assertion of independence or the like), it appears that the deleted subject noun in the underlying form of
this sentence can only have been the unmarked first-person
singular pronoun ʔin^{y}ep. In other words, (15) is a predicate
nominal sentence in which both the subject and the predicate
nouns are first person, and yet in which the verb may be either first person or third person. A similar example is

(16)   MOJAVE: man^y ʔin^{y}eč ido-pč
                   you I   be-tns
                   'You're me.'

which I have recorded only in this form (with a third-person
verb). From a superficial point of view there is no third-person NP in the underlying structure of (15) or (16) for the
verb to agree with, but if (11) is taken as the underlying
structure for these sentences, the possibility of agreement
with a third-person subject is most reasonable, since by (11)
'be' underlyingly has a sentential (hence, third-person) subject. (The problem now, in fact, is why the verb should ever
be marked for a non-third-person subject. This question is
discussed below.)

Diegueño provides a somewhat more complicated but essentially similar piece of evidence that the whole NP NP predicate nominal string functions as the subject of the following 'be'. First consider the predicate nominal sentence

(17)   DIEGUEÑO: ?əwa: m-um-vu   n^ya-?-ta:t
                     house 2-see-dem   my-1-father

                     w-čuw-č-(y)i-s
                     3-make-subj-be-emph

                     'The house you see is the one my father
                     built.'
                                                    (Langdon 1976)

in which the subject and predicate nouns are both relative
clauses -- subject ?əwa: m-um 'the house you see' and predicate n^ya-?-ta:t w-čuw 'the one my father built'. In the more
complicated (and quite rare) variant construction used in

(18)   DIEGUEÑO: ?əwa: m-um-vu   n^ya-?-ta:t
                     house 2-see-dem   my-1-father

                     w-čuw-m   yi-s
                     3-make-diff=subj be-emph

                     'The house you see is the one my father
                     built.'

                                                    (Langdon 1976)

the different-subject subordinator -m follows the last element of the predicate nominal sentence (in this case, the verb
of the relative clause n^ya-?-ta:t w-čuw), before the following verb, and unmarked (third-person) 'be'. A common way to
indicate that one clause is the subject of a following verb
in Yuman languages is to follow the first clause with -m, as
in the simpler example (19), from Mojave:

(19)   MOJAVE: ?-n^yaha?a:k-m   ?ahot-k
                   I-marry-diff=subj good-tns
                   'It's good that I'm married.'

Different-subject -m appears on the subordinate clause
?-n^yaha?a:k 'I'm married'; the subject of that clause is 'I',
while the subject of the following clause is that whole sentence 'I'm married.' Thus, the -m on w-čuw in (18) means that

the subject of the preceding predicate nominal is different
from the subject of the following verb 'be'. In other words,
the subject of 'be' cannot be the same as the subject of the
predicate nominal, which is ?əwa: m-um 'the house you see'.
The subject of the sentence 'The house you see is the one my
father built,' then, is not the subject of the following
Diegueño verb 'be', so that 'be' cannot be a member of the
same clause as that subject and thus is not a copula.

If the semantic subject of (18) (and (17)) is something
like (11), however, the use of different-subject -m just described is not surprising, since the subject of 'be' in (11)
is the whole embedded sentence consisting of the unmarked subject noun and the following predicate noun.

Another piece of evidence that (11) correctly reflects
the basic Yuman predicate nominal structure has to do with
negatives of predicate nominal sentences in Mojave.

One way to negate a Mojave sentence like (2) is by sub-
stituting a standard negative suffix like -mpotč for the -pč
tense/aspect suffix on 'be' --

(20)   MOJAVE: John k^{W}aθ?ide:-č ido-mpotč
                   John doctor-subj be-neg
                   'John isn't a doctor.'

Another way to express the same idea, however, is to use a
special negative suffix -m-, which appears between the predicate noun (here, k^{W}aθ?ide: 'doctor') and the subject-case suffix -č, as in (21) (note that again 'be' has been deleted):

(21)   MOJAVE: John k^{W}aθ?ide:-m-č
                   John doctor-neg-subj
                   'John isn't a doctor.'

Unlike the common negative suffix -mpotč used in (20), which

may follow any verb, the -m- which is used to negate sentence
(21) has quite a limited distribution. Basically it is used
to negate NPs, as in

(22)   MOJAVE: m-n^{y}ahu:?a:k-m-n^y ?-su:paw-k
                 2-marry-neg-dem   1-know-tns
                 'I know you're not married.'

where the underlined embedded clause is negated by -m- suffixed to its verb, or in (23), in which -m- is used to negate
the verb of a relative clause:

(23)   MOJAVE: ?in^{y}ep ?-ičuy-n^y kaθve:
                 my   1-husband-dem   coffee

                 u:θe:-m-n^y-c   1^{y}ahq^{w}aq-m
                 drink-neg-dem-subj bitter-tns

                 'The coffee my husband wouldn't drink was
                 bitter.'

Note, however, that this suffix -m- may only be used to negate sentential NPs.[5] It could not be used to somehow negate
a non-complex NP -- in other words, JOHN-č DOG-m HIT would
not be a way to say something like 'It wasn't the dog that
John hit,' with just 'dog' negated in the sentence 'John hit
the dog.'

    Thus, the appearance of this negative suffix -m on the
predicate noun of a sentence like (21) is an additional indication that that noun is the last element of an embedded sentence, as would follow from structure (11).

    A similar piece of evidence is provided by the form of
negative predicate nominal sentences in Diegueño. In normal
Diegueño negative sentences, the verb of the negated sentence
is followed by the irrealis suffix -x, and then by a form of
the negative verb ma:w, as in

(24)   DIEGUEÑO: John-č   a:-x   u-ma:w
                     John-subj go-irr 3-neg
                     'John didn't go.'

In negated predicate nominal sentences, 'be' does not appear;
the irrealis suffix immediately follows the predicate noun.
Note that, as in any predicate nominal sentence, the subject
noun is not č-marked:

(25)   DIEGUEÑO: John kusəya:y-x u-ma:w
                     John doctor-irr 3-neg
                     'John's not a doctor.'

This evidence from Diegueño confirms the claim that the basic
structure of a predicate nominal sentence is simply a string
of two NPs, and that, in other words, this NP NP string (from
which the first, subject, noun may be deleted in context) constitutes a complete sentence by itself.[6]

   Another piece of evidence that the NP NP string is a complete sentence by itself, without any copular 'be', is found
in the occasional occurrence in various Yuman languages of
predicate nominal sentences consisting simply of two NPs unmarked for case, as in (26):

(26)   PAIPAI: paxmi-ha ksye:
                   man-dem   doctor
                   'The man is a doctor.'
                              (Joël FN)

        DIEGUEÑO (CAMPO):   sin^y-vu   ?ən^{y}a: ?-ənsi:n^y
                             woman-dem my   1-wife
                             'The woman is my wife.'
                                        (Langdon 1976)

        HAVASUPAI: n^{y}un^{y}u muso
                      that   cat
                      'That is a cat.'
                                  (Kozlowski 1972)

All this data seems to indicate that the 'be' which may
appear in a Yuman predicate nominal sentence derived from the
pattern of (9) is not essential to the meaning of the sentence, i.e. for the establishment of an equational or copular
link between the juxtaposed subject and predicate nouns. ('Be'
has another function in these sentences, as will be discussed
below; this is related to the nonoccurrence of 'be' in sentences like (25).) In other words, the assertion of identification ('John is my father') or class-membership ('John is a
doctor') which is the essence of a "copular" sentence is accomplished in Yuman simply by the juxtaposition of two nouns.[7]

Although the N N copular structure is unchanged even if
the predicate noun is semantically definite (as in the "identification" use of such sentences), in most Yuman languages
the predicate noun usually does not carry the demonstrative
suffix which is the expected marker of definiteness -- cf.
the Campo example in (26) and the Mojave sentence

(27)   MOJAVE: k^waθide:-n^y ?in^{y}ep ?-icuy-č
                   doctor-dem   my   1-husband-subj
                   'The doctor is my husband.'

The usual marker of definiteness or prior reference for Mojave NPs, the demonstrative suffix -$\underline{n^y}$, does not show up on
the predicate noun in (27). Similarly, in Diegueño a simple
definite predicate noun apparently cannot acceptably be marked with the usual Diegueño definitizer, the demonstrative suffix -$\underline{v}$.[8]

What appears to be a striking counterexample to the
claim that definiteness is generally unmarked on predicate
nominals, however, is found in the predicate nominal constructions used in the Northern Pai group of languages (Hava-

supai, Walapai, and Yavapai). In these languages, as the
Northern Pai examples in (5)-(6) above indicate, the demonstrative suffix -v- appears between the predicate noun and
the subject suffix -č in almost every predicate nominal sentence I have seen, regardless of the definiteness of the predicate noun. Compare, for instance, the following sentences
with indefinite (28) and definite (29) predicates:

   (28)   HAVASUPAI: havasu pa-v-č   yu
                              blue   person-dem-subj be
                              'He is a Havasupai.'
                                                  (Kozlowski 1972)
           WALAPAI: n^{y}a ?apa-v-č   yu
                              I   person-dem-subj be
                              'I am a human being.'
                                                  (Redden 1966)

           YAVAPAI: John hime-v-č-yu-m
                              John boy-dem-subj-be-tns
                              'John is a boy.'
                                         (Chung, personal com-
                                               munication)
   (29)   HAVASUPAI: n^{y}a-lwa-v-č   yu
                              my-wife-dem-subj be
                              'It is my wife.'
                                                 (Kozlowski 1972)

           YAVAPAI: Bill ?n^{y}a mi:-v-č-yu-m
                              Bill my   husband-dem-subj-be-tns
                              'Bill is my husband.'
                                          (Chung, personal com-
                                             munication)

Yuman languages have from one to three demonstrative suffixes,
which may appear following the noun phrase they modify, before
any case marking. Frequently these suffixes are used almost
like definite articles -- indeed, Chung (to appear) and Kendall 1972 gloss Yavapai -v- as 'definite' in the predicate
nominal and other constructions. Given this usage, we might

expect a demonstrative like Pai -v- to appear on definite
nominal predicates like those in the identification sentences
in (29), but it would be surprising, to say the least, if
such a morpheme appeared on indefinite, generic sorts of predicates in sentences specifying class membership. Yet this
seems to be the case in (28).

Langdon 1970b hints at the reconstruction for Proto-
Northern Pai of a pair of contrasting demonstratives *v 'near'
and *θ/h 'far/anaphoric' (these reflect the Proto-Yuman demonstrative morphemes *v 'near', *s 'far', and *x 'anaphoric' --
see Langdon 1970b). Since the meaning 'anaphoric' is associated with the 'far' demonstrative suffix -h, it is not unreasonable that the opposing 'near' suffix -v should be extended to mean 'not anaphoric'. Exactly this extension is recorded for Havasupai by Hinton (1975), who has insightfully
shown how [-anaphoric] nouns newly introduced into a conversation must be nearer conceptually to the speaker, within
the discourse context, than definite nouns whose reference is
old (far-off) information. Since the [-anaphoric] use of -v
follows naturally from the spatial use of the suffix, I believe that this usage must have already been developing in
Proto-Northern Pai. (The development of the meaning 'definite'
would thus appear to be a Yavapai innovation, since it does
not fit into the general pattern indicated by the well-attested assocation of the meanings 'anaphoric' and 'far'.)

If the Northern Pai suffix -v- can have as one of its
meanings [-anaphoric], its appearance on predicate nominals
in the Northern Pai languages is not so bizarre. Recall that
in other languages no definitizing demonstrative appears,
even when the predicate is definite and unique (cf. (27)). It

appears that the use of the -v- suffix on predicate nouns
in the Northern Pai languages, where this suffix has at least
historically the extended meaning [-anaphoric], is exactly
similar to the non-occurrence of any definitizing demonstrative on predicate nominals in other Yuman languages.[9]

We should probably reconstruct for Proto-Yuman the tendency to treat all predicate nominals as syntactically indefinite -- the appearance of the 'near' demonstrative suffix -v-
on the indefinite/nonanaphoric predicate nominal, following
the extension of the meaning of this suffix, should probably
be best regarded as a Northern Pai innovation, since there
are no traces of this usage elsewhere in Yuman. In the source
for the predicate nominal construction NP_1 NP_2-č BE, then,
the predicate noun NP_2 is syntactically indefinite.

3. The Existential Identity of Predicate Nominal 'Be'

I have shown above that a predicate nominal sentence in
the Yuman languages consists simply of two juxtaposed subject
and predicate noun phrases, and that this NP NP string may be
shown to function as the syntactic subject of a following
higher verb 'be'. The 'be' that appears in Yuman predicate
nominal sentences, therefore, is not a same-clause two-argu-
ment "copula" or linking verb between subject and predicate
nouns. I believe that the 'be' which appears in Yuman predicate nominal sentences is a one-argument existential verb.
This 'be' asserts the existence or substance of its argument;
its meaning is 'be' in the sense of 'be real', 'be a fact', or
'be true'.[10]

Existential 'be' is one of the "existential auxiliaries"
whose use in all affirmative declaratives may be reconstructed

for Proto-Yuman (Langdon 1974). The primary purpose of the
presence of the auxiliary verbs 'be' or 'do' in these sentences is, apparently, to indicate that the sentence is an affirmative declarative (possibly, an affirmative declarative
with non-future reference); typically also these auxiliaries
show whether a sentence is active or stative, transitive or
intransitive. Selection of 'be' or 'do' is determined by the
semantics of the main verb which the auxiliary follows. Details vary somewhat from language to language, but Mojave is
fairly representative: 'be' is used as the auxiliary for sentences whose verbs are stative or intransitive, while 'do' is
used as the auxiliary for the remaining active transitive sentences. (A third auxiliary, 'say', is used with some verbs of
communication.) One construction in which these auxiliaries
appear in Mojave is illustrated in (30) (for 'be') and (31)
(for 'do') below:[11]

(30)   ?ahot-k   idu:-m
       good-same=subj be-tns
       'He's good.'

       su:paw-k   idu:-m
       know-same=subj be-tns
       'He knows it.'

       ipuy-k   idu:-m
       die-same=subj be-tns
       'He dies.'

(31)   MOJAVE: tapuy-k   a?wi:-m
                 kill-same=subj do-tns
                 'He kills him.'

(30)-(31) show that auxiliary 'be' occurs with sentences whose
main verbs are stative (intransitive 'good', transitive 'know')
or intransitive (stative 'good'; active 'die'), while 'do' is
used with active transitives (like 'kill').

The -k suffix which appears on the initial verbs of the
sentences in (30)-(31) is a Mojave subordinator, the same-subject marker corresponding to the different-subject -m, whose
use was discussed above. Its appearance indicates that the
"main" verbs in (30)-(31) are syntactically subordinate
to the higher auxiliaries 'be' and 'do'. The use of same-subject -k on the lexical verbs in (30) indicates that the subject of 'be' is the same as the subject of the lower verbs
(in (30), third-person singular 'he'). There is evidence, however, that the construction illustrated in (30) has evolved
historically from a simpler construction in which the existential 'be' had only one argument, the whole lower clause.
For instance, alongside sentences like the first one in (30)
one may occasionally hear sentences like (32), which are said
to have about the same meaning:

    (32)   MOJAVE: ?ahot-m   idu:-m
                      good-diff=subj be-tns
                      'He's good.'

(32) illustrates the same construction as that used in sentences (18)-(19) above. A lower clause which serves as the
sentential subject of a following verb is marked with the different-subject subordinator -m, since its subject cannot be
the same as that of the higher verb. Apparently there was
some historical rule of subject copying by which the subject
of the lower clause is raised to become the subject of the
higher existential verb (for details of this process, cf. Munro 1976).

The 'be' which appears in predicate nominal sentences in
Mojave and Yuman generally may be identified with the existential auxiliary 'be' whose use is illustrated in (30) and

(32). 'Be' appears as a higher verb above sentences which are
stative, and predicate nominal sentences are excellent examples of stative sentences. By the general statements given
above, then, we would expect that the existential auxiliary
'be' would appear above a predicate nominal sentence. There
are a number of pieces of evidence that the 'be' of the Yuman
predicate nominal sentence, the 'be' which appears in (5)-(6),
etc., is indeed auxiliary 'be'.

For instance, consider the deletability of 'be' in predicate nominal sentences in certain Yuman languages, as illustrated in (7)-(8). This is, in itself, a peculiar phenomenon.
No other non-auxiliary verb in any Yuman language that I know
of is freely deletable. But in a number of Yuman languages in
which the existential auxiliaries are used, these auxiliaries
are freely deletable. Perhaps the best language to exemplify
this deletion is Mojave--alongside sentences like (30)-(32),
we find sentences like (30')-(32'). These are essentially the
same sentences, except that the last word of each, the existential auxiliary, has been deleted:

(30')	MOJAVE:	?ahot-k	'He's good.'
		su:paw-k	'He knows it.'
		ipuy-k	'He dies.'
(31')	MOJAVE:	tapuy-k	'He kills him.'
(32')	MOJAVE:	?ahot-m	'He's good.'

The source for sentences like (30')-(32') is sentences
like (30)-(32); in other words, the -k's and -m's which follow the verbs in (30')-(32') -- which are synchronically
tense markers -- originate as same- and different-subject sub-

ordinators on these verbs. The retention of the -k and -m
dependency marking even when the following auxiliary is deleted is exactly parallel to the retention of the subject-
case marker -č when the 'be' of the predicate nominal construction is deleted, as in (7) and (8) above.

A further parallel is that in some langauges, a main
verb with no following existential auxiliary is completely
unmarked (i.e., it has no suffixed "tense" marker like Mojave
-k or -m). In such a case, apparently, deletion of the existential auxiliary causes any preceding dependency marker to
be deleted too. This sort of deletion appears to operate to
produce the simplest type of predicate nominal sentences, the
unmarked NP NP strings like those in (26). In this case, when
'be' is deleted, the preceding subject case suffix is deleted
as well.

In certain languages, 'be' may not freely be deleted
from a predicate nominal sentence, and this behavior too parallels the behavior of auxiliary 'be' and 'do' in the same
languages.

For instance, in the Northern Pai languages the sequence
of same-subject -k plus a following 'be' or 'do' (plus, addi-
tionally, in Yavapai, a final incompletive -m or completive
-n^y) has become almost frozen; the auxiliary is not freely deletable in normal affirmative declaratives in these languages.
In Tolkapaya Yavapai, in fact, it is possible to consider the
suffixes -k-yu-m, -k-yu-n^y, -k-wi-m, and -k-wi-n^y as unit "compound tense markers" synchronically (cf. Chung 1976):

(33)   YAVAPAI: vak   ?-pay-kyum
                  here   1-sit=pl-CTns
                  'We're sitting here.'

```
?a?a    ?-ma-kwim
cactus  1-eat-CTns
'I'm eating cactus.'
```

The fusion of the subject case suffix -č with following auxiliary yu 'be' to form the predicate nominal suffixes -čyu
(in Havasupai and Walapai) and -čyum or -čyun^y (in Yavapai)
is, then, exactly parallel to the fusion of same-subject -k
and the following yu 'be' and wi 'do', forming the complex
suffixes -kyu and -kwi (for Havasupai and Walapai) and -kyum,
-kwim, -kyun^y, -kwin^y (as in (33), for Yavapai). All these
suffixes are subject to the same sort of phonological reduction -- they are commonly all destressed. In the Verde Valley
dialect of Yavapai described by Kendall (1972), this reduction goes even further: the -kyum and -kwim suffixes observed
by Chung merge as unanalyzeable -kəm; -kyun^y and -kwin^y become -kin^y, and predicate nominal -čyum becomes, in the
speech of many speakers, [čüm].

Another similarity between the 'be' of predicate nominal
sentences and the standard auxiliary 'be' whose use is shown
in (30) and (32) has to do with negative sentences. As noted
above, the existential auxiliaries normally occur in affirmative declaratives. They do not occur, however, in negative
versions of such sentences (presumably because a negative is
itself a type of existential).[12] The non-occurrence of the
existential auxiliaries in ordinary declarative sentences is
paralleled by the non-occurrence of 'be' in negative predicate nominal sentences like Diegueño (25) and Mojave (21).

Something else that the existential auxiliaries and
the 'be' of predicate nominal sentences have in common is
that both are similarly difficult to embed. Although we have

postulated that all affirmative declaratives contain a higher
auxiliary verb, such verbs do not show up following the verbs
of complement clauses -- cf., for example, the Mojave example
(19). Similarly, when one attempts to embed or relativize on
a predicate nominal sentence, the verb 'be' does not show
up.[13]

A final point of similarity between predicate nominal
'be' and the existential auxiliaries is apparent when we consider the morphology of WH questions in Mojave. Normally the
verb of a Mojave question is unmarked. In WH questions, however, the main verb of the question sentence may optionally
be followed by same-subject -k plus the appropriate existential auxiliary. This existential auxiliary, in turn, may optionally be followed by a special suffix, -m. The possibilities are illustrated in (34):[14]

(34a)   MOJAVE: maki   iman
                  where come=from   'Where
                                                                       did
    b)   maki   iman-k   idu: he
                  where come=from-same=subj   be   come
                                                                       from?'
    c)   maki   iman-k   idu:-m
                  where come-from-same-subj   be-m

This optional -m suffix cannot be the same as the "tense"
suffix -m whose use is shown in sentences like (31') above,
since   ordinary verbs can never be followed by "tense" -m
(or any other tense marker) when they occur in questions --cf.
(34a) (questions like maki iman-m do not occur). The use of
the -m suffix which appears in (34c) is restricted to existential auxiliary verbs, when they appear in WH questions.
This should mean that when this special WHQ-auxiliary -m appears, the sentence in which it is used will always contain

at least two verbs. Normally this is true, but there is one
exception: the -m suffix under discussion may occur in WH
questions with only one verb if that verb is the 'be' associated with predicate nominals:

(35)   MOJAVE: makan^y k^{w}aθ?ide:-č idu:-m
                   who=obj doctor-subj be-m
                   'Who is the doctor?'

It seems best to interpret this data as further evidence
that the 'be' of predicate nominal sentences is identical
with the existential auxiliary 'be'; in other words, that
what precedes idu:-m in both (34c) and (35) is the same sort
of "complete sentence".

4. Reinterpretation of the predicate nominal construction as a one-clause sentence

In the two previous sections of this paper I strived to
show that predicate nominal sentences in Yuman consist simply
of two juxtaposed NPs and that the verb 'be' which shows up
in many Yuman predicate nominal sentences is not a copula but
rather an auxiliary whose function is to mark the type of sentence and to indicate (or perhaps to enforce) its stativity.

The tree diagrammed in (11) does, I think, reflect the
underlying semantic structure of predicate nominal sentences
at some Pre-Proto-Yuman stage, and there are many syntactic
traces of this structure which remain in the grammars of the
synchronic languages to allow for the argumentation in sections 2 and 3 above. However, even at the Proto-Yuman stage
there were a number of forces at work to change the way the
predicate nominal sentence was interpreted and constructed,
all of which may be generalized as efforts to change the complex and cumbersome structure in (11) into a single-clause

construction.

The changes which have occurred and are now occurring
may be seen as two basic types of process. In the first, the
logical subject (first noun) of the lower predicate nominal
sentence or, sometimes, the subject-marked predicate noun,
tends to become interpreted as the syntactic subject of 'be'.
In the second, the role of 'be' in the sentence changes. Either the subject -č-plus-'be' string is reinterpreted as a
unitary suffix, or else 'be' begins to lose some of its auxiliary characteristics, and to behave more like an ordinary
main verb. These two types of process are far from contradictory or mutually exclusive, as will be apparent from the examples below.

The most striking example of variable person-marking on
'be' is, I think, in Mojave, as described above (cf. sentences (13)-(16)), but I believe that a certain amount of
such variability may be observed for all Yuman languages. One
can only sympathize with the puzzled speaker confronted with
an NP_1 NP_2-č BE string and the need to mark the person of the
subject on the verb. There is a three-way conflict between
the semantic subject (the "logical" NP_1), the formal subject
(NP_2, with its -č suffix which means "subject" everywhere else
in the language),[15] and the syntactic subject (the sentence
NP_1 NP_2, according to the structure in (11)).

The conflict in person-marking is frequently resolved
in favor of the "logical" first noun,[16] as a number of the
examples above have shown, and a reasonable next step might
be for this noun to be formally marked as a subject with the
subject-case suffix -č. I believe that such innovative -č
marking was first noted by Kendall (1972) among younger

speakers of Verde Valley Yavapai, who applied it only to
third-person subjects of sentences like

(35)   YAVAPAI: n^{y}u-č   pa?ichwa:-v-č-yu-m
                              (phonetically [-vəčüm])
                   he-subj enemy-dem-subj-be-tns
                   'He is an enemy.'

Sandra Chung (personal communication; cf. also Chung to appear) has provided me with many examples of the same sort of
extention in Tolkapaya Yavapai, where the practice is not restricted to third-person subjects:[17]

(36)   YAVAPAI: ?n^{y}a-č   Bill ləwa-ha   ?umi-č   yu-m
                   me-subj Bill wife-dem neg-subj be-tns
                   'I'm not Bill's wife.'

                                      (Chung, personal com-
                                       munication)

The same sort of č- marking on the logical subject of a predicate nominal has been observed recently in Kiliwa, Paipai,
and Cocopa:[18]

(37)   KILIWA: Victoria-t   Teodoro-m   ki?swa?
                  Victoria-subj Teodoro-obj spouse
                  t-(y)u:-kha?
                  subj-be-tns

                  'Victoria is the spouse of Teodoro.'

                                      (Mixco FN)

       PAIPAI: paxmi-ha-Y   ksye: ?ic
                  man-dem-subj doctor say=pl
                  'They say that the man is a doctor.'
                                      (Joël FN)

       COCOPA: Don-pic   šk^{w}iye:-ca
                  Don-dem=subj doctor-subj
                  'Don is a doctor.'

The form and status of 'be' in predicate nominal sentences is changing too, in different ways. The normal Kiliwa 'be', yu:, becomes tu: in predicate nominal sentences with third-person subjects like the example in (37), because the preceding subject marker (-t in Kiliwa) has been reanalyzed; it is, phonologically, no longer a suffix on the predicate noun, but rather a prefix on the following 'be'.[19] The coalescence of subject -č plus yu 'be' (plus the standard preceding demonstrative -v-) into a complex 'is a' suffix which is used essentially to verbalize a predicate noun in the Northern Pai languages has been described above. A similar sort of occurrence is the fusion of subject -č plus yi 'be' plus a following emphatic suffix -s into a near-unit suffix -čis or -čəs in most northern dialects of Diegueño, and the similar treatment of -č plus yu in the Imperial Valley dialect (cf. the examples in (5) above).[20] But even when 'be' retains its status as an independent word, it may behave more like an ordinary main verb than an auxiliary (despite the evidence assembled in section 3) in certain ways.

For instance, the fact that 'be' may be followed by a negative suffix in one form of the Mojave predicate nominal construction (cf. (20)) shows that 'be' is coming to be treated less like an existential auxiliary and more like a main verb. Some other examples which show a predicate nominal 'be' with a following negative, like any other negated verb, are in [21]

(38) YUMA: Christine-c idu:-l^y?em-š
Christine-subj be-neg-tns
'That's not Christine.'

COCOPA: k^{w}akš-lo-yu-mla:x
horse-neg$_1$-be-neg$_2$
'That's not a horse.'

WALAPAI: kak k^{w}e=k=hwal=a-v-č yu-č-a=ta?op-yu
             neg$_1$ farmer-dem-subj be-pl-neg-be
             'We're not farmers.'
                                    (Redden 1975)

Normally, as noted above, existential auxiliaries may not be
followed by negatives.

   A similar process is the application to predicate nominal 'be' of tense markers and similar affixes which would
not be used with an existential auxiliary. The frequent use
of the "perfective" suffix -pč on Mojave 'be' in predicate
nominal sentences like (39a) is a case in point. I don't believe that existential auxiliaries in their normal use ever
occur with the -pč suffix -- the variant sentence (39b), in
which a form of 'be' is followed by -m, would represent a
much more common form for a true auxiliary -- cf. the examples in (30) and (32) above, where 'be' is always followed by
-m:[22]

   (39a)   MOJAVE: k^{w}aθ?ide:-č ido-pč
                       doctor-subj be-tns
                       'He's a doctor.'

   b)   k^{w}aθ?ide:-č idu:-m

Another such example is from Tolkapaya Yavapai: in the unusual
sentence (40), predicate nominal 'be' is followed by the -kyum
auxiliary/tense marker normally associated with any stative
main verb:

   (40)   YAVAPAI (TOLKAPAYA):   hwakva-čə   hayko koθiye-
                                 sibling-subj Anglo doctor-

                                 və-č   yu-kyum
                                 dem-subj   be-CTns

                                 'Her brother's a doctor.'
                                       (Chung, personal com-
                                           munication)

A final type of change that may be observed in various
languages is a change in the syntactic status of the predicate nominal, which seems in some cases to be developing verbal characteristics. I have noted that the compound predicate
nominal suffixes in the Northern Pai languages seem to be ver-
balizers -- Chung (to appear) maintains this is definitely
the case for Tolkapaya Yavapai. In various other cases the
predicate nominal may receive verbal inflections. For instance, in the Iñaja dialect of Diegueño predicate nouns appear preceded by a prefix t-, as shown in

(41)   DIEGUEÑO (IÑAJA):   pəya: t-xatəpa:-č-(y)i-s
                            that emph-coyote-subj-be-emph
                            'That is a coyote.'

This t- is an emphatic prefix whose fairly limited use in
other Diegueño dialects has been extended in Iñaja so that it
may appear on almost any verb (cf. Jacobs 1969, Langdon to
appear). Its occurrence on xatəpa: 'coyote' in (41) shows
the verbalization of the predicate noun.

If predicate nouns are coming to be felt as verbs in
some cases, a further development that would be expected
would be for predicate nouns to be marked for person as verbs
are. This happens occasionally in some languages. (42) shows
the development of second person (m-) marking on the predicate noun in Mojave, Yuma, and Yavapai:

(42)   MOJAVE: man^y m-ma:khav-č
                   you   2-Mojave-subj
                   'You're a Mojave.'

        YUMA: ma-pi?i:pa:-c m-ado-tapat-m
                  2-person-subj 2-be-no=doubt-diff=subj

                  n^y-iyu:-t-k?a
                  1=subj/2=obj-see-assert-tns

'No doubt you are human beings, as I see.'
                              (Halpern FN)

YAVAPAI (TOLKAPAYA):   ma:-čə   m-ləwa-ha
                        you-subj 2-wife-irr

                        ?umi-č-yu-m
                        neg-subj-be-tns

                        'You're not his wife.'
                              (Chung, personal com-
                                  munication)

In none of these languages is the marking of a first- or
second-person logical subject on the predicate noun obligatory.[23]

I hope to have shown in the above discussion that although the 'be' of the Yuman predicate nominal construction
is a stative/existential auxiliary which originates in a
higher clause above the predicate nominal sentence, this 'be'
is undergoing various syntactic changes which have the effect
of making it appear to be more like an ordinary main verb or,
perhaps, a special, non-existential copular suffix.

I think that these changes are quite natural ones. First
of all, the NP NP-č BE string of a typical Yuman predicate
nominal sentence is different in structure from any other sentence in the language containing two nouns and a verb (the
normal pattern, as exemplified in (3) above, is of course
NP-č NP V), and it is consequently a likely candidate for
some sort of reshaping to make it more like an ordinary sentence. Even though the analysis of the NP NP-č BE string into
a č-marked subject complement consisting of two juxtaposed
nouns, plus the following higher verb 'be' is syntactically
well motivated, as shown in section 2, there are not many
overt morphological cues in a simple predicate nominal sen-

tence to guide the hearer to this interpretation. Consequently, it is understandable that diachronic changes have occurred in the Yuman languages to bring the predicate nominal
structure more into conformity with ordinary sentences.

In a sense, such changes are language family-specific,
because few other language families start off with such a con-
fusingly marked underlying structure for predicate nominal
sentences. But there are a number of languages in which the
basic predicate nominal sentence is a string of two NPs, and
all such strings are subject to some of the same pressures I
have exemplified above. It is unusual for a sentence to have
no verb, and so given a sentence consisting only of two NPs,
we might expect two possible developments: either one of the
NPs will become less like a noun, and more like a verb, or
some other element of the sentence will be pressed into service as a verb.[24]

There are traces of both these developments in Yuman.
The fusion of the subject-case marker -č and the following
verb 'be' into a verbalizing 'be a' suffix allows a predicate
noun to be followed directly by a suffix quite similar to the
tense markers which appear on normal verbs, for instance. Examples (21) and (25) above show predicate nouns in negative
constructions where only verbs may otherwise appear. The use
of the Iñaja Diegueño (verbal) emphatic prefix t- with predicate nominals, and the occasional marking of person on predicate nominals in Mojave, Yuma, and Yavapai are further examples that show how predicate nominals are acting more like
verbs.

The second development, by which an additional element
of the sentence comes to be interpreted as its main verb (as

a copula, therefore, since the main verb of a predicate nominal construction with two nouns is by definition a copula) also occurs in Yuman, of course, as has been demonstrated above:
the higher stative/existential/fact auxiliary 'be', whose
presence in a predicate nominal sentence is somewhat fortui-
tous, is reanalyzed as the main verb of that sentence, in
some languages, as indicated by changes in person, tense, and
negative marking.

Both types of change seem psychologically well motivated,
in terms of the pressure to eliminate verbless sentences. It
will be interesting to see what comparative evidence will reveal about the likelihood of similar developments in other
language groups.

Notes

1. I use the terms "predicate nominal sentence" or
"predicate nominal construction" to refer to sentences or
clauses whose predicate is a noun (not an adjective or prepositional phrase) and whose main verb, in the English version,
is a form of 'be'.

The ten Yuman languages spoken today in Southern
California, Baja California, western Arizona, and northern
Sonora include (from, roughly, south to north) Kiliwa, Paipai,
Diegueño, Cocopa, Yuma, Maricopa, Mojave, Havasupai, Walapai,
and Yavapai. The languages are all fairly closely related,
with Kiliwa clearly the most divergent, but experts disagree
about the subgrouping of the remaining languages. The best established subgroup is the Northern Pai group (Havasupai, Walapai, and Yavapai); Mojave, Maricopa, and Yuma and Diegueño
and Cocopa respectively may also constitute subgroups.

The outline of the analysis of Yuman predicate nominal presented here was proposed in my 1974 U.C.S.D. dissertation (Munro to appear). My thanks go to Nellie Brown and the
late Robert S. Martin, my principal Mojave consultants, without whom I could never have figured out anything. My work on
Mojave and other Yuman languages has been supported at various times by the Department of Linguistics, University of California, San Diego; the Phillips Fund of the American Philo-
sophical Society; the Woodrow Wilson National Fellowship
Foundation; National Science Foundation Grant SOC74-10843;
and the Academic Senate of the University of California, Lo-
Angeles.

All Mojave data cited is from my own notes. Sources

for other data are cited in the text or in footnotes: many
of the sentences cited in the paper are from field notes
which many Yumanists have generously allowed to be reproduced
and which are now on file in the Yuman archives, University
of California, San Diego. Such field notes in the Yuman archives are acknowledged in the text as FN -- thus Mixco FN refers to Mauricio Mixco's field notes on file in the Yuman archives, etc. I am grateful to Barry Alpher, Larry Gorbet, Abraham Halpern, Roderick Jacobs, Judith Joël, Margaret Langdon,
Elke Lange, and Mauricio Mixco for making their notes available in this way.

Margaret Langdon and Sandra Chung deserve special
thanks for searching through their own notes on Diegueño and
Tolkapaya Yavapai for additional examples for me.

The responsibility for all segmentations and
glosses in cited text is mine -- in some cases I have deviat-
ed from the originals in minor ways. I have regularized transcriptions to some degree also.

The analysis given here has been a long time in evolving.
Donald Crook, Ronald Langacker, Margaret Langdon, Allen Munro,
and Susan Norwood helped me arrive at the present formulation,
and comments by Lloyd Anderson, Sandra Thompson, and Alan Timberlake were useful in revising it.

Abbreviations used in the glosses in this paper include
1 = first person subject or possessor, 2 = second person subject or possessor, 3 = third person subject or possessor, assert = assertive, comp = completive, CTns = compound tense,
dem = demonstrative, emph = emphatic, evid = evidential, loc
= locational, neg = negative, obj = object, subj = subject,

tns = tense, irr = irrealis.

2. The usual Diegueño word for 'be' is yu, not yi, as reflected here. yi is apparently a variant of yu 'be' which is used in certain specific constructions -- another example is the sentence

(i) ?əwil^y-v-k ?-yiw, ?əwa:-m ?-a:-h ?-yi-s
    rock-dem-from 1-come house-to 1-go-irr 1-be-emph
    'I'm on my way from the rock to the house.'
                              (from Christina Hutche-
                                   son, via Margaret
                                   Langdon)

3. Sandra Thompson has suggested to me that an alternative reason for why the first noun of a Yuman predicate nominal sentence is not marked with -č is that -č is only used to
mark the subjects of verbs; since by (11) there is no verb in
the same clause as the unmarked subject noun, it would receive no -č marking. This is an attractive alternative explanation which deserves consideration, but my present feeling is that the notion "subject of a predicate" is a more viable one semantically than the notion "subject of a verb", so
I will continue to claim that subjects of predicate nominals
are unmarked for the same reason that subjects of nominalized
clauses like that in (12) are unmarked -- because -č marking
is reserved for the subjects of main clauses and specific
types of subordinate clauses (subjects of adverbial clauses,
for instance, are usually č-marked). Notice that Thompson's
suggestion cannot in itself explain the lack of č-marking on
the subjects of sentences like (12), so the constraint about
the subjects of nominalized sentences will be needed independently.

4. Yuman relative clauses are "headless". See Gorbet

1973a for the standard analysis.

5. The only exception to this generalization is that -m-
is used to negate main clauses whose verbs carry the adverbial
suffix -ahay- 'still':

(ii)   isvar-ahay-k
        sing-still-tns
        'He's still singing.'

(iii)   isvar-m-ahay-k
        'He's not singing yet.'

Actually, however, I would interpret this data as evidence
that the ahay construction (which merits further study) is
not as "simple" as it might seem.

6. Sentences (24) and (25) are from Christina Hutcheson
(Margaret Langdon, personal communication).

        Margaret Langdon has told me that when she was first
developing her analysis of Diegueño syntax, sentences like
(21) were extremely puzzling for her, since they constituted
the only counterevidence to her claim that only verbs could
occur in the frame _____-x uma:w. It seems, I think, that a
better way to view this frame is as one that tests for end-of-
sentence elements, or, possibly, predicates -- either verbs
of ordinary sentences, or nominal predicates (which otherwise
do not behave like verbs).

        Confirmatory evidence has been given to me by
Sandra Chung -- in Yavapai sentences like that cited in (42)
below, irrealis -ha may similarly follow a predicate noun.

7. Several other suggestions have been made about the
structure of these sentences, which I claim to be

(iv)
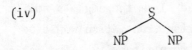

In chapter IV of Mojave Syntax (Munro to appear) I discuss
and refute a number of these, including the idea that the
sentence above contains an underlying but always deleted copular verb like BE or SAME, the idea that the predicate noun
is dominated by V in surface structure (making this sentence
an unremarkable intransitive NP V string), and a few nonsen-
tential interpretations for the NP NP string which I have
analyzed as an S.

8. Two Diegueño consultants, Mrs. Lillie Couro and the
late Rev. Ted Couro, emphatically rejected the sentence

(v)   kusəya:y-v-č-(y)i-s
       doctor-dem-subj-be-emph
       'He's the doctor.'

It appears, however, that there are sentences in
Mojave and Diegueño in which a predicate noun may be marked
as definite; examples are

(vi)   MOJAVE: hovan^y k^{w}aθ?ide: ?-u:yu:-n^y-č
                   he   doctor   1-see-dem=subj
                   'He is the doctor I saw.'

        DIEGUEÑO (SANTA YSABEL):   ?ixpa: n^y-hu:ma:y-v-č-
                                    eagle me-(have)son-dem-

                                    (y)i-s
                                    subj-be-emph

                                    'I am the eagle's son.'
                                    (Langdon to appear)

It seems that any such definite predicate noun phrases are
always complex. In the Mojave example above the predicate
noun is a relative clause, and thus a sentential NP. Although

the Diegueño example was translated 'I am the eagle's son,'
it would appear that a better English translation would be
'The eagle is my father' or, even more literally, 'The eagle
is the one who has me for a son.' n^y-hu:ma:y is, then, a relative clause itself. The prefix n^y- on this word is not one
which occurs on simple possessed nouns (e.g. ordinary Diegueño kinship terms), but rather is one which occurs on the
verbs of sentences with a third-person subject and a first-
person object. (Kinship terms are still verbs in a number of
Yuman languages (cf., e.g., Halpern 1942), and were certainly
verbs in Proto-Yuman.)

9. The only affirmative Northern Pai predicate nominal
sentences I have seen in which this -v- does not appear are

    (vii) HAVASUPAI: jan n^ya-nuwaha-č yu
                          John my-friend-subj be
                          'John is my friend.'
                                  (Kozlowski 1972)

           WALAPAI: n^yiwa čen-č   yu
                        that Jane-subj be
                        'That is Jane.'
                                  (Redden 1966)

           YAVAPAI: Sidney ?n^ya kel-č   yu-m
                        Sidney my   yo=br-subj be-tns
                        'Sidney's my younger brother.'
                                  (Chung, personal commu-
                                                 nication)

This is evidently a fairly rare construction, since -v-č-yu-
otherwise seems to be used almost as a unit in Northern Pai
today. The lack of -v- in these sentences is significant, in
the light of the discussion in the text, in that the predicate nominals in all of these sentences are, if not definite,
at least referential.

A possessive construction based on the predicate nominal construction in which the -v- does not appear in Yavapai is discussed in Kendall 1974 (p. 13).

10. A true existential sentence with a single non-sentential argument would be something like God is. Since such sentences are very rare, in many languages existentials become very closely associated with locatives like There are sheep in the field. In Yuman however, locationals are generally expressed with special verbs meaning roughly 'be located'. I will not discuss these constructions further here, although their relationship with the system of existentials deserves further examination.

11. The syntax of these and other constructions in which the auxiliary verbs appear in Mojave are discussed in Munro 1976 and Munro to appear.

Some of the general principles governing the appearance of existential verbs above "ordinary" main clauses are discussed in Langacker and Munro 1975 and Langacker 1975.

12. Like the other existentials, 'be' and 'do', the negative in Proto-Yuman took a sentential complement (cf. Munro 1973).

13. Examples get complex, but in the Mojave sentence

(viii)   ?in^{y}ep ?-θ?aw-n^y ?i:pač wa=ku:var-n^y-č
         my   1-child-dem men   love-dem-subj

              ya=amo:m-k
              crazy-tns
         'My daughter, who (is the one) the men love, is
              crazy.'

for instance, the subject NP is actually an NP NP predicate

nominal construction (subject ?in^{y}ep ?-iθ?aw-n^y, predicate,
itself a relative clause, ?i:pač waku:var-n^y), whose semantic
head is the first noun ('my daughter'). Note that no 'be' appears after the predicate noun of the relative clause.

14. This description is simplified somewhat for exposi-
tory purposes. Actually there are nine possible variants of
question (34), for each of the three given versions could optionally be terminated with an augment vowel suffix -e or -ə.
Thus the first variant given could also be maki iman-e or
maki iman-ə, etc.

15. When a relative clause (always verb-final) serves
as the subject of a main verb, the subject -č appears on the
last element of that clause, the verb; obviously, I don't
mean that in this case the verb alone is interpreted as a subject (whatever that would mean). But when a -č does appear on
a verb in most Yuman languages, the hearer's strategy is to
search for the head of the clause containing that verb, know-
ing that the subject -č will apply to that head. The predicate nominal structure is thus the only type of sentence in
these languages in which a non-subject noun is č-marked. (But
for a further complication, see fn. 16).

16. A significant reason why such a development might
occur in Diegueño and Cocopa is that in those languages the
normal Yuman same-subject subordinator (-k in other languages)
is -č. In Diegueño and Cocopa, then, the subject case -č preceding 'be' in the predicate nominal construction might be
analyzed as a same-subject marker, indicating that the subject of the clause preceding 'be' (the first or logical subject noun) has the same subject as 'be'. Since subject complements marked with -č are otherwise impossible in Diegueño

and Cocopa (see Gorbet 1973b), a real motivation for the stand-
ardization of marking the person of the logical subject on
'be' emerges.(I am grateful to Margaret Langdon for suggesting
this argument to me.)

The only examples I know of in which 'be' occurs in a
predicate nominal sentence without a preceding subject -č are
from the Jamul dialect of Diegueño (Langdon 1976), e.g.

(ix)   pəya: ?ən^ya:-vu ?-ntal^y-yi-s
        this   me-dem   I-mother-be-emph
        'This is my mother.'

This construction is evidently another way of resolving the
conflict caused by the confusing subject marking in the standard predicate nominal construction. Note that in (ix) yi 'be'
is combined with the preceding predicate nominal into a single
word, with yi apparently becoming a sort of copular suffix.
However, (ix) is still remarkably close to the original predicate nominal construction -- for instance, in this sentence,
in contrast to any other normal sentence, the subject noun
(here pəya: 'this') is not marked as a subject with the -č
suffix.

It is possible, I think, that the loss of the -č preceding 'be' in sentences like (ix) may follow from reinterpretation of -č as a same-subject marker. There are a number of
instances in Diegueño where a same subject -č may optionally
be deleted from the first of two verbs with the same subject.
In the only productive auxiliary construction in Diegueño,
where a non-existential auxiliary may follow a main verb to
express a progressive verb (in terms of person-prefixes), but
the same-subject marker -č never appears on the first verb.
The deletion of -č in (ix) may follow from an analogy with

such a construction.

17.   Chung reports that the innovative subject marking
in Tolkapaya "seems to occur more often when the 'subject' is
a pronoun/proper name.... When you think about this, it's
sort of weird, since pronouns/proper names are supposed to be
historically conservative." This example of language change
surely deserves further study.

18.   The Kiliwa sentence was recorded in July 1974 by
Mauricio Mixco; the Paipai sentence was recorded in August
1975 by Judith Joël. The Cocopa sentence reflects what is apparently a standard construction for Bertha Acebas, a young
speaker (my recording, July 1975).

19.   My description of the synchronic morphology of
Kiliwa here is based on my observations of field notes de-
posited by Mauricio Mixco and on the analysis proposed by
Mixco in his dissertation (Mixco 1971).

          I discuss other examples of the sort of reanalysis
described here in Munro 1975.

20.   In all these cases, a non-third-person subject
marker (person prefix) can intervene between -č and 'be', at
least some of the time for some speakers. Even in these cases,
however, 'be' is generally destressed and suffixal.

21.   The Yuman and Cocopa negatives are complex and can
be further segmented -- see Munro 1973 and Slater 1976. I recorded the Yuman sentence cited here from Christine Wilson in
October 1974, and the Cocopa sentence from Bertha Acebas in
July 1975.

22.   In Munro 1976 and Munro to appear I claim that the

Mojave suffix -pč is derived by deletion of an existential auxiliary (the underlying string is -p AUX-č), which would explain why this suffix would not be expected to occur follow-ing an auxiliary.

I owe to Judith Crawford the observation that Mojave idu: and ido are morphophonemically determined vari-ants of 'be'.

23. Halpern (1946, p. 210) treats the ma- second-person prefix in this example as a "referential pronominal prefix". The situation with this construction in Yuman is evidently complex, and merits further study.

24. For instance, see Charles Li and Sandra Thompson's paper (this volume), in which they describe the development of a copula from a demonstrative.

References

Chung, Sandra. 1976. Compound tense markers in Tolkapaya.
    Proceedings of the First Yuman Languages Workshop, ed.
    by James Redden, 119-128. Carbondale, Ill.: Southern
    Illinois University.

Crawford, James N. 1968. Meaning in Cocopa auxiliary verbs.
    Ms.

Gorbet, Larry. 1973a. How to tell a head when you see one:
    disambiguation in Diegueño relative clauses. Linguistic
    Notes from La Jolla, University of California, San Diego,
    5.63-82.

_____. 1973b. Case markers and complementizers in Diegueño.
    Working Papers in Linguistic Universals 11.219-222.

Halpern, Abraham. 1942. Yuma kinship terms. American Anthrop-
    ologist 44.425-441.

_____. 1946. Yuma 3. International Journal of American Lin-
    guistics 12.204-212.

Hinton, Leanne. 1975. Havasupai language in song. Ph.D. dis-
    sertation, University of California, San Diego. (Prelim-
    inary version.)

Jacobs, Roderick. 1969. The rabbit and the coyote: analysis
    of a text in the Iñaja dialect of Diegueño. Ms.

Joël, Judith. 1975. Handout prepared for presentation at the
    Yuman Workshop. University of California, San Diego,
    June 1975.

Kendall, Martha B. 1972. Selected problems in Yavapai syntax.
    Ph.D. dissertation, Indiana University.

_____. 1974. Preliminary survey of Upland Yuman dialects. Presented at the American Anthropological Association Annual Meeting, Mexico City. Ms.

Kozlowski, Edwin. 1972. Havasupai simple sentences. Ph.D. dissertation, Indiana University.

Langacker, Ronald W. 1975. Functional Stratigraphy. Papers from the Parasession on Functionalism, ed. by Robin Grossman, et al., 351-397. Chicago: CLS.

_____, and Pamela Munro. 1975. Passives and their meaning. Language 51.789-830.

Langdon, Margaret. 1968. The Proto-Yuman demonstrative system. Folia Linguistica II.61-81.

_____. 1974. Auxiliary verb construction in Yuman. Presented at the American Anthropological Association Annual Meeting, Mexico City. Ms.

_____. 1976. Syntactic diversity in Diegueño dialects. Proceedings of the First Yuman Languages Workshop, ed. by James Redden, 1-9. Carbondale, Ill.: Southern Illinois University.

_____. to appear. The story of eagle's nest -- a Diegueño text. To appear in Yuman Texts, ed. by Margaret Langdon.

Mixco, Mauricio. 1971. Kiliwa grammar. Ph.D. dissertation, University of California, Berkeley.

Munro, Pamela. 1973. Reanalysis and elaboration in Yuman negatives. Linguistic Notes from La Jolla, University of California, San Diego, 5.36-62.

_____. 1975. Comitative conjunction: a syntactic reinterpretation in Yuman. Presented at the Linguistic Society of America Annual Meeting, San Francisco. Ms.

_____. 1976. Subject copying, predicate raising, and auxiliarization: the Mojave evidence. International Journal of American Linguistics, 42.99-112.

_____. to appear. Mojave syntax. Garland Publishing, Inc.

Redden, James. 1966. Walapai II. International Journal of American Linguistics 32.141-163.

_____. 1975. Handout prepared for presentation at the Yuman Workshop, University of California, San Diego, June 1975.

Slater, Carol E. 1976. Not, in Yuman, I say. Proceedings of the First Yuman Languages Workshop, ed. by James Redden, 71-77. Carbondale, Ill.: Southern Illinois University.

V Clisis and Verb Morphology

11 The Evolution of Third Person Verb Agreement in the Iroquoian Languages

Wallace L. Chafe

The languages of the Five Nations of the Iroquois (from east to west, Mohawk, Oneida, Onondaga, Cayuga, and Seneca) have an elaborate system of prefixes within the verb to express agreement with one or more of the nouns associated with the verb. This system of so-called pronominal prefixes is one of the most salient features of the verb morphology of these languages. Each language has on the order of sixty-five or seventy such prefixes, and one of the joys of Iroquoian linguistics has been to unravel their form and function in each language.

An equally complex system existed in the closely related, now extinct language Huron, and one nearly as complex appears in Tuscarora, a somewhat more divergent language. All these languages together constitute the Northern Iroquoian branch of the Iroquoian family. The only other language in the family is Cherokee, which also has agreement prefixes, but considerably fewer of them than its relatives to the north. The Iroquoian family as a whole is probably remotely related to the Caddoan and Siouan language families (Chafe 1964, 1973). Those families, too, show a certain amount of agreement of a similar type, but as with Cherokee there are many fewer prefixes than in the Northern Iroquoian languages. Figure 1 indicates the major relationships within and between the Iro-

quoian and Caddoan families. (Siouan is not included, and
will not enter into the discussion here.)

The question arises as to whether the complexity of the
Northern Iroquoian systems is an innovation among these languages, or whether it is a retention from a much earlier stage
--perhaps from Proto-Macro-Siouan, the remote ancestor of Iroquoian, Caddoan, and Siouan. In the latter case, simplification would have taken place in both the Siouan and Caddoan
families, as well as in Cherokee and to some extent in Tuscarora. This paper relies on the opposite hypothesis that
the complexity was an innovation in the Northern Iroquoian
languages. I believe that a more plausible overall picture
emerges if we accept this direction of development, and I
attempt here to reconstruct some of the milestones which led
to the complexity. The attempt is necessarily speculative,
since we have only the modern languages to look to for evidence and the evidence they provide is often incomplete and
perplexing. Nevertheless, the exercise is an intriguing one
and I feel reasonably confident that the main outlines of
what I suggest here are correct, even though there may be various particular suggestions which are misguided. In order to
keep the discussion within bounds, I will restrict it to third
person agreement, since that is where most of the changes from
simplicity to complexity have taken place.

Why should this exercise be of any interest to those who
are not specialists in Iroquoian languages? For one thing,
it is not only Iroquoian languages which are characterized
by an elaborate form of verb agreement; the phenomenon is common among polysynthetic languages, and even languages with
simpler morphological patterns may show some similar kinds of

development in their systems of independent pronouns. In addition, these developments suggest a source for at least some of the agreement markers which is different from the kind of origin usually assumed. It is generally thought that agreement markers arise from forms that were independent pronouns at an earlier stage of the language, those forms having later become attached as clitics or affixes to the verb. As stated by Givón (1975:155): "The morphological binding of the pronoun to the verb is an inevitable natural phenomenon, cliticization, having to do with the unstressed status of pronouns, their decreased information load and the subsequent loss of resistance to phonological attrition." But in the Iroquoian case, if the reconstruction here is essentially correct, the agreement markers arose instead from a reinterpretation of affixes that were already being used for other purposes. They came from material already present in the verb morphology, rather than from material originally outside it. Instead of cliticization, they illustrate processes of reinterpretation.

The particular directions of reinterpretation we find in this material may illustrate some more general principles of language change. The most general principle which suggests itself is simply that agreement systems may be prone to increase in complexity, all other things being equal. A decrease in complexity, as in the history of English, perhaps takes place primarily as a result of phonological erosion, although it may also be produced by acculturation, as in the case of American Indian languages which have lost dual number and/or the inclusive/exclusive distinction as a result of contact with English (as I believe has happened for some speakers of Cherokee, for example). But we are concerned here with

developments in which phonological change was not a determining factor, and in which the role of contact with other languages is unknown but need not be assumed to have been an important factor either. Under these circumstances the drift
was clearly toward greater elaboration.

Other directions of development illustrated here involve extensions from one semantic category to another, or
the elaboration of distinctions within a category. Some of
the agreement markers with which we will be concerned, for
example, seem to have originated as markers of number, and to
have been extended, first, to become markers of person, and
subsequently to have become gender markers. We will see a
parallel development from an original function as a marker of
nonspecific reference to use for specific reference as well,
and then an extension to human reference and finally to feminine gender. We will see that complexities are most apt to
be present in first and second person agreement, to be extended only later to third person; that they are likely to
apply earlier to agents than to other roles; and that they
are likely to apply first to masculine referents before they
are extended to feminine or nonhuman.

In the systems of the Northern Iroquoian languages,
agreement is in terms of number, person, case, and gender (in
the third person). Number includes singular, dual, and plural, though in some combinations dual and plural are merged
into a single category which will be called nonsingular. Person includes first, second, and third, but also a distinction
between exclusive and inclusive in the dual and plural. Case
is essentially a matter of distinguishing agents and patients,
though these terms are more specific than they ought to be.

For example, 'agent' includes not only doers, but also per-
ceivers (those who see and hear) and the subjects of certain
epistemic verbs, while 'patient' includes also certain recip-
ients and beneficiaries. Gender includes masculine, feminine,
and nonhuman, though here too certain qualifications are necessary and will be mentioned as we proceed.

Agreement may be with one or with two of the nouns associated with a verb. Roughly speaking, if there is both an
agent and a patient noun, the verb will contain a complex
prefix which indicates the number, person, case, and gender
of both nouns. Iroquoianists have traditionally distinguished
three classes of pronominal prefixes: agent prefixes, patient
prefixes, and transitive prefixes, the last category including
those which relate to both agents and patients. The transitive prefixes present many problems of detail which are best
left to a discussion directed at Iroquoian specialists. The
treatment here will be limited to the history of the intransitive third person agent and patient prefixes.

Obviously, sixty-five or seventy different prefixes do
not provide unique representations for all possible combinations of numbers, persons, cases, and genders relative to two
possible nouns. There is a great deal of merging of these
dimensions in particular combinations. For example, although
there is a unique prefix which indicates a first person singular agent with a second person singular patient, when either the first person or the second person, or both, are dual,
these three different possibilities are represented with only
a single form. There is another single form which is used
when the first person, the second person, or both are plural.
This form covers five possible combinations, since the refer-

ent which is not plural may be either singular or dual, or
may in fact itself be plural. In other words, for nine possible combinations there are only three different forms.

In the above example there was a merging of numbers, but
in fact there is sometimes a merging of the exclusive-inclu-
sive distinction, of case distinctions, and of genders. One
of my guiding principles will be that at least some of these
merged categories provide evidence as to how things were at
an earlier stage. It will appear that further elaboration
of the system has taken place in areas of greatest salience
or most frequent use, whereas often these elaborations have
not been extended into the less salient or less used areas.
For example, in most of the Northern Iroquoian languages
there is a three-gender distinction in the third person <u>sin-
gular</u> only. In the dual and plural there is only a distinction between masculine and nonmasculine; feminine and nonhuman are merged. Comparative evidence, I think, tends to confirm the hypothesis that the three-way gender distinction is
fairly recent, and that at an earlier stage there was a two-
way distinction (although earlier it was probably between human and nonhuman), still earlier no gender distinction at all,
and, if we go back far enough, no third person agreement marker of any kind.

Information on the Mohawk prefix system comes from Bonvillain (1973), on Oneida from Lounsbury (1953), on Onondaga
from Chafe (1970), on Cayuga from field notes provided me by
Floyd Lounsbury, on Seneca from Chafe (1967), on Huron from
Barbeau (1915) and Blin-Lagarde (in preparation) as well as
unpublished discussions by Roy Wright, on Tuscarora from an
unpublished description by Lounsbury and from Williams

(1976), and on Cherokee from Pulte and Feeling (1975) and
King (1975). For Caddoan languages I rely for Wichita on
Rood (1976, in press), for Pawnee on Parks (1976), and for
Caddo on my own notes and Chafe (1976).

Proto-Iroquois-Caddoan

I will start with the hypothetical proto-language from
which emerged the Caddoan and Iroquoian families. It is likely that in Proto-Iroquois-Caddoan there existed the same system for first and second person agreement that we find in the
languages of these families today: a system with singular,
dual, and plural number, with exclusive and inclusive distinguished in the dual and plural, and with agents distinguished
from patients. The modern forms are not all cognate, even
though the same distinctions are made. We can be fairly confident, however, that *k- was used to mark first person, *s-
second person, and *wa- plurality. The other details are
more problematic.

In general there was no marker in the verb to express
agreement with a third person noun, other than agreement with
its number. This is pretty much the case today in the Caddoan
as well as the Siouan languages. Of the exceptions which exist to such a blanket statement, only one of them has a bearing on the development of third person agreement in Iroquoian.
The relevance of that one, however, is great. It seems indis-
putable that Proto-Iroquois-Caddoan had a nonspecific or indefinite prefix. The appropriate translation would be 'one' or
'you,' as in 'one eats it' ('you eat it'). The Caddoan languages today have such a prefix, as do the Iroquoian. Strictly speaking it was not an agreement prefix, since it never

agreed with a nominal referent expressed outside the verb, but
it occupied the same position in the verb morphology as the
first and second person agreement prefixes, and in fact it developed into an agreement prefix as we will see. Its shape
must have been *yi- for an agent and *yu- for a patient, if
we assume a three-vowel system for that stage. It still appears as yi- and yu- in Caddo. In Wichita the nonspecific
prefix is -i- (either accented or lengthened or both), apparently cognate with the Caddo form. In Pawnee there is a form
-ir- which may also be cognate. In summary, the third person
system in Proto-Iroquois-Caddoan was as shown in Figure 2.

There must also have been a variety of number markers,
some of which at least must have marked the number of third
person referents. It is easier to say something about their
form than to specify precisely their function, since their
modern reflexes are too functionally diverse to lead to any
very clear reconstructions in that respect. I believe that
the following forms, all marking number in some way, were present: *hi-, *hra-, *ka-, *na-, *ni, *ti-, and *wa-. Iroquoianists will recognize all except *na-. I will mention briefly
how these forms are reflected in the Caddoan and Iroquoian
languages.

*hi- seems to have been lost in Caddo and Pawnee. A num-
ber morpheme with this shape occurs in Wichita to indicate
principally that a first or second person subject or a third
person agent is nonsingular. The same shape occurs in the
Northern Iroquoian languages to indicate nonsingularity of a
first person referent when combined in a transitive prefix
with a third person that is not masculine singular.

*hra- is a more problematic reconstruction. I am posit-
ing it as underlying, in combination with *ka-, a Proto-Caddoan form *hraka-. In Caddo this form appears as haka- 'non-
singular patient' (restricted to certain verbs). In Proto-
Northern-Caddoan it appears as *rak-, marking plurality with
a first or second person, as this form does in both Pawnee
and Wichita. The form ha- appears in Huron to mark nonsingularity of a masculine referent in a transitive combination.

*ka- is postulated as part of the Proto-Caddoan form
*hraka- just mentioned, and perhaps it also has a reflex in
Proto-Northern-Caddoan *(?)ak-, leading to Pawnee ak-, marking plurality with a third person animate object or indirect
object, and Wichita ?ak-, marking nonsingularity with a third
person patient. In Iroquoian the form ka- marks nonsingularity of third person in a transitive combination. In Huron it
is restricted to a nonmasculine third person (cf. ha- above).
This form has been lost or is only vestigial as a number marker in the Four Nations languages (Mohawk, Oneida, Onondaga,
and Seneca).

*na- appears in Caddo in that form as a marker of a non-
singular patient with those verbs which do not take haka-
(see above).

*ni- appears in the Iroquoian languages meaning either
'nonsingular' or 'dual.' If the vowels need not be taken too
seriously, perhaps it is ultimately related to *na-.

*ti-, so far as I know, has no plausible reflex in the
Caddoan languages, unless it can be identified with the final
consonant in Caddo wiht-, the usual dual marker in that language. In Iroquoian languages it is a common marker of plu-

rality, either for first and second persons as in Cherokee, or
for third persons as in Northern Iroquoian. Whether it was
present as a number marker in Proto-Iroquois-Caddoan and was
then lost before the Proto-Caddoan stage, or whether it was
an innovation in Iroquoian is uncertain.

   *wa-, on the other hand, is a satisfying reconstruction
for Proto-Iroquois-Caddoan. It appears in Caddo as the regular marker of plurality with animate referents. In Wichita
it is something of a relic form, appearing as a marker of
duality with third person patients, but only with the verbs
meaning 'come' and 'sit' and a few others. It has evidently
been lost in Pawnee, as well as in Cherokee. In the Northern
Iroquoian languages, however, it is the regular marker of plurality with first and second person agents and patients.

Proto-Iroquoian

   The proposed system of intransitive third person agreement for Proto-Iroquoian is shown in Figure 3, posited as the
most likely system to have led from that shown in Figure 2 to
both the Cherokee and the Northern Iroquoian systems. In comparison with Figure 2 we have really three innovations. One
is the extension of *yu- in the patient category to include
specific as well as nonspecific referents. Quite possibly
that was what happened with *yi- in the agent category as
well, although we must assume that the distinction between
specific and nonspecific was always preserved in some fashion,
if only as a covert semantic distinction. (It may be noted
that in some of the modern languages there is still a semantic distinction between nonspecific and feminine, even though
the form ye- is used to express both.)

The second development was the introduction of a marker
with the shape *ka- to indicate agreement with a third person
singular specific agent. It would appear that the form *ka-
was extended to this function from its original use as a number marker in Proto-Iroquois-Caddoan, and that this is only
the first of several cases where a form that began by marking
number came to be used also to mark some category of singular
third person referent.

The third and final innovation was an analogic one. It
can be seen in Figure 3 that most third person marking was
accomplished with forms exhibiting an initial y. The introduction of *ka- produced the first deviation from this pattern,
and it is not surprising that a form *ya- came to be used a-
longside it. Probably some verbs came to take *ya- while others remained with *ka-. That is essentially what is true now
in Cherokee (allowing for phonological change), while in the
Northern languages *ya- has been preserved as a relic with the
verb 'die.' (However, it appears elsewhere in the non-third
and in the transitive prefixes of those languages.)

Cherokee

The general pattern of third person agreement in Cherokee
is shown in Figure 4, which differs from Figure 3 chiefly in
the presence of -ni- as a marker of nonsingularity. However,
it is entirely likely that -ni- was already performing this
function at the Proto-Northern-Iroquoian stage. As mentioned
above, -ni- shows up in the Northern Iroquoian languages as
the marker of duality. In any case, it occurs in Cherokee
together with a- for agents (by phonological change from
*ya-), and together with u- for patients (by phonological

change from *yu-). The several markers of singular agent evidently arose predictably from a system in which some verbs
used *ka- and others *ya-. With consonant stems Cherokee
shows either ka- or a- (with the regular loss of initial y).
Vowel stems caused the loss of the prefix vowel, so that for
them Cherokee shows either k- or zero.

Proto-Northern-Iroquoian

We need now to consider how a plausible system for
Proto-Northern-Iroquoian could have developed out of that
shown in Figure 3. The system I will eventually posit for
Proto-Northern-Iroquoian is shown below in Figure 7, but it is
necessary to discuss several intermediate stages in its development. It should be pointed out that there were also vowel
system changes along the way, with the result that earlier i
and u came to be reflected as e and o. In particular, the
reflexes of *yi- and *yu- are in Northern Iroquoian *ye- and
*yo-.

In Figure 3 we hypothesized that the form *ya- was an
analogic reshaping of *ka-, with *ya- and *ka- functioning as
alternate forms of the same morpheme. That remained true in
Cherokee. Prior to the Proto-Northern-Iroquoian stage, however, there was evidently a realignment whereby *ya- became
an alternate of *ye- instead, as can be seen from a comparison
of the agent portion of Figure 5 with that of Figure 3.

The other development which distinguishes Figure 5 from
Figure 3 is the extension of the specific-nonspecific differentiation overtly to patient prefixes, where an analogic form
*ko- has appeared as the patient counterpart of *ka-. Thus,
at this stage the system was a fairly regular one, with y

marking nonspecific and k specific, and a marking agent and o patient, except that *ye- was maintained as a slight irregularity.

At some point, however, there must have occurred a semantic reinterpretation, whereby the nonspecific agent marker *ye-/*ya- came to be used for agreement with any specific human referent as well, and the earlier specific agent marker *ka- came to be restricted to nonhuman referents, as indicated in Figure 6. Since the original nonspecific category was probably used largely or even exclusively when nonspecific humans were involved ('one' meant a nonspecific person), this development was a natural one. Because 'nonspecific' is still preserved as a separate category in the modern languages, however, it seems necessary to assume that it remained as a separate semantic category at the stage of Figure 6, even though it was no longer formally distinct from 'human.'

But Figure 6 shows a curious fact about the patient markers. For agents it was the nonspecific category that came to be extended to humans. For patients it was just the reverse. The new human marker was based on the earlier specific marker, the new nonhuman marker on the earlier nonspecific one. How might this apparent reversal in the patient markers have taken place? As suggested above, we can imagine that nonspecific agents were usually or always persons. But we might also imagine that the nonspecific patient category was an uncommon one. It seems at least intuitively plausible that patients are usually specific. (How often is French on or German man used to refer to a patient?) If we can assume at the same time that human referents were more common than nonhuman ones, we can imagine that it was on that basis of

relative frequencies that the *ko- of Figure 5 came to be
assigned to human patients, while the less frequently used
*yo- was assigned to nonhumans. Whether or not this is the
correct explanation, the reversal of the patient markers certainly did occur. It is striking that in many environments
the human patient prefix came to be not just *ko- but *yako-.
It is as if the Pre-Northern-Iroquoian speakers felt some
qualms about using *ko- in a function that was the opposite
from that of *ka-, so that they added the extra *ya- (producing a form that was anomalous in this set of otherwise monosyllabic prefixes) as if to specify clearly that *ko- was the
patient counterpart of *ya-, and not of *ka-.

Figure 7 shows the final system posited for Proto-Northern-Iroquoian. It differs from that shown in Figure 6 chiefly
by the addition of a special form for agreement with masculine
singular referents, both agents and patients. The most likely
source of this form is the number marker *hra-, discussed a-
bove for Proto-Iroquois-Caddoan. Presumably this form was
introduced as a masculine singular agent marker, and subsequently the patient form *hro- was created by analogy to the
other forms in which patient o corresponds to agent a. The
addition of this masculine singular form meant that in the
singular the human category was split into masculine and feminine. Thus, in the singular there was now a three-way distinction between masculine, feminine, and nonhuman, and nonspecific reference was marked with the same form as feminine.
For nonsingular referents, on the other hand, there was only
a distinction between human and nonhuman.

The other innovation in Figure 7 is the addition of a
new alternate for the nonhuman agent prefix, with the shape

*wa-. There seems no way to know whether this innovation pre-
ceded or followed the introduction of masculine singular
*hra-, but I have included it at the same stage because both
markers seem to have had their origins in number marking, wa-
being preserved in the modern languages as a number marker for
first and second person. The present distribution of nonhuman
ka- and wa- is roughly that ka- occurs before consonant stems
and i- stems, while wa- occurs before other vowel stems. However, the a is missing before vowels, so that the prefix now
appears to be w-. It is likely that its a was lost through
overlap with the initial a of a-stem verbs, by far the most
common vowel stems. The origin of this prefix as *wa- is confirmed in the nonsingular (later plural) form *wati- which we
will first meet in Figure 11. A parallel development occurred
with masculine *hra-. That is, before most vowel stems its
shape seems to have been reinterpreted as hr-. And again we
will later find a form *hrati- parallel to *wati-.

Proto-Tuscarora-Cayuga

It is not customary to posit a unique common ancestor for
Tuscarora and Cayuga, the latter language usually being considered to be a member of the Five Nations subgroup and most
closely related to Seneca. However, as discussed by Chafe
and Foster (in preparation), there are reasons to believe that
the Cayuga split off from the parent Northern Iroquoian community at an early date and subsequently returned to become
closely associated with the Seneca, to the extent that the
Seneca and Cayuga languages now share uniquely a number of
common features. The evidence of agreement prefixes, however,
coupled with a small amount of uniquely shared lexicon, makes

it appear that at this much earlier time the Tuscarora and
Cayuga were a single people.

The system shown in Figure 8 for Proto-Tuscarora-Cayuga
differs from the Proto-Northern-Iroquoian system in only one
respect: the use of *ka- as a marker of nonsingularity for
human agents. The *ka- was in use from Proto-Iroquois-Caddoan
times as a marker of nonsingularity, but this development in
Tuscarora-Cayuga seems to have been its only extension to
third person intransitive prefixes. That is, its use was
otherwise restricted to nonthird person and/or transitive prefixes. It was of course assumed above to have been the source
of the nonhuman marker *ka- at a much earlier stage, but certainly by the time it was introduced to form the nonsingular
human agent prefix *kaye- any association with nonhuman *ka-
must have been lost.

Tuscarora

The modern Tuscarora system of intransitive third person
agreement is shown in Figure 9. It differs from the Proto-
Tuscarora-Cayuga system in two respects. First, by the pattern of extending innovations already present in the agent
prefixes eventually to the patient prefixes as well, the *ka-
marker of nonsingularity has been extended to human patients,
yielding the form kako-.

Second, Tuscarora has developed a unique way of marking
dual number, which it does by adding the 'duplicative' or
'dualic' prefix before the pronominal one (Chafe 1967:30-31,
Lounsbury 1953:48-49). This prefix serves a variety of other
functions in all the Iroquoian languages. These functions
include the enumeration of two objects (with a verb root

used for enumeration), and obligatory occurrence with verbs
indicating 'twoness' of some kind. Among them are verbs involving two agents, such as 'meet' or 'wrestle,' and verbs
denoting a binary change of state, such as 'cross over (to the
other side)' or 'take off (clothing).' It is also used sometimes to indicate simply the multiplication of some action;
for example, when added to a verb that would otherwise mean
'cut down (a tree)' it changes the meaning to 'cut up (logs).'
Tuscarora is the only Iroquoian language, however, in which
this prefix is used to mark agreement with dual referents,
although this use seems to be a natural extension of its other
functions. As can be seen from the arrangement in Figure 9,
no distinction is made in the dual between masculine and feminine, but only between human and nonhuman. That fact might
suggest that the development of this dual marker occurred
prior to the stage shown in Figure 8. On the other hand
there is no trace of third person dual agreement in Cayuga,
and I am inclined to attribute the absence in Tuscarora of a
separate masculine category in the dual to a strong identification of *hra- with purely singular reference.

Cayuga

The present Cayuga system of intransitive third person
agreement, shown in Figure 10, can also be seen as a natural
and simple outgrowth of the system shown in Figure 8, but in
a different direction from that taken by Tuscarora. In general, Cayuga has simply changed the somewhat sloppy and ir-
regular system of Figure 8 into a very regular system with
three genders and two numbers across the board. Essentially
it has done so by making use of a regular nonsingular marker

-ti- (on which more presently), and by applying it to all
three genders. However, the one place in the system where
-ti- is not used, the feminine nonsingular agent prefix kae-
(from *kaye-), provides a clear link to the system shown in
Figure 8. The presence of this reflex of *kaye- in both
Tuscarora and Cayuga (and nowhere else in the family) is the
single most important piece of evidence that these two languages shared a unique common history.

The nonsingular marker *-ti- must have been present in
Proto-Iroquoian, and perhaps in Proto-Iroquois-Caddoan, as
noted above. It appears in Cherokee in nonthird person agreement prefixes, and in some of the transitive prefixes linking
third and nonthird person referents. In most of the Northern
Iroquoian languages it is one of the most common markers of
third person nonsingularity or plurality. It has largely
dropped out of use in Tuscarora, however, although Marianne
Williams has discovered a few relics of its earlier presence
in that language. The best hypothesis seems to me to be that
-ti- had largely fallen into disuse at the stage of Proto-
Tuscarora-Cayuga (Figure 8), and that it was reintroduced into
Cayuga in the regular manner shown in Figure 10 as a result of
the renewed contact between Cayuga and the Five Nations languages (especially Seneca) which is hypothesized to have taken
place more recently. Thus, the almost completely regular use
of -ti- in Figure 10 was not an independent development within
Cayuga, but rather a result of diffusion.

Proto-Lake-Iroquoian

After the splitting off of Tuscarora-Cayuga, the other
branch of Northern Iroquoian seems to have undergone the de-

velopments summarized in Figures 11 and 12. First, the form
-ti- was regularized as a marker of nonsingularity in third
persons, as shown in Figure 11. Ignoring gender developments
for the moment, we can pass on to Figure 12 which shows that
-ni- was subsequently introduced as a marker of duality in
third person agents only. This dual marker has still not been
extended to third person patients in any of the modern languages. The source of -ni- is clear: it existed previously
as a dual marker for first and second person referents. Its
introduction to the third person markers was simply a generalization of an already existent pattern.

It is intriguing to try to relate Cayuga to this sequence
of developments in number marking. If it were not for the
presence of kae- in the Cayuga system, the simplest hypothesis
would be that Cayuga shared in the development shown in Figure
11, and that it split off before the introduction of duality
shown in Figure 12. But the sharing of the *kaye- innovation
with Tuscarora forces us to hypothesize the earlier split described above, while the absence of duality in Cayuga suggests
a borrowing of -ti- from Lake Iroquoian at the stage represented by Figure 11. One can speculate, therefore, that the Cayuga returned to the parent group at the Figure 11 stage, only
to leave again before the introduction of duality, with a
subsequent return at a still later time. In other words, the
relationships between these prefixes in Cayuga and the other
languages suggest the hypothesis that the Cayuga bounced in
and out of the mainstream of Northern Iroquoian development
several times.

Gender developments in Lake Iroquoian are centered
around the marking of feminine referents. If Figure 7 is

essentially correct, there was in Proto-Northern-Iroquoian
basically a distinction between human and nonhuman referents,
with the same marker being used for human as for nonspecific.
In addition there was the beginning of sex gender, represented
by the intrusion of a special form for masculine singular referents. This special attention paid to masculine referents
became more predominant in Lake Iroquoian. For nonsingular
referents, as shown in Figures 11 and 12, Proto-Lake-Iroquoian
had shifted to a pattern in which the distinction was between
masculine and all else. This result was achieved through the
development of a system in which nonsingular feminine referents had come to be marked with the same prefixes as nonhuman.
For singular referents, however, there was still a three-way
distinction, no different from that which had existed in Proto-Northern-Iroquoian. It is interesting that this is the
one case among all the developments posited here where an innovation seems to have occurred in the nonsingular category
first. It may be relevant that the innovation was not the
introduction of a new form, but a realignment of old forms.
Specifically it was a reassignment of feminine, whereby its
earlier closeness to masculine within the human category was
replaced by a new association with nonmasculinity. But presumably frequency of usage was strong enough in the singular
to preserve the three-way distinction.

   One curious aspect of Figure 12 is the monosyllabicity
of the dual agent forms. One might have expected the extension of -ni- to third person to have produced forms like
*hrani-for masculine and *kani- or *wani- for nonmasculine,
but in fact the first vowel is missing. The only explanation
I can offer is that *hra- had by this time largely been rein-

terpreted as *hr- or *h- (in certain environments the *r is
missing), especially because of the apparent loss of its a
with the very frequently occurring a-stems (see the discussion of Proto-Northern-Iroquoian above). The nonmasculine
*kni- would then have been formed by analogy to *hni-. It
seems at least clear that the dual forms arose as an innovation in the Lake languages, and that they were modeled, not
on the plural (earlier nonsingular) forms, but by some kind
of extension from the forms in the singular.

Huron-Wyandot

Huron went the farthest of the Lake languages in con-
verting the gender distinction into one between masculine and
all else, extending this pattern into the singular as well.
Figure 13 shows the completion of this realignment. (Among
phonological changes in the Wyandot dialect were the loss of
y and the conversion of k into y.) It may be noted that one
result of this development was the narrowing of the function
of *ye- to nonspecific reference only, the sole function which
it originally had in Proto-Iroquois-Caddoan. Having passed
through stages in which its meaning embraced all third person,
then human third person, and then feminine, but having always
retained its nonspecific function as well, in Huron it was
brought by the complete masculine-nonmasculine dichotomy in
that language to return to its original function alone.

Four Nations

Among the Four Nations languages, Seneca has preserved
exactly the system shown in Figure 12 (allowing for certain
phonological changes which need not be described here). Mo-

hawk, Oneida, and Onondaga can be said to vacillate between
that system and the one shown in Figure 13, a fact which suggests either diffusion between these languages and Huron or
a drift toward the Huron system which already existed at the
Proto-Lake-Iroquoian stage. What this means is that in these
three languages feminine singular referents are sometimes
marked by ye-/ya- and sometimes by ka-/wa-. As described by
Bonvillain (1973:86-87) for Mohawk, ye-/ya- is used for "female human beings who are regarded in some prestigeful or re-
spectful way by the speaker," or "for whom the speaker has
feelings of affection or closeness." The alternative ka-/wa-
is used otherwise. "It may or may not reflect a momentary or
general negative feeling on the part of the speaker toward
the female who is spoken about. Some speakers feel that . . .
a girl or woman who is awkward or aggressive may more readily
fall into this category, whereas one who is graceful and
quiet may tend to be classed in the other way." The situation in Onondaga is similar, though speakers of that language
have emphasized to me that ka-/wa- is not derogatory, but
only detached and impersonal. A rather special distinction
has arisen in Oneida, where ka-/wa- is typically used for
women of child-bearing age while ye-/ya- tends to be restricted to young girls and old women (Lounsbury 1953:51-52).

It is easy to speculate that the masculine orientation
which is particularly evident in the Lake languages, and
above all in Huron, arose during a period when male referents
were especially salient in the society. The same focus is if
anything even more pronounced in the transitive prefixes of
these languages. It might be thought that this development
was paradoxical in the light of the well-known matrilineal

emphasis of Iroquois society. On the other hand, the identification of feminine with nonspecific reference has sometimes
been taken to express an association of women with mankind as
a whole. Certainly there is a sense in which feminine is the
'unmarked' category in these languages whereas masculine is the
strongly 'marked.' In any case it seems reasonable to suppose that these conspicuous grammatical differences reflect
something about relative sex roles at the time the systems
arose, whatever the precise nature of the differences may
have been.

To summarize, the systems shown in Figure 12 and 13
are hypothesized to be the culmination of a series of developments beginning with an original Proto-Iroquois-Caddoan
stage at which there was no third person agreement except for
number, and even then presumably only for singular and non-
singular. There was, however, from the outset a nonspecific
marker differentiated for agent and patient. That marker has
maintained its nonspecific function through all these millen-
ia, as it has in the Caddoan family also. In the history of
Iroquoian it was first extended to general third person reference, later restricted to the category human, and eventually
further restricted to feminine, only to be finally banished
from that category altogether by Huron and partially by Mohawk, Oneida, and Onondaga. Three of the other third person
markers seem to have arisen from forms which were number markers originally, and which still retain that function in some
or all of the modern languages. One of them is ka-, first a
marker of specific third person agent, later restricted to
nonhuman agents, and finally extended to feminine referents
in the nonsingular, and in Huron everywhere. Another is

hra-, which has always been a marker for masculine agreement.
And the third is wa-, which came to function as an alternate
of ka-. The remaining forms in the modern systems were created from these by analogy: ya- reformed from ka- on the a-
nalogy of other forms with initial y, and ko- and hro- created according to the pattern by which o expresses patient
status.

*After the first version of this paper was presented at
the Symposium on Mechanisms of Syntactic Change in Santa Barbara, I was able to benefit from a discussion of it at the
Conference on Iroquois Research held in Albany in October
1976. The present version was completed at the Center for
Advanced Study in the Behavioral Sciences.

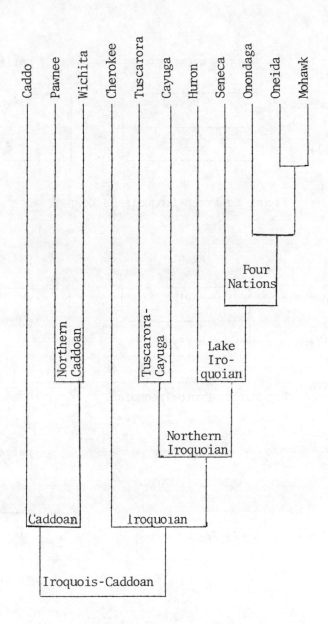

Figure 1: The Iroquois-Caddoan Languages

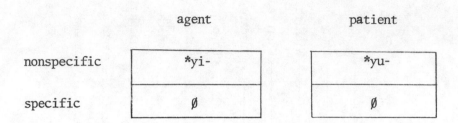

Figure 2: Proto-Iroquois-Caddoan

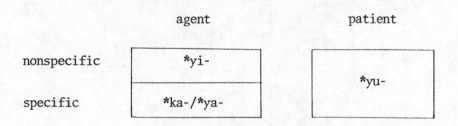

Figure 3: Proto-Iroquoian

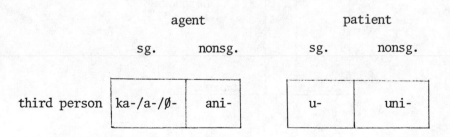

Figure 4: Cherokee

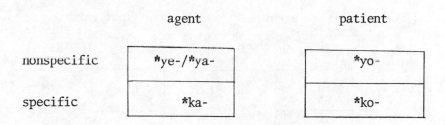

Figure 5: Pre-Proto-Northern-Iroquoian I

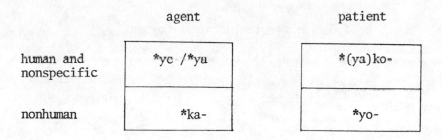

Figure 6: Pre-Proto-Northern-Iroquoian II

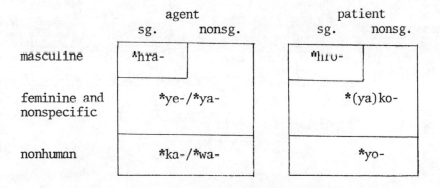

Figure 7: Proto-Northern-Iroquoian

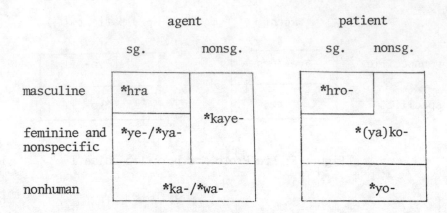

Figure 8:   Proto-Tuscarora-Cayuga

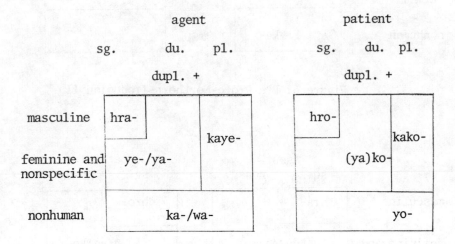

Figure 9:   Tuscarora

	agent		patient	
	sg.	nonsg.	sg.	nonsg.
masculine	ha-	hati-	ho-	hoti-
feminine and nonspecific	ye-/ya-	kae-	(ya)ko-	(ya)koti-
nonhuman	ka-/wa-	kati-	yo-	yoti-

Figure 10: Cayuga

	agent		patient	
	sg.	nonsg.	sg.	nonsg.
masculine	*hra-	*hrati-	*hro-	*hroti-
feminine and nonspecific	*ye-/*ya-	*wati-	*(ya)ku-	*yoti-
nonhuman	*ka-/wa-		*yo-	

Figure 11: Pre-Proto-Lake-Iroquoian

| | agent | | | patient | |
	sg.	du.	pl.	sg.	nonsg.
masculine	*hra-	*hni-	*hrati	*hro-	*hroti-
feminine and nonspecific	*ye-/*ya-	*kni-	*wati-	*(ya)ko-	*yoti-
nonhuman	*ka-/*wa-			*yo-	

Figure 12:   Proto-Lake-Iroquoian

| | agent | | | patient | |
	sg.	du.	pl.	sg.	nonsg.
masculine	ha-	hi-	hati-	ho-	hoti-
nonspecific	e-/a-			ayo-	
nonmasculine	ya-/wa-	i-	wati-	o-	oti-

Figure 13:   Huron

References

Barbeau, C. Marius. 1915. Classification of Iroquoian radicals with subjective pronominal prefixes. Canada Department of Mines, Geological Survey, Memoir 46, Anthropological Series 7. Ottawa: Government Printing Bureau.

Blin-Lagarde, Pierrette. In preparation. Le verbe huron. Etude morphologique d'après une description grammaticale du 17ème siècle.

Bonvillain, Nancy. 1973. A grammar of Akwesasne Mohawk. Mercury Series, Ethnology Division, Paper 8. Ottawa: National Museum of Man.

Chafe, Wallace L. 1964. Another look at Siouan and Iroquoian. American Anthropologist 66:852-862.

_____. 1967. Seneca morphology and dictionary. Smithsonian Contributions to Anthropology 4. Washington: Smithsonian Press.

_____. 1970. A semantically based sketch of Onondaga. International Journal of American Linguistics, Memoir 25.

_____. 1973. Siouan, Iroquoian, and Caddoan. In Current trends in linguistics, ed. by Thomas A. Sebeok, 10.1164-1209.

_____. 1976. A brief look at the Caddo language. In The Caddoan, Iroquoian, and Siouan languages, 55-82. The Hague: Mouton.

Givón, Talmy. 1975. Topic, pronoun, and grammatical agreement. In Subject and topic, ed. by Charles N. Li. New

York: Academic Press.

King, Duane H. 1975. A grammar and dictionary of the Cherokee language. Ph.D. dissertation, University of Georgia.

Lounsbury, Floyd G. 1953. Oneida verb morphology. Yale University Publications in Anthropology 48. New Haven:
   Yale University Press.

Parks, Douglas. 1976. A grammar of Pawnee. New York: Garland
   Publishing.

Pulte, William, and Feeling, Durbin. 1975. Outline of Cherokee grammar. In Cherokee-English dictionary. Tahlequah,
   Oklahoma: Cherokee Nation of Oklahoma.

Rood, David S. 1976. Wichita grammar. New York: Garland
   Publishing.

____. In press. Wichita. In Handbook of North American
   Indians 17. Washington: Smithsonian Press

Williams, Marianne M. 1976. A grammar of Tuscarora. New
   York: Garland Publishing.

12 From Auxiliary Verb Phrase to Inflectional Suffix[1]

Mary R. Haas

1. The development that I am about to trace took
place over a period of not less than 3-5 millennia. Some of
the information has been gleaned from comparing several extant related languages. But in order to give substance to
the extrapolation of the probable proto-forms out of which
the modern forms have developed, it has been necessary to
take examples from neighboring languages which may perhaps
be related, though at a very great time depth.[2]

The extant related languages are the Muskogean languages, formerly spoken in several southern states east of
the Mississippi River, now spoken in eastern Oklahoma and
southern Florida. The two neighboring languages from which
examples are drawn are Natchez, formerly spoken in the vicinity of Natchez, Mississippi, and Tunica, formerly spoken
somewhat to the north of the Natchez (though later in central
Louisiana). Both of these languages are now extinct.

The several Muskogean languages conjugate their active
verbs for subject by means of (1) prefixes and suffixes
(Choctaw), (2) infixes and suffixes (Koasati), and (3) suffixes (Hitchiti-Mikasuki and Creek). Careful study has
shown that the affixes of the several systems are related
but not in a simple one-to-one correspondence. Two of the
Koasati paradigms and the Hitchiti-Mikasuki and Creek paradigms show extra elements that need to be accounted for.

The hypothesis has been developed that these extra elements are remnants of old auxiliary verb stems. In other words, the changes are a result of a series of morphological rein- terpretations, or reanalyses.

2.   In order to develop this hypothesis I shall show the kind of paradigmatic structure exhibited in Natchez, whose principal paradigmatic device is the combination of active verb stem (VS) plus a conjugated auxiliary verb (= auxiliary verb phrase). In addition I shall show a similar structure characteristic of Tunica[3] but with a slight devia- tion which gives us a clue to one unusual feature of the Pro- to-Muskogean (PM) structure.

A model of the elements of the principal intransitive conjugation in Natchez is shown below:

(1)   Act. VS = Pres. Subj. Pron. - Aux. Root - Prog.
      yuku   t(a)-   -ak(i)   -a·
      stand   I   (intr.)   progressive
      yuku-taka·^{n}
      'I am standing.'

The elements of the principal transitive conjugation are sim- ilar but a different auxiliary is used and the object pro- noun is added:

(2)   Act. VS = Pres.Subj.- Obj.Pron. - Aux.Root - Prog.
                Pron.
      cak   t(a)-   -p(i)-   -al-   -a·
      stick   I   you(s.)   (tr.)   progres-
                                                sive
      cak-tapila·^{n}
      'I am sticking you.'

In Natchez the subject pronouns are semantically complex
morphemes in that they express not only person (1st, 2nd,
and 3rd) but also tense-mode (present, past, and optative).
The several subject prefixes all occupy the position of the
1st person subject pronoun of the present tense shown in (1)
and (2).

The last point is significant because Tunica, whose
periphrastic conjugations are in general structurally similar to those of Natchez, shows deviation in its placement
of the 1st person singular subject pronoun, although the
other subject pronouns exhibit the same order as in Natchez:

(3)   a.   Act. VS = Aux.Root - 1st Pers.Subj.

             hára   ʔahki-   -nı

             sing   EXIST   I

             hárʔahkini.   'I have sung.'

        b.   Act. VS = Subj.Pron. - Aux.Root

             hára   ʔu-   -hki

             sing   he   EXIST

             hárʔuhki.   'he has sung.'

3.   The periphrastic structures shown in the preceding section are those of actual languages which may be
distantly related to PM but are in no sense to be considered
ancestral to it. They are necessary and useful, however, to
serve as a realistic basis for comparison with the reconstructed model of the periphrastic structures of pre-PM.[4]
However, before showing these periphrastic models it is important to point out that pre-PM also had nonperiphrastic
conjugation for some verbs. In other words, the VS could
be conjugated directly and the arrangement of the elements

in such conjugation was similar to the Tunica model in (3)
except that VS is substituted for Aux.Root as follows:

(4)   a.   VS - 1S Subj.
             VS - 1i   VS-1i

       b.   Other Pron. Subj. - VS
             iš (2S)   - VS   iš-VS
             ∅ (3S)   - VS   VS
             ili (1P)   - VS   ili-VS
             haš (2P)   - VS   haš-VS

Besides this direct conjugation of the active VS, there was
periphrastic conjugation with a transitive auxiliary, as
shown in (5) and with an intransitive auxiliary as shown in
(6). Note that the arrangement of the subject pronouns follows the Tunica model given in (3) while the actual phonetic
nature of the transitive and intransitive auxiliaries is similar to that of the Natchez models shown in (1) and (2).

   The transitive model is:

(5)   a.   VS - Aux.Root - 1S Subj.
             VS   LI   1i   S1) VS-LI1i

       b.   VS - Other Subj. - Aux.Root
             VS   ši (2S)   LI   2) VS-šiLI
             VS   ∅ (3S)   LI   3) VS-LI
             VS   (hi)li (1P)   LI   P1) VS-(hi)liLI
             VS   haši (2P)   LI   2) VS-hašiLI
             (Cap letters are used to distinguish the Aux.Root
             from an affix.)

   The intransitive model is:

(6)   a.   VS - Aux.Root - 1S Subj.

           VS   KA   li   S1) VS-KAli

      b.   VS - Other Subj. - Aux.Root

           VS   (h)iš (2S)   KA   2) VS-(h)išKA

           VS   Ø (3S)   KA   3) VS-KA

           VS   (h)ili (1P)   KA   P1) VS-(h)iliKA

           VS   (h)aši (2P)   KA   2) VS-(h)ašiKA

The conjugational models shown in (4), (5), and (6) then undergo reinterpretation to give three classes of verb inflection. Class I, shown in (4), remains a nonperiphrastic conjugation with one suffix and three prefixes to indicate pronoun subject. Classes II and III, shown in (5) and (6), respectively, are reinterpreted as two different sets of inflectional affixes, shown in (7) and (8).

(7)   S1)   -lili   (8)   S1)   -kali

      2)   -šili   2)   -(h)iška

      3)   -li   3)   -ka

      P1)   -hilili   P1)   -(h)ilika

      2)   -hašili   2)   -(h)ašika

4.   The three distinct types of inflection shown in (4), (5) → (7), and (6) → (8) are retained in only one extant Muskogean language, namely Koasati (and its very close relative, Alabama). The other languages have chosen just one of the three, though not the same one always. Choctaw uses the model shown in (4), while Hitchiti-Mikasuki and Creek use (8). If it were not for Koasati and its three classes of verb inflection, the model of (7) would be unattested and therefore unreconstructible.

Although the Koasati system remains closest to the PM

system, there has been some reanalysis even here. Except for
Class I, based on (4), the other two classes exhibit subvarieties. And the subvarieties of Class III, based on (8), are
very important because they enable us to trace the evolution
of this type of inflection from its most transparent form to
its most opaque, as represented in Hitchiti-Mikasuki.

Koasati Class I, as mentioned above, remains close to
the model shown in (4). The paradigm shown in (9) is built
on the VS hica 'to see', capitalized to set it off from the
affixes.

(9)   S1)   HICA-li   hicali
       2)   is-HICA   ishica
       3)   HICA   hica
       P1)   il-HICA   ilhica
       2)   has-HICA   hashica

Koasati Class II conjugations show a suffixed 1st person
but the other personal pronouns are infixed, not prefixed as
above. In Classes IIA and IIB the inflection for 1st person
is attached to the remnant of the old LI auxiliary. Otherwise LI does not appear except in the 3rd person, where person is unmarked. Class IIB differs from IIA in that another
morpheme, causative CI follows LI. The paradigm illustrating
Class IIA, built on kalas.li 'to scratch' is shown in (10).

(10)   S1)   KALAS   LI-li   kalaslili
        2)   KALAS-ci   kalasci
        3)   KALAS   LI   kalasli
        P1)   KALAS-hili   kalashili
        2)   KALAS-haci   kalashaci

The paradigm illustrating Class IIB, built on bok.li.ci 'to

thresh', is shown in (11).

(11)	S1)	BOK	LICI-li	boklicili
	2)	BOK-ci	CI	bokcici
	3)	BOK	LICI	boklici
	P1)	BOK-hili	CI	bokhilici
	2)	BOK-haci	CI	bokhacici

Note that LI is lost in S1, P1, and P2.

There is still one more Class II paradigm, namely Class IIC. There is here no trace whatever of LI. However, in canonical shape the VS resembles those of Classes IIA and B. Note that ka̧lasli is CVCVCCV and boklici is CVCCV with added CI (caus.). The stems conjugated in Class IIC are also CVCCV (or CVCVCCV). However, since in Class IIC there is no remnant LI to prefix the nonfirst pronominal elements to, these nonfirst personal pronouns are infixed before the medial consonant cluster and the 1st person pronoun is suffixed, as usual. These nonfirst pronouns, then, have at this stage become true infixes. The paradigm illustrating this, built on hohca 'to dig', is shown in (12).

(12)	S1)	HO	HCA-li	hohcali
	2)	HO-ci-	HCA	hocihca
	3)	HO	HCA	hohca
	P1)	HO-li-	HCA	holihca
	2)	HO-haci-HCA		hohacihca

Koasati Class III verbs also exhibit some important subvarieties. Class IIIA conjugations are based on verb stems ending in -ka (which may very well be a remnant of the old intransitive auxiliary KA) or on any other verb stem ending in -ki or -ko. These latter have nothing whatever to do with

the old intransitive auxiliary. The first type, i.e. the one
ending in -ka, is illustrated by the stem yas.ka 'to chew',
as shown in (13)a. But the paradigm is clearly undergoing
reanalysis, as shown in (13)b.

(13)   a.   S1)   YAS   KA-li   b. YASKA-li   yaskali

            2)   YAS-is-KA   YAS -iska   yasiska

            3)   YAS   KA   YASKA   yaska

          P1)   YAS-il-KA   YAS -ilka   yasilka

            2)   YAS-as-KA   YAS -aska   yasaska

The reanalysis, indicated in (13)b, shows that the infixes of
(13)a plus -ka have become suffixes. That this reanalysis is
productive is clearly seen in the paradigms of any and all
other verb stems ending in -kV, e.g. imfi·ki 'to pay', shown
in (14)a and isko 'to drink', shown in (14)b.

(14)   a.   S1)   IMFI·KI-li   imfi·kili

            2)   IMFI· -hiska   imfi·hiska

            3)   IMFI·KI   imfi·ki

          P1)   IMFI· -hilka   imfi·hilka

            2)   IMFI· -haska   imfi·haska

That reanalysis has taken place is confirmed by the fact that
S2) is IMFI·-hiska, not *IMFI·-his-KI, P1) is IMFI·-hilka,
not *IMFI·-hil-KI, and P2 is IMFI·-haska, not *IMFI·-has-KI.
The same type of reanalysis applies to isko, as shown below.

(14)   b.   S1)   ISKO -li   iskoli

            2)   IS   -iska   isiska

            3)   ISKO   isko

          P1)   IS   -ilka   isilka

            2)   IS   -aska   isaska

An even more radical reinterpretation is seen in Class IIIB.

Here the reanalysis giving a set of inflectional suffixes
mostly ending in -ka shows this set used with a VS which has
never had -ka or -kV as its final syllable. The example
shown in (15) is based on imponnaci 'to teach' (-ci is caus.
suff.).

(15)   S1) IMPONNACI-1i   imponnacili
        2) IMPONNAC -iska   imponnaciska
        3) IMPONNACI   imponnaci
        P1) IMPONNAC -ilka   imponnacilka
        2) IMPONNAC -aska   imponnaska

Note, however, that causative verbs containing LI (e.g.
boklici above) must be conjugated as shown in (11), never as
shown in (15). The latter is used only when -ci is not added to LI.

The paradigmatic treatment shown in Class IIIB makes it
clear that the amalgamation of the personal pronouns and the
old auxiliary KA is now complete. There is no longer a morpheme boundary in S2) -iska and there is no meaning whatever
attached to the -ka in -iska. The unit is simply S2).

5.   Hitchiti and Creek each have only one set of
paradigmatic affixes. This single set in both languages corresponds to the set in Koasati Class IIIB. But unlike
Koasati, Hitchiti and Creek have no choice but to use them
with old LI verb stems (where Koasati requires Class IIA, B)
as well as verb stems corresponding to Koasati Class I conjugations. Thus Hitchiti patapli- 'to hit' (an old LI stem)
and pocka- 'to touch' (an old KA stem) are conjugated exactly alike, as shown in (16)a and (16)b. Both paradigms
are followed by the indicative marker -s.

(16)   a.   S1)   PATAPLI-li   -s   pataplilis
              2)   PATAPL -icka   -s   pataplickas
              3)   PATAPLI   -s   pataplis
              P1)   PATAPL -i·ka   -s   patapli·kas
              2)   PATAPL -a·cka   -s   patapla·ckas

        b.   S1)   POCKA   -li   -s   pockalis
              2)   POCK   -icka   -s   pockickas
              3)   POCKA   -s   pockas
              P1)   POCK   -i·ka   -s   pocki·kas
              2)   POCK   -a·cka   -s   pocka·ckas

The conjugation shown in (16)b shows that ka in S2) -icka,
etc., is simply a part of the pronominal suffix and this is
further reinforced by the fact that the ka which is a part
of the stem pocka is kept intact and not truncated as in the
Koasati Class IIIA forms.

     Like Hitchiti, Creek also has only one set of paradigm-
atic suffixes as subject pronouns. However, this single set
is not quite identical in the two languages. Both the 1st
person singular and the 1st person plural differ in interesting ways. While the Hitchiti 1st person singular -li can be
said to be truncated from either the old transitive LIli
form as in (5)a, or the old intransitive KAli form, as in
(6)a, the Creek 1st person singular -ay- is clearly from the
old intransitive KAli form. The Creek 1st person plural
-iy-/-i·- form, however, is not so simple. A form *-i·k-,
similar to Hitchiti -i·ka-, would be expected if it is derived from the old intransitive (h)iliKA, shown in (6)a.
Two explanations are possible. (a) At some point in pre-
Creek, -ka was dropped, giving the -iy-/-i·- that we actually
have, perhaps on the superficial analogy of the 1st person

singular -ay-. (The analogy is superficial because the vowel
of -ay- is actually the remnant of the old KA.) (b) The k
in a possibly earlier form *-i·k- was absorbed into the -iy-
/-i·- that we actually have. In accordance with these suggestions the single set of Creek subject pronouns is derived
from the old PM intransitive model as shown in (17).

(17)   PM   Creek   Reanalysis
        S1) *-kali   -ay-   Morpheme cut after k
        2)   *-(h)iška   -ick-   Loss of final a
        3)   ∅   ∅
        P1) *-(h)ilika   -iy-/-i··   Absortpion or loss
                                        of ka
        2)   *-(h)ašika   -a·ck-   Loss of final a;
                                        long V unexplained;
                                        cf. Hitchiti

This set of Creek subject pronouns are used with all verbs,
including transitive, intransitive, and causative. Old LI
stems end in -y (<-li) in Creek and old KA stems end in -k.
Causative stems end in -yc. The Creek stem wanay- 'to tie
one' is a LI stem, atotk- 'to work' is a KA stem, and lasti·c-
'to blacken one' is a causative stem. Their conjugations are
shown below in (18) a, b, and c. The tense-aspect used in
the examples is present progressive and this requires the
lengthening of the last vowel of the stem if it is not already long.[5] The final suffix -(i)s is the indicative mode
marker.[6]

(18)   a.   S1) WANA·Y   -ay-   -s   wana·yéys
              2)   WANA·Y   -íck-   -is   wana·yickis
              3)   WANA·Y   -is   wana·yís
              P1) WANA·Y   -iy-/-i··   -is   wana·yi·s
              2)   WANA·Y   -á·ck-   -is   wana·yá·ckis

b. S1) ATO·TK   -ay-   -s   ato·tkéys
    2)   ATO·TK   -íck-   -is   ato·tkíckis
    3)   ATO·TK   -is   ato·tkís
    P1) ATO·TK   -iy-/-i·-   -is   ato·tkí·s
    2)   ATO·TK   -á·ck-   -is   ato·tká·ckis

c. S1) LASTI·C   -ay-   -s   lasti·céys
    2)   LASTI·C   -íck-   -is   lasti·cíckis
    3)   LASTI·C   -is   lasti·cís
    P1) LASTI·C   -iy-/-i·-   -is   lasti·cí·s
    2)   LASTI·C   -á·ck-   -is   lasti·cá·ckis

6.   It has now been demonstrated that in Hitchiti and
Creek an old conjugated auxiliary used with intransitive
verbs has been transformed into a set of subject pronoun suffixes that can be used to conjugate all verbs, including
transitive and causative as well as intransitive. But without the several conjugational classes of affixes in Koasati
and the model of inflected auxiliaries in Natchez and Tunica,
it would not have been possible to trace out with sufficient
accuracy the path of such an interesting development.

Notes

1.   Grateful acknowledgment is made to the Committee on Research, University of California, Berkeley, for financial aid used to provide clerical assistance needed in processing some of the materials used in this paper.

2.   The data presented here on Tunica, Natchez, Choctaw, Koasati, Hitchiti, and Creek are taken from my own field notes on these languages collected in Louisiana and Oklahoma in the course of several field trips between 1933 and 1941. Only a portion of this material has been published.

3.   See M. R. Haas, A grammatical sketch of Tunica. Linguistic Structures of Native America.   VFPA 6:337-66 (1946), esp. pp. 349-51.

4.   See M. R. Haas, A Proto-Muskogean paradigm. Lg. 22: 326-32 (1946).

5.   See M. R. Haas, Ablaut and its function in Muskogee. Lg. 16:141-50 (1940).

6.   There is good evidence to indicate that this suffix was formerly characteristic only of men's speech. See M. R. Haas, Men's and women's speech in Koasati. Lg. 20:142-49 (1944).

13 Clisis and Diachrony

Susan Steele

0. Introduction

0.0   A number of Uto-Aztecan languages have clitic subject pronouns which follow the first element of the clause.[1] (1) is an example from Luiseño, a Uto-Aztecan language of Southern California.[2]

```
LS    (1)    hunwuti=pum ¢c?iwun
             bear:object=they(CP) are:shooting
             'They are shooting a bear.'    (LS-S-FN)
```

Other Uto-Aztecan languages have clitic subject pronouns which are proclitic (or prefixed) to the verb. (2) is an example from Classical Axtec, a Uto-Aztecan language of Mexico.[3]

```
AZ (2)    an-teečLaso?La
          you(CP)-love:us
          'You love us.'    (AZ A-R-21)
```

This paper examines the development of both types of clitic pronouns. Specifically, it makes two claims. (1) Second position clitic pronouns are diachronically derived from independent pronouns which move to second position as they become clitics. (2) All the pronouns which are proclitic (or prefixed) to the verb are derivative from other bound pronominal forms, most from previously cliticized second position pronouns.

The position of bound grammatical elements, of which

clitic pronouns are simply one type,[4] has been argued to be
a relic, a frozen reflection of the position of independent
elements at an earlier stage of the language.[5] The proof of
the two claims above will demonstrate this hypothesis to be,
at best, too simplistic a view of diachronic change. Second
position clitic pronouns have a different position than their
diachronic source; verbal proclitic (or prefixed) clitic pronouns are secondary developments, and their position is not,
therefore, a reflection of the position of independent pronouns at some earlier stage of the language. Rather than
clitic pronouns reflecting the position of the independent
elements from which they descend, clitic pronouns in Uto-
Aztecan move to certain "good" positions. Whether the histories of other grammatical elements parallel the histories
of clitic pronouns -- and whether the histories of clitic
pronouns in other language families parallel Uto-Aztecan --
remains an open question.

0.1   The Uto-Aztecan language family is presented in I.

I.

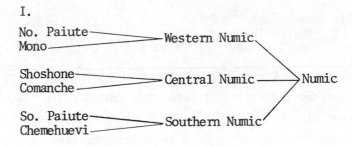

Tubatulabal

Hopi

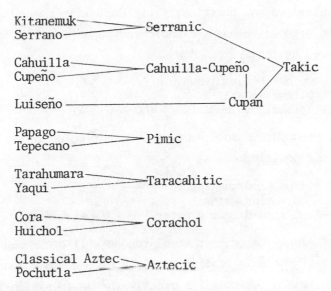

Although some Uto-Aztecan languages do not have clitic pronouns, the majority of them do. II presents the distribution of clitic subject pronouns in the language family.

II.

Clitic Subject Pronouns	Comanche, So. Paiute, Chemehuevi, Tubatulabal, Serrano, Kitanemuk, Cupeño, Cahuilla, Luiseño, Papago, Tepecano, Tarahumara, Yaqui, Cora, Huichol, Classical Aztec, Pochutla,
No Clitic Subject Pronouns	Northern Paiute, Shoshone, Hopi
Borderline	Mono

The pronouns of Mono can only be described as somewhere between clitics and independent forms. There is one set of
pronouns in the language; these pronouns occur generally in
sentential second position.

MO (3)   nopihweeh nɨɨ miyawaih
         to:home I will:go
         'I shall go home.'   (MO-L-G-377)

In sentential second position, first dual and first plural inclusive pronouns alone are indicated as attached to the word preceding them.

MO (4)   nopihweeh=taa miyawaih
          to:home=we will:go
          'We shall go home.'   (MO-L-G-377)

However, pronouns in some sentences do not occur in sentential second position.

MO (5)   nɨɨ=po?o poyanahipitɨh
          I=but drink:water
          'But I am drinking water.'   (MO-L-G-380)

It is not simply the case that a pronoun will occur sentence initially if the only other non-clitic element in a sentence is a verb, since (6) contains exactly the postpositional phrase of (3) and (4).

MO (6)   ?ɨɨ hsahqwa nopihweeh ?ika
          you modal to:home go
          'You ought to go into the house.'   (MO-L-G-389)

Rather it appears that certain elements like the conjunction po?o and the modal hsahqwa are more necessarily sentential second position elements than are pronouns.

As I stated earlier, clitic pronouns either occur in sentential second position, e.g. (1); or they are verbal proclitics (or prefixes), e.g. (2). Some languages, however, exhibit both -- Cupeño, Tepecano, Tarahumara, Yaqui, and Cora.

III.

Second Position   Comanche, So. Paiute, Chemehuevi,
                       Tubatulabal, Serrano, Luiseño,
                       Papago

Proclitic/Prefix   Kitanemuk, Cahuilla, Huichol,
                          Classical Aztec, Pochutla

Both   Cupeño, Tepecano, Tarahumara,
                          Yaqui, Cora

Tepecano clitic pronouns can fill both positions simultaneously.

TE (7)   ndedos n=an=ahohoinda
          my:fingers introducer=CP=will:shake:them
          'I will shake my fingers.'   (TE-M-PL-403)

For the other four languages with both types, the two positions are independent possibilities. (8), (9), and (10) are
examples from Tarahumara, Yaqui, and Cora respectively of
the two types of clitic pronouns cooccuring; (11) contains
two Cupeño sentences, one with a second position clitic pronoun, another with a verbal proclitic/prefix clitic pronoun.

TR (8)   čú mu šika ké mu naki muhé ko ba
          WH CP WH neg CP want you emphatic emphatic
          'Why don't you want it?'   (TR-B-G-53)

YA (9)   kwarénta péso dyáryota=ne ne=kóba iani inine
          forty peso daily=CP CP=earn now here
          'Now I make forty pesos a day here.'   (YA-L-S-20)

CR (10)   n-a'ana'iⁿ yiiche'e nú
          CP-was:going:to:build:a:fire CP
          'I was going to build a fire.'
                    (Casad, personal communication)

CU (11)   a.   nə?ə=n yəkwinqa
                I=CP be:scared
                'I'm scared.'   (CUP-J-SC-65)

          b.   čəm=əp čə?-mamayəw
                we=aux CP-help
                'We helped.'   (CUP-J-SC-77)

1.   Second Position Clitic Pronouns

1.0   This section is devoted to substantiating the claim
that second position subject clitic pronouns are diachronically derived from independent pronouns which move to second
position as they become clitics. The important part of this
claim for the purposes of this paper is that such clitics result from the movement of independent pronouns into second
position. But before the evidence which bears on the issue
can be considered it is necessary to substantiate the claim
that second position clitic pronouns and independent pronouns
are related and that for most Uto-Aztecan languages the relationship is diachronic.

1.1   The appendix lists the clitic subject pronouns and the
independent subject pronouns of each Uto-Aztecan language
that has second position clitic pronouns. An examination of
the two sets will reveal clear resemblances. /n/ shows up
regularly in the first person singular of the clitic pronouns; /n/ shows up regularly in the first person singular
of the independent pronouns. Reflexes of */t/ occur in the
first person plural of the clitic pronouns; reflexes of */t/
show up in the first person plural of the independent pronouns. The relationship between third person singular clitic pronouns and demonstratives is inescapably obvious. In
Chemehuevi and So. Paiute there is no distinction in form between certain of the demonstratives and the third person
singular clitic pronouns. The Cupeño third person singular
clitic pronoun pə and the Luiseño third person singular
clitic pronoun up are clearly related to various third person pronouns and demonstratives found throughout the language family.

   More particular resemblances are apparent. In some lan-

guages the independent subject pronouns and the clitic pronouns are related to each other by the presence or absence
respectively of an affix. In Comanche, the independent pronouns and the clitic pronouns differ by the presence or absence respectively of a demonstrative or some other clitic
element. In Tubatulabal the independent subject pronouns
differ from the clitic pronouns by the presence of the prefix in- in the former. Papago, Tepecano, Tarahumara, and
Yaqui are somewhat less transparent examples of a similar
type. In Papago and Tepecano, clitic pronouns and independent pronouns differ primarily by the absence or presence respectively of a prefix ?a- or a-. Tarahumara and Yaqui clitic pronouns and independent pronouns differ from one another
primarily by the absence or presence respectively of a suffix, -he in the former and usually -po in the latter.

The other languages don't exhibit a regularity of any
obvious sort in the relationship between the set of clitic
pronouns and the set of independent pronouns, although, of
course, the broad phonological correspondences suggested at
first still pertain. But in some persons in some languages
the relationship between the two types of pronouns is regular.
For example, in So. Paiute t becomes r after a spirantiz-
ing vowel. First person dual and plural independent pronouns
begin with t ; the first person dual and plural clitic pronouns begin with r .

The evidence above suggests that clitic pronouns and
independent pronouns are related; the question now is how.
A first hypothesis might be that clitic pronouns are the synchronic reductions of otherwise free independent forms. English clitic pronouns seems to be exactly that. In (12) the

pronoun subject -- and the auxiliary verb <u>be</u> -- is a (pro)
clitic; in (13) the pronoun subject is a (en)clitic.

(12)   'tsraining.

(13)   I fought'em.

Spanish and French clitic pronouns have been analyzed to be
the result of a synchronic rule which moves the independent
pronouns into clitic position (and changes their form). (14)
and (15) below are examples respectively of clitic (object)
pronouns in these languages.

(14)   Elena la vio.   'Elena saw her.'
              CP

(15)   Paul le lira   'Paul will read it.'
              CP

    English clitic pronouns differ from Spanish and French
clitic pronouns in that reduction in the latter requires a
different position.[6] They are similar, however, in that neither co-occurs with a noun to which they refer or an independent pronoun with the same referent.[7] If these two types
exhaust the synchronic possibilities -- an assumption which
admittedly needs much more study -- we can use co-occurrence
as diagnostic of a synchronic relationship between clitic
pronouns and independent pronouns. If clitic pronouns are
the synchronic reduction of independent pronouns, we would
not expect the two to co-occur.

    In all Uto-Aztecan languages, except for Tubatulabal
and Comanche, the clitic pronouns co-occur with an independent pronoun with the same referent. The first example sentence of this paper is a Luiseño sentence with a clitic subject pronoun; the following sentence with both independent

pronominal subject and clitic subject pronoun is equally
good.

LS (16)   wunaalum=pum hunwuti ʃe?iwun
           they=they(CP) bear:object are:shooting
           'They are shooting the bear.'   (LS-S-FN)

(17) to (21) are examples paralleling (16) from a number of
other Uto-Aztecan languages.

SP (17)   qaču=anga=ni ni? iminčuxwavaang?wain.iaanga
           neg=object:CP= CP I shall:give:him:to:you
           'I shall not give him to you.'   (SP-S-G-226)

SR (18)   ?imi?=ta=m? payika? miib
           you=modal=CP away will:go
           'You'll go away.'   (SR-H-G-10)

CU (19)   nə?=nə ?əməmi ?əməhiwčəqa
           I=CP you know:you
           'I know you.'   (CUP-S-SC-146)

PA (20)   ?áañi=?áñ ñiok
           I=CP speaking
           'I am/was speaking.'   (PA-H-IN)

YA (21)   ínepo ka=ni aman nóitik
           I neg=CP there went
           'I did not go there.'   (YA-M-PS-205)

The clitic pronouns in all but two Uto-Aztecan languages are
to be distinguished from those of English, Spanish, and
French. Hence, given the hypothesis above that the characteristics of these are diagnostic of a synchronic relationship between clitic pronouns and independent pronouns, the
relationship between the two must not be synchronic in all
Uto-Aztecan languages but Tubatulabal and Comanche.[8]

1.2   We are ready now to consider the diachronic process by
which independent pronouns become second position clitic
pronouns.

The beginnings of the cliticization of independent pronominal forms can be witnessed synchronically in Mono. As
discussed above, pronouns in Mono generally follow the first
non-clitic element of a clause. (See (3) and (4).) Although these pronouns generally occur in sentential second
position, they are not the clitic elements of, say, Luiseño.
They are the only subject pronouns in the language; they can
occur initially under certain, not totally clear, conditions.
(See (5) and (6).)

It appears that the beginning of the cliticization of
independent pronouns is indicated by their appearance in
sentential second position. The synchronic situation in
Mono is mirrored in an Australian language, Warramunga.
Hale (1973) says that Warramunga pronouns "...are in fact
independent pronouns in the sense that they can appear as
isolated fully stressed words...." (341) However, "...the
independent pronouns become unstressed and cliticize, that
is, become enclitic to the first non-pronominal constituent
of the sentence." (340)

Now the question is why independent pronouns occur in
sentential second position as they become clitics. There
are two possibilities that suggest themselves immediately,
both of which depend on the following scenario. Assume
that independent subject pronouns were initial to the clause.
With the appearance of some other element at the beginning
of the clause -- because it is a topic or somehow emphasized
-- this independent pronoun would occur in sentential second
position.

(22)   John, he never does anything for me.

(23)   Into the woods he ran.

The first hypothesis is that the position of the clitic pronoun is a relic of the position of the independent pronoun
in such constructions. Perhaps independent subject pronouns
in sentences like (22) and (23) are essentially stressless
and, hence, subject to cliticization.[9] The position of clitic pronouns, under this hypothesis, would be an accident of
the original clause initial position of the independent pronoun and the process of topicalization. This hypothesis
loses its force when we consider that sentential second position in many languages of the world, and, most importantly,
in Uto-Aztecan, is the position for certain grammatical elements. In an earlier paper, I discussed the fact that modal
elements also have a strong tendency toward sentential second
position.   In fact, elements which correspond roughly to what
has been analyzed as the AUX in English -- tense, aspect, and
modality -- commonly occur in sentential second position, as
do conjunctions, negatives, and question-markers. (24) is
an example from Luiseño of second position modality and aspect; (25), of a second position negative; (26), of a second
position question marker.

LS (24)   nanatmalum xu=m=po henge?malumi ?ari
           girls MODAL=CP=ASPECT boys kick
           'Girls should kick boys.'   (LS-S-FN)

LS (25)   nawitmal qay hengeemali ?ariq
           girl NEG boy is:kicking
           'The girl isn't kicking the boy.'   (LS-S-FN)

LS (26)   nawitmal=ʃu hengeemali ?ariq
           girl=Q:MARKER boy is:kicking
           'Is the girl kicking the boy?'   (LS-S-FN)

Any hypothesis which posits that the position of clitic

pronouns in second position is an accident will have to explain why all of these elements occur in second position as
well.

The second hypothesis acknowledges the importance of
sentential second position. It argues that if some topic or
emphasized element of the clause precedes the independent
subject pronoun, this pronoun occurs in second position,
the position of clitics, and hence becomes a clitic. That
is, cliticization is the result of the accidental occurrence
of some (potentially cliticizable) element in sentential
second position. This hypothesis, while more satisfactory
than the first, must be rejected -- and the arguments
against it seal the fate of the first hypothesis as well.

If independent pronouns accidentally occurred in second position -- and therefore cliticized -- because they
were preceded by a topic or some otherwise emphasized element, we would expect at least those languages with relatively recent cliticization to show some signs of such a
stage. Mono pronouns are in the process of cliticization.
The clitic pronouns of Tubatulabal and Comanche are in the
early stages of cliticization, if the assumptions about the
difference between synchronically related clitic pronouns
and independent pronouns and diachronically related clitic
pronouns and independent pronouns discussed above are correct and if we can further assume that languages develop at
least from the type exemplified by Spanish and French to the
type exemplified by Luiseño. In none of these three languages is there indication that the clitic pronouns have
arisen from a topic-comment construction. First, languages
in the early stages of cliticization have clitic pronouns

occurring after what would be difficult to argue is a topic.
For example, in Tubatulabal clitic pronouns follow a clause
initial subordinate clause which contains a single word:

TU (27)   aanayuwibɨ=gi iimi
           fight:subordinate=1sgCP went
           'Without fighting, I went.'   (TU-V-G-124)

and a clause initial time adverbial.

TU (28)   piš=bum pinahi tohiilin tuguwayin
           then= 2plCP must:bring deer's meat
           'Then you must bring the meat of the deer.'
                                            (TU-V-T-218)

Moreover, if independent pronouns accidentally occurred in
second position because they were preceded by a topic, we
might expect to find clitic pronouns serving the function of
clearly partitioning the sentence into topic and comment at,
at least, some early stage in their history. But there is
no Uto-Aztecan language, at any stage, where second position
clitic pronouns unambiguously serve to so partition the sentence -- and I know of no language with second position phenomena where the clitics can be said to always do so.[10] Second,
consider sentences with a topic and a resumptive pronoun referring to the topic such as (22). (29) below is such an example from Classical Aztec.

AZ (29)   in tolteka? ye?waantin senka wel Layakana
           article Toltecs they very emphatic they:took:lead
           'The Toltecs took the very lead.'   (AZ-L-PCN-179)

If clitic pronouns resulted from the reduction of resumptive
pronouns in such sentences, we would expect to find clitic
pronouns co-occurring with nouns at the early stages of their
development. But we do not. The Mono borderline clitic pronouns do not co-occur with nouns. Nor do the Tubatulabal or

Comanche clitic pronouns.

In sum, then, it appears that pronouns move into sentential second position as they cliticize. Accepting this
as a diachronic fact, accepting that neither second position
itself nor the fact that certain elements occur there synchronically is an accident of diachrony, the question becomes: Why second position? I will return to this question
in the last section of this paper.

2.   Derivative Clitic Pronouns

2.0   I have argued that the clitic pronouns of a certain
set of Uto-Aztecan languages descend from independent pronouns that have moved into second position in the clause.
This section discusses the development of proclitic (or prefixed) clitic pronouns. Five languages in the language family have clitic pronouns of this type only -- Kitanemuk,
Cahuilla, Huichol, Classical Aztec, and Pochutla; others
have this type in addition to second position clitic pronouns
-- Cupeño, Tepecano, Tarahumara, Yaqui, and Cora. The proclitic (or prefixed) clitic pronouns found in all these languages are secondary developments, albeit developments of
two different sorts. The prefixed pronouns of Cahuilla,
Cupeño, and Kitanemuk are descended from possessive pronominal prefixes. I am not going to discuss the diachrony of
these here; it is the development of clitic pronouns in the
other languages that is of concern.[11] These are secondary
developments from second position clitic pronouns.

Excluding Cahuilla, Cupeño, and Kitanemuk, there remain seven languages with pronominal elements which are proclitic (or prefixed) to the verb -- Tepecano, Tarahumara,

Yaqui, Cora, Huichol, Classical Aztec, and Pochutla. Although the development of these from second position clitic
pronouns is ultimately attributable to a single factor, it
followed one course in Tarahumara and Yaqui and another in
the other five languages.

Tarahumara and Yaqui each have two series of clitic pronouns. The sentences below each have two clitic subject pronouns, one proclitic to the verb, the other in sentential
second position.

TR (30) čú mu šika ké mu nakí muhé ko ba
         WH CP WH neg CP want you emphatic emphatic
         'Why don't you want it?'   (TR-B-G-53)

YA (31) kwarénta péso dyáryota=ne ne=kóba íani ininc
         forty peso daily=CP CP=earn now here
         'Now I make forty pesos a day here.'   (YA-L-S-20)

Note that both clitic pronouns in each case have the same
shape; this I take as indicative that they are not descended
from different sources, but rather that one is derivative
from the other. There is strong evidence for arguing that
the proclitic is derivative from the second position clitic.
An 18th century grammar of Yaqui states explicitly that clitic pronouns are second position elements. "...Velasco states
as one of his most infallible rules that the pronominal subject [read clitic pronoun] must be the second word or element
in the sentence...." (YA-M-PS) Thus, the verbal proclitic
pronoun of Yaqui has developed since the 18th century. Although there is no nice straightforward evidence of this sort
for Tarahumara -- there is no early grammar -- there is evidence that the proclitic clitic pronouns of Tarahumara are
dependent on the presence of second position clitic pronouns,
in a fashion that suggests the former are more recent. Both

languages can have both types of clitic pronouns in the same
sentence, as demonstrated above; both can have second position clitic pronouns alone.

TR (32)   semati ne napaha rarimea aré
           nice CP shirt gonna:buy probably
           'I am probably gonna buy a nice shirt.' (TR-L-SE-29)

YA (33)   tuká=ne antónyta bičak
           yesterday=CP Antonio saw
           'Yesterday I saw Antonio.'   (YA-L-S-178)

But only Yaqui can have proclitic clitic pronouns alone.

YA (34)   ?inepo ne=?a=me?ak
           I CP=IT=threw
           'I threw it.'   (YA-J-I-29)

In Yaqui then, the presence of a clitic pronoun preceding
the verb apparently allows the second position clitic pronoun to be absent. That sentences like (34) exist in Yaqui,
but not in Tarahumara, is good evidence that the direction
of development in this language as well has been from second
position clitic pronoun to verbal proclitic.

     Synchronically, then, in these languages we can posit
an optional copying rule which spreads the clitic pronoun
from sentential second position to preverbal position.

     X CP Y V ⟶ X CP Y CP V

In the other five languages with proclitic (or prefixed)
clitic pronouns, a second position clitic pronoun which is
also contiguous to the verb has been reanalyzed as a proclitic to the verb.

     I noted in the first section that Tepecano clitic pro-
nouns can be both proclitic to the verb and in sentential
second position simultaneously. The proclitic status of

clitic pronouns has developed secondarily. Clitic pronouns
can still be separated from the verb by, for instance, a
noun object.

TE (36)   an=ti nauw kiis
           CP=tense/aspect napal transplanted
           'I transplanted napal.'   (TE-M-PL-341)

It is unlikely that a verbal proclitic would shake loose
from the verb. More importantly, though, the beginnings of
procliticization of second position clitics can be witnessed
in Papago, a closely related language. In Papago, the clitic pronoun occurs initial to the clause if the verb is the
only other element in the clause and is preceded by some proclitic element which cannot be clause initial -- in the example below o.

PA (36)   n=t o mnii
           CP=aspect proclitic see:you
           'I will see you.'   (PA-H-IN)

Putting the clitic pronoun after the verb in such a sentence
would make the necessarily non-initial proclitic initial, so
the clitic pronoun remains initial to the clause and directly
precedes the verb.

PA (37)   * o mnii ?ant
           proclitic see:you CP:aspect   (PA-H-IN)

    Clitic pronouns in Huichol, Classical Aztec, and Pochut-
la are always and only prefixed to the verb; one set of Cora
clitic pronouns is as well. Although it is possible that
these clitic pronouns developed from a system like that hypothesized for Tarahumara and Yaqui, fairly good evidence exists that the clitic pronouns of these languages have arisen
in a fashion similar to that hypothesized for Tepecano, that

is, by the reinterpretation of second position clitic pronouns as verb prefixes. Most languages in the language family have an unmarked word order SOV, but none of these languages do. The word order SOV is almost unattested in Classical Aztec; rather SVO or VOS word order are most common. Pochutla word order appears to be like Classical Aztec. Huichol
is described as having regular OSV word order. In Cora, Eugene Casad has informed me, VSO word order is most common.
With a second position clitic pronoun and a (potentially)
clause final verb, the clitic pronoun can be separated from
the verb by a noun.

    S=CP O V

But if the object nominal is moved out from its position between the clitic pronoun and the verb, the two will be contiguous. The clitic pronoun is potentially reanalyzable as proclitic to the verb.

    S=CP V O > S CP=V O

The SVO word order of Classical Aztec and Pochutla falls in
nicely with this hypothesis. I assume that the OSV word order of Huichol is derivative from an older SVO word order
just as Classical Aztec, at least, regularly exhibits VOS
word order.

    S CP=V O > O S CP=V
                CP=V O S

And I assume that the VSO word order of Cora is further derivative from VOS; in Classical Aztec VSO is less common
than VOS.

    CP=V O S > CP=V S O

Although the evidence for the development of proclitic
clitic pronouns from second position clitic pronouns is good,
I have yet to offer a reason for such a development in the
first place. The reason for the development is that the
verb exhibits a certain attraction for the grammatical elements -- and some of the non-grammatical elements -- of a
sentence. In English, for example, words like only and just
can occur in front of the verb even when their scope is restricted to a particular item in the predicate.

(38)   Mary only caught one fish.

(39)   Mary just caught one fish.

In other languages an object noun may be incorporated in the
verb. The following are examples from Classical Aztec and
Onondaga.

AZ (40)   ni-naka-kwa
           I-meat-eat
           'I eat meat.'   (AZ-A-R-104)

   (41)   wa?-ha-ye?kwa-hniinu
           tense-he/it-tobacco-buy
           'He bought tobacco.'   (Woodbury, 1975)

I have argued for the attraction of the verb as it pertains
to the position of modal elements. (Steele, 1975b) It is the
attraction of the verb for grammatical elements that encour-
ages the development of clitic pronouns that are proclitic
(or prefixed) to the verb from second position clitic pronouns, whether by copying them there or by reanalysis.

I argued above that the proclitic clitic pronouns in
Cora, Classical Aztec, Huichol, and Pochutla could have developed from second position clitic pronouns; I didn't show,
however, that they could not be directly descended from in-

dependent pronouns. The attraction of the verb for grammatical elements certainly could -- and in some (non-Uto-Aztecan)
languages does -- cause independent pronouns to cliticize to
it. The evidence for Uto-Aztecan, however, is that it does
not. First, we can see second position subject clitic pronouns from independent pronouns being created over and over
again in Uto-Aztecan; there is no indication of similar waves
of creation of subject proclitics on the verb. The beginnings of second position clitics in Mono were discussed a-
bove; Tubatulabal and Comanche were suggested to have created
second position clitic pronouns relatively recently. Even in
languages with verbal proclitic subject pronouns, second position clitic pronouns are created. Eugene Casad (personal communication) has suggested that the clitic pronouns which are
prefixed to the verb in Cora are older than the second position clitics. Cahuilla and Classical Aztec, both languages
with prefixed/proclitic pronominal elements, have pronominal
forms -- reductions of independent pronouns -- which are more
restricted in their position than the full independent pronominal forms, are, hence, on their way to cliticization. Second, if the dissimilarity between clitic pronouns and independent pronouns can be taken as evidence of the length of
time they have been separated (but see footnote 6), the pronominal elements on the verb are older than second position
clitic pronouns. (Compare the sets in (13) to (16) in the
appendix to those in (1) to (12).) However, the proto language can be reconstructed to have had second position clitic
pronouns. The evidence in support of this reconstruction is,
first, the recreation discussed above. If a particular feature is created time and again in the members of a language
family, I would suggest it points to a characteristic of the

proto-language. In this case, the recreation of second position clitics points to the existence of second position clitics in the proto language. The second piece of evidence in
support of the reconstruction is a hypothesis about language
change. While many -- probably all -- languages evidence an
attraction of the verb for certain grammatical elements of
the clause, fewer show an equally strong attraction of such
elements into sentential second position. It follows, then,
that the presence of the latter characteristic is dependent
on certain other, as yet unknown, characteristics and, further, that the development of the latter in a language which
didn't originally evidence it would be less likely than the
reverse development. In Uto-Aztecan languages, much of the
grammatical information about the sentence is found in second
position (See (24), (25), and (26) above for examples.) If
the chain of hypotheses above is correct, it is unlikely that
numbers of such languages would have developed from a proto-
language where grammatical elements were found primarily on
the verb, where attraction to the verb was dominant. Now,
given this reconstruction, the pronominal elements on the
verb, the oldest extant clitics, would not be directly descended from independent pronouns; they would, rather, be
derivative from even older second position clitics.

3.   Conclusion

3.0   This paper has examined the diachronic process by
which clitic subject pronouns are formed. The two claims
made at the beginning of this paper have been substantiated.
In Uto-Aztecan, clitic pronouns move into second position as
they become clitics; second position clitic pronouns can be
attracted out of second position to the verb. Any reconstruc-

tion which depends on the assumption that the position of
grammatical elements is a relic should be viewed dubiously.

The question raised earlier in this paper -- why second
position? -- remains to be answered. While second position
is clearly not a diachronic accident, it could be argued to
be a synchronic one. Clitics, being unstressed and reduced
forms, have to attach to something. There are no languages,
as far as I know, where a clitic procliticizes to whatever
element follows it, regardless of its category. Hence, if
what ends up as second position clitics are generated clause
initially, they will have to move around the first element
to sentential second position -- or some element will have
to be moved around them to clause initial position.This is not
a totally satisfactory hypothesis, however. First, it begs
the question of why clitics cannot procliticize to the first
element in the clause. Second, it requires that everything
which ends up in second position begin someplace else. If
these problems are disconcerting enough, we have two choices,
which are not necessarily mutually exclusive. We can reject
a theory of grammar which forces us into this analysis. And/or
we can say that asking the question: Why second position? is
like asking the question: Why adjectives?

* Thanks to Eugene Casad, Donald Crook, Joan Hooper,
Charles Li, and Richard Oehrle for generous comments on an
earlier version of this paper. Research for this paper was
supported by a research fellowship from the American Council
of Learned Societies.

Notes

1. The first element, most generally, is either the first word or the first constituent. In some languages, like Luiseño, clitic pronouns have either option. (See Steele 1975a) The details of the positional possibilities remain to be worked out for the other Uto-Aztecan languages; it may be that only one of the two positions is possible in some of them.

2. Except for the Classical Aztec example sentences, all example sentences appear in the (regularized) transcriptions of their source. The Classical Aztec sentences have been changed to a broad phonemic transcription from a Spanish orthography. The source for each example sentence is identified in a code which follows the English gloss; the code refers to an item in the bibliography. A number of conventions are used in the literal glosses: - indicates a morpheme boundary; = indicates a clitic boundary; : connects the words in a multiple word gloss for a single word in the example sentence; CP is an abbreviation for clitic pronoun.

3. The distinction between being proclitic to the verb and prefixed to the verb is, at least in the Uto-Aztecan languages, not always possible to make. I'm not going to try to make the distinction and will equivocate by referring to such pronominal elements with both terms.

4. The class of clitics is a subset of the class of grammatical elements. Many grammatical elements -- elements indicating modality, tense, and aspect; negatives; conjunctions, etc. -- either have clitic counterparts or are necessarily clitic.

> a.   She'll know the answer.
>
> b.   She's racing down the field with the ball.
>
> c.   I don't want it.
>
> d.   me 'n Bobby McGee.

But some are always stressed, unreduced, and unattached.

5.   Givón (1971) is the most radical proponent of this
view; few historical linguists -- and probably no longer
Givón himself -- subscribe to the position set forth in his
paper. While this paper argues that the strongest form of
the hypothesis -- all grammatical elements reflect the position of the independent element from which they descend --
could not possibly be correct, it also suggests that the
weaker form of the hypothesis -- some grammatical elements
reflect the position of the independent element from which
they descend -- must be carefully reexamined in light of data
on the positional tendencies of grammatical elements.   It
also requires that we consider why grammatical elements do
not reflect the position of some earlier independent element,
if they do not.

6.   There is also a more transparent relationship between independent pronouns and clitic pronouns in English
than between the independent pronouns and the clitic pronouns
of Spanish and French. But we cannot assume that the transparency of the relationship varies with the change in position.   In Mono, as discussed above, independent pronouns can
occur in second position, become clitics, and there is no
change in form.   (There are, no doubt, stress differences between the two however.)

7. They can co-occur with the oblique object to which
they refer and with other nouns or pronouns under conditions

of emphasis, in Spanish and French.

8. Tubatulabal and Comanche also have the most transparent relationship between clitic pronouns and independent
pronouns of the language in the language family with second
position clitic subject pronouns; in the former the independent pronouns are the clitic pronouns plus the prefix in- and
in the latter the independent pronouns are the clitic pronouns plus some emphatic element. It is probably the case
that the more time that separates the independent pronouns
from the clitic pronouns, the more different the two sets
will be. For example, the second person singular independent pronoun in Luiseño is ?om and the clitic pronoun is up.
up is also the third person singular clitic pronoun, a form
which is obviously descended from a demonstrative. It appears then that the third person singular clitic pronoun has
invaded the second person singular. Similar kinds of shifts
are evidenced throughout the language family. Deciding what
to ascribe to phonological reduction and what to temporal separation is difficult, however. ?om and up are certainly no
more different, in some undefined sense, than will not and
its contraction won't; the latter here is supposed to be the
synchronic reduction of the former. (The comparison was
suggested to me by Joan Hooper.)

9. They might be stressless simply because they themselves are obviously not the topic. Stresslessness certainly
accompanies cliticization; clitic forms cannot be stressed.
Compare:

     a.   Them, I like

     b.   *'em, I like.

10. In Steele (1975a), I argued that the second posi-

tion clitics of Luiseño developed from delineating topic and comment. With this paper, I renounce that hypothesis.

11. Examples of the verb prefix pronominal elements of Cupeño, Cahuilla, and Kitanemuk are given below.

CU   čəm=əp čə?-mamayəw
            we=aux CP-help
            'We helped.'   (CUP-J-SC-77)

CA   čem čem-hičiwe
            we CP-are:going
            'We are going.'   (CUP-J-SC-44)

KT   ni-kwara=mat pākwiñiñ
            CP-plaster=aux with:mud
            'I will plaster (cracks) with mud.'
                                (KT-A-PR-18)

These were once prefixed to subordinate verbs, verbs of sentential subject complements embedded under the equivalent of English be; the construction indicated past tense. Possessive prefixes were reanalyzed when the subordinate verb to which they were prefixed lost its subordinate status. The embedding verb disappeared and the suffix on the verb which indicated its subordination came to indicate tense/aspect.

[poss-V-subordinator] V > subject:marker-V-tense/aspect
(See Jacobs, 1975)

Appendix

(1) to (12) list the clitic pronouns and the independent pronouns of each Uto-Aztecan language that has second position
clitic subject pronouns; (13) to (16), the independent pronouns and the proclitic (or prefixed) pronouns of Cora, Huichol, Classical Aztec, and Pochutla. The third person forms
in the independent pronominal systems of Uto-Aztecan are generally, but not always, demonstratives. Demonstratives are,
therefore, included in the lists of independent subject pronouns below.

1.   Comanche Clitic Pronouns

	sg	dl	pl
1.	nɨ?	nɨkwi (excl)	ninɨ
		takwɨ/ (incl)	ta/tamɨɨ
		tah	
2.	ɨnɨ	mɨkwɨ	mɨɨ
3.	ma? (vis)	marɨkwi	marɨɨ
	?u? (invis)	urɨkwi	?urɨɨ
	?i? (close)	irɨkwi	?irɨɨ
	?o? (distant)	orɨkwi	?orɨɨ

Comanche independent pronouns are formed from the clitic pronouns by the addition of some other clitic.

```
nɨ=?u           'It is I.'
CP-demo:clitic  (CM-OS-F-97)
```

2.   So. Paiute Clitic Pronouns

	sg	dl	pl
1.	n·i	ram·i	rangwa (incl)
			nɨm·wi (excl)
2.	?		ngwɨ
3.	anga (vis anim)		am·ɨ
	?...ngwa (invis anim)		?...m·ɨ
	aq·a (vis inanim)		
	?...q·wa (invis inanim)		

Independent Pronouns

	sg	dl	pl
1.	nɨ	tam·i	tangwa (incl)
			nɨm·wi (excl)
2.	im·i		mwɨm·wi
3.	anga (anim indef)		am·ɨ
	manga (anim vis)		mam·ɨ
	inga (anim here)		im·ɨ
	ungwa (anim invis)		um·wɨ
	arɨ, aq·a (inanim indef)		
	marɨ, maq·a (inanim vis)		
	icɨ, ik·a (inanim here)		
	uru, uq·wa (inanim invis)		

3.   Chemehuevi Clitic Pronouns

	sg	dl	pl
1.	nV	raami	rawɨ (incl)
			mɨmi (excl)
2.	ukV/?		wV
3.	inga (anim here)		imɨ
	anga (anim vis)		amɨ
	unga (anim invis)		umɨ
	ika (inanim here)		
	aka (inanim vis)		
	uka (inanim invis)		

Independent Pronouns

	sg	dl	pl
1.	nɨɨ/nɨɨnɨ	tami	tawɨ (incl)
			mimi (excl)
2.	ɨmi		mɨmi
3.	inga (anim here)		imɨ
	manga (anim vis)		mamɨ
	unga (anim invis)		umɨ
	icɨ/ika/i (inanim here)		
	marɨ/maka/ma (inanim vis)		
	urɨ/uka/u (inanim invis)		

4.   Tubatulabal Clitic Pronouns

	sg	dl	pl
1.	g(i)	gil(a) (incl) gila?ang (excl)	(gi)luuc (incl)
2.	b(i)		bu(u)m(u)
3.	∅		da

Independent Pronouns

	sg	dl	pl
1.	nik	inggila (incl) inggila?ang (excl)	inngiluuc
2.	imbi		imbuumu
3.	in		inda

As a comparison of the clitic pronouns and independent
pronouns in (4) will show, Tubatulabal independent subject
pronouns are formed from the clitic pronouns with the prefixation of in-; the first singular form is, however, irregu-
lar.)

5.   Serrano Clitic Pronouns

nɨ	čɨmɨ
çɨ	çɨmɨ
vɨ	mɨ

Independent Pronouns

1.	nɨ?	?ačam
2.	?ɨmi?	?ɨɨm
3.	?ivi(near)	?iim
	pɨta(close)	pɨm
	?ama (far)	?aam

(The Serrano clitic pronouns listed above are extracted
from the subject clitic pronoun/object clitic pronoun combinations. The forms are taken from Langacker (TAK-L-RPE).)

6.   Cupeño Clitic Pronouns

The form of the clitic pronoun in Cupeño differs depending primarily on whether the verb is intransitive or transitive. Both forms are listed below, respectively.

ən	čə
ʔət	məl
pə	məl
nə	cǎmə
ʔə(pə)	məl
pə?	məl

Independent Pronouns

nə?(ə)	čəm(əm)
ʔə?(ə)	ʔəm(əm)
pə?ə(ə)	pəm(əm)

7.   Luiseño Clitic Pronouns

n	ča
up	um
up	pum

Independent Pronouns

noo	čaam
ʔom	ʔomom
po/wunaal	pomom/wunaalum

(The clitic pronouns of Luiseño have slightly different
forms depending on the tense of the sentence. Those given
above are the present tense forms.)

8.   Papago Clitic Pronouns

n	č
p	m
∅	∅

Independent Pronouns

1.   ?aañi   ?aačim

2.   ?aapi   ?aapim

3.   ?iida(near)   ?iidam
     higai(distant)   higam

9.   Tepecano Clitic Pronouns

     n(i)   t(i)
     p(i)   pim
     Ø   m

     Independent Pronouns

     ani   ati
     api   apim
     higa   higam

10. Tarahumara Clitic Pronouns

     ne, ni   ta, ti, ra, tamu
     mu, mi   tu, tumu, emi
     Ø   Ø

     Independent Pronouns

     nehé, nehéri   támu, tami, tamuhé, temuhéri
     muhé, muhéri   tumuhé, tumuhéri
     eči, era   (?)

(Different grammars list different forms for the clitic
pronouns of Tarahumara. All the possibilities are listed
above.)

11. Yaqui Clitic Pronouns

     ne   te, itom
     e, ?en   em, ?eme
     Ø   Ø

Independent Pronouns

1.   ?inepo   ?itepo
2.   ?empo   ?eme?e
3.   ?apo   bempo

(Again, different grammars list different forms for the
clitic pronouns and independent pronouns of Yaqui. All the
possibilities above are from Lindenfeld.)

12.   Cora Clitic Pronouns

nu   tu

pa   šu

pu   mu

Independent Pronouns

1.   (í)nʸáa   (í)tʸan
2.   mwáa   mwán
3.   aí, here   aíɲe
     amɨ there   amɨ̇me
     aɨ́ out of   aɨme
          sight

13.   Cora Proclitic Pronouns

na   ta

pa   sa/ša

Ø   ma

Independent Pronouns
(See (12) above.)

14.   Huichol Proclitic Pronouns

ne   te

pe   ze

Ø   we/me

Independent Pronouns

1. nee   taame
2. ?eekɨɨ   zeeme
3. ?iikɨ near ?iime
   mɨɨkɨ distant mɨɨmɨ
   ?iya general

15. Classical Aztec Proclitic Pronouns

   ni   ti
   ti   an
   ∅   ∅

Independent Pronouns

   ne?waaL   te?waan(tin)
   tc?waaL   ame?waan(tin)
   ye?waaL   ye?waan(tin)

16. Pochutla Proclitic Pronouns (intransitive sentences)

   n   t
   t   ?
   ∅   ∅

Proclitic Pronouns (transitive sentences)

Subject clitic pronouns are part of a subject/object clitic combination. PO-B-DMP gives only the singular forms.

		Object		
		1	2	3
S				
u	1	--	nc	nk
b				
j	2	tič	--	ti
e				
c	3	nič	moc	k
t				

Independent Pronouns

Only the singular forms are given in the source.

    nen
    muen
    na

References

Abbreviations

AASP American Academy of Arts and Sciences, Proceedings

IJAL International Journal of American Linguistics

UCPAAE University of California Publications in American Archaeology and Ethnology

UCPL University of California Publications in Linguistics

Primary Sources

Cupan (CUP)

Jacobs, Roderick A. 1975. Syntactic Change: A Cupan (Uto-Aztecan) Case Study. UCPL 79. Berkeley and Los Angeles: University of California Press. (CUP-J-SC)

Takic (TAK)

Langacker, Ronald W. 1973. 'Reconstruction of Pronominal Elements in Takic'. Manuscript. (TAK-L-RPE)

Classical Aztec (AZ)

Anderson, Arthur J. O. 1973. Rules of the Aztec Language. Salt Lake City: University of Utah Press. Translation of Francisco Xavier Clavigero, Reglas de la Lengua Mexicana. (AZ-A-R)

Dibble, Charles E., and Arthur J. O. Anderson. 1961. Florentine Codex, Book 10--The People. [Translation of Fray Bernardino de Sahagún, General History of the Things of New Spain.] Santa Fe, New Mexico: School of American

Research and University of Utah. Monographs of the
School of American Research, No. 14, Part 11. (AZ-DA-
FC10)

Garibay, K., Ángel María. 1961. Llave del Nahuatl. Mexico
City: Editorial Porrua. (AZ-G-L)

Langacker, Ronald W. 1972. 'Possessives in Classical Nahuatl'. IJAL 38. 173-186. (AZ-L-PCN)

Molina, Fray Alonso de. 1571. Arte de la Lengua Mexicana y
Castellana, facsimile edition 1943. Madrid: Ediciones
Cultura Hispánica. Colección de Incunables Americanos,
Siglo XVI, Vol. 6. (AZ-M-A)

Cahuilla (CA)

Seiler, Hansjakob. 1965. 'Accent and Morphophonemics in Cahuilla and in Uto-Aztecan'. IJAL 31. 50-59. (CA-S-AM)

Seiler, Hansjakob. 1970. Cahuilla Texts with an Introduction.
The Hague: Mouton. Indiana University Publications, Language Science Monographs, 6. (CA-S-T)

Chemehuevi (CH)

Press, Margaret L. 1974. A Grammar of Chemehuevi. Los Angeles: University of California doctoral dissertation.
(CH-P-G)

Comanche (CM)

Osborn, Henry, and William A. Smalley. 1949. 'Formulae for
Comanche Stem and Word Formation'. IJAL 15. 93-99. (CM-
OS-F)

Cora (CR)

Gomez, Ancieto M. 1935. 'Estudies Gramaticales de la Lengua

Cora que se Labla en el Territorio de Tepic'. Investigaciones Linguistica III. 79-142. (CR-G-EG)

Preuss, Konrad Theodor. 1912. Die Nayarit-Expedition, Text-
aufnamen und Beobachtungen unter Mexicanischen Indian-
ern, Vol. 1. Leipzig. (CR-P-NE)

Preuss, Konrad Theodor. 1932. 'Grammatik der Cora-Sprache'.
IJAL 8. 81-102. (CR-P-W)

Cupeño (CU)

Hill, Jane H. 1966. A Grammar of the Cupeño Language. Los
Angeles: UCLA doctoral dissertation. (CU-H-G)

Hopi (HO)

Jeanne, LaVerne Masayesva. 1974. Hopi Data. Informal
Notes. (HO-J-IN)

Whorf, B. L. 1946. 'The Hopi Language, Toreva Dialect', in
Harry Hoijer et al. (eds.), Linguistic Structures of
Native America, pp. 158-183. New York: Viking Fund
Publications in Anthropology, 6. (HO-W-TD)

Huichol (HU)

Grimes, Joseph E. 1964. Huichol Syntax. The Hague: Mouton.
janua linguarum series practica, 11. (HU-G-S)

Kitanemuk (KT)

Anderton, Alice. 1975. 'A Grammatical Sketch of Kitanemuk'.
Informal Notes. (KT-A-GS)

Anderton, Alice. 1974. 'A Progress Report on Research into
Kitanemuk'. Manuscript. (KT-A-PR)

Luiseño (LS)

Steele, Susan. 1970-6. Luiseno Field Notes. (LS-S-FN)

Mono (MO)

Lamb, Sydney M. 1958. Mono Grammar. Berkeley: University
of California doctoral dissertation. (MO-L-G)

Northern Paiute (NP)

Liljeblad, Sven. 1967. Northern Paiute Manual. Course notes,
University of Nevada, 1966-67. (NP-L-M)

Nichols, Michael J. P. 1974. Northern Paiute Historical
Grammar. Berkeley: University of California doctoral
dissertation. (NP-N-HG)

Papago (PA)

Hale, Kenneth. 1974. Papago Data. Informal Notes. (PA-H-IN)

Mason, J. Alden. 1950. The Language of the Papago of Arizona. Philadelphia: University of Pennsylvania Museum
Monographs. (PA-M-LPA)

Saxton, Dean and Lucille. 1969. Dictionary, Papago & Pima
to English, English to Papago & Pima. Tucson: University
of Arizona Pres. (P-SS-D)

Pochutla (PO)

Boas, Franz. 1917. 'El Dialecto Mexicano de Pochutla, Oaxa-
ca'. IJAL 1. 9-44. (PO-B-DMP)

Shoshone (SH)

Daley, Jon P. 1970. Shoshone Phonology and Morphological
Sketch. Pocatello: Idaho State University master's
thesis. (SH-D-PM)

Miller, Wick. 1975. 'A Sketch of Shoshoni Grammar (Gosiute Dialect)'. Manuscript (to appear in Handbook of American Indians, Vol. XV). (SH-M-S)

Southern Paiute (SP)

Sapir, Edward. 1930. 'Southern Paiute, A Shoshonean Language'. AAASP 65. 1-296. (SP-S-G)

Sapir, Edward. 1930. 'Texts of the Kaibab Paiutes and Uintah Utes'. AAASP 65. 297-535. (SP-S-T)

Sapir, Edward. 1931. 'Southern Paiute Dictionary'. AAASP 65. 537-729. (SP-S-D)

Serrano (SR)

Crook, Donald. 1975. 'Complements and Adverbial Clauses in Serrano'. Manuscript. (SR-C-CAC)

Hill, Kenneth C. 1967. A Grammar of the Serrano Language. Los Angeles: UCLA doctoral dissertation. (SR-H-G)

Tarahumara (TR)

Brambila, David, S. J. 1953. Gramatica Raramuri. Mexico: Editorial Buena Prensa. (TR-B-G)

Llaguno, Jose A. 1970. El Tarahumara sin Esfuerzo. (in collaboration with David Brambila and Ernesto Uranga.) Manuscript. (TR-L-SE)

Tepecano (TE)

Mason, J. Alden. 1916. 'Tepecano, A Piman Language of Western Mexico', Annals of the New York Academy of Science 25. 309-416. (TE-M-PL)

Tubatulabal (TU)

Voegelin, C. F. 1935. 'Tubatulabal Grammar'. UCPAAE 34. 55-189. (TU-V-G)

Voegelin, C. F. 1935. 'Tubatulabal Texts'. UCPAAE 34. 191-246. (TU-V-T)

Voegelin, C. F. 1958. 'Working Dictionary of Tubatulabal'. IJAL 24. 221-228. (TU-V-WD)

Yaqui (YA)

Johnson, Jean B. 1962. El Idioma Yaqui. Mexico City: Instituto Nacional de Antropologia e Historia, Departamento de Investigaciones Antropologicas, Publicaciones 10. (YA-J-I)

Lindenfeld, Jacqueline. 1969. A Transformational Grammar of Yaqui. Los Angeles: UCLA doctoral dissertation. (YA-L-TG)

Lindenfeld, Jacqueline. 1973. Yaqui Syntax. Berkeley and Los Angeles: University of California Press. UCPL 76. (YA-L-S)

Mason, J. Alden. 1923. 'A Preliminary Sketch of the Yaqui Language'. UCPAAE 20. 195-212. (YA-M-PS)

de Velasco, J. B. 1737. Arte de la Lengua Cahita. (Edited and Reprinted by Eustaquio Buelna. 1890. Mexico.) (YA-V-A)

Secondary Sources

Boomer, D. S. 1968. 'Hesitation and Grammatical Encoding'. Language, R. C. Oldfield and J. C. Marshall, eds. 159-170. Baltimore: Penguin Books.

Emonds, Joseph. 1969. Root and Structure Preserving Trans-
    formations. Cambridge: MIT doctoral dissertation.

Givón, Talmy. 1971. 'Historical Syntax and Synchronic Morph-
    ology: An Archaeologists' Field Trip'. CLS7. 394-415.

Hale, Kenneth. 1973. 'Subject Marking in Walbiri'. A Fest-
    schrift for Morris Halle, Stephen Anderson and Paul Kip-
    arsky, eds. 308-344. Cambridge: MIT Press.

Kayne, Richard. 1975. French Syntax: The Transformational
    Cycle. Cambridge: MIT Press.

Perlmutter, David. 1971. Deep and Surface Structure Con-
    straints in Syntax. New York: Holt.

Steele, Susan. 1975a. 'On the Count of One'. Manuscript.

Steele, Susan. 1975b. 'On Some Factors that Affect and
    Effect Word Order'. Word Order and Word Order Change.
    Charles Li, ed. 199-268. Austin: University of Texas
    Press.

Woodbury, Hanni. 1975. 'Onondaga Noun Incorporation: Some
    Notes on the Interdependence of Syntax and Semantics'.
    IJAL 41. 10-20.

VI Multiple Analyses

14 Multiple Analyses

Jorge Hankamer

0. Introduction

The purpose of this paper is to expose, examine, and reject a particular assumption about the nature of linguistic knowledge, or "competence". That knowledge means, as usual, whatever principles enable the speaker of a language to determine the sound-meaning correspondences of the language and use it as a means of communication.

It has been a fundamental and, so far as I know, unquestioned methodological assumption in the theory and practice of syntactic investigation that for a given body of data there is one correct analysis (which may, of course, have several notational variants), and that our job is to find that analysis. In this paper I will present a number of cases where, I claim, no such single analysis can be found, or rather, any one of two or more distinct analyses might be proposed, but each of them leaves some subpart of the facts unexplained which another analysis does explain. In the face of such cases syntactic investigators have always been baffled, for our methodological assumption (and tacitly our underlying theory of the nature of linguistic knowledge) tells us that we <u>must</u> choose between two competing analyses, unless they are notational variants of each other. I suggest that in view of facts such as those I am going to present, we must give up the assumption that two or more conflicting analyses cannot be simultaneously correct for a given phenomenon.

   If we are forced to this conclusion, as I hope to demonstrate, we must reexamine our fundamental assumptions about
the knowledge that a native speaker must have internalized a-
bout his language. The classical assumption is actually a very
strong claim about the nature of this knowledge, and about
the properties of the learning mechanism that allow a speaker
to acquire it. Linguists have long marvelled at the apparent
ability of a child to acquire the grammar of his language in
so short a time and on the basis of such incomplete and confusing data. I suggest that the child does not have such a putative ability at all. In the face of confusing and conflicting data, I believe he constructs conflicting analyses, and
does not necessarily ever choose between them. There are, of
course, certain universal constraints on the analyses he can
construct; but I suggest that in the quite frequent cases
where the analysis, even within these constraints, is under-
determined by the available data, the mind of the speaker does
not, at least not always, choose one at random (or by any other choice procedure either). The classical assumption about
the uniqueness of syntactic analyses in effect assumes that
he does.

1. The Cases
1.0 The cases to be presented in this section constitute only
a small sample of those available. As it would be impossible
to give in full the arguments for so many analyses in a paper
of this scope, in each case I will present merely a sketch of
the arguments, indicating specifically the facts which require
the adoption of a multiple analysis; in those cases where the
arguments have been published in any form, the presentation

here will be correspondingly more elliptical.

1.1 The Negative Imperative Construction in English

The double analysis presented here is based on the work of Ava-Robin Cohen (1976). She observes that the negative imperative construction exemplified in (1) appears at first glance to be the product of an inversion rule, deriving it from (2). This is the analysis assumed by Emonds (1970).

(1) Don't you blow that thing any more.

(2) You don't blow that thing any more.

This analysis accounts for several properties of the construction in terms of an inversion operation, a type of process which we know to be necessary for many syntactic constructions in English and other languages. It explains straightforwardly, for example, the ungrammaticality of (3), where don't appears in two places:

(3) *Don't you don't blow that thing when I tell you to.

And it accounts, of course, for the shape of the first word, which is derivable straightforwardly by do-support and contraction with the negative before inversion.

There are, however, properties of this construction which are not accounted for under the inversion analysis. One is the fact that inversion in positive imperatives is impossible:

(4) *Do you blow your horn when you see the enemy.

Another is the fact that even in negative imperatives, inversion without contraction is impossible:

(5) *Do you not blow that thing.

Compare the quite different behavior of yes-no questions,

where an inversion analysis is established:

(6)   Don't you have a car?

(7)   Do you have a car?

(8)   Do you not have a car?

Cohen proposes an analysis of this construction which posits the existence of a special negative imperative particle with the shape of don't, which is generated with that shape and in sentence-initial position; in this analysis no inversion is assumed. The imperative particle analysis accounts for the ungrammaticality of (4) and (5) straightforwardly; since no inversion rule is assumed to be defined on imperative constructions, there is no reason to expect such sentences to be derived.

The analysis does not, on the other hand, explain the ungrammaticality of (3). Note that it is not simply that there can be no double negation in imperatives:

(9)   Don't you not go into the water when you're told to, or you'll get a bash on the head.

A doubly negated sentence like (9) is not at all bad, for many speakers at least; a double don't sentence like (3) is absolute garbage. The inversion analysis would account for these facts, since under that analysis the normal operation of do-support will provide only one do even if there are two not's. It would also account for the shape of the don't, which the particle analysis does not.

Cohen provides a detailed discussion of the properties of this construction, which I will not attempt to reproduce here. What is of interest is that the construction exhibits properties which can be accounted for under one analysis but not under the other, and at the same time exhibits other properties which can be accounted for under the second analysis but not under the first. It is clear that neither of the two analyses under consideration, by itself, is adequate.

There is always the possibility (and under the classical assumptions there is no other) that neither of these analyses is correct because there is some third, as yet undiscovered analysis which accounts for everything about the construction in a unified manner; according to the classical methodological assumptions we have to go and seek this third analysis. I suggest that an alternative which must be considered is that the classical assumption is wrong, and the right way to account for the properties of the negative imperative construction is to treat it according to both of the apparently conflicting analyses simultaneously.

I am suggesting, in effect, that the native speaker of English, or rather that part of his mind which is concerned with such matters, regards the don't you negative imperatives as related by inversion to the corresponding positive imperatives, and at the same time regards the word don't in such constructions as an invariant negative imperative particle. If this is accepted, it is no wonder that the construction exhibits properties attributable to both analyses.

This suggestion immediately raises a multitude of questions regarding the interaction of multiple analyses with each other and with other processes in a grammar. Obviously I will not be able even to satisfactorily discuss, much less examine closely or attempt to provide answers for, the range of questions which emerge instantly as soon as such a possibility is contemplated; especially in a paper of this scope, which must perforce be intended more as suggestive and provocative than conclusive. In the present case I will note only that the construction would seem to be correctly described, and all of its known properties accounted for, if we say that every sentence in it has two derivations (one through inversion and one by way of base generation of a negative particle in initial position) and in order to be grammatical, a negative don't-initial imperative sentence must be derivable both ways. Thus the interaction of the two analyses is expressible in terms of a transderivational condition.

I will term a multiple analysis of this type, where the properties of a construction are determined by two analyses operating in conjunction, conjunctive multiple analysis; we shall see in the next case that there exist multiple analyses in which the two analyses interact disjunctively as well.

1.2 Reduced WH Questions

A very clear example of disjunctive multiple analysis is that of reduced direct questions. A detailed and thorough study of the properties of such questions is presented in Bechhofer (1976).

(10) I just hired somebody to walk my dog.
      -- Oh yeah? Who?

Bechhofer shows that reduced questions like Who? in (10) are ambiguously derived, one derivation involving Sluicing (cf. Ross, 1969) and the other involving Stripping (cf. Hankamer, 1971). Each of these rules is independently motivated, and each has quite distinct and fairly well-established properties (see Bechhofer, 1976 and Hankamer, 1971 for discussion). The

motivation for the double analysis, as in the case above, is
that while the two analyses have exactly the same consequences
for the mass of cases, there are cases which can be accounted
for only under a Sluicing analysis, and at the same time there
are other cases which can be accounted for only under a Stripping analysis.

For example, a reduced question containing a stranded
preposition betrays the application of WH-movement and subsequent Sluicing:

(11)   Slinky Sue just walked in.
       --Oh yeah? Who with?

A question like (11) can be derived under a Sluicing analysis
because that analysis involves WH-movement fronting the WH
constituent and subsequent deletion of the WH-clause except
for the WH and a stranded preposition; it is not derivable
under a Stripping analysis because Stripping can be shown in
general not to leave a nonconstituent survivor.

Given this, one might propose to maintain a unique analysis by assuming that all direct reduced questions are derived
unambiguously by Sluicing. This turns out to be impossible,
however, because there are reduced WH questions in which the
survivor of the reduction is something which cannot have been
fronted by WH movement, and consequently cannot be a survivor
of Sluicing:

(12)   Dick has a picture of [inaudible] on his desk.
       -- A picture of who?

NP's such as a picture of do not pied-pipe under question
movement; furthermore, Bechhofer points out that when a fronted WH pronoun is accompanied by a pied-piped preposition, it

cannot appear as <u>who</u> but must take the objective form <u>whom</u>.
For these reasons, reduced questions like (12) cannot be derived under a Sluicing analysis, but they can be derived by
Stripping. The reader should consult Bechhofer's paper for
the full argument, which is only partially represented here.

In this case, the situation seems to be that whereas the
great mass of reduced questions are ambiguously derived,
there are some grammatical questions which are derivable only
under a Sluicing analysis, and other grammatical questions
which are derivable only under a Stripping analysis. Note the
difference between the interaction of the analyses in this
case as opposed to the previous one: there neither analysis
alone was restrictive enough, and I proposed that compliance
with both was required to account for all the ungrammatical
sentences; here neither analysis alone is capable of accounting for the existence of all the grammatical sentences, so it
is necessary to say that compliance with either is insuffi-
cient for a sentence to be grammatical.

There are many clear examples of disjunctive multiple
analyses of this kind, whcih result from partial overlap in
the classes of sentences derived by distinct grammatical processes. I will not present any more here, but two which have
been discussed explicitly as multiple analyses and demonstrated convincingly, I believe, to be such, are the reduced comparative construction <u>than NP</u> in English (Hankamer, 1973) and
the WH-Cleft construction (Hankamer, 1974).

1.3 Two further examples of Conjunctive Multiple Analysis

Examples of conjunctive multiple analysis are more difficult to establish, and so far as I know no cases are recog-

nized as such in previous literature. Nevertheless, I believe
that several cases of conjunctive multiple analysis have been
discussed in the literature, and recognized as troublesome
for the standard theory of transformational grammer. I will
not discuss these cases in any detail, but I will cite two in
particular which would cease to be mysterious and troublesome
under a theory which allows conjunctive multiple analysis.

The first is the infinitival relative construction in
English, exhibited in (13):

(13)   I have a stool for you to sit on.

Berman (1974) argues that the for-phrase (for you in this example) is underlyingly a matrix phrase, and that the subject
of the infinitival clause is deleted by Equi under identity
with this matrix for-phrase. She also argues, however, that in
surface structure the for-phrase is in fact the complementizer-
plus-subject of the lower clause. In order to account for the
full range of facts within the confines of standard theory,
she has to posit a transformation lowering the matrix for-
phrase into the infinitival clause after deletion of the subject there, so that the originally matrix for- phrase, after
controlling deletion of the embedded subject, then moves down
and in superficial structure serves as the subject of the infinitival clause. This derivation is quite bizarre (in the
sense that similar operations have never been found to be necessary elsewhere) and calls for an explanation.

The mystery disappears, however, if we adopt a general
theory which allows multiple analyses. The fact which has to
be accounted for is that the speaker of English regards the
for-phrase as a matrix dative phrase and at the same time re-

gards it as representing the subject of the embedded infinitival clause (rather, he regards the NP in it as representing
the subject of the infinitival clause; the for in this case
is regarded as a complementizer). All this is accounted for
straightforwardly if we say that such constructions have both
analyses at once (in the conjunctive sense); any process which
requires that the for-phrase be part of the matrix clause will
treat it as such, and any process which requires that the for-
phrase be treated as the embedded complementizer and subject
will find it analyzed as required.

A more complex case is that of the temporal adverbial
construction in Turkish, discussed in Hankamer (1972), which
for some speakers has properties indicating that it should
have an analysis as a relative clause construction, while at
the same time having properties appropriate only to a class
of adverbial constructions. In that paper I argued that the
properties of the construction could only be accounted for if
it were given basically an analysis as a relative clause construction, and allowed to acquire its non-relative clause
properties by analogy with other adverbial constructions in
the language. In order to state such analogical relations in
the grammar of Turkish, it would be necessary to allow rules
with transderivational reference.

Briefly, the problem is that when an adverbial relative
clause like

(14)   Hasan -in gel-diğ -i   zaman
        Hasan-GEN come-PRT-POSS time
        'when Hasan came'

is used with inceptive force, the genitive suffix does not
appear on the subject as generally required in this type of

relative construction, so that in such cases we find

(15)   Hasan gel-diğ-i zaman
        'when Hasan came'

Here the rule of case-marking treats such constructions not
as relative clause constructions but as parallel to the syn-
onymous inceptive adverbial constructions which do not take
genitive case marking on their subjects:

(16)   Hasan gel -ince
        Hasan come-ADV
        'when Hasan came'

    Once again the facts that have to be accounted for are
that the speakers of the language simultaneously regard the
constructions in question as relative clause constructions,
thus accounting for their relative-clause properties, and as
adverbial constructions of a type not generally produced by
the same mechanism as relative clauses, thus accounting for
their strictly adverbial-clause properties. These facts can
be accounted for under a theory of multiple analysis by assigning the constructions in question two analyses at once; in
this case, however, it must be stipulated that the case-marking of the subject of the clause is controlled according to
the requirements of the adverbial analysis and not of the relative analysis.

    Here is not the place to develop these ideas in full,
but it seems that the theory of multiple analyses provides a
way to develop at last a theory of analogy which will have
some restrictive force. An initially attractive proposal would
be that all observed cases of syntactic "analogy" are describ-
able in terms of conjunctive multiple analysis, perhaps holding up to or after only a certain point in the derivation.

This would clearly allow us to maintain a theory which prohibits arbitrary transderivational reference, while still allowing a lucid treatment of the analogical phenomena which have been observed and discussed in recent syntactic literature. Other examples of such cases, in addition to the one discussed here, are the nominalization constructions in Ewe discussed in Clements (1975) and the object-agreement phenomenon in Spanish (Otero, 1972, Aissen, 1973).

2.   Relational and Nonrelational Analyses

The position I am assuming is that when the universal constraints on linguistic structure permit two analyses of a given construction, no matter how they differ, it may be the case that the construction simultaneously has both analyses. In this section I will discuss a case which is of particular theoretical interest because it involves conflict between an analysis formulated in strictly positional terms and an analysis formulated in relational terms (cf. Postal and Perlmutter (forthcoming) and references cited there).

The construction is the permutation known as locational-adverb preposing with concomitant subject-verb inversion:

(17)   Into the path of the truck darted a zebra.

(18)   Under the chestnut tree stands an old woodshed.

These have been regarded (cf. Emonds, 1970) as simple shifts in word order. Recently Postal (1976) argues that the subject is not only shifted to post-verbal position but demoted from subjecthood by There Insertion (or a related process). Postal's proposal thus relates sentences like (17)-(18) to the corresponding There-Insertion versions:

(19)   Into the path of the truck there darted a zebra.

(20)   Under the chestnut tree there stands an old tool-
        shed.

Postal provides several arguments for this analysis.

The proposed analysis seems to be contradicted, however,
by the fact that such permuted sentences are grammatical with
definite subject NP's as well:

(21)   Into the path of the truck darted the zebra.

But sentences of this type should not be derivable under
Postal's analysis, because the corresponding There-Insertion
version is ungrammatical:

(22)   *Into the path of the truck there darted the zebra.

Postal has no explanation for this discrepancy.

I argue that (21) is derived by a permutation process
distinct from the relational process which Postal posits for
(17); and that (17) is in fact ambiguously derived, on the
one hand by a relational demotion process and on the other
by a simple permutation which so far as I can tell affects
only linear order. The construction thus exhibits a case of
disjunctive multiple analysis, with one analysis relational
and the other non-relational.

The evidence for this is the following: it is fairly well
established that in cases where a relational demotion has
taken place, removing the subject of a sentence, certain adverbial constituents can, at least apparently, undergo raising operations into higher clauses just as the subject
would have done if it were present. Such cases are discussed
in Breckenridge (1975), Andrews (1975), and Thrainsson (1976).

The same behavior is evident in the construction under discussion here, if the former subject is indefinite:

(23)   Into the path of the truck seemed to dart a zebra.

(24)   Under the chestnut tree appears to have stood an old toolshed.

When the subject is definite, however, such migration of adverbial elements does not take place:

(25)   *Into the path of the truck seemed to dart the zebra.

(26)   *Under the chestnut tree appears to have stood the old toolshed.

These facts can all be accounted for if it is assumed that there is a subject-demotion process (There-Insertion or a related process) which affects only sentences with an indefinite subject, and that when this process has applied an adverbial constituent of the sentence can appear in the place where a raised subject would be in complex examples like (23)-(24); and that there is a distinct permutation process which is insensitive to the definiteness or indefiniteness of the subject, and that this process derives (21) without occasioning the subject-demotion which allows nonsubject adverbial constituents to be raised.

The discussion presented here is regrettably but necessarily sketchy, and is intended to be more suggestive than conclusive. I believe, nevertheless, that the case cited is representative of a large class of multiple analyses in which relational and nonrelational analyses coexist for a given construction, and that the existence of such multiple analyses is instrumental in the acquisition of relational rules by a language.

Consider the fact referred to above, that in cases where a subject has been demoted some non-subject (even a non-NP) can apparently undergo Raising:

(27)   Under the chestnut tree appears to have stood an old toolshed.

(28)   In this forest are believed to have been buried many martyrs of the revolt against the bad king.

One might attempt to avoid the conclusion that the adverbial phrases in these examples have undergone Raising by assuming that the inversion process has simply applied to the complex structure after raising of the original subject. This is contradicted, however, by the fact (noted by Emonds, 1970) that in general this inversion takes place only about simple verbs, and by the fact noted above that the inversion is sensitive to the indefiniteness of the subject just in case a Raising structure is involved.

My proposal is that the adverbial phrases in such constructions actually undergo Raising (whether this means that they are subjects is an open, and perhaps merely terminological, question). If this is correct, we have to ask why something that is originally not a subject should be able to undergo a process which is normally restricted to subjects, just in case there is no genuine subject present in the sentence. My conjecture is that this phenomenon results from the partly positional nature of subjects, and that the raised constituents in these cases get to undergo raising just because they happen to get into subject position (i.e. immediate pre-verbal position) by way of the adverbial-fronting rule which preserves the verb-medial word order.

In the same way, we can regard the <u>there</u> of There Insertion, which now behaves like a subject in many respects (particularly with regard to relational rules like Raising) as
historically the relic of a noncyclic, nonrelational adverb-
preposing rule (with concomitant subject inversion), owing
its present status as a dummy subject to a reanalysis of the
linear adverb-preposing rule as a relational rule, largely as
a result of its successfully masquerading as a subject in
many cases.

I will cite as a final case in support of this proposal
the impersonal Object-Raising construction in German discussed in Breckenridge (1975). Ordinary Object-Raising is exemplified in (29); we also find (30):

(29)   Elefanten sind mit Doppeldeckern schwer zu
         'Elephants are with biplanes   hard to

              transportieren.
              transport.'

(30)   Nach Berlin wird leicht zu fliegen sein.
         'To Berlin will easy   to fly   be.'

In (29) an object has been raised to become the subject of
the predicate <u>schwer</u>, exactly as in the English Tough-Move-
ment construction. In general, only direct objects undergo
this rule. In (30), however, it looks like a non-object (in
fact, a non-NP) has been raised in the same fashion. Breckenridge argues that the PP <u>nach Berlin</u> in a sentence like (30)
is not in fact a derived subject, but merely one of many constituents which can be fronted to sentence-initial position
by a general preposing rule (which has nothing to do with
grammatical relations). Her proposal, which seems in general
to be convincingly established, is that there is no derived

subject in such constructions, the raising operation having applied vacuously. The only thing she cannot explain is that in such an impersonal object-raising construction, the fronting of some non-subject constituent is <u>obligatory</u>:

(31) *Wird leicht nach Berlin zu fliegen sein.

One might try to make the verb-second constraint account for this, but that will not do because even the question is bad:

(32) *Wird leicht nach Berlin zu fliegen sein?

It is also impossible to insert the impersonal <u>es</u> in these constructions:

(33) *Es wird leicht nach Berlin zu fliegen sein.

The arguments that the constituents in the initial position of these sentences are not subjects are convincing; on the other hand, the observed odd constraint would be unnecessary if in fact the constituent that ends up in initial position had been raised there. Again the facts seem to indicate that a normally relation-sensitive Raising rule has taken, for lack of anything better, a non-object in the underlying structure and moved it into the position of a subject in the derived structure, without actually making it into a derived subject. In other words, the rule in these cases operates as if it were a rule effecting only a reordering of the affected constituents.

Cases like these are of particular interest because they indicate that there is perhaps not the strict differentiation between relational and positional rules assumed in current versions of relational grammar, but rather that a given rule may have both aspects. If this is true, it will be easier to see how languages can acquire particular relational rules where they did not have them before. All that we need to assume is that the learner and user of a language has at his disposal both relational and positional ways of analyzing grammatical constructions, which seems at present to be clearly true; and that a given construction may have multiple analyses involving one positional analysis and one relational analysis.

3. Consequences

The consequences of adopting a theory of multiple analyses are rather far-reaching:

a. In the practice of syntactic investigation, we have a potentially much more complex task than we thought. On the other hand, there is a whole class of questions which we have been struggling in vain to answer which in fact we don't have to answer at all.

b. In syntactic argumentation, it will no longer count as an argument against a particular analysis that there are facts which it leaves unexplained, even if there exists an alternative analysis which explains those facts perfectly. This result will probably cause many linguists, rightly concerned for the preservation of our already pitiful supply of valid means of argumentation, to recoil in horror. Nevertheless, you cannot make a mode of argumentation valid by refusing to contemplate the possibility that the assumptions on which it rests are unsupportable.

c. In the general theory, in giving up a strong

(albeit rather covert) claim about the fundamental nature of linguistic knowledge, we reduce the explanatory power of our theory from nothing to less than nothing, it seems. The final comment under (b) is also applicable here.

d. On the other hand, we have a new claim about the psychological reality of linguistic analyses, and about the nature of linguistic knowledge, which may allow us to make sense of such phenomena as variation within an idiolect (any practicing syntactician who has done informant work on any complicated construction can attest that this exists), much of the most baffling dialect variation, the squishiness of many syntactic phenomena, and (perhaps most fundamentally) our general failure to establish some of the most basic features of syntactic structure.

e. Finally, the conclusion drawn here has immediate and far-reaching consequences for the theory of syntactic change. It has these consequences partly by virtue of the different conception it imposes on the nature of what changes, and partly by virtue of the new possibilities it raises for mechanisms of change.

I suggest that one of the most instrumental factors in syntactic change is the existence of multiple analyses in the grammars even of adult speakers of any language. The existence of such multiple analyses poses for the child learning the language an even more difficult task than

has previously been thought, and his chance of
reproducing exactly the grammar of his parents
or peers is negligibly small. The judgments and
behaviors associated with the different grammars
will differ only in a few fringe areas of the
construction, the core of judgments being sub-
stantially the same. Unfortunately for syntacticians, it is just in those fringe areas where we
look for evidence to decide between conflicting
theories; I suggest that we now have an explanation for why we are so frequently stymied, finding nothing there but uncertain and conflicting
judgments. There are cases where people disagree
firmly on the crucial examples, and cases where
a single speaker cannot agree with himself. I
suggest that this is exactly what is to be expected; since the evidence which would distinguish between two analyses for a given case is
often to be found only in marginal or infrequent
constructions, it is likely to happen that a
child will never encounter or assimilate the data which would decide between them. In at least
some of these cases he ends up having made no
choice at all, and is consequently baffled when
a linguist asks him for a judgment which depends
on having made the choice.

How this situation provides a mechanism
for syntactic change is obvious, and need not be
elaborated further at this point. With regard to
the results of such change, I will cite just

two examples of very generally observable phenomena which have always been baffling from the
point of view of the classical theory, but which
make perfect sense in a framework of multiple a-
nalyses. First, the striking and frequently observed fact that syntactic "dialect" variation
often fails to correlate with any discernible
geographic or sociological parameters. In this
it is entirely unlike phonological and lexical
variation. Second, the fact that we frequently
find cases of closely related dialects with formally very different analyses of the same construction. The question of the mechanism of syntactic reanalysis -- how does a language get
from one analysis of a given construction to a
quite different one? -- is answered almost directly once we grant that the language may have
both analyses at once.

It is also evident that the argument, which
has appeared from time to time in historical syntax, that because a language at a given stage
can be shown to have had such and such an analysis for a given construction, we should accept
the same or a similar analysis for the construction at a later stage, can be rejected.

Conclusion

In all of the cases cited, I argue that the following
situation obtains: there is a body of data, representing what
we may call a "construction" in the language. For a substantial subclass of the data (in some cases almost all of it)

there are two formally quite different analyses which account
equally well for the facts. There exist, however, facts in
the data left unaccounted for by each of the analyses but
accounted for by the other. The general situation may be represented as follows:

(34)

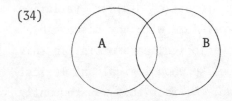

The leftmost circle represents the portion of the data accounted for by analysis A; the rightmost circle represents
that portion accounted for by analysis B. The whole body of
data is the union of that accounted for by A and that accounted for by B (we should be so lucky).

The area of overlap may be greater or smaller, as represented below:

(35)   (36)

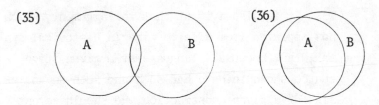

Everybody is aware of the existence of cases like (35),
where there is overlap between two analyses only in a restricted subclass of the cases; these are annoying, but have
never been thought much of, except that once in a while somebody worries about the fact that some sentences are getting
two derivations instead of one, without being semantically
ambiguous. Given the existence of cases like (35), it should

hardly be surprising that there exist cases like (36) as well.
I think I have demonstrated that such cases are far from rare.

Finally, given the fairly common occurrence of cases
like (36), I see no reason why we should not assume that there
are cases like

(37)

References

Aissen, J. (1973) "Shifty Objects in Spanish", CLS 9.

Andrews, A. (1975) "On the VP-Complement in Icelandic",
    paper delivered at the Sixth annual meeting of the North
    Eastern Linguistic Society, Montreal.

Bechhofer, R. (1976) "Reduction Processes in WH-Questions"
    to appear in J. Hankamer & J. Aissen, Eds., Harvard
    Studies in Syntax and Semantics, vol. II. (Harvard Uni-
    versity)

Berman, A. (1974) "Infinitival Relative Constructions", CLS
    10.

Breckenridge, J. (1975) "Rules Which Nothing Undergoes: A
    Study of Impersonal Passive and Object Raising Construc-
    tions in German" unpublished undergraduate thesis, Har-
    vard University.

Clements, G. (1975) "Analogical Reanalysis in Syntax: The
    Case of Ewe Tree-Grafting" Linguistic Inquiry 6.1

Cohen, A-R. (1976) "Don't You Dare" unpublished paper, Har-
    vard.

Emonds, J. (1970) Root and Structure-Preserving Transforma-
    tions unpublished doctoral dissertation, MIT. Ditto, Indi-
    ana University Linguistics Club.

Hankamer, J. (1971) Constraints on Deletion in Syntax unpub-
    lished doctoral dissertation, Yale University.

_____ (1972) "Analogical Rules in Syntax" CLS 8.

_____(1973) "Why There are Two than's in English" CLS 9.

_____ (1974) "On the Noncyclic Nature of WH-Clefting" CLS 10.

Otero, C. (1972) "Acceptable Ungrammatical Sentences in Spanish" Linguistic Inquiry 3.2

Postal, P. (1976) "About a 'Nonargument' for Raising" unpublished paper, IBM.

_____, and D. Perlmutter (forthcoming) Relational Grammar

Ross, J. (1969) "Guess Who" CLS 5.

Thrainsson, H. (1976) "Remarkable Subjects in Icelandic" unpublished paper, Harvard University.

Author Index

A

Abramowitz, D., 312

Acebas, B., 486

Aissen, J., 594

Allen, W.S., 330

Alpler, B., 449, 478

Andersen, H., 13, 49, 142, 170, 172, 173, 301

Anderson, L., 478

Andrews, A., 595

Anderson, S., 320, 321, 328, 350, 351

Anttila, R., 146, 172

Applegate, R., 257

Ard, J., 240, 296

B

Bauman, J., 438

Bailey, T., 344

Barbeau, C. M., 498

Beaglehole, E. & P., 20, 48, 52

Bean, M., 296, 312

Bechhofer, R., 588-591

Beeler, M., 257

Benveniste, E., 337, 338

Berman, A., 592

Berman, R., 427-429, 431, 438

Bickerton, D., 20, 198, 243

Blin-Lagarde, P., 498

Bloch, J., 331, 333

Bokarev, A., 351

Bonvillain, N., 498, 514

Brathwaite, K., 347-349, 351

Bolinger, D., 181, 183, 187

Breckenridge, J., 595, 598

Brown, N., 477

Butorin, D., 174

C

Canale, M., 296

Casad, E., 544, 557, 558, 560

Catford, 374

Chafe, W.L., 439, 493, 498, 499, 507, 508

Chikobava, A.S., 347

Chung, S., 9, 10, 17, 24, 28, 43, 47, 50-52, 150, 172, 285, 325-327, 329, 448, 459, 465, 466, 470, 472-474, 478, 480, 482, 486

Clark, D.R., 9

Clark, T., 334

Clements, G., 594

Cohen, A-R., 585, 586

Comrie, B., 286

Conklin, H., 395

Coseriu, E., 142

Couro, L., 481

Couro, T., 265, 448, 481

Crawford, J., 448

Creiter, C., 241

Crook, D., 285, 478, 560

D

de Velasco, J., 553

Devens, M., 438

Dixon, R., 321, 322, 329, 355,
    369, 374, 382, 383, 386,
    393, 395, 399

Dyen, I., 43, 48, 51

E

Emonds, J., 50, 320, 585, 594,
    597

F

Faltz, A., 430, 431, 438

Feeling, D., 499

Fromm, H., 153

G

George, L., 375

Givón, T., 181-189, 192, 194,
    205, 211, 238, 240, 284,
    292, 310, 311, 438, 495, 562

Glover, B., 438, 442

Golab, Z., 375

Gorbet, L., 265, 447, 478, 479,
    485

Gordon, A., 438

Green, G., 170

Greenberg, J., 255, 286

Grierson, G., 343

Grossman, R., 137

Grosu, A., 427, 429, 431

H

Hadad, F., 442

Haiman, J., 292, 293, 311,
    313

Hakulinen, A., 146, 154, 171

Hakulinen, L., 153

Hale, K., 9, 286, 318, 319,
    354, 383, 394, 400, 548

Halpern, A., 276, 280, 447,
    474, 478, 482, 487

Hankamer, J., 45, 50, 172,
    588, 590, 592

Harris, A., 332

Haas, M., 274, 285

Hausenblaus, K., 174

Hetzron, R., 435, 442

Heusler, A., 291

Higgins, F.R., 50

Heath, J., 383

Hinton, L., 277, 447, 460

Hohepa, P.W., 9, 53

Hooper, J., 185, 195, 560,
    563

Householder, F., 317

Hutcheson, C., 479, 480

Hyman, L., 242, 298

Hkonen, T., 145

J

Jackendoff, R., 320

Jacobs, R., 447, 473, 478, 564

Jakobsen, R., 158

Joël, J., 447, 449, 457, 470,
   486

Johnson, C.D., 437

K

Keenen, E.L., 41, 183, 184, 286

Kendall, M., 265, 459, 466, 469,
   483

King, D.H., 499

Kiparsky, P., 13

King, R.D., 3, 15

Klima, E.S., 3, 49, 151

Kozlowski, E., 449, 457, 459,
   482

Kuroda, Y., 274, 285

Kuz'mina, I., 173

L

Labov, W., 19, 34, 35

Langacker, R., 150, 170, 478,
   483

Langdon, M., 256, 265, 277, 447,
   449, 454, 457, 460, 462, 473,
   478-480

Lange, E., 449, 478

Lea, W., 282

Lehmann, W., 182, 296

Li, C., 242, 255, 439, 487, 560

Lindenfeld, J., 570

Lorimer, D., 344

Lounsbury, F.G., 498, 508,
   514

M

Martin, R., 477

Mathew, J., 399

Mathews, W.K., 330

McKay, G., 384

McKnight, G., 291-293, 296,
   298

Mebarkia, M., 442

Meillet, A., 9

Mixco, M., 447, 470, 478,
   486

Morevesik, E., 438

Moreau, J.L., 170

Mulder, J., 170

Munro, A., 170, 478

Munro, P., 133, 135, 173,
   265, 281, 283, 285, 286,
   419, 438, 445, 463, 481,
   483, 486

N

Nemčenko, E., 173

Norwood, S., 285, 478

O

Oehrle, R., 560

Ojansuu, H., 144, 154, 170

Otero, C., 594

P

Parks, D., 499

Pawley, A., 5, 41

Perlmutter, D., 37, 321, 375, 594

Pilhofer, G., 356

Pinkham, J., 50

Platero, P., 274

Postal, P., 37, 321, 375, 594, 595

Pullum, G., 376

Pulte, W., 499

R

Redden, J., 447, 459, 472, 482

Reid, L.A., 41

Rigsby, B., 384

Robertson, J., 351

Rood, D., 274, 499

Ross, J., 32, 544

Runeberg, A., 170

Rybarkiewicz, W., 311

S

Sapir, E., 323, 325, 356, 384

Schmidt, J., 9

Schachter, P., 184, 194

Schuh, R., 438

Schwartz, A., 170

Silverstein, M., 323, 391, 392, 398, 401

Siro, P., 170

Slater, C., 486

Smith, A., 302, 303

Smith, J., 296, 297

Somersal, L., 442

Southworth, F., 334

Strakova, V., 174

Steele, S., 557, 561, 563

Stuebel, O., 39

Sudeniemi, M., 153

Sundheim, B., 265

T

Taylor, A., 274

Thompson, S., 185, 195, 242, 439, 478, 487

Thrainsson, H., 595

Timberlake, A., 146, 154, 170, 350, 478

Traugott, E., 3

V

Vendryes, J., 337

Vennemann, T., 292, 294, 295, 299, 301, 310-312

Visser, F., 301

W

Wackernagel, 294, 295

Wang, L., 420, 422, 424-426

Wasow, T., 320

Wiik, K., 170

Williams, M., 498, 510

Wolfram, W., 20

Woodbury, H., 557

Wright, R., 498

Y

Yen, S., 440, 441

Z

Zhou, F.G., 420, 422, 425

Language Index

A

Akkadia, 242

Alabama, 529

Algonquian, 439

Altaic, 420

Arabic, 437

Arabic (Algerian), 434

Arabic (Egyptian), 338

Arabic (Palestinian), 420, 431-436

Aramaic, 189

Armenian, 330

Armenian (Classical), 328, 340

Athapaskan, 274

Austronesian, 241, 242, 437, 439

Australian, 286, 318, 321, 328, 329, 382, 391-393, 408, 437, 439

Avar, 319, 351

Aztec, 73, 81, 84, 93, 94, 104, 105, 109, 131

Aztec (Classical), 539, 541, 543, 551-553, 555-558, 561, 565, 571

Aztecan, 131

B

Balti, 343, 344, 346

Bambara, 436

Breton, 337

Burashaski, 330, 344

Burmese, 436

Bᵶedugh, 351

C

Caddo, 500-502, 517

Cahuilla, 69, 78, 131, 541, 543, 552, 558, 564

Cahuilla-Cupeno, 97, 541

Cayuga, 493, 498, 507, 509-511, 517, 521

Celtic, 241, 243, 291, 296, 337

Chadic, 439

Chemehuevi, 540-542, 544, 566

Cherokee, 493, 495, 499, 502-504, 510, 527, 528

Chinese, 427

Chinese (Archaic), 420, 422, 424, 426, 441, 442

Chinese (Mandarin), 242, 420, 426, 429, 434, 435

Chinook, 323, 325, 326, 355, 356

Choctaw, 525, 529, 537

Chuckchee, 338

Chumash, 257

Cocopa, 259, 262, 267, 278,

279, 285, 448, 470, 471,
477, 484-486

Cora, 131, 541-543, 552-557,
565, 571

Corachol, 131, 541

Creek, 525, 529, 533, 534-537

Cupan, 131, 133, 541

Cupeño, 69, 78, 131, 541-544,
552, 564, 568

Czech, 174

D

Dardic, 343

Diegueño, 259, 262, 267, 269-271,
273, 275, 278, 279, 285, 439,
447, 448, 453-458, 466, 471,
473, 475, 477-482, 484, 485

Diola-Fogny, 439

Djingli, 439

Dyirbal, 354, 365-369, 372-382,
384-388, 393-397, 401, 402,
404-408, 439

Drās, 344, 345

Dravidian, 439

E

English, 65, 71, 181, 182, 186,
261, 282, 291, 303, 337, 338,
348, 350, 352, 369, 374-376,
380, 382, 405, 406, 437, 477,
495, 546, 547, 549, 557, 562,
587, 591, 598

English (Old), 291, 295, 297-299,
301, 305, 307, 309, 310, 311

F

Fijian, 241, 242

Finnish, 143-155, 158, 170-
172, 350

Finno-Ugric, 421

French, 134, 337, 339, 546,
547, 550, 563, 564

G

Gabi, 399

Georgian, 330, 347-352

German, 181, 186, 293, 295,
299, 309, 310, 311, 598

Giramay, 403, 404

Gothic, 297

Greek, 189, 294

Gumar, 435

Gura, 435

Gurēsi, 344, 345

H

Hanunóo, 395

Havasupai, 259, 263-265,
268, 279, 285, 447, 448,
457-460, 466, 477, 482

Hawaiian, 6

Hebrew, 181-190, 209, 215,
223, 228, 236, 292, 420,
427, 429, 431, 432, 434-
438, 442, 443

Hindi, 330-339, 340

Hitchiti-Mikasuki, 525,
529, 530, 533-537

Hittite, 337

Hokan, 257, 439

Hopi, 74, 75, 93, 94, 104,
109, 131, 540, 541

Huichol, 77, 85, 95, 103, 131,
    135, 542, 544, 552, 553,
    555, 557, 565, 570

Hungarian, 436

Hurrian, 321

Huron, 493, 498, 501, 513-515,
    517, 522

I

Icelandic, 292

Ijo, 439

Indic, 329, 333, 339, 341, 342,
    344, 345

Indic (Middle), 334

Indo-European, 58, 291, 293,
    294, 296, 318, 329, 331,
    338, 420, 438

Indonesian, 42, 43, 241

Indonesian (Bahasan), 4, 14,
    38, 41, 42, 46, 47, 51

Iranian, 329, 337, 341, 342,
    344, 345

Irula, 439

Italian, 186

Irish, 241, 242

J

Jacaltec, 439

Japanese, 274

K

Kanuri, 439

Kartvelian, 318, 347, 352

Kashmiri, 342

Kâte, 356

Kawaiisu, 71, 90, 131, 137,
    439

Kiliwa, 262, 263, 268, 270,
    285, 447, 470, 471, 477,
    486

Kipigis, 421, 242

Kitanenemuk, 541, 543, 552,
    564

Koaseti, 525, 529-531, 533,
    534, 536, 537

Kohistanti, 345, 347

Konkow, 438

L

Lakota, 274, 276, 278

Lardil, 336

Latin, 319, 337

Laz, 352

Luganda, 439

Luiseño, 59-63, 67, 78, 94,
    98, 131, 133, 436, 539,
    542, 544, 546, 549, 550,
    563, 564, 568

Luo, 241

M

Macro-Algonkian, 274

Maidu, 439

Maiduan, 438

Malagasy, 14, 41, 241, 242

Maori, 6, 316, 317, 350

Maranungku, 439

Maricopa, 285, 446, 449, 478

Mayan, 439

Mingrelian, 353, 355

Mohawk, 493, 498, 501, 514, 515, 517

Mojave, 259, 262, 266, 267, 269-271, 278, 279, 281, 285, 445-456, 458, 462-269, 471-473, 475, 477, 481, 483, 487

Mono, 65, 66, 92, 131, 133, 539-541, 548, 550, 551, 558, 562

Muskogean, 525, 529, 537

Muskogee, 537

N

Naga, 439

Nahuatl (Classical), 439

Nandi, 241, 242

Natchez, 525-527, 536, 537

Navajo, 274, 276, 278, 350

Nepali, 334, 335, 340, 341, 343

Ngizm, 439

Niger-Congo, 439

Nilo-Saharan, 439

Nisenan, 438, 439

Nivean, 325

Numic, 59, 86, 90, 94, 97, 109, 131, 540

Numic (Central), 131, 540

Numic (Southern), 131, 540

Numic (Western), 92, 131, 540

Nyawaygi, 400, 404

O

Onandaga, 493, 498, 501, 514, 515, 517, 557

Oneida, 493, 498, 501, 514, 515, 517

Otomanguean, 439

P

Pai, 265, 285, 460

Pai (Northern), 458-461, 465, 473, 477, 482

Paipai, 259, 262-264, 267, 271, 278-281, 285, 447, 449, 457, 470, 477, 486

Paiute (Northern), 88, 131, 540, 541

Paiute (Southern), 71, 73, 83, 95, 107, 131, 540-542, 544, 545, 565

Papago, 131, 541, 542, 545, 555, 568

Pashto, 337, 340

Patañjali, 333

Pawnee, 500-502, 517

Persian (Old), 338, 340

Pimic, 90, 131, 541

Polynesian, 318, 325-327, 329

Portugese, 186, 337

Pochutla, 131, 541, 543, 552, 553, 555-557, 565, 571

Proto-Aztecan, 67, 133

Proto Australian, 328, 329, 354, 365, 395, 399, 407

Proto-Caddoan, 491, 492, 517

Proto-Cahuilla Cupeno, 69, 71, 86, 87, 97

Proto Central Numic, 89

Proto-Cupan, 78, 103

Proto-Germanic, 291

Proto-Iroquoian, 492, 510, 517, 518

Proto-Iroquois-Caddoan, 499-501, 503, 508, 510, 513, 515, 517, 518

Proto-Lake-Iroquoian, 510-512, 514, 517, 522

Proto-Macro-Siouan, 494

Proto-Muskogean, 526, 527, 529, 535, 537

Proto-Northern-Caddoan, 501, 512, 517

Proto-Northern-Iroquoian, 503, 504, 506, 508, 512, 513, 517, 519

Proto-Northern Pai, 460

Proto-Numic, 72, 86, 87, 94, 107

Proto-Pimic, 89

Proto-Polynesian, 8, 10-14, 49, 316

Proto-Southern Numic, 72, 89, 107

Proto-Takic, 74, 78, 89, 93, 94, 104

Proto-Taracahitic, 89

Proto-Tuscarora Cayuga, 507, 508, 510, 517, 520

Proto-Uto-Aztecan, 58-60, 65, 69, 76, 77, 85, 86, 88-91, 95-98, 104, 106, 108, 109, 132, 135, 138

Proto Western Numic, 89, 92

Proto-Yuman, 263, 269, 272, 277, 283, 446, 449, 452, 460, 462, 468, 482, 483

Pukapukan, 3, 4, 6, 14, 17-21, 24, 26, 27, 32-37, 46, 47, 49-51

R

Rennell-Bellona, 10

Romanian, 186

Russian, 157, 159, 160-168, 174, 181, 338, 350, 436

S

Samoan, 4, 38, 39, 46, 47, 241, 325

Sanskrit, 294, 331-333

Semitic, 434

Semitic (Ethiopian), 242, 434, 435

Seneca, 18, 21, 25, 493, 498, 501, 507, 510, 513, 515

Serrano, 78, 131, 541, 542, 565

Shina, 341-346

Shoshone, 131, 133, 540, 541

Siouan, 274

Slavic, 291, 296

Spanish, 181-183, 186, 292, 546, 547, 550, 562, 563

Swahili, 181

T

Tagalog, 242

Takic, 69, 90, 131, 541

Taracahitic, 131, 541

Tarahumara, 75, 76, 88, 94, 106, 131, 136, 137, 541-543, 545, 552-555, 569

Telegu, 439

Tepecano, 131, 541-543, 545, 552, 554, 555, 569

Tepehuan (Northern), 131

Tibetan, 343, 347

Tibeto-Burman, 439

Tiwi, 439

Tolkapaya, 486

Tongan, 241, 242, 315, 316

Tubatulabal, 69, 98, 131, 540-542, 545-547, 550, 551, 558, 563, 567

Tunica, 274, 276, 525-528, 536, 537

Turkish, 436-438, 582

Tuscarora, 493, 498, 508-511, 517, 520

U

Uto-Aztecan, 57, 64-67, 76, 87, 90, 91, 94, 108, 116, 131, 132, 134, 439, 539-541, 544, 546, 547, 549-551, 558, 559, 561, 565

W

Walapai, 260, 263, 268, 269, 279, 459, 466, 472, 477, 482

Walbiri, 328, 350, 355, 389, 394

Wappo, 420, 434, 444

Warramunga, 548

Wargamay, 400, 404

Welsh, 241, 242

Wichita, 499-501, 517

Wiyot, 439

Wyandot (Huron), 513

Y

Yaqui, 57, 80, 93, 95, 98, 109, 131, 439, 541-543, 545, 552-555, 569

Yavapai, 259, 263, 268, 270, 278-280, 285, 448, 459, 460, 465, 466, 470, 472, 473, 474, 475, 477, 478, 480, 482, 483

Yidin, 365, 367, 376, 377, 379-383, 388, 393-397, 404-408

Yukian, 433

Yuma, 258, 261, 262, 266, 269-271, 276, 278-285, 446, 447, 449, 471, 473, 475, 477

Yuman, 172, 256-258, 260, 266, 269, 272, 274-278, 280, 282-286, 445, 446, 451 452, 454, 455, 457-459, 461, 463, 464, 468, 469, 474-479, 482-484, 486, 487

Yuman (Upland), 264, 265

Z

Zapotec (Isthmus), 439

Zway, 434, 435, 443